# SATELLITE LIFELINES

## MEDIA, ART, MIGRATION AND THE CRISIS OF HOSPITALITY IN DIVIDED CITIES

ISABEL LÖFGREN

Theory on Demand #38

**Satellite Lifelines: Media, Art, Migration and the Crisis of Hospitality in Divided Cities**

Isabel Löfgren

Academic Editing: Roman Horbyk

Production and graphic design: Marijn Bril
Cover design: Katja van Stiphout

Supported by the Amsterdam University of Applied Sciences, Faculty of Digital Media and Creative Industries.

Published by the Institute of Network Cultures, Amsterdam, 2020
ISBN epub: 9789492302687
ISBN print-on-demand: 9789492302694

**Contact**
Institute of Network Cultures
Phone: +3120 5951865
Email: info@networkcultures.org
Web: http://www.networkcultures.org

This publication is published under the Creative Commons Attribution-NonCommercial-NoDerrivatives 4.0 International (CC BY-NC-SA 4.0) licence.

This publication may be ordered through various print-on-demand-services or freely downloaded from http://www.networkcultures.org/publications.

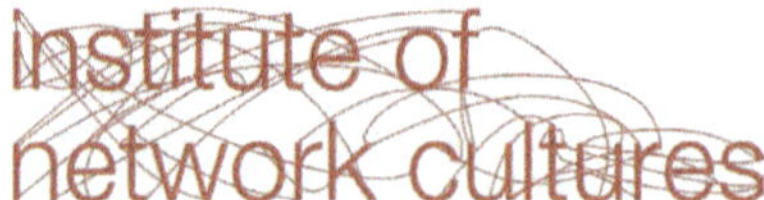

# TABLE OF CONTENTS

# A (FORE)WORD OF WELCOME

This book is an adapted version of my PhD dissertation titled 'Hospitality and Its Other: Migration, Media and the Divided City' defended in the summer of 2015 at the Division of Media and Communication (now renamed Division of Philosophy, Art and critical Thought (PACT)) of the European Graduate School (EGS), in Saas-Fee, Switzerland. The thesis is renamed to better reflect the notion of satellites in two ways. First, the notion of divided city in the original title can be implicated in the term *satellite city* which I explore in a variety of ways in this book, and to refer to the title of the artistic project *Satellitstaden*, which included interventions on satellite dishes on building façades of a Swedish suburb and is the central axis of this intellectual journey. Secondly, the term *satellite subjects* coined in the thesis refers to the type of subjectivities that develop in multiethnic peripheral urban formations and embrace multiple ways of being and becoming that orbit around each other.

As with any book, this work reflects who I was, what I was reading, what I was doing, and what was happening in the world when I was writing between 2008 to 2015, the duration of my doctoral studies. This inquiry begins with the year of the global financial crisis and the expansion of social media, spans the years of new forms of protest and significant social movements such as Occupy, the Arab Spring, and the Journeys of June in Brazil, the rise of neo-fascist politics globally, the beginning of the devastating war in Syria, and the resulting flows of migration from these and other world conflicts towards Europe.

In 2008, the effects of the financial crisis were relatively unfelt in the industrious and prosperous island-state of Singapore where I was living and teaching. I had already begun to observe the dynamics of contemporary migration patterns in Southeast Asia and its diasporic populations by way of researching its colonial history, the policies regarding cultural and religious co-existence under single-party rule, and the differential policies regarding guest-workers and qualified labor in the island.

By contrast, when moving to Sweden in 2011 to conduct the field research for the doctoral thesis, I found the effects of the financial crisis were met there with sharp critiques against neo-liberalism and the resulting politics of austerity and rise of social inequalities. In addition, the increased migration by asylum-seekers from conflict zones, especially from the Middle East, stimulated anti-immigration rhetoric and polarization. In Stockholm, these effects could be felt locally in the steady rise of urban segregation in its suburbs where I would do my fieldwork. This discontent towards immigration, whether real or imagined, put into question the notion of multiculturalism and the politics of hospitality in Europe – about who is allowed to be a 'European' or a 'Swede' and who is not. This metaphysical turn in the public discourse paved the way for the political representation of extreme-right 'otherphobic' nationalist politics in the past decade. This is best exemplified by the entry of neo-Nazi party Sverige Demokraterna (SD) in the Swedish parliament in 2010 which ushered the country into what I call an 'inhospitable turn' which is increasingly becoming normalized in a global dimension. This phenomenon makes evident that racial, environmental, and cultural differences sit at the core of nationalist discourses and programs. How this is reflected in urban form, and how media cultures relate to this phenomenon, and lastly how artistic interventions help illuminate this issue, are the motivations behind this research.

When I began this research, Sweden had one of the most generous migration policies in Europe. The arrival of thousands of refugees and migrants combined with previous waves of humanitarian migration to the country, forcibly led the country to reassess the openness of its democracy and welfare system while redefining what it means to be 'Swedish'. The same period also saw a rise in anti-racist movements, the spread of the rhetoric of identity politics, and a complexification of notions of belonging that aims to be more inclusive. Who belongs *here* anyway, and on what terms? What are the possibilities and limitations of this belonging? Democracy *for whom*? This led me to examine these questions through the philosophical perspective of the ethics of hospitality, that is, the complex relation between hosts and guests, from a macro perspective of countries and populations, cities and inhabitants, to the micro perspective of how we embrace familiarity and otherness within our own being.

A few weeks after I defended the dissertation in late July 2015, the migration discourse in the media and public policies regarding migration took a sharp turn due to an unprecedented intensification of refugee crossings in the Mediterranean towards Europe. Sweden became one of the most desirable destinations and the number of asylum claims grew fourfold. This figure is high in European terms, while the amounts of refugees in neighboring countries to conflict zones is beyond compare. That moment was also a political tipping point in terms of restrictive measures and political discourse against migration, in time for the election of a new class of political leaders worldwide with the 2016 elections of Rodrigo Duterte in the Philippines and Donald Trump in the USA. In addition, the rise of far-right populism coupled with data manipulation, disinformation campaigns and social polarization has radicalized anti-refugee and anti-immigrant sentiment in a network of globally coordinated nationalisms. In Sweden, this *crisis of hospitality* as I call it (as opposed to the more mediatic term *crisis of migration*) has turned the extreme-right Sweden Democrats into Sweden's second largest party. One of my suggestions in this book is to examine this controversial debate about immigration, its political, spatial and cultural implications and its effects through the ethics of hospitality as a possibility of peaceful, or at the very least, bearable coexistence as societies, collectivities and subjects, in order to become vigilant to the social and political mechanisms that may plunge us into a state of perpetual violence.

For it is surely not a crisis of the migrant, or of migration, as the news media claim. Rather, it is the crisis of a specific type of relation, of how we relate to the Other – a *crisis of hospitality* – or as Franco 'Bifo' Berardi suggests, a crisis in how we relate with *another* in times of complex issues such as migration, religious intolerance, militarization, financial speculation, structural racism, land assassination, and climate change. An *otherness* which is not necessarily embodied in individuals and populations with whom we may or may not share origins or affinities, but an otherness which means recognizing life in the other – about who is considered human and who is not. Humanness is the foundation of all hospitality; hospitality begins by becoming human.

The aim of this book is to outline a philosophy of hospitality by examining shifting host-guest relationships as they are reflected in peripheral urban form and in the uses of social aesthetics coupled to transnational media manifest in these formations by populations who are statistically, culturally and subjectively considered foreigners, or others, from nationalist perspectives. The research is an assemblage of theoretical analysis and situated research presented in a non-linear approach and written within an essayistic tradition in philosophy and the humanities, far from the more pragmatic formats more appropriate to the social sciences. The field research includes a site-specific participatory art installation in a Swedish suburb, *Satellitstaden*, which doubled up as a framework for media ethnographic research about transnationality, migration and urban form, specifically looking at transnational satellite television practices as they relate to immigrant communities living in Stockholm suburbs. One of my contentions is that art, through the specific modality of participatory artistic practices, is a form of knowledge production, which together with philosophical inquiry contributes to further problematize, redefine and recontextualize Otherness today.

This book is similarly a result of an age of expansion for artistic residencies and nomadic strategies for art production and research in the past decade. The research was developed through three forms of residencies: first the European Graduate School (EGS) summer academy in Saas-Fee, Switzerland in 2008-10 where I attended philosophy, art, media, and film theory PhD seminars with an array of world-renowned scholars. EGS residencies are based on the concept of isolating the philosopher for periods of time, removing her from everyday life and entering an intellectual journey only achievable in such intensive conditions. Following that, I enrolled in the Konstfack CuratorLab program in Stockholm, Sweden, a year-long low-residency academic program intended for art curators and managers that provided the opportunity to plan the field research and seek initial funding to develop the art project in partnership with an range of artistic and public institutions in Stockholm. And finally, Residence Botkyrka, an artist's residency located in the satellite city of Fittja in Botkyrka municipality which provided the location, time, space, and support necessary for executing the art project and conducting the field research. This structure of temporary intensive 'stays' as a guest-artist has indeed become the *modus operandi* for so-called nomadic artistic practices and revealed another set of complexity for artists working with hospitality, especially in participatory approaches, which is also explored.

Lastly, this book is written with the understanding that the philosopher's task is to be *the stranger in the house*, the intruder, the uninvited guest who observes the house and cuts through the habitual to see it more clearly and denounce its uncanniness. I am aware that the research between the correlation of migrancy, cities, architecture, art and media is centered on human relations within a Western paradigm. We may soon need to shift our focus from the borders of nation-states to think in more planetary dimensions where we could become exiles from the Earth, members of a permanent diaspora. We need to urgently re-imagine an ethics of hospitality and habitability for the future of the planet. The 2020 pandemic also forces us to reassess our philosophy and practice of contact, re-engineering how we relate to the Other and what hospitality means in face of a global halt.

Stockholm, October 2020

# INTRODUCTION

# INTRODUCTION

> The new is horrifying for being new. The new man that is emerging around us and within us horrifies us, because we cannot sympathize with him in the exact meaning of the term. We do not oscillate with his vibration. His gestures are not ours. His models do not square with ours. We cannot decipher the codes through which he symbolizes the world. And, since we are, as of now, new men; we cannot sympathize with ourselves. We are out of tune. A civil war without precedent is being fought within us: the new that is rebelling against us. It is as if we were, each one of us, going through an agony that we experience sometimes as the final stage of mortal illness and sometimes of birth. The new is horrifying and we are ourselves, new.
>
> – Vilém Flusser[1]

Hospitality, in practice and theory, relates to crossing boundaries or thresholds between dimensions: Self and Other, private and public, inside and outside, individual and collective, emotional and rational, political and economic. All these couplets overlap each other's territories without any one exactly mapping another. Hospitality is central to the question of political frontiers where admittance and refusal across state borders may be a matter of life or death, and also touches on the fundamental ethical question of the boundaries of the human, the constitution of the subject, how and why we set these up, and why we attempt to bring them down.

The displacement of populations across the Earth have historically been occasioned not only by climate change such as droughts, floods and earthquakes, but also by changes in cultural, political and economic climates where war and displacement force painful and costly movements in a cadre of persistent inequality that requires a leveling movement between different parts of the world. Over the past decade, the number of people forced to flee their homes in search of safety has nearly doubled. In 2019, The UNHCR reports that 26.2 million are refugees, who have turned to a country other than their own for hospitality and protection, 45.7 million are uprooted within their own countries, and 4.2 million are asylum seekers and more, making the total number of displaced population almost 80 million people, or, the stunning proportion of 1 in 97 people in the world's population, and rising at a rate that outpaces global population growth.[2] A majority of migrants now seek refuge in cities rather than in camps, prompting us to reconsider the way in which we need to rethink urban space to accommodate newcomers more long-term. This certainly puts pressure on existing infrastructures and has been a major concern in host societies, but also presents new opportunities for reflecting on which new modes of habitation and co-existence that arise from these frictions, as well as how a new set of identifications and subjectivities are played out.

---

1 Vilém Flusser, *Post-history,* trans. Rodrigo Maltez Novaes, Siegfried Zielinski (ed.) Minneapolis: Univocal, 2014, p. 163.

2 *Global Trends: Forced Displacement in 2019*, UNHCR, https://www.unhcr.org/globaltrends2019/.

The so-called 'migration crisis' in the past decade has been aggravated and propagated by the media discourses and to a large extent happens therein. In recent years, public opinion about migration in Europe has been increasingly influenced and polarized by some overtly conservative views that have succeeded in hijacking public discourse and increasingly dominate media and political agendas against immigration that have given rise to a populist anti-immigrant vote throughout Europe. This results in part from the distributional inequalities in European societies, and the increased competition among workers in deregulated labour markets which puts the burden of the crisis on the middle- and lower-income groups. Migrants, then, are not the cause of the problem, but for many they become the face or the symptom of the problem. It has also been claimed that populist anti-immigrant sentiment is a reaction against the failure of previous multiculturalist policies that fall short in successfully embracing diversity.[3] It follows that there is an overflow of mediation and representation of the migrant as the Other, as the unwelcome, the intruder, as a parasite, or as a threat to national values. There is, however, little space for migrant's voices to be heard and less so a reflection from host societies to turn around this perception. Here there is ample room for philosophical reflection about the complexity of host-guest relations as they expressed in the media, as they are embodied in the city, and as they experienced in everyday life.

Multiculturalism is the term used to describe public policies in which several groups hailing from different cultures coexist side-by-side and are acknowledged in their diversity with rights and protections in favour of a multitude of cultural expressions and safeguarding against structural discrimination. While the term points to the recognition of communities or localities where individuals and groups from multiple cultures live, multiculturalism has been claimed to be insufficient in addressing the dynamics and processes in which exchanges between these cultures may take place. The extent to which multiculturalist policies are able to establish the terms of relationship between different groups and guarantee each group's cultural autonomy, the right to self-determination and democratic participation in relation to the hegemonic national culture has been an intense source of debate in the continent.[4]

In 2010, Angela Merkel, chancellor of the largest destination country for immigrants in the European Union, declared that 'attempts at creating a multicultural society in Germany have been an utter failure. (...) Living happily side-by-side did not work, and immigrants need to do more to integrate to German society,' she says, 'including learning German'.[5] Former British Prime Minister David Cameron also pronounced his country's long-standing policy of

---

3 Kenan Malik, 'The Failure of Multiculturalism: Community Versus Society in Europe', *Foreign Affairs*, (March/April 2015), https://www.foreignaffairs.com/articles/western-europe/2015-02-18/failure-multiculturalism.

4 'Multiculturalism is a body of thought in political philosophy about the proper way to respond to cultural and religious diversity. Mere tolerance of group differences is said to fall short of treating members of minority groups as equal citizens; recognition and positive accommodation of group differences are required through 'group-differentiated rights,' a term coined by Will Kymlicka (1995).' See Sarah Song, 'Multiculturalism', in Edward N. Zalta (ed.) *The Stanford Encyclopedia of Philosophy,* Summer 2015 Edition, https://plato.stanford.edu/archives/sum2015/entries/multiculturalism/.

5 'Merkel says German multicultural society has failed', *BBC News Europe*, 17 October 2010, https://www.bbc.com/news/world-europe-11559451.

multiculturalism a failure, 'calling for better integration of young Muslims to combat home-grown extremism'.[6] Former French President Nicholas Sarkozy called for more stringent measures on immigration and cultural integration by advocating a respect for difference insofar as it does not affect an environment of shared core values at the national level. He claimed that 'we have been too concerned about the identity of the person who was arriving and not enough about the identity of the country that was receiving him'. In other words, Sarkozy believes there has been far too much tolerance for the immigrant's origins at the expense of a national identity and national values considered essential by the majority population. All of these discourses seem to put the blame on the immigrants and migrants and exempt national politics from responsibility for diversity, inclusion and justice, leading to an asymmetrical representation in discourses of power, but hardly ever a reflection on how national politics presents migrants with systems that are structurally discriminatory and histories that have created these inequalities.

Brazilian theorist Denise Ferreira da Silva writes that the "welcomes' from German and British authorities (...) disguise the inability of Europeans to comprehend that they have produced the circumstances forcing millions out of their homes, to risk their lives crossing the dangerous Mediterranean waters and unfriendly lands in Eastern and Southern Europe'.[7] While multiculturalism may arguably not be the ultimate solution to peaceful coexistence between populations of different origins and the clash with pre-existing 'national values', whichever those may be, the problem is that Merkel's claim leaves us with a political vacuum in the future articulation of identities and identifications within a politics of difference. We are then tempted to ask: what happens after multiculturalism?

By the mid-2010s as I was writing this manuscript, the 'migration question' in Europe had intensified to such an extent that governments in Europe reevaluated their positions. In the five-year interim since Merkel's infamous claim, thousands of lives have been lost in the Mediterranean Sea in capsized clandestine boats, adding pressure on the European Union (EU) to rethink its role in safeguarding its borders. By the end of 2014, the number of refugees arriving by land and sea in the Mediterranean towards Europe was 225,455. In 2015, this figure escalated to over one million individuals, then diminishing to nearly one third to 373,652 in 2016 and reaching an estimate of 100,000 by the end of 2019.[8]

---

6 'Nicolas Sarkozy joins David Cameron-Angela Merkel view that multiculturalism failed', *Daily Mail*, 11 February 2011, https://www.dailymail.co.uk/news/article-1355961/Nicolas-Sarkozy-joins-David-Cameron-Angela-Merkel-view-multiculturalism-failed.html.

7 Denise Ferreira da Silva, 'The 'Refugee Crisis' and the Current Predicament of the Liberal State', in *L'Internationale Online, Subjects and Objects in Exile*, 2017, p.157. Available at: https://d2tv32fgpo1xal.cloudfront.net/files/05-subjectsandobjectsinexile.pdf.

8 Arrivals include sea arrivals to Italy, Cyprus and Malta and both sea and land arrivals to Greece and Spain. Afghanistan and Syria top the list with the highest numbers of refugees, UNHCR, https://www.unhcr.org/.

## The Boat People

The intensification of migration to Europe alone in mid-2015 is in part explained by the escalation of conflict in the Middle East, especially in Syria, and other neighboring conflict zones, which precipitated an unprecedented rise in flights to Europe by land and sea.

In 2015 alone, thousands of refugees drowned in the Mediterranean trying to reach the EU, but it was only after the picture of a single lifeless body of the 3-year-old Syrian boy Alan Kurdî on September 2nd, 2015 in Greece, making headlines and front pages around the world, that the tide of the public opinion turned and forced the authorities to go public and react to it. This reveals the macabre workings of the 'society of spectacle' we live in, reflecting in a dramatic media intervention how mediatized all these fields have become as well as the power that the media hold in the debate around this issue. 'The waves of the Aegean are not just washing up dead refugees, dead children, but the very civilization of Europe', as the Prime Minister of Greece Alex Tsipras claimed on 30 October 2015.[9]

The prototypical image of the boat filled beyond capacity with refugees and their neon orange life vests became an icon of the decade. After Alan Kurdî's photograph published widely in world media in September 2015, mainstream contemporary artists like the Ai Wei Wei quickly created monuments using life vests, appropriating disaster aesthetics and using their notoriety to raise awareness about the issue. At the same time, other independent and less visible cultural initiatives in refugee camps along the Aegean attempted to address some of the effects of this humanitarian catastrophe by setting up projects including film and storytelling projects.[10] Others, like the Slovakian artist and filmmaker Tomas Rafa, has since 2011 documented the passage of refugees through the Eastern European corridor from Greece towards Germany and Sweden showing dramatic sequences of refugees facing resistance by police and border patrols through barbed wire fences and violent reaction of white suprematist nationalists in the series 'New Nationalism'.[11] Such exhibitions were attempts at giving voice and agency to narratives and perspectives otherwise not mediatized in the mainstream media.

The narratives are well known from the media with liberal or progressive reputation: risk-filled journeys undertaken by hundreds of migrants often ending up in thousands of deaths on the shores of the European Union or off the Australian coast and elsewhere. Those who manage to survive register asylum claims at the nearest port of entry, waiting to be sent elsewhere

---

9 'Greek Premier Condemns Europe's Response to Migrant Crisis', *New York Times*, 30 October 2015. https://www.nytimes.com/2015/10/31/world/europe/tsipras-migrants-aegean-eu.html.

10 See the Swedish collective Historiebrättarna's EU-funded project 'Refugee Arts with Participants and Practitioners Open to integRaTion', *Historieberättarna*, http://historieberattarna.se/kontakt/.

11 In 2016, the exhibition *The New Human* curated by Joa Ljungberg at Moderna museet in Stockholm addressed the need to redefine what it means to be human in times of contested geopolitics and presented artworks by Slovakian artist Tomas Rafa and other artists. I moderated a panel discussion between Albanian artist Adrian Paci and Tomas Rafa in this context on September 30, 2016. See the event at https://www.modernamuseet.se/stockholm/sv/aktiviteter/adrian-paci-och-tomas-rafa/, and Tomas Rafa's website http://your-art.sk/.

in what will be a long journey as migrants towards safety and legality. While humanitarian aid and favorable reception to migrants are consistent with international conventions, this very thrust towards international hospitality is what also causes potential host societies to adopt stricter control measures, border patrols, and population registers that protect borders instead of expanding them. The extent of the maritime tragedy is so extensive[12] that the EU sees itself laying resources in sea rescue operations, trying to put a halt to human trafficking, and setting policies and quotas restricting the number of asylum seekers to be taken in by European countries. This moment in contemporary history has been repeatedly referred to as the 'European migration crisis'.[13]

One of the countries along the Mediterranean most implicated in these dilemmas has been Italy, due to its proximity to the North African coast, with the island of Lampedusa having become the first destination of many clandestine frigates. Former Italian Prime Minister Enrico Letta (2013-14) created the operation *Mare Nostrum* in late 2013 after one such tragedy, an operation launched to search and rescue migrants attempting the perilous crossing from Africa to Italy, and discontinued after one year.[14] Letta writes that the migrant crisis was the 'gravest issue' under his administration and is quick to point out that 'doing something about those deaths wasn't just about putting an end to our shame or sense of guilt. It had to do with a certain conception of civic and political duty. Those *boat people* in the Mediterranean came as a reminder that there were things that simply had to be done: there were moral obligations'.[15]

Fast-forward seven years and Italy has now had one of the most migration-hostile governments in Europe under the extreme-right Lega Nord Prime Minister Matteo Salvini (2018-2019), aggressively pursuing an anti-refugee border policy. This dramatic shift in the politics of hospitality towards the populist right has been heavily predicated on yet another development in the media landscape with increasingly polarized and politically clientelist media which is also increasingly fragmented thanks to the advent of social media, personal data manipulation and weaponized oligarch-controlled television.

The year 2015 also marked the reversal in the orientation of the laws of hospitality in the European Union towards more restrictive measures, which helped boost the rise of anti-

12 Between January and June 2015, over 1800 lives have been lost in the Mediterranean Sea. Dozens of other boats with refugees have been known to sink in South Asia, Africa and the coast of Australia.

13 Many magazines and newspapers have had special sections called 'Migration Crisis' as an umbrella term for series of articles about reactions and effects regarding the phenomenon.

14 Letta published the book *Andare insieme, andare lontano* (Going Together, Going Far) in which he describes his experience as head of the Italian government in 2013-14, including the experience with *Mare Nostrum*. Letta writes in his book that there is a much larger issue at play here, and one that no one seems quite ready to confront: the question of why millions of people decide to uproot themselves from Africa in search of a better life in Europe. *Mare Nostrum* had been replaced by *Operation Triton* lasting until 2018, which in its turn was replaced by *Operation Themis* See Enrico Letta, *Andare insieme, andare lontano*. Rome: Mondadori, 2014.

15 Natalie Nougayrède, 'Europe's tide of migrant tragedy can be stemmed only in Africa', *The Guardian*, 15 May 2015, https://www.theguardian.com/commentisfree/2015/may/15/europe-migrant-tide-tragedy-africa.

immigration sentiment in public opinion. In parallel, however, we also evidence the rise of solidarity and social movements against these sentiments, such as *Refugees Welcome, No Person is Illegal,* and many more.[16] The extent to which societies should express and practice solidarity was amply discussed, as well as a reassessment of the meaning of democracy in times of crisis and what it means to be human in contested times. These examples point towards where we find ourselves historically and help us to delineate why we should be addressing the ethics of hospitality with a sense of urgency even though the term hospitality is rarely used to define this ongoing problematic in public discourses. Hospitality, as the ethics governing the relationship between hosts and guests, is especially relevant as the conflict about who is eligible to live where reverberates in every sphere of private and public life and, I contend, implicates all citizens in any given society, whether foreign or national.[17]

## From a 'European Migration Crisis' to a Global Crisis of Hospitality

This should forcibly change the media discourse, in my view, from a 'migration crisis' to a 'crisis of hospitality' where receiving countries are equally implicated in the equation between refugees and host societies, and shifts the culpability of mass migrations from its victims to their perpetrators, including the responsibility of host societies in the aftermath of such dramatic shifts. The repercussions of the photograph of 3-year old Alan Kurdî's body washed ashore in Greece in September 2015, for instance, forced politicians sensitive to the popular sentiment of the moment to take a softer stance on the European border policies and commit the EU to alleviating the human cost of the refugee crisis. Only three days after the boy's tragic death, Angela Merkel announced there would be no upper limit on the refugee intake in Germany, a claim she herself retracted two years later.[18]

These media discourses are of course neither created nor distributed by migrants and refugees themselves, but by host societies, thus forcing the divide between natives versus outsiders in public opinion. Even though migrants are a minority in overall European populations, they are disproportionately overrepresented, discussed and perceived as problematic subjects of media discussions. Remembering Nick Couldry's critique of the myth of mediated centers – the myth in which the media occupies the central position in present-day societies – one may see how this mythological thinking elevates anything that is talked about

---

16 In September 2020, a new migration policy was launched by the EU which creates a new form of cooperation between EU states regarding migration, where states can choose how many newcomers are allowed. For those states who impose more restrictive measures, they must instead provide exonomic or other resources to other states. The new policy also puts strong emphasis on repatriation and deportation.

17 *Refugees Welcome in Sweden* is a movement to facilitate housing for stateless persons, and *No Person is Illegal*, an international network of groups representing stateless and paperless persons initiated in 1997 at Documenta X in Kassel, Germany, to bring attention to the precarious political situation of refugees. See *Refugees Welcome,* https://refugees-welcome.se/, https://www.refugees-welcome.net/, and *Ingen människa är illegal*, https://www.ingenillegal.org/.

18 'Germany Opens Borders, Expects 7,000 Refugees and Migrants from Hungary Over Weekend', *NBC News*, 5 September 2015, https://www.nbcnews.com/storyline/europes-border-crisis/germany-opens-borders-expects-7-000-refugees-migrants-hungary-over-n42233.

in the media to the status of everyone's personal issue.[19] These debates have of course been used as an opportunity by nationalist conservatives to build their political agendas centered on the immigration issue and profiting from this polarization between 'us' and 'them'. It is therefore not surprising that the rise of nationalist politics in Europe goes hand in hand with the intensification of migration in recent years as well as the advance of mediatization and the resultant strengthening of the myth of mediated center. Furthermore, the lack of resolutions and palliative bureaucratic solutions on these fronts leads us to examine the paradoxes of international solidarity.

Media – as well as media studies – remain largely fixated on the nation-state as a unit of analysis, whereas the local, regional, cross- and supranational phenomena are often ignored. It is exactly these 'media thickenings'[20], that is, media practices that cross national boundaries[21] thanks to a globalized world or by virtue of their cross-border character (surpassing the limits of communities, such as media practices by migrants on the go), that I propose are the central locus where the mediation of hospitality is happening. This shifts the focus from a 'migration crisis' which puts the migrant on center stage as an unwanted guest in a nation-state and its imagined homogeneous community, to a *crisis in hospitality* where the behavior of host societies is implicated as part of the crisis.

The aspect of hospitality, however, is not something explicit in media debates or in the discourse of migration in general. Even though migration politics have everything to do with aspects hospitality, it is precisely the lack of a vocabulary of hospitality and the lack of an overt recognition of the relationality between host societies, migrants and refugees that leads to polarizing debates. This book is an attempt at looking at what this vocabulary of hospitality could be. Hospitality is here introduced as an ethics as well as a practice.

Transnational hospitality, in this case, does not presuppose a universal hospitality as advocated by Kant as early as 1795, that is, the foundation for a cosmopolitan politics aimed to foster 'perpetual peace' between nations.[22] The framework of refugee protection, which is part of the Human Rights framework and international law[23] based in part in Kant's cosmopolitical universality, and the ideals of democratization secure themselves through the foundational category of the nation-state and the citizen. This leads to important questions, of a political but also of a philosophical nature. Can hospitality be extended to people and populations who are not considered citizens and whose existence is not confirmed by nation-states?

---

19 Nick Couldry, 'Transvaluing Media Studies: Or, Beyond the Myth of the Mediated Centre', in James Curran and David Morley (eds) *Media and Cultural Theory*. Abingdon: Routledge, 2009, p. 178.

20 Nick Couldry, 'Theorising Media as Practice', *Social Semiotics*, *14*(2), 2004, p. 116.

21 This includes, for instance, transantional satellite television used in immigrant communities, which is the object of this research in Chapter 5.

22 Immanuel Kant, *Perpetual Peace: A Philosophical Essay,* trans. M.Campbell Smith, New York: The Macmillan Company, 2017 (1795). Available at: https://www.gutenberg.org/files/50922/50922-h/50922-h.htm.

23 United Nations Human Rights, Office of the High Commissioner (OHCHR), https://www.ohchr.org/EN/Issues/Migration/Pages/HumanRightsFramework.aspx.

The fact that there seems to be no natural place for migrant subjects to belong to in host societies, both existentially and politically, is one of the arguments that sustain the shift towards exclusionary politics in fragile European democracies. Where do these individuals and populations fit in the grand scheme of national narratives and recognized national identities? In this case, citizenship becomes synonymous to humanity, and anyone outside of that realm may fall under the rule of no protection. The 1951 Convention states that a refugee is defined as a person with a well-founded fear of persecution because of their race, religion, nationality, membership in a particular social group, or, political opinion; who is outside their country of origin; and who is unable or unwilling to avail themselves of the protection of that country, or to return there, for fear of persecution.[24] This leads us to revisit Giorgio Agamben's concept of 'bare life' as a concept possibly capable of describing all regulated life (as opposed to simply life in refugee camps, for instance) under the current regimes of exceptional insecurity.

The response of Europe to the crisis of the summer of 2015 was the European Agenda on Migration, a migration management program that allocated extra financial resources for countries of arrival as well as the places of origin most refugees came from. This extension of EU jurisdiction for managing the 'migration crisis' focused more on the borders of 'Fortress Europe' with a European Border and Coast Guard, systems of resettlement and relocation, and systems of return/deportation. Jean-Claude Juncker, the president of the European Commission, introduced the measures by saying,

> In spite of our fragility, our self-perceived weaknesses, today it is Europe that is sought as a place of refuge and exile. This is something to be proud of, though it is not without its challenges. The first priority today is and must be addressing the refugee crisis. The decision to relocate 160,000 people from the most affected Member States is a historic first and a genuine, laudable expression of European solidarity. It cannot be the end of the story, however. It is time for further, bold, determined and concerted action by the European Union, by its institutions and by all its Member States.[25]

As in any legal document, the refugee protection framework acts defensively and establishes a negative right at the heart of the politics of hospitality as an obligation: the right *not* to be returned or the right to stay. Over the years and in particular since 9/11, juridical structures of law enforcement and management have increasingly focused on keeping refugees away, including the outsourcing of asylum seekers to neighboring countries, or keeping them in detention centers that put individuals into a state of social and legal limbo. Media theorist Nicholas Mirzoeff describes this 'social death' in Denmark where asylum seekers are isolated in camps on islands deprived of any sense of comfort or agency. The immigration minister declaredly wants to make life for a refugee in Denmark unbearable: no access to communications or simple comforts such as a rug or pictures on the wall, no possibility of cooking

---

24 UNHCR, https://www.unhcr.org/1951-refugee-convention.html.

25 'Managing the refugee crisis: Immediate operational, budgetary and legal measures under the European Agenda on Migration', *European Commission*, 23 September 2015, https://europa.eu/rapid/press-release_IP-15-5700_en.htm.

own food, restricted visits, etc., denying her the right to host. Mirzoeff recounts meeting an Eritrean woman on one of these offshore detention centers:

> When I entered her room, Lily had arranged hot water to make tea or instant coffee and spread a paper plate with a packet of saltines. It was heartbreaking: Not because she had relatively little to offer, but because it made clear that the intent of the Danish state was to deny her the human impulse to hospitality.[26]

In the seminal essay *We, refugees*, Giorgio Agamben claims that the refugee is a subject that glitches all existing systems, forcing these systems to reevaluate themselves and face uncomfortable truths regarding how they represent, care for, and (legally) recognize the Other. An ethics of hospitality is thus necessary to understand the dilemmas at the heart of this question.

## Identities, Identifications

Most theories of identity understand it as relational and moveable, contextual and flexible, fragmented, discontinuous and contingent to conditions of modernity. In the media and political discourses against multiculturalism however, notions such as 'national identity' and 'cultural integration' keep resurfacing and calling into question what identities best serve to reify identity as something *a priori* fixed and immutable. The longing for this readily definable and even biologically defendable 'identity' – a sort of essential 'master identity' – is part of the backlash specifically against immigration and multiculturalism. This is rhetorically expressed in fear and anxiety about foreign 'others' and nostalgia for an imaginary past when everyone supposedly shared thick bonds of identity and solidarity.[27] This mindset has and is still being used to justify genocides on the basis of national virtues. Migrants, who are themselves often escaping genocide at home precisely due to their non-hegemonic cultural, religious, ethnic affiliations or sexual identities, thus often meet the necropolitics[28] of genocidal ideologies in their host societies as well.

Stuart Hall outlines three conceptions of identity. First, the Enlightenment subject, a subject based on the idea of the unified individual with the capacity of reasoning, conscience and action that remains continuous and identical along her existence. Secondly, the sociological subject, reflecting the complexity of the modern world whose conscience is no longer autonomous and self-sufficient. Identity and identification are formed in the interaction between

---

26 Nicholas Mirzoeff,' 'Social Death' in Denmark - The European country is isolating and excluding asylum seekers until they disappear from society completely', *The Nation,* 20 January 2019, https://www.thenation.com/article/denmark-refugees-asylum-europe/.

27 Please note that immigrant multiculturalism is different from multiculturalism related to indigenous peoples, for example. While there has been a retreat from immigrant multiculturalism, the same cannot be said about the recognition of indigenous populations, which is not in the scope of this monograph.

28 Achille Mbembe theorizes the enactment of sovereignty in cases where 'the generalized instrumentalization of human existence and the material destruction of human bodies and populations' is the central project of power, rather than autonomy. See Achille Mbembe, *Necropolitics*, Duke University Press, 2019.

the self and society, filling the gap between 'inside' and 'outside', private and public worlds – we project ourselves onto these cultural identities making them a 'part of us.' In this case, identity is what 'stitches' the subject to a structure in such a way that both subject and the cultural worlds they inhabit are reciprocally unified and predictable. Lastly, with the post-modern subject, structures once considered stable and defineable collapse, and the process of identification through which we project our cultural identity becomes provisional, variable and problematic, resulting in a subject that is not fixed, essential or permanent.[29] As such, the post-modern subject is rather defined historically and not biologically, allowing for an individual to take up different identities at different moments, containing contradictory and multiple identities. The effects of such fragmentations yield a crisis of the morphology of the subject, which is a crisis between the historical subject and the biological subject – a crisis of *Being*.

Societies in late modernity are characterized by difference and are formed through a series of clashes and antagonisms where individuals are required to take different 'subjective positions', so-called identities. Brubaker and Cooper's critique of the very concept of identity as contradictory and vague (in lumping together essentialist and fluid qualities) results in the use of the term *identifications*, which are mutable, instead of identities.[30] The ambivalence and uncertainty from this destabilization of fixed categories has, as observed by the Polish-English philosopher Zygmunt Bauman, given rise to demands for protection and a return to a familiar and predictable world that creates boundaries holding the 'outsider' at bay.[31] When stable identities of the past are disarticulated, new identities are recomposed into the production of new political subjects, amalgamating identities and identifications in a transformative process of *Becoming*.

The challenges in cross-cultural communication between rising nationalism and predominance of more fixed cultures ('Finns for the Finns', 'Swedish*ness* for Sweden' debates, etc.) and newcomers to established societies calls for a more flexible and tolerant understanding of what it means to belong anywhere. In *We, Refugees*, Agamben goes even further by claiming that the refugee represents the avant-garde as her presence as the 'stranger in the house' beckons a radical reassessment of belonging, being and becoming.

And yet, what of the subject that articulates her existence and identifications between a double or even multiple belongings? They may be identifications which are constantly orbiting between homelands and countries of arrival and the path in between them. Identities which transform into a multiple set of coexisting identifications while in exile, in the double bind of existence between places and narratives mediated in a variety of ways. What is a subject that oscillates between being-host and being-guest, becoming-host and becoming-guest? Is there a possible resting place in this in-betweenness? Is it possible to break from permanent guesthood philosophically, historically and existentially?

29 Stuart Hall, *Questions of Cultural Identity*, London: Sage, 1996, p. 65.
30 Rogers Brubaker and Frederick Cooper, 'Beyond 'Identity', *Theory & Society*, 29(1), (2009), p. 23.
31 See Zygmunt Bauman, *Community: Seeking Safety in an Insecure World*, Cambridge: Polity Press, 2001.

## Life-worlds

In the essay *Taking up Residency in Homelessness*, the Czech-Brazilian media philosopher Vilém Flusser writes that when the migrant finds herself in the limbo-like state between the world she left behind (or was expelled from) and the new place of arrival which is unknown to her, she enters a state of existential *white noise* where all referential signals – the language, customs, people, etc. of the place of origin that were known to her-have been lost. In this state of 'signal failure', no new inputs can be synthesized. But if we look at this state as *white noise*, a transitional stage between the old referential worlds and a new possibility of existence, Flusser claims that there is a great productive capacity in this transformation.[32]

In fact, Flusser sees the migrant as the embodiment of a creative capacity which may be unleashed in her new freedom. If we look at exile and migration as the movement between circumstances of extreme pressure where flight (forced or not) is the only solution for survival, the journey of the exile can be a metaphor for projecting oneself into freedom. From the perspective of the migrant and the exile such as himself, he claims that freedom is not to be seen as a freedom *from* something, but a productive one, a freedom *for* something. Essentially, Flusser is using the theory of communication, phenomenology and the positive aspects of migration to arrive at creativity as a condition of survival for the migrant. Once the host realizes that the migrant is there not to intentionally disrupt the common order as nationalists often claim, but to inject it with a positive difference, a transformation in both the native/host and the migrant/guest subject may occur. It is here that an ethics of hospitality begins to take hold where migration flows disrupt the orders of both hosts and guests, and opens up for new identifications. The process of hospitality in the constitution of the subject affects both sides of the host-guest equation, not always symmetrically.

Flusser's theory of the migrant subject and its relationship to survival is reflected in the biopolitics of the city and in social, political and media infrastructures. They constitute systems of life supports, such as the *lifeworlds* in Husserlian phenomenology, where, 'intersubjective experience plays a fundamental role in our constitution of both ourselves as objectively existing subjects, other experiencing subjects, and the objective spatio-temporal world. The term 'lifeworld' denotes the way the members of one or more social groups (cultures, linguistic communities) use to structure the world into objects'.[33]

It is no coincidence media theorists Andreas Hepp and Friedrich Krotz speak about the mediatization of the *Lebenswelten/Alltagswelt*, and eventually of 'mediatized worlds' as inspired by Husserl.[34] These uses are not accidental. They are also inspired by my reading of German philosopher Peter Sloterdijk's concept of immunology in the *Spheres* trilogy, especially in *Volume III: Foam*, and in *You Must Change Your Life*, where he takes this concept of

32 Vilém Flusser, 'Taking up Residence in Homelessness', trans. Erik Heisel, in Andreas Ströhl (ed.) *Writings*, Electronic Mediations, vol. 6. Minneapolis: University of Minnesota Press, 2002, p. 93.

33 See Christian Beyer, 'Edmund Husserl', in Edward N. Zalta (ed.) *The Stanford Encyclopedia of Philosophy*, (Summer 2015), http://plato.stanford.edu/archives/sum2015/entries/husserl/.

34 See Andreas Hepp and Friedrich Krotz (eds) *Mediatized Worlds: Culture and Society in a Media Age*, Basingstoke: Palgrave Macmillan, 2014.

lifeworlds and metaphorical immunological systems even further. Sloterdijk claims that if the 19th century can be viewed as standing under the sign of production, and the 20th century under the sign of reflexivity, then we need to grasp the future-the 21st century-under the sign of the exercise, or practice. The human being is a creature that results from repetition, no longer as *homo faber,* a human of labor, or as Agamben's *homo sacer,* a human of sacrifice, but above all as a creature of repetition and artistry, a 'human in training' that shapes and self-shapes. This is close to Huizinga's *homo ludens,* the human of play, but with a dimension of recursivity and reflexivity. This is also close to Schirmacher's *homo generator,* the human that creates, the being that can engender new life-forms that inhabits new lifeworlds which leads us to, again, a creative and generative capacity. Schirmacher writes, 'What can a self, which doesn't care about having a fixed outlook and a secure place in society do? It has to become a creative self'.[35] Sloterdijk's aim is ambitious: with the aid of the notion of practice, he seeks to overcome the gap between biology and culture, or between natural processes, on the one hand, and human actions, on the other. It is an attempt to write the history of *homo immunologicus,* the self-protecting human or the self-caring human, by focusing on the mental and physical methods by which human beings from diverse cultures and civilizations have sought to optimize their 'cosmic and immunological status' in the face of the risks of life and the certainties of death. In short, immunology is a tactics of survival for the subject. For him this remains an ethical task, as opposed to one of mere genetic or social engineering.[36] In this sense, Flusser's description of migrancy and creativity seems to combine aspects of *homo generator* and *homo immunologicus*: a Self that creates as a condition of survival and immunity.

For Sloterdijk, the novelty of the *new* (and I would extend this to anyone who is referred to as 'new' in an established society as in the term '*new*comer') stems from what he sees as an unfolding of what is known, and as such innovation in an absolute sense is not possible. The *new* is always a continuation of that which already exists. The human being, he continues, is made up of a multiplicity of immune systems-systems of self-protection-besides the biological one, including socio-immunological methods as well as symbolic or psycho-immunological practices. Hence, systems of solidarity and the ethics of hospitality can be said to be examples of immunological practices that show how collectivities can become mutually protective. The design of our physical living environments like cities can also be considered immunological systems that embrace and protect collectivities and populations. Media, welfare, and other institutions can also be part of socio- and media-immunological methods.

There are other theories of the subject that are worth mentioning in the context of media theory and modernity to complement Sloterdijk's concept of immunology. According to the Dutch media theorist Mark Deuze, contemporary life is not simply becoming ever more mediatized, it is becoming 'media life',[37] that is, centered toward routinely performed media practices and

35 See Wolfgang Schirmacher, *Homo Generator: Media and Postmodern Technology*, New York, 1994.

36 See also Peter Sloterdijk, *Sphères: Écumes, sphérologie plurielle, Volume 3*, Paris: Pluriel, 1982; and *You Must Change Your Life: On Anthropotechnics*, Polity Press, 2013; Johan Huizinga, *Homo Ludens: A Study of the Play-element in Culture*, Boston: Beacon Press, 1955.

37 Mark Deuze, 'Media Life', *Media, Culture and Society*, 33.1 (2011), p.138.

rituals[38] built within the structure of life itself. The discourse of migration becomes one of such rituals while the very practices of migration and hospitality encompass an increasing number of media practices, rituals and routines outside the mainstream spotlight. Artistic projects, for example, and other practices may help in making visible the issues which mediatization may hide. What does it mean to survive, or even be reborn, in a media landscape or *mediascape*[39] as combination of both software content and hardware technological structure which produce a certain image of the world? Altogether, these constitute the *lifeworlds* in Husserl's definition, where the generative and self-immune subjects may find themselves at home.

Yet are these systems always designed to provide adequate socio-immunity? For example, the failure of cities in providing adequate housing for all their inhabitants may leave disenfranchized populations, including migrants, vulnerable to all forms of abuses and exploitations. Along the lines of Zygmunt Bauman's ideas on the vulnerable subject, these exiled populations may continue to remain unprotected and therefore both practically and ontologically.

For an exile who has lost her home and who is in the process of contructing a new home in the country of arrival, reconstructing a connection to the homeland and forging a new identification with the host society may well happen via media life practices. These include media-immunological systems, networks, infrastructures and apparatuses facilitated by a creative, generative capacity proper to the generative and self-immune subject described earlier. Transnational satellite television in European immigrant suburbs, for instance, may be a type of a media life world. Suburbs in major European cities display façades dotted with satellite dishes pointing in every direction. This phenomenon reflects the use of satellite television as a means to reconnect to homelands via TV broadcasts. They become a lifeworld when the satellite dishes act like a *lifeline* to the homeland and serve in part to mitigate the loss of one's referential environment, and as such provide a sense of immunity from a state of referential 'white noise' as Flusser noted. This is also in agreement with the findings of scholars working in media diaspora studies such as Myria Giorgiou, who describe similar phenomena that constitute *diasporic media lifeworlds* enabled by globalized, deterritorialized mediascapes.[40]

Different media practices and uses tend to concentrate in different locations creating 'media textures' (involving media from a remote homeland), and combine in different ways to produce 'media amalgamations'.[41] In this book we will look deeper into the spatial dimensions of these diasporic media lifeworlds, exemplified by transnational satellite television cultures reflected in urban peripheries. In Bruno Latour's actor-network theory (ANT), these combinations can be considered as networks and become actors in their own right when they

---

38 Couldry, *Media Rituals: A Critical Approach*, and Stina Bengtsson, 'Symbolic spaces of everyday life', *Nordicom Review*, 27.2 (2006), p. 120.

39 Arjun Appadurai, 'Disjuncture and Difference in the Global Cultural Economy', *Public Culture*, 2.2 (1990), p. 4.

40 See Myria Georgiou, *Diaspora, Identity and the Media: Diasporic Transnationalism and Mediated Spatialities*, NY: Hampton Press, 2006.

41 André Jansson, 'Indispensable Things: On Mediatization, Materiality, and Space', in Knut Lundby (ed.) *Mediatization of Communication*. Berlin: De Gruyter, 2014, p. 274.

create an assemblage with other actors, including but not limited to humans.[42] How do these technological actors determine the subjectivity of refugees, asylum seekers, migrants and immigrants in their host countries? What are the ethics of hospitality within these media lifeworlds, who is guest and who is host?

Undoubtedly, the rise of social media and the corresponding addition of 'new media logic'[43] to the more traditional media logic[44] in which new subjectivities and identifications unfold needs to be briefly considered. New modes of interaction and media participation enable complex participatory cultures[45] which puts new pressures on the constitution of the subject. Among migrants, social media becomes an important *media lifeworld* as it acts as an interface of identification and creates recognizability among peers in flight, in diaspora and in exile. Social media practices may become a locus of belonging in and of themselves as a site of new subjectivities while, at the time, serving to reify and crystallize *a priori* national identifications. Moreover, in diasporic social media specifically, to be connected also implies visibility, and visibility for a migrant both confers a means of subjective existence and mutual protection as well as exposure to danger – the network today can more effectively trace back the expelled in the absence of a passport number at a physical border control. All selves become traceable, trackable, retrievable, with nowhere to hide. What sort of immunity do we have against this overall visibility?

The abyss that separates city centers and puts immigrant areas out of sight or in remote detention centers such as in Denmark is the same abyss that separates the media discourses from the human experience of migration, from both the host's and the guest's perspective. If we continue to encounter the migrant in its mediatized version as an image, a news article or in a social media feed, she will continue to be part of a faceless flow, which is the side effect of inhabiting media lifeworlds: they result in abstractions. The social media flows offer us continuous perceptions and glimpses of other worlds, but we are unable to conceptualize them, and even less establish a dialogue with them. In *Networks without a Cause*, Dutch media theorist Geert Lovink gives a detailed analysis of the ways in which subjectivity is shaped online, and the effects of the accelerated nature of a connected life on a sense of self. The multiple platforms we use to connect to the world, whether it is the Internet or satellite television, enable a sense of self that reveals itself in different ways depending on which channels we are surfing on. While the connected self may become empowered by the multiple ways in which it can express itself, Lovink argues that these identifications 'may leave one "flat"'. For him, the debate about information overload, not just in the way we consume information but also in how information consumes us, comes down to 'the loss of the Self'.[46]

---

42 See Bruno Latour, *Reassembling the Social: An Introduction of the Actor-Network Theory*, Oxford University Press, 2005.

43 Dana M. Boyd, and N. B. Ellison, 'Social Network Sites: Definition, History, and Scholarship', *Journal of computer‐mediated Communication*, 13.1 (2007), p. 213.

44 See David L. Altheide and Robert P. Snow, *Media Logic*, Beverly Hills: Sage, 1979.

45 See Henry Jenkins, *Convergence Culture: Where Old and New Media Collide*, New York: NYU Press, 2006.

46 Geert Lovink, *Networks Without a Cause: A Critique of Social Media*, Cambridge: Polity Press, 2013, p. 33.

The central question of an ethics of hospitality is the humanity implied in this encounter. Philosopher Emmanuel Lévinas describes the encounter with the face of the Other, not as represented by others or mediatized by apparatuses, but as encountered by oneself as a foundation of the ethics of hospitality. Himself a representative of Otherness as a Jewish émigré, Lévinas' ideas of alterity open up a discussion about the parallels between the status of migrant versus citizen, native versus foreign, but also a more intimate dimension that occurs in the unplanned, unforeseen, un-mediated hospitality embodied in gestures and in the face. The face, according to Lévinas, is the ultimate and most concrete instance where we meet the Other, a confrontation where we acknowledge someone's presence and acquire a responsibility before it. This way, that face can no longer be ignored. Facing the other then implies a welcoming of the other and establishes a relationship with them. Jacques Derrida recalls Maurice Blanchot's words about Lévinas's philosophy of alterity in *Totality and Infinity* as a foundation for thinking itself, where

> (...) we are called upon to become responsible for what philosophy essentially is, by welcoming, in all the radiance and infinite exigency proper to it, the idea of the Other, that is to say, the relation with *autrui*. It is though there were here a new departure in philosophy (...).[47]

If the politics of hospitality are created to defend the host, the counter-narrative can only be created by combatting the facelessness of existing discourses and looking at them face to face. The face becomes the locus of our responsibility that cuts across media surfaces, where we rely on our human capacity to understand the Other, reconcile with the Other, and coexist with the Other by way of presence. According to Lévinas, facing another face is at the precognitive stage of an embodied sensibility which is what he means by the ethics that lies in the foundation of philosophy. Thus, here is the essence of an ethics of hospitality for Lévinas: not the distance that separates the host from the guest and that which keeps them in their separate spheres of host-*ness* and guest-*ness*, but the human sensibility that can only be reached by the closeness to another face.

It is in the day-to-day occurrence of city life, in the everydayness of the city lifeworld where we encounter a stream of faces, voices, bodies, objects that compose this phenomenon – of a hospitality which can be found in the encounter with the human, where there is a possibility for a dialogic encounter and to be able to perceive and conceive reality. The city is where this encounter of faces and of humanity occurs at close proximity embedded in the immunological apparatuses and lifeworlds described earlier.

47 Jacques Derrida, *Adieu to Emmanuel Lévinas,* Palo Alto: Stanford University Press, 1999, p. 20.

## Contextualizing Hospitality, in Stockholm and Beyond

In this book, I will investigate this global phenomenon of migration in a specific European city, Stockholm, Sweden, as the main case study,[48] where much of the debate surrounding immigration revolves around issues of race, religion and the toll on the welfare system, as well as the culprit of social inequality and urban segregation. In trying to accommodate individuals and groups with different needs and different histories within densely populated areas, systems of protection and immunity may become slowly eroded, not by the presence of refugees or newcomers alone, but also by the effects of privatizations, new public management,[49] and financial speculation that blurs the definition of the public sphere.

Whereas in many European countries much of the current crisis in hospitality stems from the consequences of a long-drawn financial crisis begun in 2008, it is important to note that Sweden, exceptionally, did not suffer the same consequences and its middle class has remained quite stable during this period – it is by no means a bankrupt country. What occurs, perhaps, is an existential crisis when faced with this demographic shift towards a more cosmopolitan, or globalized, society which puts any notion of the 'national' to a test. While many Swedes support a generous open-door policy, the sharp rise in popularity of the extreme-right and its anti-immigrant political platforms in a short period of time[50] points to a larger trend of retreating slowly into a closed-borders nationalism, thus putting hospitality as the ethical relationship governing the rights and duties between guests and hosts, to the forefront. By looking at a small community in a specific periphery, or satellite city, of Stockholm, we can more easily gauge all of these effects.

Over the course of an entire generation, forty-something Swedes like myself have watched profound changes in the country's demographic makeup. Since the late 1970s, immigration has risen dramatically in an egalitarian society that has practiced one of the most liberal immigration policies in the world and built a national self-image of being a sanctuary for refugees, victims of persecution and poverty around the world. This has made the country's largest cities positively more multicultural, but the effects of its multicultural policy have also resulted in the negative development of ethnic concentration in suburban areas. Stockholm is today considered one of the most segregated cities in Europe. As Stockholm's non-native population continues to grow both in size and proportion, by 2030 immigrants

---

48 According to recent statistics; one-third of the immigrants and first-generation Swedes in Stockholm are from Asia (including Middle East and Turkey), 9% from Africa, 4% from South and Central America, and 2% from North America, Australia and other parts of the world. Almost 53% have origins in Europe, most of those from Finland and the remaining from Eastern Europe. Swedish Migration Authority, http://www.migrationsverket.se

49 Part of an effort to make the public service more 'businesslike' and to improve its efficiency by using private sector management models, creating 'customer-centered' services. This mode of administration has been very successful in Sweden, where many state-owned companies and service providers within the system of welfare have been privatized in the past two decades.

50 *Sverigedemokrater*, Sweden's extreme-right party has risen from less than 3% of voters before 2010 to 23,4% of voter preference in February 2020. It is today the third largest party in the Swedish Parliament. The party defines its program on a more restrictive refugee policy, which has been gaining more and more supporters in recent years, as the numbers show.

and their descendants are projected to account for 40% of all the city's residents.[51] Given that a large part of this heterogeneous population today finds itself in the lowest income brackets, this also means that Stockholm may become a city with considerably more poverty than today – unless measures towards making it a more hospitable city are taken.

Of all babies born in 2014 in Stockholm – my son's generation – nearly 50% have at least one foreign-born parent, like myself, or have half-Swedish parents, like my son. In the media, this generation is called *andragenerationare*, 'second-generationers,' the children of immigrant parents. This term is rejected by this generation, like a student of mine, of Malay-Singaporean heritage, who asks himself: 'I was born here, I live here, I have no other homeland, but I am still not Swedish-what does it take to become Swedish?' Even though nationalist and conservative agenda-setting has progressively gained more space in the media in recent years, opening this wound in national conscience and its troubled relationship to the foreign Other, this has also created an opportunity for an array of writers, artists and politicians who are themselves immigrants or children of immigrants, to appear under the media spotlight. As such, there is an increased agency and a multitude of voices in the public sphere that constitute a growing counter-public to mainstream mediatized narratives in equal proportion to the growing nationalism.

Stockholm is used here as a case in point to illustrate the possibilities and limitations of hospitality vis-á-vis current migration policies, the strategies of multiculturalism and cultural integration, and its effects on urban form, as well as outlining how art may be able to reveal aspects of hospitality in practice. One of the aspects this book will investigate in detail is how segregation based on cultural, racial, and class lines is embedded in urban planning by design and how overcoming this may become part of an 'hospitable turn' where art and urban design are mediums where host-guest relationships are performed, mediated, and problematized.

Home to nearly one third of the country's immigrant population, Stockholm's suburbs have become the epicenter of immigration in Sweden, followed by Gothenburg and Malmö. Cross-cultural communication has become increasingly challenging within Swedish cities, many of which have *de facto* segregated areas, or, neighborhoods and regions in the peripheries where there is a majority of foreign-born populations paired with lower income populations.[52] These peripheries follow the morphology of 'satellite cities' – smaller suburban areas which are relatively locally autonomous but largely dependent on city centers for work or services. Those satellite cities on the lower end of the socio-economic scale are sometimes labeled by sensationalist media as 'no-go zones', but are formally called 'extremely disadvantaged areas'[53] that the public regards unruly and controlled by local criminals,

---

51 *Potential Nordic population in 2030*, Nordregio (Nordic Centre for Spatial Development), 2014, https://archive.nordregio.se/en/Metameny/About-Nordregio/Journal-of-Nordregio/2008/Journal-of-Nordregio-no-1-2008/Potential-Nordic-population-2030/index.html.

52 The most famous such areas in Sweden are Rosengård in Malmö, Bergsjön in Göteborg, and Tensta/Rinkeby and Fittja/Alby in Stockholm, where the foreign-born population is over 85% in all cases. These areas are all located at the end of the line of the public transportation lines that service them.

53 'Extremely disadvantaged areas' is the name given by the police and replicated in the media to identify those areas showing socio-economic problems and levels of relative (in)security.

and 'where the police is unable to fulfill its duties', very often mediatized in direct correlation to foreign-born populations.[54] The city centers are well to do areas seemingly impermeable to these discourses: immigration is something that always seems to exist somewhere else.

In many of these suburbs, the predominant building type is a neo-brutalist architecture from the late 1960s and early 1970s used for fast, cheap and large-scale construction of affordable housing that built one million new living units between 1964 and 1975, also known as the *miljonprogrammet*, or 'The Million Program'. Like similar housing programs elsewhere in Europe, in *miljonprogram* neighborhoods in the peripheries of Stockholm, where the case study takes place, we see the problematic encounter between large-scale government investments to solve the housing crises of the past and the large-scale immigration that allegedly creates a 'population crisis' of the present. What served as a subsidized housing solution for the working class one generation ago is now perceived as an eyesore and a burden in the eyes of today's middle class. The commonly held view that criminality is high in these segregated areas, largely due to the mediatization of violence in these suburbs, allegedly made them undesirable for their original intended tenants, partly causing a middle class, or white flight,[55] to move out from these neighborhoods which were originally designed with innovative living technologies and intended as the rising middle-class, touted as the architectural avant-garde of the day. While not clearly instituted by the State, the availability of social housing, lower living costs and proximity to one's ethnic/religious/social group foster in many diasporic populations a preference to live together, and thus the formation of local bonds and local beloinging within suburban communities is very strong.

---

54 In 2014, the Swedish police released a report listing 55 such 'no-go zones'. See Per Gudmunsson, '55 'no go'-zoner i Sverige', *Svenska Dagbladet*, 28 October 2014, https://www.svd.se/55-no-go-zoner-i-sverige; and the report *En nationell översikt av kriminella nätverk med stor påverkan i lokalsamhälle* (A national overview of criminal networks with strong influence in local communities), Rikskriminalpolisen, Underrättelsesektionen, October 2014, p. 8. Available at: https://polisen.se/siteassets/dokument/ovriga_rapporter/en-nationell-oversikt-av-kriminella-natverk.pdf.

55 'White flight' is most often referred to as a past-tense phenomenon in the United States: the decades in which fearful mid-century whites in the United States moved to the suburbs, such as what ensued after the 1967 race riots in Detroit, where most white residents of the inner city moved to the new suburbs. New research suggests that white flight is far from over and is acquiring new dimensions and definitions. The result is the creation of segregated areas, or 'ethnoburbs' as in Wei Li's definition. See also Wei Li, *Ethnoburb: The New Ethnic Community in Urban America*, Honolulu: University of Hawaii Press, 2009.

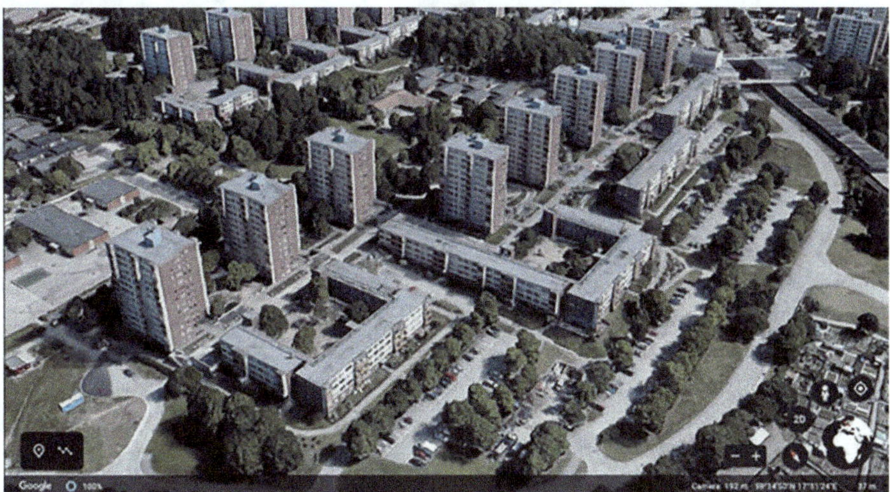

*Figure 1 – Fittja, Sweden, 59'14N, 17'51E. Source: Google Earth*

During the time I spent living in Fittja, I witnessed how the access to and contact with the host country and culture is an abyss. The noticeable absence of Swedish nationals in the residential population contrasts with the overrepresentation of Swedes as figures of authority such as the police, politicians, bureaucrats and administrators. Whether by design or by pattern of occupation, the suburbs have become islands of diversity separated from a historically monocultural landscape. These territories have developed a distinct character and culture which can be called heterotopias, to use Michel Foucault's concept of 'othered' spaces.[56]

As such, the contemporary effects of global conflict and its resulting migrations acquire an important symbolic and aesthetic dimension this book will try to address. It is important to note that the relationship of these housing complexes reflects both a need to solve a housing crisis of the past, but also to enter a project of modernization via the aesthetic regime of modernism and the feasibility and 'planability' of social progress.[57] In fact, such utopian architecture as that of the city of Brasília in Brazil is among the modernistic precursors of *miljonprogrammet* carrying with them the promise of new social models which often fail to become realized, as we will see later.

These neighborhoods do not simply express an architectural ideal based on a social ideology; I argue that they also work as a media form, the organization of space that mediates social relationships in a similar fashion to what Walter Benjamin observed in the 19th century Paris. In his classical reading, Baron Haussmann's replanning of the city resulted in both ghettoization and alienation, but at heart was aimed at preventing urban riots and physical clashes by rendering the construction of barricades impossible (the hopes proved futile by

---

56 Michel Foucault, 'Of Other Spaces', in Nicholas Mirzoeff (ed.) *The Visual Culture Reader*, London: Routledge, 2002.

57 Tom Avermaete and Serhat Karakayali Marion von Osten (eds) *Colonial Modern: Aesthetics of the Past, Rebellions for the Future*, London: Black Dog Publishing, 2010.

the Parisian Commune's barricades).[58] In a similar way, the 20th century grand architectural visions (including *miljonprogrammet*) were aimed at fostering certain social interactions and disabling others within a conception of a utopic future. As ironic as their bourgeois counterparts, they often resulted in unpredictable constellations and also acted as spaces where struggles for urban and social justice took place.

Beginning in 2011, and parallel to the intensification of migration flows along the decade, Sweden would see a string of uprisings in suburbs, along with the rise of urban justice movements taking stride in these areas, to make a claim for several misconceptions and the well-known underrepresentation of immigrants and persons with foreign backgrounds in every sphere of society. This period thus marks not only a political shift ushered in by conservative and progressive fronts, but also a reevaluation of a national self-image that had been closely identified with a social democracy and social equality, that no longer exists as such since it was imagined for a more homogeneous society.

And yet, it is exactly this historical element which creates the frictions between new populations and the host population. In Reinhart Koselleck's vision, even the historical time itself is generated by similar frictions between 'space of experience' as whatever we know about the world and the past, and a 'horizon of expectations', that is, what we envisage in the future.[59] Hosts and the newcomers have dramatically different spaces of experience, and as a result they also have very different horizons of expectations. It can even be said that they live in different historical times. How can these radically different worlds of experience and expectations coexist? Are there common grounds? Can we live together?

## Mapping the Satellite City

In order to witness this phenomenon where media, art and architecture intersect with migration in Stockholm, I created a research device in the form of participatory art and media intervention in the satellite city of Fittja, located south of Stockholm, between 2010 and 2012. The research, planning, and execution of *Satellitstaden* ('Satellite City', in Swedish) was done under a post-professional art curating program CuratorLab at Konstfack University of Arts, Crafts, and Design in Stockholm, Sweden. *Satellitstaden* included a site-specific art intervention on satellite dishes hanging on building facades, community engagement strategies, and an ethnographic field research with interviews with local residents about their transnational media habits symbolized by the satellite dishes that hang on the façades of every building in this area.

The most interesting institutions visited during this time were active in Stockholm suburbs and exemplified artistic practices and curatorial programs related to the 'social turn' in contemporary art, a term coined by the art historian Claire Bishop in 2006. This included socially oriented projects with community engagement, artist residencies and artist-initiated projects

58 See Walter Benjamin, *The Arcades Project*, New York: Belknap Press, 2002.

59 See Reinhart Koselleck, *Futures Past: On the Semantics of Historical Time*, NY: Columbia University Press, 2004.

responsive to and engaged with areas dominated by *miljonprogram* building typologies and its residents. Bishop identifies the 'social turn' in contemporary art as a 'surge of artistic interest in collectivity, collaboration, direct engagement with specific social constituencies'.[60]

In Botkyrka, a municipality south of Stockholm, the local art center *Botkyrka konsthall* had an exhibition space and an artist residency program called *Residence Botkyrka* in Fittja, a *miljonprogram* neighborhood built in 1973. This area is otherwise known for having the highest percentage (97%) of immigrant residents in any constituency in Scandinavia. All the artistic activity done by this artistic residency program somehow responded to this urban and social context, whose landscape is dominated by a single architectonic design that houses 7,500 people in identical highrises and rowhouses over only four streets spread across a park area.

Moving to Sweden to do this project on a more permanent basis was not without estrangement. It was confusing as well as exhilarating to 'migrate' somewhere new, especially as this 'new' was something I was supposed to already call home. Even though I am Swedish by birth and speak Swedish without an accent, because of a lack of exposure to my supposed homeland prior to my arrival, my vocabulary was somewhat limited. At first, I identified more with the immigrants in Fittja than with my Swedish family and with Swedish society, whose values and traditions I was familiar with but could not relate to.

Even though Fittja is sometimes defined as a place where no one is 'originally' from (since in its current form it is a satellite city that was erected on rural grounds in 1973), this aspect is what enabled an entry point into the research project, even though the subculture of Stockholm suburbs and the cultures of those countries where most residents in Fittja come from, mainly the Middle East, were largely unknown to me. Skeptical of the misrepresentation of places like Fittja in the media, *Satellitstaden* became a device to discover the issues faced by this community from the inside out. Newspaper articles and several studies about the representation of migration in the media and Fittja specifically were relatively easy to find. In fact, Fittja has been exhaustively researched by sociologists, journalists and political scientists because of its demographic uniqueness. As such, many residents already had an initial resistance to anything and anyone that looked like a journalist or researcher and expressed animosity towards being considered 'study objects' and expressed 'research fatigue'.

Even though news reporting and studies were important as background material, I was not initially interested in the media representation of migration or migrants in suburbs *per se*, nor in the role of the press in shaping Fittja's identification by external sources. The existing data was often biased or distanced, tainted by academic and journalistic objective coldness. I was missing material that expressed a perspective that came from direct involvement with the community and agency from members of the community itself – a more human dimension which could only be achieved by the direct encounter with residents, without an institutional interface or editorial agenda.

60 Claire Bishop, 'The Social Turn: Collaboration and its Discontents', *Artforum*, February 2006, p. 179, https://www.artforum.com/print/200602/the-social-turn-collaboration-and-its-discontents-10274.

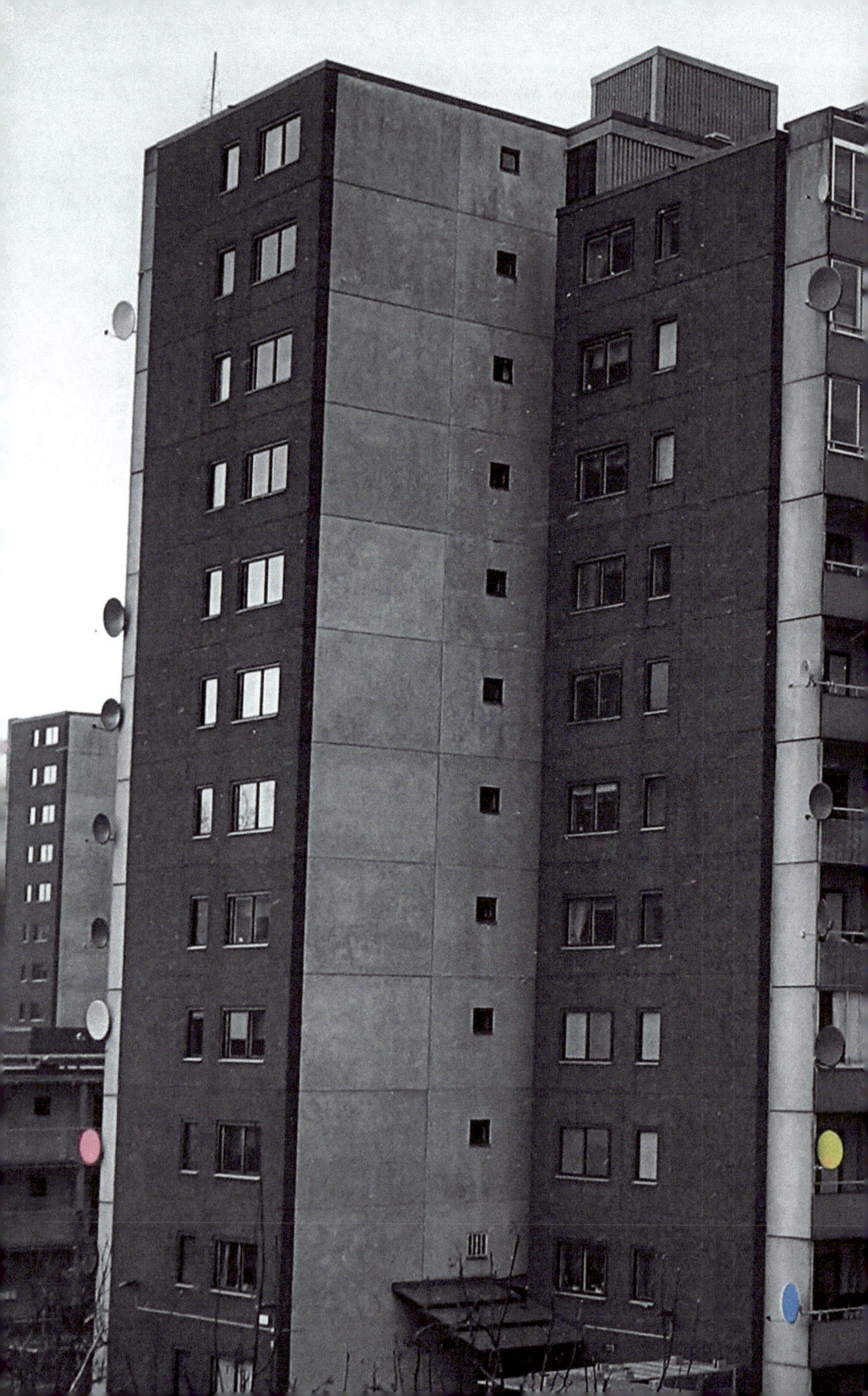

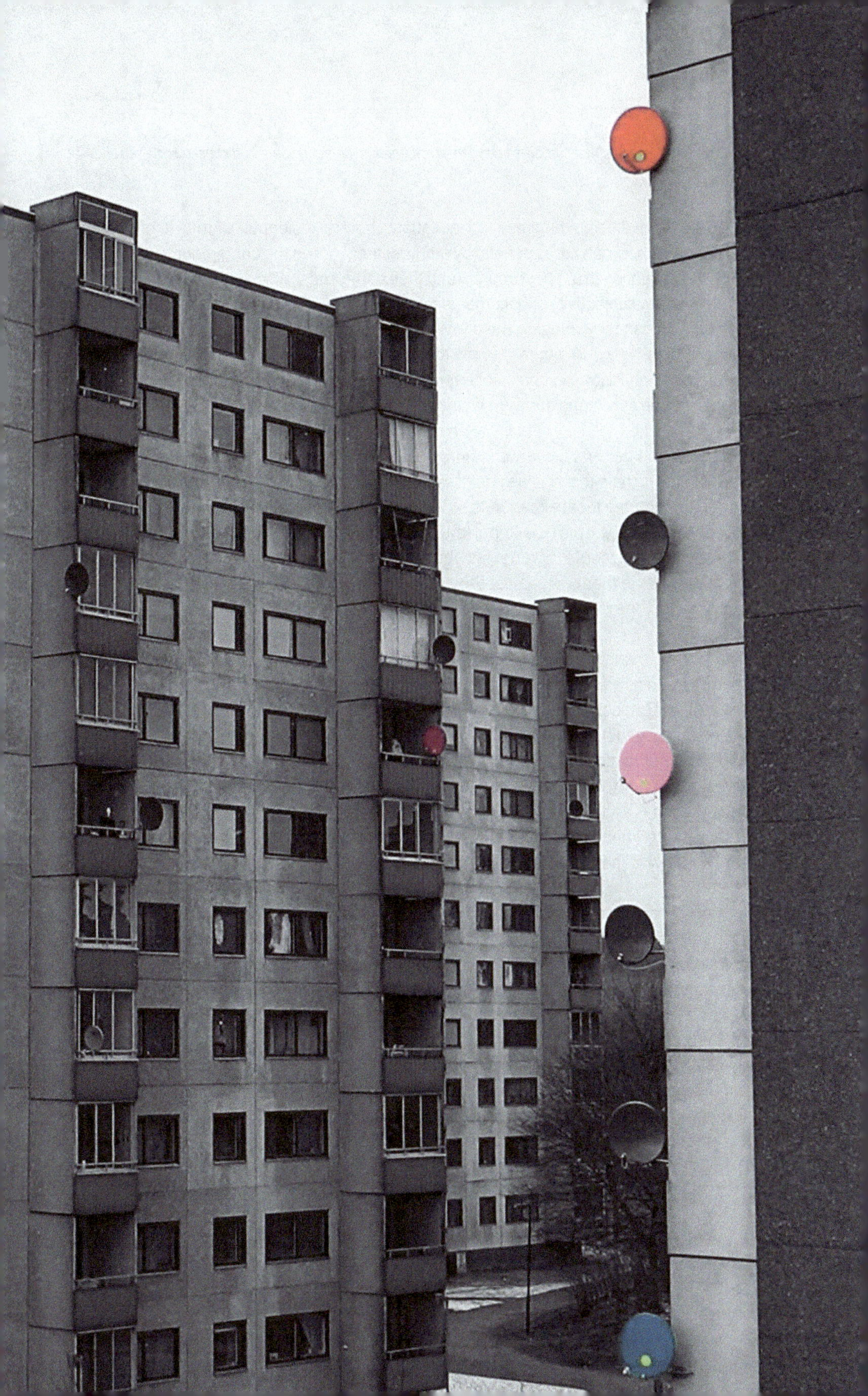

*Figure 2 – Street-wide installation Satellitstaden which entailed coloring satellite dishes in Fittja, 2011-2012. Image by the author.*

This led me to develop guiding research questions: how do residents of Fittja, or of any other *areas of exclusion,* urban areas defined by ethnic segregation in the contemporary city, define themselves in relation to the host country and their homelands? Who are the new subjects and what are the new subjectivities that emerge from new forms of living and *media life supports*?[61] With what tools do they mitigate the dilemmas of exile, home and homeland? How do they respond subjectively and spatially to the ever-shifting terms of engagement to newcomers in the host society? How can host societies be structured differently if those who do not fit mainstream norms of behavior were included in decision-making and world-designing?

In trying to avoid generalities about immigration and urban segregation in the study, I narrowed my playing field to a single street in Fittja. This allowed me to be as specific as possible in understanding the local experience of 'landed' immigrants and their life in a microcosm within a satellite city. This was important in rebating the *representation* of immigration – the image of immigrants in Sweden as observed and interpreted from the outside, i.e. the general view in the media – against the *experience* of living in this area – the self-image of the community, the point of view of singularity.

The means to conduct the field research was to engage residents in a participatory art project that also served as an ethnographic research device for the entire investigation. The interpellation of the art project as a device for approximating the relationship between the philosophy of the migrant, media and political realities, was largely inspired by the way in which Flusser applies communication theory and aesthetics to his philosophy of migration-the three fields of investigation for the ethics of hospitality: hospitality as moral philosophy, hospitality as artistic practice, and hospitality as media practice. More importantly, I was interested in Flusser's formulation of the subject in what he called 'the migrant condition' as a transformative, creative capacity, as mentioned earlier.

The aesthetic premise was quite straightforward: to put color on satellite dishes dotting the façades of the highrise buildings and rowhouses along the street. In contrast, the execution was very complex and required funding, logistics, collaborations, the buy-in of administrators and residents, and several strategies of reaching out to people over time.[62] Indeed, as we shall see later, involving individuals and communities in so-called 'participatory' art projects (reminding once again of Jenkins' participatory culture problematic and Bishop's concept of the 'social turn' in contemporary art) is far from simple, and where philosophy of hospitality again is concerned, it involves ethical dilemmas as well. How does one approach the Other inside a territoru that is not one's own? Does a participatory art project contribute to more *othering* of the community or is it able to create a new image for itself? What does participation

61 Deuze, 'Media Life', p. 141.

62 Strategies involved creating situations for meeting people and generate participation: neighborhood meetings, workshops, being a member in local clubs, attending the local gym and leisure facilities, eating in local restaurants, etc.

mean in a community like Fittja and what does it bring in terms of change (if any) in such environment? What is the guest artist-researcher's positionality in this context?

The artistic project aimed to investigate how the transnational media practices of this community relate to the notion of home, focusing specifically on the community's relationship to the ubiquitous satellite dishes on façades, to gauge the level and nature of belonging and identification with host society and homeland. *Satellitstaden*, which is described at length in Chapter 4, was a site-specific intervention consisting of coloring satellite dishes with neon colors hanging on the balconies of highrises and rowhouses on a single street. The satellite dishes, hung on balcony railings or pierced through the concrete façades adjacent to the balconies, could only be reached for the aesthetic intervention from inside the apartments, which required the permission of the resident and entry into the home. Due to this physical constraint, a greater part of the time was spent in meeting residents interested in participating in the project through a variety of strategies. In exchange for coloring their satellite dishes with a 'parabol dress' (as the seamstresses that manufactured the textile cover used to 'color' the dishes called them), I asked for a one-hour semi-structured interview in return where I would gauge the significance of satellite television in that family's everyday life as well as their relationship to their living environment, community, city, host country, and their homeland.

Much time was spent communicating in Swedish or in other languages on kitchen tables, usually with fresh coffee and cakes, and sometimes even watching television together. Indeed, much of the study continues the line of inquiry initiated by David Morley's analysis of how television watching is practiced as a family-centered activity revealing complex dynamics of power relations, gender, and other aspects.[63] In this light, the media and media use are regarded as rituals, close to what Nick Couldry views as *media rituals* typical of the television-dominated mediascape. Instead of the powerful social center, the media become a set of practices oriented towards issues of belonging. In this sense, what is found in the media is less important than what people do with the media and around the media.[64]

Entering the homes of so many people allowed me to also loosely perform what French philosopher Gaston Bachelard called *topoanalysis*, 'the systematic psychological study of the sites of our intimate lives'.[65] In considering space as not being an order among things but rather a *quality* of things in relation to us, this phenomenological orientation allowed me to glimpse, in several house visits, the objects, smells, tastes, sounds, images, words, presences, and rhythms that constitute the distinct universes inhabited by each family in Fittja. The visits confirm Vilém Flusser's theory of objects acting as extensions of the homeland for the exiled subject.[66] The homes felt like space-time capsules inhabiting entirely different worlds, each one a *heterotopia* in its own right.

---

63 David Morley. *Family Television: Cultural Power and Domestic Leisure*, London: Comedia Publishing Group, 1986, p43.

64 See Couldry, '*Media Rituals*' and 'Theorising Media as Practice'.

65 Gaston Bachelard, *The Poetics of Space*, trans. Maria Jolas, Boston: Beacon Press, 1969, p. 8.

66 Flusser, 'Taking residence in Homeslessness', p. 99.

Between 2011 and 2012, the colors spread on satellite dishes, one by one, along the streets of Fittja, with one participant recommending another participant throughout the entire period. Participation in the project was the result of spontaneous adhesion, recommendations, active recruiting in community meetings, workshops, mouth to mouth, and other approaches. Essentially, the project became a media intervention as much as an art intervention, using the power of media to mobilize research and facilitate positive changes in society, along the lines of Löwgren and Reimers' principle for collaborative media.[67] According to them (theoreticians and practitioners of intervention projects), art and media interventions are typically combined in complex, layered projects, just as this one.

As the installation became increasingly visible from several vantage points in the neighborhood, it caught some media attention, which in turn generated more participation and also created a renewed and more positive representation of Fittja in the press. This way, a new network of affinity emerged within the project while using existing ties of kinship, friendship or proximity between residents. At the same time as these intimate connections unfolded, each resident's relationship to their homelands as media diasporas or 'mediatized migrants'[68] also became clearer for the purposes of the research, and the ethics of hospitality emerged as a philosophical framework that could encapsulate this complex and active experience. Transnational television as a medium for of hospitality (media *as* a home), also became a device for an art and media intervention, not simply a contemplative and analytical project. In practice, television was used in the spirit of the collaborative media approach at once to examine the problem academically and contribute to a tangible, visible reflection of the situation by virtue of media intervention.[69] Furthermore, the legitimating of my role as an artist-researcher or perhaps, my *imposition* as an artist-researcher, always needed to be confronted. Indeed, during the project where I conducted fifty interviews, it felt like I was the one being interviewed fifty times. Curiosity was reciprocal: if I wanted to know more about their stories, I had to be prepared to also share mine.

The theory toolbox in this monograph begins with philosophical speculations that traverse media philosophy, architectural theory and history, sociological analysis, media and art theory, as well as a personal account of the face-to-face meetings I had with some of the total of fifty participating individuals and families resident in Fittja, who kindly allowed me to enter their homes. I also aimed to avoid the trap of mono-disciplinarity and the reduction of an otherwise complex topic to the narrow vision of a single specialist field. Likewise, I position it as an attempt to open the possibility of philosophy to shed light on contemporary issues and the development of a philosophical vocabulary of hospitality with which to examine a contemporary phenomenon.

---

67 Jonas Löwgren and Bo Reimer, *Collaborative Media: Production, Consumption, and Design Interventions*, Cambridge, Mass.: MIT Press, 2013.

68 See Andreas Hepp, Cigdem Bozdag, and Laura Suna, 'Mediatized Migrants: Media Cultures and Communicative Networking in the Diaspora', in Leopoldina Fortunati, Raul Pertierra and Jane Vincent (eds) *Migrations, Diaspora, and Information Technology in Global Societies*, London: Palgrave, 2012, pp. 172-188.

69 Löwgren and Reimer, '*Collaborative Media*', p. 23.

**Chapter 1**, 'On Hospitality', traces a philosophical lineage of the ethics that governs the relationship between guest and host, self and the other, or better, between several Others in the context of the city, perhaps where a dissolution of the notion of Self facilitates the possibility of coexistence between others, the concurrent process of claiming space should not be merely seen as related to delineating a geographical, or physical, territory. The ethics of hospitality is approached first through Kant's treatise on hospitality and cosmopolitanism as a means for the perpetual peace between nations, and later on Derrida's speculation on unconditional hospitality and Lévinas's meeting of the ethics of hospitality in the encounter with the human. The insufficiency of language in naming otherness reverberates in Flusser's and Sassen's speculations on a vocabulary capable of representing the 'other' as a way to create a political subject. The notion of difference and otherness is also represented in spatial terms and goes through a discussion of heterotopias and spaces of difference.

The definitions of home, homeland and belonging as ever shifting notions are further viewed through Flusser's approach to migration and nationalism as a problem of communication to draw a framework for the hospitable city and the subject that inhabits it. This has to do with issues beyond identification and belonging: it is perhaps a matter of sharing resources with the Other that ultimately determines the level of permeability of a host culture towards its guest: how wide open or wide shut are the doors to the city? As David Harvey inspired by Henri Lefevbre's question suggests: who has the right to the city? Who *does not* have the right to the city and why? Is spatial justice possible? Does hospitality come before or after the city, or is hospitality, if considered in a phenomenological sense, always in process, always in a state of *becoming* and therefore able to transform the city? Can we think of a 'hospitable city'? Lastly, Ulrich Beck's *Cosmopolitan Manifesto* provides a set of clues as to how we can begin to speculate on a cosmopolitan subject as a possibility that helps dissolve borders.

**Chapter 2**, 'The City as an Act of Hospitality', is an essay that begins with the act of writing as an act of hospitality and the imagination of the city. It bridges the more philosophical first chapter with the more case-study oriented third chapter and contains a series of metaphors serving to contextualize the relationship of hospitality to utopia and the relationship of utopia to exclusion poetically, philosophically and in practice. The examples given are the Astral City, known as 'Our Home', transcribed by the Brazilian psychic Chico Xavier, and the city of Brasília as examples of new cities that contain futuristic and progressive views on society and technology while at the same time falling prey to their historical contexts. This comparison reveals the failure of planned communities, utopian visions, the failures of modernist aspirations and the programmatic exclusion of the Other in modernity. While the essay reflects on the failures of public housing propositions, it also puts into question the ability of architects and planners to bridge the gap between theory and practice when it comes to planning for 'unplanned' subjects such as migrants. Here, some narratives from the construction of Brasília in the 1950s until today are presented. The chapter also includes instances where residents of segregated and peripheral areas have been given agency to voice their concerns, with examples from documentary films that exemplify this critique.

**Chapter 3**, 'Hospitality, Modernity and the Subject', I examine the socio-immunological life support institutional systems such as welfare and the architecture of social housing in relationship to migration in specific contexts, notably in Sweden which is where the case study takes place. When did, for example, the Swedish suburb typology, originally meant to facilitate housing for the working class, become a synonym for ethnic enclave? By extension, what is the genealogy of the space of the Other in the modernist and contemporary city, as a space of exception, segregated *by design* to contain those who for some reason or another, voluntarily or not, for economic, political, religious or ethnic reasons cannot live in the main city? I examine the social engineering behind the urban typologies of social housing and where the politics of 'open door' migration and its relationship to welfare and the built environment situates particular instances of hospitality, host-guest relationships and its contradictions. The chapter ends with a discussion of the notion of spatial justice, the subaltern and the importance of grassroots movements as a means of empowering the Other to become visible, heard and situated in places that 'talk back'.

**Chapter 4**, 'Satellite City: Art and Hospitality', begins with a positioning of culture as an aggregative agent in a segregated environment, and the triangulation between a participatory art project, satellite network cultures, and architecture in satellite cities. This leads into the detailed description of the research environment of Fittja where *Satellitstaden* takes place. In this area, one of the most visible physical markers of immigrant residents are the hundreds of satellite dishes hanging from balconies, a common feature in similar satellite cities across the continent. Due to the significance of transnational satellite television in immigrant communities, these objects became the chosen elements for an aesthetic and media intervention, done with the participation of, or, as I argue, *co-generation* with the local community. The art project is described at length within the vocabulary of hospitality and discusses guest-host relationships in several levels: a guest artist temporarily living in the artist residency; the relevance of art projects in blighted communities; the tactics for gathering participants and modes of address; the situations in which I met participants; and the results of these interactions. Because *Satellitstaden* depended entirely on the involvement of the community, the issue of participation in art projects is addressed from a critical standpoint drawing on art theories that situate the anthropological approach to art, the 'social turn' of socially-engaged and community-based art projects. At the end of the chapter, I oppose art criticism of participation to the citizen perspective of 'experimental' art in the suburbs and speculate on the possibility of introducing the notion of a 'hospitable turn' in the realm of participatory art projects.

**Chapter 5**, 'Transnational Media and Hospitality', is an account of the experience of interviewing participants and house visits in Fittja during *Satellitstaden* for one year strung along with more media theoretically oriented analysis. The chapter follows a narrative format in first person as a walkthrough in the neighborhood that consists of reflections, stories, impressions and contextual aspects which straddle the aesthetic intentions of the art project and deal more directly with the philosophical aspects introduced in Chapter 1. The interviews themselves focused first on television habits, the resident's satellite dishes and television program preferences, and secondly on their lives in the neighborhood and in Sweden. The material is grouped according to themes that arose from conversations, focusing on the relationship between the individuals I met and the contexts they inhabit – real, symbolic and imaginary. Mostly, the interviews recount stories of isolation, flight, and the doubleness of longing for the homeland and the difficulty of inhabiting a new *lifeworld*, that is, the difficulty of acquiring a second (or third) home and the journey towards normalizing life within a new set of references, a new language, new laws, and new values. In some cases, this 'clash of civilizations' resulted in an existential impasse, persons who have become 'lost in translation,' often finding comfort in the building of a personal universe within the space of their home, while others have more easily adjusted to new realities. The television set with the homeland channels in this case act as a view towards the world, a window to look through and gain an understanding of possible lifeworlds, and as such, becomes a *media-immunological* device in exile.

While satellite television is used to mitigate some of the negative existential aspects of life in exile, it also informs diaspora communities of the struggles of the homeland. This in turn informs the shaping of necessary *media lifeworlds* in this community. The rapidly escalating violence in current war zones in the Middle East, for example, which precipitates one of the largest migrations flows into Sweden in the past decades, mobilizes diaspora communities into acting on behalf of their homeland, and acting on behalf of a sense of belonging, and more so – acting according to a duty of belonging. One of the observed effects of urban segregation in so-called 'ethnic enclaves' is that the sense of cultural belonging and identification to the host country are weak when compared to the strong connection to homeland identities as well as to local communities – the 'national' aspect of the host country is something threatening, remote and abstract, and often enters the domestic space in media forms, but are not conceived as tangible realities. The host country is thus a place of estrangement and distance. Lastly, the consequences of a type of multiculturalism that has purposefully concentrated migrant populations in specific public housing areas in the city has yielded, in fact, a new type of political subject which is rewriting the 'national' narrative of the host with a new language being formed in these areas away from hegemonic discourses.

Even though areas like Fittja are the symptom of increasingly segregated cities, I contend that suburbs are where a cosmopolitan sense of belonging can actually take place against the growing nationalistic conservatism that uses the existence of diasporic and by extension segregated communities as a political linchpin. This ability to envision and experience worlds beyond one's own has been lost in the closed-mindedness of the middle class, and the wanton gentrification of wealthy downtown areas that tend to make communities closed in themselves, distant from the 'other' (or many 'others') who have been ejected to the periphery, far from view. While the real estate realtors sell an image of emancipated lifestyles, the trap is that this emancipation can only occur within gated communities, where safety means sameness. In this sense, I contend that the crisis of hospitality is also a crisis of visibility and representation. It is ultimately a crisis of mediation, especially in the light of the fact that migration entails a media thickening,[70] a particular set of media practices associated with particular actions in particular locations, and a 'media texture'[71] that binds physical

70 Andreas Hepp and Nick Couldry, 'What Should Comparative Media Research Be Comparing? Towards a Transcultural Approach to 'Media Cultures', in Daya Kishan Thussu (ed.) *Internationalizing Media Studies*. Abingdon: Routledge, 2009: 32-48.

71 André Jansson, 'Indispensable Things', p. 277.

spaces with specific activities using specific media and types of media (for example migrant suburbs with satellite television), perhaps not only for the migrant but for the host as well.

I end this introduction by no longer asking if there is a possibility of living together, but with the hopefulness that we can live together... if so, how? Is there a place that we can call home, 'our home'?

If we cannot escape living together, we must address what constitutes a 'we', perhaps a 'we' that is a complex multitude of several 'others', and reflect on possibilities to share common goals of peaceful co-habitality alongside difference within a paradigm of mutual humanity.

Where integration politics and multiculturality based on older paradigms can be said to have failed, there is an opportunity to rethink a hospitality for the future beginning with the recognition of the Other as a new subject that can envision and later build a society based on new social paradigms. This self-representation includes citizen movements that also imply the transformation of the urban environment suitable to these new ways of life, new technologies, subjectivities and new urban personae-and in this sense the 'loss of Self' may become the starting point for a process of becoming. It is, in fact, in the segregated areas with the paradoxes[72] and clashes of diversity and multiple life-forms that a new subject and this new subjectivity may emerge, stemming from what Homi Bhabha calls a 'border situation'. The segregated suburb may as well be such a border situation that generates a new subject, a *satellite subject*, a subject that orbits around multiple identifications, by ways of critically inhabiting the city and setting agendas for media discourses and as a way of projecting an ethics of hospitality into the future.

72 André Jansson, 'Indispensable Things', p. 277.

# CHAPTER 1: ON HOSPITALITY

# CHAPTER 1: ON HOSPITALITY

> (...) it is a word of welcome, yes, a word of welcome that I will thus dare to pronounce.
>
> – Jacques Derrida[1]

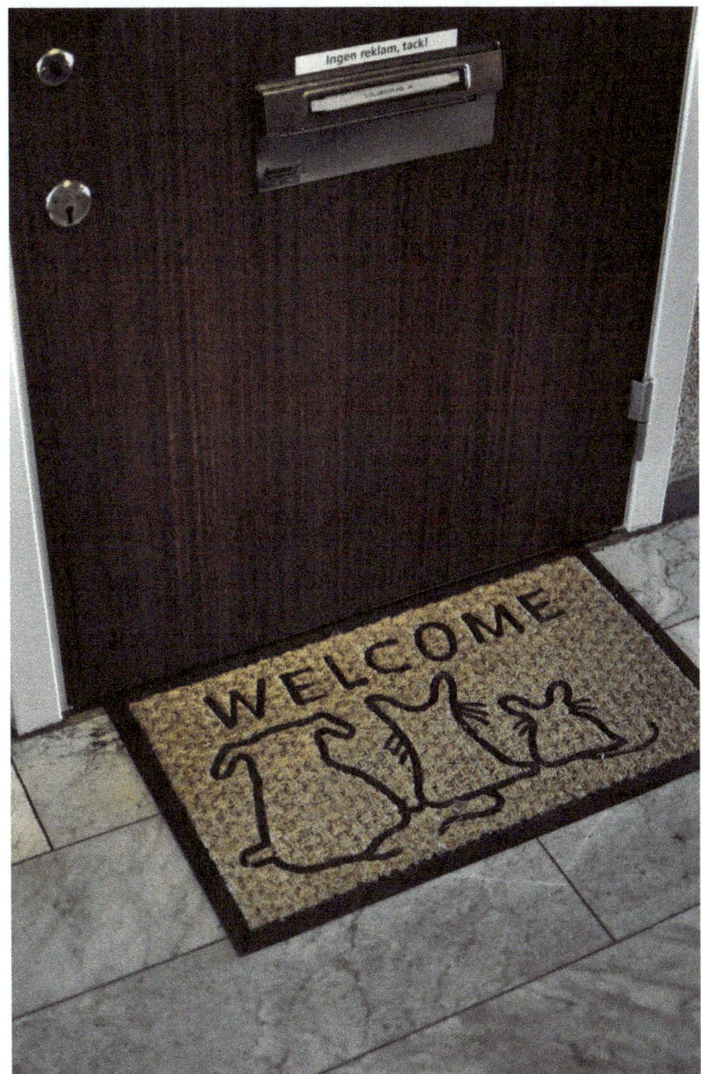


*Figure 3 – Front door to an apartment in one of Fittja's many highrise buildings. Image by the author*

---

1 Derrida, *Adieu to Emmanuel Lévinas*, p 18.

Hospitality implies an ethical relationship: it is how we, as individuals, communities, institutions and nation-states deal with the Other, the Other as a foundation of our own being – the inverted mirror of who we are. The roles in this equation are the host and the guest. The guest is a temporary entity in the house of the host, which is permanent. Their worlds views are inverted. Whereas for the host her surroundings are familiar, and any change becomes an alteration of the world-as-is, the guest may perceive the same surroundings as completely new. Lifted from habit, for the guest everything is unusual. A home is a network of habits that together organize and order the environment and determine modes of relating. Since we do not notice what is habitual, from a communications perspective all new information becomes immediately visible – habit recognizes the 'strange' as information.

The host also perceives the guest as someone unusual, and her exceptionality may put into question the stable world of the host where permanence is constant, and change is readily perceivable. By contrast, the world of the guest has change as its constant, not permanence. The transience of the guest is what defines her, unfixed, moveable – an entity which comes and goes. The host may often assume that the guest will leave one day, at which point her world may return to normalcy, unshaken by the interpellation of the guest, except a few traces left behind, which soon become erased. Sometimes guests stay longer than predicted, and by so doing begin to take ownership of the world of the host. As they adapt to each other, habits may change, and a new situation emerges where the new habits become normalized. However, the host may become nostalgic of the previous order and decide to expel the guest after all, and seek to restore her previous world view, leaving the guest homeless anew.

As Vilém Flusser reminds us, the migrant carries the mysteries of all homes she has once inhabited, but she does not embody any of these mysteries, she 'does not live in mystery, but in evidence'.[2] The homeless is thus a subject in the order of the uncanny, and as such it is unknown to the native which system she belongs to. The loss of the original mystery of the home opens the migrant to a different mystery: the mystery of Being with the Other. The opacity of the migrant arouses a sentiment of deep distrust, and thus laws are created to contain the migrant into what Flusser calls the traps set up by the 'apparatus'.

Hospitality, as a system of laws and governance, stems from the ethics of alterity, on the one hand, as internalized as cultural practices, on the other, and also a set of policies governing terms of belonging relative to nation-states. Hospitality could very well begin when we welcome strangers in our house with kindness – when the contact with the stranger, which is another name for the Other, is first established at one's doorstep. As an action, to *be hospitable* may begin with an invitation, welcoming friends and relatives into one's home with compassion and friendliness. In this simplicity lies the complexity of the host and guest relationship, even among members of the same family or group. The host has the duty to take in the stranger [to the home] and make sure that she is met with compassion. Symmetrically, the guest has the duty to not damage the home of the host nor to outstretch the host's resources. Hospitality is not only an act between humans but has a spatial dimension – it extends the home to those who temporarily are far from home. Hospitality can also occur in

2 Flusser, 'Taking Up Residence in Homelessness', p.102.

a more abstract dimension, such as when we welcome the 'strange' in our lives with curiosity: a new word, a taste or a sight, the meeting of a new person on the street, the sound of a new note, the encounter with all that is unfamiliar to oneself. It expresses itself as a gesture of inclusion as the act of greeting another is a commonplace everyday experience when exchanged without violence.

The reciprocal relationship between guest and host may be expressed in both material benefits, such as the exchange of gifts to each party, as well as immaterial ones, such as protection, food, shelter, favors, or certain normative rights. This reciprocity involves a contract, whether formally as prescribed by law and a set of rights and duties; or informally as a cultural coding of sorts where this relationship is often ritualized.[3] Hospitality means extending oneself towards the Other. Should this contract be broken, such as when the host denies access to the house, or when the guest takes advantage of the kindness of the host, the relationship may become a transgression – a situation where there is a trespassing of limits that may lead to conflict. In this sense, the ethics of hospitality can be said to regulate this relationship as to avoid potential conflict and to also be an instrument in conflict resolution.

Furthermore, it may also involve a degree of freedom, such as when we have access to all parts of the city without having to cross walls or gates, or when we are admitted to spaces unfamiliar to us without trials or barriers. On a global scale, this includes the ability to cross national borders without discrimination or excessive controls. Where freedom of crossing borders is not accorded, hospitality also means the right to seek refuge and to be met with humanity. Thus, hospitality always begins with an act of opening up, of reception and care, and ends with an act of being taken care of.

In Ancient Greece, the idea of hospitality was related to the divine. The hospitality extended to a guest, or *xenia*, defined as *guest-friendship* between strangers, was important because the guest could be a deity in disguise. One would therefore be unsure if one was hospitable because of the kindness of their nature, or if one was being hospitable for fear of the gods. In doubt, one would extend hospitality as a gesture of friendship between strangers as gods in disguise. For instance, hospitality is an important theme in Homer's *Iliad* and the *Odyssey*. In the *Iliad*, the Trojan war begins due to a break in the contract of hospitality, a break in *xenia* whence Paris transgresses his rights as a guest with the infamous Trojan horse, a gift disguised as a weapon, abducts his host's property and spouse, Helen, and precipitating ten years of war for avenging this transgression. Once the war ends and it is time for Odysseus to return home as recounted in the *Odyssey*, a voyage that takes ten years to complete. In the epic poem, every step taken in the direction of his home meets an obstacle that requires a negotiation in the terms of hospitality and the constant reapplication of *xenia* during the seemingly endless quest for home.

3 In addition, greetings, words, the custom of offering food and shelter, the rules of three days for guests, in Islam called *hadith*, the spaces in a house designated to visitors, the public sphere of the house as the part that is created for the well being of the guest, and how religion has dictated treating the Other, the formalities in giving and receiving.

In his journey, Odysseus embodies several capacities of the stranger. He spends time as a guest, captive, refugee, or as a visitor to his own kingdom upon his return. In the epic tale, Circe and Calypso take him in as a lover while he waits to be able to continue voyage; the parents of the Princess Naussica take him in as an honored guest; and he cleverly avoids being eaten by the Cyclops Polyphemus by disguising himself as a 'Nobody' while held hostage and waiting to be eaten. Perhaps, the process of becoming oneself necessarily undergoes a process of *un*becoming oneself in the guise of a *Nobody*. When he finally reaches his own island, Ithaca, after twenty years of absence, he is no longer recognized by his own wife or son, except for a blind man, and is forced to prove his worth as a suitor to hiw own queen among all others who are trying to usurp his throne. Even inside his own home, Odysseus takes the disguise of a guest to regain his rightful place by proving his identification as the host in front of others.

The welcoming of the other, even with kindness and curiosity, does not exclude the possibility of threat where the guest – the welcomed foreigner – once inside, may abuse his right of stay and destroy the home of the host that has welcomed her. This is the tragic 'Trojan horse' paradox of hospitality: that it opens itself to its own destruction. A new arrival, or guest, stands at the door, at the border, and is welcomed inside unconditionally. This very welcoming opens up into a violence. Such violence turns the home inside out. The host is forced into becoming a guest in his own home, he is taken hostage. Inversely, the guest, now invader, occupies the host's house and becomes its master.[4] In the words of Jacob Racek,

> The guest, in his purest form, would thus be our beloved enemy, the *hostis*, (...) this 'other' always remaining an intruder from the outside – only through him as the 'other' does our self acquire its meaning. No sooner has he crossed the threshold into our courtyard than he starts to make demands; he wants to eat, entertain (and be entertained) and to spend the night. If we are unlucky, the guest will leave traces behind him; before he departs again, he uses – that is to say irreparably moistens and soils – our home. He is a true parasite, one who stands aloof and is never entirely here or there. As a figure on the threshold, he opens our house to the outside, giving entry to that which we sought to exclude.[5]

## WORDS OF WELCOME OR OTHERWISE

Algerian-born French philosopher Jacques Derrida's book on Emmanuel Lévinas, *Adieu to Emmanuel Lévinas* (1997), can be said to lay out the most penetrating logic of the *same* and *other* through a discussion of hospitality in contemporary thought. Derrida writes 'hospitality is an ethics without law and without concept', and as such any law or concept would impose on hospitality and would cause it to no longer be absolute, or unconditional.

---

4 Mark W. Westmoreland, 'Interruptions: Derrida and Hospitality', *Kritike*, 2.1 (June 2008), p. 6.

5 Jacob Racek, 'Strategies of Weakness', in Anna Ptak (ed.) *Re-tooling Residences: A Closer Look at the Mobility of Art Professionals*, Warsaw, Poland: Centre for Contemporary Art Ujazdowski Castle, 2011, p. 137.

Derrida defines ethics as hospitality, and hospitality as ethics. Hospitality is not removed from ethics, nor is it a specific area of ethics, it is the foundation, or 'the whole and the principle of ethics'. [6]

For Lévinas, philosophical work meant trying to find a first philosophy, the one that lies at the foundation of all philosophical thought, which he believed to be ethics, not ontology. In other words, ethics relies on hospitality so much that one cannot speak of ethics without speaking of hospitality, although the relationship between the two may be at once both hidden and calling to be seen. Lévinas developed his philosophy in opposition to an ontological approach, by describing and interpreting the event of encountering another person where one's response is revealed to other human beings as they are embodied, quite literally, in their faces, as a primary philosophical category, as it elicits an act of responsibility. Lévinas reduces the essential relationship with the other to the singularity of the encounter with an other's face – a face in the flesh, a face brought forward to one's field of vision by way of physical presence, a face that addresses me, calls to me, and acts in response to and according to my own face in such a way that is not possible by its mere representation. Lévinas presents his ethics as something that happens in a concrete encounter with the Other, and not an abstracted one. 'To situate philosophy in the face-to-face encounter is to choose to begin philosophy not with the world, not with God, but with what will be argued to be the prime condition for human communication'. It is what we do with this encounter, how we handle this communication that matters: 'the relationship between the same and the other, my welcoming of the other, is the ultimate fact, and in it the things figure not as what one builds but as what one gives'. Lévinas's ethics is thus 'an interpretive, phenomenological description of the rise and repetition of the face-to-face encounter, or the intersubjective relation at its precognitive core; (...) being called by another and responding to that other'.[7] The pre-cognitive core is the necessity of that encounter from which all other cognition, and therefore thought can be built upon.

Lévinas' ethics is thus based on an action, *facing* the other, which preconizes both a reflective activity and a practical interest. If human sensibility can be characterized conceptually, he believes, then it must be described in what is most characteristic to it: a continuum of sensibility and affectivity. In other words, he refers to the interconnection between sentience and emotion that concerns the encounter with the world, with the human other, and a reconstruction of a layered interiority characterized by sensibility and affectivity.[8] This sentient encounter in the face-to-face meeting is the ultimate instance of hospitality, and of the responsibility involved in this encounter:

> Someone who expresses himself in his nakedness – the face – is in fact one to the extent that he calls upon me, to the extent that he places himself under my responsibility: I must already answer for him, be responsible for him. Every gesture of the Other was

6 Derrida, *Adieu to Emmanuel Lévinas,* p. 20.

7 Emmanuel Lévinas, *Totality and Infinity: An Essay on Exteriority,* trans. Alphonso Lingis, Pittsburgh: Duquesne University Press, 1969, p. 77.

8 Bettina Bergo, 'Emmanuel Levinas', in Edward N. Zalta (ed.) *The Stanford Encyclopedia of Philosophy*, Summer 2015 Edition. https://plato.stanford.edu/archives/sum2015/entries/levinas/

> a sign addressed to me. To return to the classification sketched out above: to show oneself, to express oneself, to associate oneself, to be entrusted to me. The Other who expresses himself is entrusted to me (and there is no debt with regard to the Other – for what is due cannot be paid; one will never be even). The Other individuates me in my responsibility for him.[9]

The concept of the face has been developed in a number of theories of the self. Whereas for Lévinas the face is a site of original and ultimate hospitality from which to develop an ethics of reciprocity and encounter, the face has also been developed as a concept that acts as a medium towards reaching the Other, not just the physical presence of another, but *through* the Other as an image or by performativity. Jacques Lacan's psychoanalytic theory of the mirror stage introduces the notion of the image of the mother's face as a locus for individuation that establishes the ego as fundamentally dependent upon external objects, on an 'other'.[10] Inspired by Lévinas, Erwing Goffman developed an idea of 'face' and 'face-work' in a sociological rather than in a philosophical context as incessant self-presentation in social situations, as a staging and performativity which is not always conscious. According to Goffman, 'the term 'face' may be defined as the positive social value a person effectively claims for herself by the line others assume, she has taken during a particular contact'. *Face* is a basic prerequisite or condition for interaction, a means to display the awareness of others and accountability.[11]

However, in Guy Debord's view of a world of mediated encounters in the terms of capitalist logic[12], or in Jean Baudrillard's theory of simulations and simulacra, this encounter with a physical face has become abstracted and mediated, entering the realm of a virtual *facelessness*. Whereas we encounter faces in the city by our physical presence (faces are *presented* to us), for instance, in electronic and social media, this encounter occurs with the *image* of this face, whether real or simulated (faces are *represented* for us). Furthermore, the face is currently increasingly becoming securitized, instrumentalized and weaponized through the technologies of facial recognition and biometry for a variety of disciplinary, regulatory and commercial purposes. In the surveilled city, with surveillance cameras capturing biometric data on the streets, there is a desirability in becoming faceless, in order to avoid being traceable. In our discourse about hospitality and the face, the use of such technologies in the realm of migration and administration of migration, the electronic surveillance apparatus that begins with facial recognition becomes a means to classify migrants and determine the legitimacy of asylum and the right to exile, and thus of belonging. Yet, within a discourse of hospitality and representation, could there exist something like a hospitable image, an image that is, or that symbolizes, the welcoming of the Other? Can an image, as representation, establish a relationship of reciprocity and solidarity?

---

9 Lévinas, *Existence and Existents*, transl. Alphonso Lingis, The Hague: Martinus Nijhoff, 1978, p. 40.

10 Jacques Lacan, 'The Mirror Stage as Formative of the Function of the I as Revealed in Psychoanalytic Experience' (1966), *Écrits: A Selection*, trans. Bruce Flink, New York: W. W. Norton & Company, 2004.

11 See Erwing Goffman, 'On Face-work: An Analysis of Ritual Elements in Social Interaction', *Psychiatry*, *18*.3 (1955): 213-231.

12 See Guy Debord, *The Society of Spectacle*, trans. Ken Knabb, Berkeley: Bureau of Public Secrets, 2014 (1957).

## THE BELOVED ENEMY

In 1993, French philosopher René Schérer published a landmark book, *The Hospitable Zeus*, in which he presents a series of extensive readings of Homer's Odyssey, Kant, deProudhon, Fourier and others in praise of hospitality in a time, he claimed, when hospitality seemed to be rather absent, referring to the Balkan war and ensuing migrations of that decade. Four years later, Jacques Derrida published *Of Hospitality* with French philosopher Anne Dufourmantelle, where hospitality is viewed as a question of what happens 'at the border', albeit an epistemological one, and in the initial surprise of the encounter with the Other, a stranger, a foreigner. The book consists of two texts on facing pages written by each author, where Dufourmantelle's essay 'Invitation' appears on the left, clarifying and inflecting Derrida's 'response' on the right, in an enactment of the notion and the problems of the notion of hospitality being discussed. Dufourmantelle as the host inviting the guest Derrida, sometimes but not always in synch, as a metaphor for the potential misalignments of both sides of the mutually dependent relationship between host and guest, between the act of welcoming and being welcomed.

In both works, which represent only two of several works by philosophers dedicated to hospitality, the critique of this concept provides a philosophical ground that elucidates the observable hostility of European countries against refugees and invites us to question the meaning and practice of hospitality in the contemporary world. Nowadays, we have, for example, a crisis in the media representation of migrants that have caused a polarization in public opinion about the divisive issue of immigration, and increasingly segregated cities where hosts and guests are spatially estranged from each other. In times where ideas of the national are being openly contested, Schérer believes that hospitality is becoming an impossible luxury, a madness, a hyperbole – true hospitality is a utopia. Schérer's utopian idea of a general hospitality involves the unconditional, absolute permission of movement and permanence to be offered to everyone, without exception:

> About the hospitality issue of our time, posed by the welcoming of foreigners, the consensus seems to believe in a selective admission, the fact that there are national guidelines for imposing restrictions and conditions upon entry. (...) I take the opposite position, thinking and outlining the idea of an unconditional hospitality, alien to all laws, (...) the idea of a universal and absolute hospitality.[13]

The idea of unconditional hospitality is also proposed by Jacques Derrida, who presents the unconditionality of hospitality to probe the limits of this notion – which is as much a part of moral philosophy as a practical reality for the thousands of individuals met with the shifting selectivity of admission across borders everyday.

Unlike Schérer, Derrida does not believe in a utopian ideal as something to aim for, but rather exposes the concept of hospitality as being governed by *aporia*. On the one hand, there are the laws of hospitality under conditions that underpin a right to hospitality while in transit

13 René Schérer, *Zeus hospitalier: l'éloge de l'hospitalité*. Paris: La Table Ronde, 2005.

within legal, political and ethical restrictions upon admission, and on the other, the terms and conditions of settlement and living somewhere different from one's place of origin or citizenship. Between these two poles is a zone of uncertainty and doubt where the definition of hospitality dismantles, deconstructs itself and undermines its own foundations.

The right to hospitality is normally conditional within a restrictive framework. On the other hand, there is also the question a 'hyper-ethical' law of real and absolute hospitality that commands the reception of the foreigner, of whatever provenance and legal status, to be offered refuge without conditions, restrictions, obligations or compensations. However, within this absolute admittance of the foreigner, Derrida writes, 'one must accept the danger that the foreigner will come and destroy the host, may begin a revolution, steal everything, and kill everyone. This is the danger of a pure hospitality'.[14] The perceived threat of the foreigner as something or someone that can harm the host is what makes us recede to a conditional hospitality. When prone to excess, the host-guest relationship needs to be regulated by an instrument of mediation, a law, which will make it objective. The regulation of this excess can also result in a law of no-hospitality, where the admittance of the guest is so restricted that she becomes marginalized, faceless, unnamed and yet again, expelled.

## THE CONTRADICTIONS OF HOSPITALITY

The taking over of guest as master which Derrida refers to is perhaps the risk Kant wished to avoid in *Perpetual Peace: A Philosophical Sketch* (1795),[15] where he outlines the foundation for a peace program among governments, and where he also specifies the rights a universal hospitality can be afforded to strangers – these rights being necessary to accomplish the ultimate goal of intercommunication and peaceful relations between nations. As one of the first of the modern philosophers to inscribe the notion of hospitality in a treatise of moral philosophy, Kant defines hospitality as the 'right of a stranger not to be treated as an enemy when he arrives in the land of another, but, so long as he peacefully occupies his place, one may not treat him with hostility'.[16] Foreigners can certainly be turned away: this is not part of what is meant by *treating him with hostility.*[17] They cannot, however, be turned away if this means that doing so will lead to their destruction. This means that a foreigner may not be denied permanence and sent back to conditions where his life is at risk. It is not the right to be a permanent visitor that one may demand; it is only a right of temporary sojourn, a right to associate, which all persons have.

But there are limitations: 'the nation may send [the visitor] away again, if this can be done without causing his death" and that it is "not a right to be treated as a guest to which the stranger can lay claim'.[18] The hospitality conceded to a foreigner is a 'right to visit' but not

---

14 Derrida, 'On Cosmopolitanism', in Garret W. Brown, Garrett and David Held, eds., *The Cosmopolitanism Reader*. Cambridge: Polity Press, 2013, p. 313.

15 Kant, *Perpetual Peace,* p. 32.

16 Kant, *Perpetual Peace,* p. 137.

17 Note the same etymological root of *host* and *hostile, hospital,* the confinement of the ill; and *hospice,* the confinement of the mad.

18 Kant, *Perpetual Peace,* p.138.

the right to visit *permanently* and is thus always conditional. The realm of a law of hospitality inherited from the Enlightenment that regulates a relationship between guest and host, which, as Derrida's aporetic claim shows, contains in and of itself the possibility of violent transgression:[19]

> (...) to put it in different terms, absolute hospitality requires that I open up my home and that I give not only to the foreigner, but to the absolute, unknown, anonymous other, and that I give place to them, that I let them come, that I let them arrive, and take place in the place I offer them, without asking of them either reciprocity (entering into a pact) or even their names.[20]

In the third definitive article in this piece, Kant concludes that a cosmopolitan right of universal hospitality and calls for world citizenry as part of the means through which 'a perpetual peace between nations' can be achieved:

> The intercourse, more or less close, which has been everywhere steadily increasing between the nations of the earth, has now extended so enormously that a violation of right in one part of the world is felt all over it. Hence the idea of a cosmopolitan right is no fantastical, high-flown notion of right, but a complement of the unwritten code of law-constitutional as well as international law-necessary for the public rights of mankind in general and thus for the realisation of perpetual peace. For only by endeavouring to fulfil the conditions laid down by this cosmopolitan law can we flatter ourselves that we are gradually approaching that ideal.[21]

Kant's essay has gained importance in the context of postcolonial studies, for instance, as he denounces very early on the abuses of colonial power and how laws of hospitality may redeem the common right 'to the face of the earth (*sic.*)' and what is the natural law, a sort of universal commons:

> Uninhabitable portions of the surface, ocean and desert, split up the human community, but in such a way that ships and camels – 'the ship of the desert' – make it possible for men to come into touch with one another across these unappropriated regions and to take advantage of our common claim to the face of the earth with a view to a possible intercommunication. The inhospitality of the inhabitants of certain sea coasts as, for example, the coast of Barbary – in plundering ships in neighbouring seas or making slaves of shipwrecked mariners; or the behaviour of the Arab Bedouins in the

19 The relationship of hospitality to violence cannot be understated and would yield an entire monograph alone. For it seems that it is this very transgression of the tenuous limits of hospitality, the degrees of permission, of permanence and compensations, of rights and duties, of spatial and economic grants or constraints become the source of enduring conflicts that characterize coexistence and cohabitation, from the most intimate to the most public spheres. Hospitality as culture is above the juridical and is dictated by culture.

20 Derrida, *Of Hospitality* (*Cultural Memory in the Present),* Palo Alto: Stanford University Press, 2000, p. 14.

21 Kant, *Perpetual Peace*, p. 142.

> deserts, who think that proximity to nomadic tribes constitutes a right to rob, is thus contrary to the law of nature. This right to hospitality, however – that is to say, the privilege of strangers arriving on foreign soil – does not amount to more than what is implied in a permission to make an attempt at intercourse with the original inhabitants. In this way far distant territories may enter into peaceful relations with one another. These relations may at last come under the public control of law, and thus the human race may be brought nearer the realisation of a cosmopolitan constitution.[22]

Alongside the developments of moral philosophy that includes a notion of universality, inspired as well by the *Declaration of the Rights of Man* (1791), Kant makes explicit the relation between violence, hospitality and the rivalry between cultures and the need for a common law for all humanity that unnaturalizes the assumed violence caused by proximity between peoples, as stated above. However, establishing a cosmopolitan right or world citizenship would also require a reflexive position from those considered 'civilized', and Kant notably points out the asymmetry of these power relations. He was inspired by the transformative spirit of the French Revolution while European colonialism in Africa, Asia and the Americas were still in full swing in an imperial world order. Kant uses a specific vocabulary of hospitality by calling the European colonizer the 'civilized intruder', thus problematizing the division between civilized and barbarian, and the common regard for the humanity of others 'as nothing', and writes,

> Let us look now (...) at the inhospitable behaviour of the civilised nations, especially the commercial states of our continent. The injustice which they exhibit on visiting foreign lands and races – this being equivalent in their eyes to conquest – is such as to fill us with horror. America, the negro countries, the Spice Islands, the Cape etc. were, on being discovered, looked upon as countries which belonged to nobody; for the native inhabitants were reckoned as nothing. (...) And this has been done by nations who make a great ado about their piety, and who, while they are quite ready to commit injustice, would like, in their orthodoxy, to be considered among the elect.[23]

Kant's imagination of a world in which hospitality is a common and universal law that paves the way to a state of 'perpetual peace' also needs to be understood in the context of the phenomenon of mass forced migration in his own time. In fact, the decades following the first publication of *Perpetual Peace* in 1795 would be the most intense period in the trafficking of slavery to the Americas,[24] also concurrent to the growing forces that include

---

22 Kant, *Perpetual Peace*, p. 143.

23 Kant, *Perpetual Peace*, p. 141.

24 In Brazil, for instance, the most intense period of the slave trade was between 1799 and 1831, at which point the international slave trade begins to wind down due to the pressure by the British Empire to abolish international slave trading. A similar expansion of the slave trade can be noted in the United States in the same period. This intensification of the slave trade is due to the rise of exports of raw materials to global markets and precedes the first industrial era, when Europe begins to mechanize its workforce. Nevertheless, the escalation of the slave trade in the 18th century, and its systematization in the 19th century coincides precisely with the period of Enlightenment and the revolutionary spirit in Europe, causing a split consciousness about notions of humanity and freedom. *Slave Voyages Database* https://www.slavevoyages.org/assessment/estimates.

slave insurgencies (such as in Haiti in 1805) and the rising movements for the abolition of slavery. By the end of the 19th century, slavery had finally become abolished (as late as 1888 in Brazil), at which point the world had become for the most part organized into nation-states under republican values, with a framework of international law, including the rights between nations and hospitality. However, some of these nation-states remained imperial powers which would hold on to their colonies well into the 20th century, where the logic of colonial violence still reverberates in contemporary societies with pervasive structural racial discrimination. In the 21st century, this logic can be evidenced in the persisting police and state violence against African Americans and Afro-Brazilians, for instance, not coincidentally the two countries, the United States and Brazil[25], where slavery was the most widespread and most enduring.

In the article 'Hegel in Haiti', Susan Buck-Morss describes how 'slavery had become the root metaphor of Western political philosophy, connoting everything that was evil about power relations. Freedom, its conceptual antithesis, was considered by Enlightenment thinkers as the highest and universal political value'.[26] Buck-Morss highlights the fact that despite the awareness of necropolitics at the time, the blind spot of the Enlightenment project accounted for freedom and universality from the standpoint of those subjects considered worthy of freedom, where degrees of humanness act as the foundation for defining terms of belonging, as seen in Kant above. Whereas today we debate the level of belonging through citizenship and national affiliation, the biopolitical foundation relies on who is considered to be human. Kant's belief was, perhaps, that a cosmopolitan order, a law of hospitality above all else would help pave the road to freedom for all subjects, and as such confer humanity to all.

If Kant's cosmopolitan project is taken to its ends, it aims to define the basis of all humanity as the right to be human, and therefore to be free. The idea of who gets to be human, however, is highly contested. In the case of slavery, the notion of humanness is precisely what is at stake. Slaves were not considered fully human, they were a commodity. It is this struggle for the recognition of the humanity of the Other which is the basis of emancipation struggles. This leads us to question what liberation can mean, is it a path towards humanity and freedom that breaks the logic of perpetual violence towards perpetual peace, or, to follow Frantz Fanon's call for liberation through violent struggle, is it a path towards a self-perpetuating violence?

In addressing Kant's statement for perpetual peace to the emerging nation-states – 'the law of cosmopolitanism must be restricted to the conditions of universal hospitality' – René Schérer claims that Kant was self-delusional. If the individuals and the peoples around the world were generally hospitable, states and nations were not.[27] For whom did the Kantian notion of the 'universal' serve? How can we redefine what 'universal' means today?

---

25 According to the *Slave Voyages Database*, of an estimated total 10,702,654 disembarkment of slaves from Africa in the Americas from 1650 to 1866, 45% of the total, or 4,864,373 persons disembarked in Brazil alone with Rio de Janeiro as the main port of arrival for half this amount, and 2,706,999 persons disembarked in North America and the British Caribeean, *Slave Voyages Database*, https://www.slavevoyages.org/assessment/estimates.

26 Susan Buck-Morss, 'Hegel and Haiti', *Critical Inquiry*, 26.4 (Summer 2000), p. 821.

27 Schérer, *Zeus hospitalier*, p. 82.

Inasmuch as Kantian cosmopolitics lay the foundation for regulating the interdependence of nation-states, it is precisely this universality which today is criticized as an oppressive structure that favors hegemonic groups and leaves the Other at bay. In fact, Fanon's deeper criticism is that the supposedly universal values function as weapons in the hands of the colonizers by means of which they atomize and divide the colonized, and the only path to liberation for the colonized is to completely crush the colonial world.[28]

## DECOLONIZING HOSPITALITY

The colonial situation is one where hospitality appears inverted: the colonizer comes to a foreign land and becomes its host by force as a 'civilized intruder' using barbaric force to establish his civilized world order. The indigenous (named as such by the intruder) becomes a guest, held hostage by the colonizer in her own (former) home through enslavement and other tactics of domination and control. The goal of the Conquistadors was to conquer land by exterminating its occupants. The idea of rootedness, according to Èdouard Glissant, is not important in the Conquistadors' 'devastating desire for settlement' and arrowlike nomadism, which is preconized in the real uprooting of circularly nomadic societies'.[29]

This new order is only possible through extreme violence and the installation of necropolitics as a law. In the postcolonial world, the order of host and guest aims to either revert to the pre-colonial structure by recalling the status of the indigenous as the original host and expelling the colonizer as an unwanted guest, or to create new conditions of hospitality between the former colonizer and the former colonized as these two may have generated, through time, a hybrid subject that has superseded the original conditions of colonization. A *hybrid* subject represents a 'doubling up of a sign' as it acquires new meanings in different contexts. For Homi Bhabha, 'hybridity is a form of incipient critique; it does not come as a force from 'outside' to impose an alternative a priori ground-plan on the pattern of the present. Hybridity works with, *and within*, the cultural design of the present to reshape our understanding of the interstices – social and psychic – that link signs of cultural similitude with emergent signifiers of alterity'.[30]

However, the colonial tactics behind the creation of a hybrid subject lies at the heart of a project of biopolitical power based on necropolitics and institutionalized violence in conquered territories. As a case in point, the resulting miscegenation of colonizer and colonized in Brazil generated an array of such new 'hybrid' subjects within the logic of colonization

28 Frantz Fanon, *The Wretched of the Earth*, trans. Constance Farrington, New York: Grove Weidenfeld, 1991 (1961), p.36.

29 Édouard Glissant, *Poetics of Relation*, transl. Betsy Wing, Ann Arbor: The University of Michigan Press, 1997, p 12-13. Here, Glissant refers to Deleuze and Guattari's definition of arrowlike and circular nomadism. In circular nomadism, each time a part of the land is exhausted, a population moves around to find another territory to explore, like the Yanomami communities in the Amazon, driven by a specific need to move. In arrowlike or invading nomadism, the goal is to conquer land by exterminating its original occupants and sparing no effects towards definitive settlements.

30 Homi Bhabha, 'Foreword', in Pnina Werbner and Tariq Modood (eds) *Debating Cultural Hybridity: Multicultural Identities and the Politics of Anti-Racism*, Zed Books Ltd, 2015, p. II - VII.

with enduring legacies in the present. In the language of hospitality, the indigenous populations, who were originally the hosts of the land, were turned into captives by Portuguese colonization. Inversely, the Portuguese colonizer as the intruders, claimed themselves as hosts by claiming ownership of the land, its resources, and its people. More precisely, the colonizers establish themselves as hosts through the initial process of converting 'heathen souls' into Christianity by the first Jesuit missionaries that fulfilled the Papal edict of expaning Christianity[31] to the *terra incognita anthropophagorum*[32], in exchange for financing the first voyages and initiating the process of exploitative colonization. The host-guest relations become further complicated as one of the Portuguese tactics of colonization was to break down the Indigenous identities and cultures genetically through intermarriage, and at the same time increase the colonial population. Nonetheless, the necessity of African slaves to fully develop an extraction economy proved necessary very early on. By dismantling the identities and identifications of subjugated peoples, it was believed that they would more easily conform to the colonial order.[33]

The resulting hybrid subject is then assumed to be docilized by its own hybridity as the two poles that constitute it – the captive guest and the intruding host – have been merged into a new historical subject. This merging, however, does not result in a uniform amalgam. Rather, it results in a complex assemblage of conflicting identifications and loyalties, with a doubling and trebling of signs and split identities, that are also exploited for the sake of the colonial project. Within modernity, the necessity of defining Brazilian*ness* became paramount in the 1930s, when the violent logic of colonial hybridization was rebranded as a harmonic exchange between races (between captives and captors) resulting in a fictional 'racial democracy' – an ideological device constructed to build a notion of modern nationhood. Today, we know that the régime that engendered this hybrid *Brazilian* subject has not ceased to exist and still reverberates in the memory and expression of multiple diasporas. This régime is in fact replicated in contemporary forms, i.e. in the colonial approach to the indigenous in the Amazon region, whose ecocide may turn the region inhospitable, and the persistent presence of black lives in police statistics as a continuation of the systematic violence affecting the African diaspora. This reveals that despite republican values of universality and freedom inherited from the Enlightenment, what is at stake is not a definition of the national (of who is a 'Brazilian' and who is not), but the very definition of who has the right to be human.[34]

31 *Inter caetera*, papal bull given in Rome by Pope Alexander VI on 4 May 1493, https://www.papalencyclicals.net/alex06/alex06inter.htm.

32 Translated from Latin, 'unknown land of the Cannibals'. This was the name given to the part of the New World that would later become Brazil as found on a map from the late 1400s, as seen by the author inside the Ducal Palace in Venice.

33 The Brazilian population today is said to be the result of the interbreeding of successive generations of guests as migrants, from the first Portuguese colonizers in the 16th and 17th centuries, the indigenous populations, the millions of enslaved Africans up to the 19th century, to the arrival of impoverished white Europeans and Japanese in the early 20th century, after the abolition of slavery in 1888.

34 The history of miscegenation in Brazil can be said to constitute the foundation of the country's cultural and genetic identification. With the arrival of the Portuguese men in the caravels in 1500, the native populations went through successive transformations due to the mixing of Portuguese colonizers with native, and later, with the African slaves. In the nineteenth century, the country would receive a large influx of Europeans, followed by the arrival of thousands of Japanese in the early twentieth century,

The consequences of decolonization in the mid-20th century have brought many thinkers from former colonies/newly independent countries to rethink the basis for the laws of hospitality previously established within an imperial world order. While expressed in particular postcolonial contexts, these critiques have much potential for the broad range of postcolonial experiences because they represent powerful calls for the gaze of the Radical Other as a critique of the hegemonic Euro-centric gaze. In an interview given in the context of Documenta XI, Cameroonian philosopher Achille Mbembe states:

> There is no doubt that postcolonial theory, under its many guises, has decisively contributed to the 'unmasking' of Western hegemony in the field of the humanities and in other disciplines. It has forced Western discourses on the self and the other, on difference and alterity, or on particularity and universality, to become accountable. In the process, postcolonial theory has revealed the violence of Western epistemologies and the dehumanizing impulses at the heart of their definition of the human. This task is far from over.[35]

For instance, Dipesh Chakrabarty's suggestion to de-Westernize Indian history and stop applying European concepts and schemes to get rid of the postcolonial subject's self-incurred split, is still relevant far beyond the field of Indian history proper.[36] Likewise, Mbembe's critique of the modes of anti/postcolonial history writing exposes a longing for African subjectivity against the representation and mediatization of the African subject mostly as victimized; it seeks to move away from imagining African history as 'sorcery and stuttering' and focuses on the emergence of an 'Afro-cosmopolitan' culture, including its associated creative processes. While African historiography has been shadowed by connotations of the continent as the 'Dark Continent,' recent post-colonial approaches are concerned with a locally informed rewriting of these externally imposed negations.

## EXILE, COMMUNICATION, AND THE EXPELLED

In *Poetics of Relation* (1997), Édouard Glissant offers a thorough account of the subjectivity of exile from a poetic and decolonial perspective. In describing the myths of errantry, such as epics like the *Odyssey* in the tales of the great colonial voyages, as founding myths of incipient Western civilization in the former and the solidification of an advanced Western ideal in the latter, these function paradoxically as tales of uprootedness and an affirmation of settled societies and the fixity of cultural identifications. He observes that,

---

Syrian, Turkish, Armenian, Lebanese, etc. Brazil's racial makeup to date is 42.7% white, 9% Black, and 46,8% mixed-race, 1,1% Asian and Indigenous. *IBGE*, https://educa.ibge.gov.br/jovens/conheca-o-brasil/populacao/18319-cor-ou-raca.html.

35 Christian Höller and Achille Mbembe, 'Africa in Motion: An Interview with the Post-colonialism Theoretician Achille Mbembe', *Metamute*, 17 March 2007, https://www.metamute.org/editorial/articles/africa-motion-interview-post-colonialism-theoretician-achille-mbembe.

36 See Dipesh Chakrabarty. *Provincializing Europe: Postcolonial Thought and Historical Difference.* Princeton University Press, 2008.

> (...) the reality of exile is felt as a (temporary) lack that primarily concerns, interestingly enough, language. Western nations were established on the basis of linguistic intransigence, and the exile readily admits that he suffers most from the impossibility of communicating in his language. The root is monolingual.[37]

He continues, 'the conquered or visited peoples are thus forced into a painful quest after an identity whose first task will be opposition to the denaturing process introduced by the conqueror. A tragic variation for the search for identity'.[38] Glissant points to an important part of the experience of the exile, who in a state of uprootedness and errantry is the Other to the consolidation of the discoverer/conqueror's drive to claim his root as the strongest and most explicit value, whereby a person's worth (and humanity) is determined primarily by his root. One of the vectors for the primacy of his root was the systematic exportation of a single language from the civilized metropolises to become dominant in opposition to the multilingual realities of *elsewhere*.

Another contemporary thinker who has made the connection between exile, language and communication explicit is Vilém Flusser. What does migrancy and the existential dilemmas faced by the exile have to do with communication? Communication begins with language. Its negation, *ex-communication*, signifies the expulsion from the realm of meaning, which is constructed by language. When language is obliterated and insufficient, there is an accentuation of a longing for communion, of life as a missing subject, a longing for what is *not here*. *Ex-pulsion* (from the Latin *expellō*, *ex-* out of and *pellō* drive out), *ex-ile* (with the same Latin etymology, even though rather obscure) and *ex-communication* share the same grammatical template, conveying the conceptual link of physical displacement, disappropriation, and then communication deprivation (in religion, this means the prohibition of communication with God and the Church).

There is a linguistic dimension to the ethics of hospitality, which becomes a matter or reading and writing, speaking and listening, of how to call things by what names. Language becomes the enunciation of this ethics and has been frequently related to this textual dimension and the act of naming, and much political debate as well. What is the appropriate pronoun for those who are not 'us'? Is the expression 'the Other' a name or designation, noun or adjective, singular or plural? The list is extensive and inexhaustible: exile, migrant, floater[39], guest-worker, boat-people, stranger, foreigner, foreign-born, non-native, expatriate, apatriate, refugee, displaced, stranger, outsider, *retirante*[40]. I read them in the news everyday, often

---

37 Glissant, *Poetics of Relation*, p. 15.

38 Glissant, *Poetics of Relation*, p. 17.

39 'Floaters,' 'floating population' or '*bei piao'* are unregistered rural migrants turned urban construction workers in China as they are called by Beijing Police. Every year, 200,000 'floaters' arrive in Beijing. China is the country that has undergone one of the largest migration shifts in history. Over 100 million people have migrated from countryside to 'new' cities that in the matter of a few decades have grown from towns to megalopolises with populations the size of a Scandinavian country each, with staggering poverty despite the expansion of the Chinese economy. Mike Davis, *Planet of Slums*, London: Verso, 2006, p. 17.

40 *Retirante* is the name given to the internal migrant from the poor Brazilian northeastern drylands to the

interchangeably – migrant, immigrant, refugee – often three of these in the same article, as if redundancy itself indicates the confusion caused by the notion of the Other as a diffuse subject in her host society. Or else, the condition of the Other is always unnameable, and any adjectives serve only to classify and to tell the *Other* apart from the *Same*.

In *Exile and Creativity*, Vilém Flusser begins to sketch a philosophy of difference by way of further understanding the migrant as 'the 'Other' in relation to the native, the 'different one', and inversely the native is also the 'Other' to the migrant.[41] In Derrida's definition, the migrant is an interruption in the identitarian life of the native – a disturbance and a rupture.[42] *The Other* thus can have several names, it is general and blurred in opaque multitudes while 'the Same' is almost always indivisible, transparent and singular. The Other becomes marginal, or as Gayatri Spivak recalls from Gramsci, it is the *subaltern,* an Other that is subjugated by hegemony. In a state of subalterity, language becomes a contested site. She asks, can the subaltern speak? What is the language with which the subaltern can make themselves listened to? Lévinas calls for a recognition of the Other within language:

> To recognize the Other is therefore to come to him across the world of possessed things, but at the same time to establish, by gift, community and universality. Language is universal because it is the very passage from the individual to the general, because it offers things which are mine to the Other. To speak is to make the world common, to create commonplaces. Language does not refer to the generality of concepts but lays the foundations for a possession in common.[43]

Flusser differentiates the emigrant from the refugee by explaining that while the body has been freed from the expeller, the mind of the refugee is still prey to the context she had to abandon. Because she has not freely taken the decision of leaving, the refugee drags her homeland with her, remembering it with both love and resentment, yet defined by the motives of the expeller. Differently, the emigrant has transcended her previous condition by having made a choice to leave. This difference is crucial: what differs the emigrant and the refugee is choice. The refugee – who is often involved in a traumatic displacement – is defined according to conditions external to her and is placed outside any of the host society's existing stratifications. A third figure, the *im*migrant, which is the landed emigrant already settled in the host society, positions herself partially open to the new reality. The things that remind her why she left her previous residence are precisely those things that she can best assimilate in her new context, and even, in due time, actively influence it. This to-and-fro between the expelled and the expeller, and this third emergent entity, is pushed even further:

> The expelled is the Other of others. Which is to say, he is the other for the others, and the others are other for him. He himself is nothing more than the Others of him.

prosperous south. The word comes from the verb 'retirar' which means 'to withdraw.' *Retirantes* would then mean 'the withdrawn.'

41 Flusser, 'Exile and Creativity', p. 124.

42 Flusser uses the term native as the opposite of the migrant. The native is sedentary, fixed, traceable to its origin. The migrant is moveable, uncertain, flexible, dynamic.

43 Lévinas, *Totality and Infinity*, p. 65.

> In this manner, he is able to 'identify.' His advent in exile allows the original natives to uncover that they are unable to identify without him. Because of the advent in exile, the self is rent asunder, opening it up to others, to a being-with-others. This dialogic atmosphere that characterizes exile is not part of a mutual recognition, but rather, it is mostly polemical (not to mention murderous). For the expelled threatens the 'particular nature' of the original natives; this strangeness calls him into question. But, even such a polemical dialogue is creative; for it leads to the synthesis of new information. Exile, no matter what form it takes, is a breeding ground for creative activity, for the new.[44]

An exile,[45] according to Flusser, is one who has been uprooted and expelled from his original place of being, forcibly or not. To be in exile means to be *ex-ilos*, outside one's former place. To be in exile is to be in a state of negation of something else, to be somewhere else as a representative of the original expulsion.[46] This involves several stages of severance from home. First, the event that precipitates the expulsion itself, often turning some action of the population or the individual that has been criminalized or targeted for exclusion in some sense. Then the journey undertaken as a refugee. Upon arrival on another shore, the status of becoming paperless, the self that is not formally quantified as part of any nation. Then the self in waiting for permission to reside, the asylum-seeker. Lastly, the approval of asylum which turns one into an immigrant, with or without full citizenship. In this epic trajectory, Flusser claims, the exile's life is constantly defined by the motives of the expeller. Therefore, the name of this subject should not be restricted to the phenomenon which she is a part of, but a name that grasps the totality of this state. He writes,

> I use the word expelled rather than refugees or emigrants, to bring the totality of the problem before our eyes. For I do not only refer to phenomena like the 'boat people', Palestinians, or Jewish emigration from Hitler's Europe, but also, the expulsion of an older generation from the world of their children and grandchildren – or even the expulsion of humanists from the world of apparatuses. We find ourselves in a period of expulsion. If one values this situation positively, the future will appear a little less dark.[47]

This process may be in equal parts a source of freedom and strength but also of confusion and discontentment. This balance is asymmetric. While the exile carries with her the weight of her expulsion, the expelled has, in the meantime, been successfully erased from the homeland by the expeller. The expeller thus permanently haunts the expelled. Inversely, the expelled sheds light onto the expeller's motives and modes of action. Flusser believes that the expelled says more about the expeller than about herself, and as such those expelled hold a potential of revelation, of demasking the systems of expulsion which have victimized her, but to which they bear witness.

---

44 Flusser, 'Exile and Creativity', p. 126.

45 Saskia Sassen ironically says that when refugees are 'very fancy' they are called 'exiles.' In Saskia Sassen, Keynote speech at the *2014 Creative Time Summit,* Stockholm, 13-16 November 2014, https://www.youtube.com/watch?v=EwqNuFugYRg.

46 Flusser, 'Taking Residence in Homelessness', p. 76.

47 Flusser, 'Exile and Creativity', p. 105.

Flusser corroborates this position by claiming that a differential process is necessary for a process of communication and a dialogue between cultures to take place, and for each to affirm themselves and to become open to the exchange of knowledge, the transference of experience and information, and the expression of subjectivity. Contrary to the perception of the migrant or the *expelled* as a depressed condition, confused and undefined, Flusser then poses a challenge: the condition of the difference, and of the migrant, is at the end, a productive and creative experience. The exile is forced to translate new signals from a new culture and a new place into a vocabulary of her own and reconstruct a new set of identifications beyond their known references. An exile, as an expelled has this synthetic capacity as a mode of survival and existence, and this capacity is by definition a creative act.[48]

Decades later, the sociologist Saskia Sassen similarly claimed about the migrant condition: 'it is not immigration, it's expulsion' and reaches a similar conclusion about the naming of the migrant as the expelled.[49] Sassen is concerned with a call to disambiguate the naming of the immigrant, refugee and asylum-seeker subject by claiming that the current political mediatized vocabulary is insufficient to describe this subject, and therefore insufficient to create adequate politics around this subject. It is as if the very act of naming is a fundamental act of recognizing the existence of these subjects so they can have agency in the public sphere. She believes that the vagueness of the terms used in public discourse leads to a vagueness of political action. She suggests that we call the immigrant, refugee, displaced, etc. by what they really are, by what led them to their status as non- or quasi-citizens in the world, as products of multiple expulsions. Like Flusser, she suggests that we use the term, the 'expelled' to mark the radicality that this condition requires. It does justice to the phenomenon of non-returning migrants, as many of them, like the paperless minor refugees living in Sweden, have nowhere to return safely. In this case, the paperless refugee is from the outset haunted by the prospect of a return to the expeller, a condition that extends the status of expulsion to an excruciating level of homelessness.[50] In this condition, Sassen makes a specific reference to where those *expelled* may take up residence, who in host countries are not simply housed, but are 'warehoused', she writes,

> I use the term "expelled" to describe a diversity of conditions. They include the growing numbers of the abjectly poor, of the displaced in poor countries who are warehoused in formal and informal refugee camps,[51] of the minoritized and persecuted in rich

48 Flusser, 'Exile and Creativity', p. 108.

49 Sassen, *2014 Creative Summit: Stockholm*.

50 In the case of under-age Afghani refugees in Sweden, many of them are the victims of double expulsions and after the flight to Europe, they are already twice exiled. Many of them come from refugee families in Iran, having been expelled from Afghanistan earlier. When faced with deportation from Sweden to Kabul, these youths claim that they have never been to Afghanistan proper, and fearing the continued status as the expelled in Kabul, become panic-stricken at the prospect of homelessness and being at the mercy of the original expellers of their family. Deportation is often confused with repatriation, but what does repatriation mean for a person who has no country of origin? They do have a community of origin, a place of belonging which does not get officially recognized by the law.

51 See the documentary *Förvaret: Migrationsverkets låsta rum*, (dir. Anna Persson and Sharon Chakraborty, 2014), About the Migration Authorities detention facility in Flen, Central Sweden and the circumstances of those who have been denied permanence in the country, but who refuse to leave for a variety of

> countries who are warehoused in prisons, of workers whose bodies are destroyed on the job and rendered useless at far too young an age, of able-bodied 'surplus populations' warehoused in ghettoes and slums.[52]

The *expelled* is a category of citizen or quasi-citizen that inhabits a particular precarious space within the urban cosmos, where she is marginalized by what Sassen calls 'systemic edges', which are 'hidden deep inside the territory of the national', and become thresholds of invisibility. For once the expelled cross this systemic edge, they are less likely to inhabit a statistic, to be counted in a census, to exist inside a legitimated system. Becoming invisible means to fall through the systemic edges into a form of forgetfulness and a facelessness (to recall Lévinas foundational ethical philosophy), and thus entering a space which is beyond naming – the space of invisibility, which is a space of non-representation. Sassen extends the terms by which someone is thrust into expulsion, and underpins this condition by pointing out that there is no home to return to, because that home is non-existent as it has been replaced by something else:

> Our language must recognize that the 52 million people identified by The United Nations High Commissioner for Refugees (UNHCR) as "displaced people" are almost never returning home, because their "homes" have been replaced by a new luxury building, a plantation, a war zone. Both the long-term unemployed and the long-term displaced have, in fact, been expelled from society.[53]

Sassen further declares that 'expulsions don't simply happen; they are made.' In her article *The Language of Expulsion* (2014), she focuses on the real estate bubbles that have caused mass eviction of many families in the United States, for instance, in the past decade as one possible story of expulsion machinated by very sophisticated instruments: 'The instruments for this "making" range from elementary policies to complex techniques requiring specialized knowledge and intricate organizational formats, and repressive apparatuses'.[54] If we take Flusser's instructions on tracing the path from the expelled back to the expeller, we arrive at the conditions of expulsion, usually a violent phenomenon of extermination or substitution, which leads us not to focus on its effects, but on its causes.

Who are the *expellers* then? They may be oppressive words, other subjects, acts of violence, economic scarcity, land speculation, land assassination, or embodied as family members or enemies. They may be specific leaders of nations who implement austerity

reasons. This detention center is an in-between space where people are 'warehoused' (in Swedish, 'förvaring') until their situation is decided upon by police, lawyers, both and neither. The filmmakers compare the bureaucratic system to the efficiency of Nazi Germany, and Hannah Arendt's conclusion of the Eichmann trials in 'The Banality of Evil' - the bureaucrat, unknowing of the entire machinery, cannot be held accountable for the overall results of the apparatus.

52 See Sassen, 'Expelled: Humans in Capitalism's Deepening Crisis', *Journal of World Systems Research*, 19.2 (2013): 198-201. Available at: https://doi.org/10.5195/jwsr.2013.495.

53 Sassen, 'The Language of Expulsion', *Truthout*, 30 April 2014, https://truthout.org/articles/the-language-of-expulsion/.

54 Sassen, 'The Language of Expulsion'.

policies, as in Greece or Spain, causing many citizens to seek better opportunities elsewhere, or even the austerity principles themselves. They may be the policies of companies which displace their labor production, causing unemployment and therefore migration. They may be environmental catastrophes where resources are compromised to the point where a place becomes uninhabitable, inhospitable. Or they may be wars and threats of genocide based on a variety of factors.

As I write, I think of those *expelled* individuals I have met during the course of this research: Dhikra, Muhammad, Malik[55] and Shakhlo who live in the microcosm of the immigrant suburb in Fittja, south of Stockholm, Sweden.[56] Their short biographies of exile are interwoven with the narratives of the expellers. Dhikra, a Christian Assyrian from Iraq who has been expelled from her ancestral homeland sheds light on the power of her expeller's intolerance that has driven nearly all her people out of their homeland, a people who are the original inhabitants of Iraq but who have been a persecuted minority for centuries. Muhammad, a refugeed Indonesian national from the island of Aceh sheds light on the brutality of the Indonesian government towards ethnic and political minorities. Malik, a Muslim from Western China who arrives in Sweden after anti-Muslim 2009 riots in Urumqi, reveals the brutality and cultural intolerance of the Chinese State. Shakhlo, a Muslim woman from Uzbekistan who finds freedom of religion in Sweden and reflects on the religious prohibitions in her post-Soviet homeland. While they have been freed from their condition of oppression in their homelands and redeemed into a life of more freedom in a more tolerant host society, in this case Sweden, the expeller is still part of their shadow while in exile. Is the expelled indissociable from the expeller? Can this dialectical relationship between the expelled and expeller ever be resolved? The expelled may express the radicalness and brutality of the situation of all migrant subjects in a variety of conditions and circumstances, but this points to the generalization we should try to avoid. Is this generalization a confession of our inability to name the specificity of these subjects? Does our language become invisible when trying to name those on the verge of becoming invisible?

As Sassen writes, 'today, despite movements of resistance around the globe, such opposition is often prevented by the way in which the oppressed have been expelled and survive at a great distance from their oppressors.' And further, 'addressing this reality full on will require recognizing the radical character of these expulsions. A bit more job growth, a bit more help with housing, none of this will be enough to restore a measure of social justice in this world'.[57] But perhaps, the most radical definition of the expelled which serves to describe a particular condition of otherness, is given by Giorgio Agamben in *We, refugees*: 'the novelty of our era, which threatens the very foundations of the nation-state, is that growing portions of humanity can no longer be represented within it. (...) The refugee should be considered for what he is, that is, nothing less than a border concept that radically calls into

55 Malik has since been deported back to China when he was denied asylum in Sweden. He and a group of fellow Uyghurs demonstrated in front of the Chinese Embassy who retaliated with strict measures towards the asylum seekers and the Swedish authorities.

56 I will return to these characters in Chapter 3 and 4.

57 Sassen, 'The Language of Expulsion'.

question the principles of the nation-state and, at the same time, helps clear the field for a no-longer-delayable renewal of [ontological] categories'.[58] In my view, when highlighting the fact that the refugee makes the glitches of nation-states visible while themselves subjugated to a regime of conditional visibility, Agamben seeks to shed light on the need to dialectically address the role of the host in the equation of expelled and expeller and critically assess the role of the ethics of hospitality within a larger questioning of borders and statehood. It becomes clear that it is not the refugee who is in crisis, for the refugee knows her condition, nor is there something like a migration crisis where the blame is put on the effects of a series of expulsions as outlined above. The crisis is rather in the regime of host-guest relationships which are at the root of these expulsions, and therefore I propose that it is a *crisis of hospitality,* in which host societies are explicitly implicated.

## WHAT IS IT WE CALL HOME?

The relationship between hosts and guests necessarily implies that there is a place, a space and a temporality where this relationship occurs. The guest is the one who enters this space with the consent of the host, such as the wanderer who needs refuge for a night, or the refugee granted asylum and permission to stay. In other words, the relationship between guest and host, its benefits and abuses are always context dependent. In the past decade, in many countries we have witnessed states of friction resulting from the affirmation of homelands and identities and the series of wars and expulsions resulting from what Giorgio Agamben would term a state of exception. The political dimension of the notions of home and homeland may also provide an access point towards understanding hospitality in the context of migration and spatiality that straddles the notions and myths of the national, in which the migrant finds herself trapped in.

Once the subject has been displaced, is there an existential condition which we can call the migrant condition? It is difficult to present solutions to the Gordian knot of entangled identities and diasporic movements, between notions of emplacement and displacement, depatriation, expatriation and repatriation. To speak of a 'migrant condition', we must first relate the migrant to her previous rooted self, and to the notion of *heimat* – the German word for homeland that entangles the notions of home and homeland together, and which carries with it original connotations lost in any simple translation. The migrant (or the expelled), who can be lost or found in the translation of this concept, is in a constant state of understanding the double bind implied in *heimat,* what constitutes her nationality and the homeland, and what constitutes a space and being of belonging and, ultimately, a home.

*Heimat* must be considered historically, especially in relation to the idea of Germanness and its application in the context of the affirmation of a specific identification defined by a clearly delineated territory. Although in English *heimat* is often used synonymously with 'home' or 'homeland,' it has been claimed that this word is particularly ill-equipped for use outside the German-speaking community, owing to its specific cultural baggage as a myth that has

58 See Giorgio Agamben, 'We refugees', *Symposium: A Quarterly Journal in Modern Literatures,* 49.2 (1995): 114-119.

created the basis for an ideology of purity and superiority connected to modern nationalism, or nationhood based on the inclusion of certain subjects at the expense of the exclusion of undesirable Others in a given territory. Any claim in favor of searching for roots of a mythically constructed past has a historical dimension in which the uprooted, the migrant and the newcomer have no place of belonging. The newcomer, lacking history in a national context, becomes ontologically and concretely 'homeless'. Is it possible to liberate this term from its original meaning and the nationalistic connotations it carries?

As a Jewish émigré from the German speaking tradition in Prague, Vilém Flusser was forced to migrate to Brazil during the war while his family was murdered in Nazi death camps. In his writings on exile he builds a philosophy of homelessness and rootlessness (*Heimatlosigkeit*) and groundlessness (*Bodenlosigkeit*). Upon arriving in São Paulo in the early 1940s, he was at the same time orphan, expatriate, migrant, refugee, and without a fixed residency, a nomad. Cut off from his origins and expelled from the European landscape by genocide, he was thrust into a new culture whose parameters were unknown to him and felt 'unhoused' (*Heimatlos*). As with thousands of other victims of the Holocaust, Flusser needed to redefine his own being and place in the world in order to deal with entirely new circumstances. In his philosophical autobiography, *Bodenlos* ('groundless', in German), Flusser reveals his pain of migration and the process he underwent to find a new intellectual and philosophical *heimat* in a dialogical format, writing with and through others. This philosophical place of belonging becomes a critique of a territorial *heimat*, and the very nationalism that caused his initial displacement.

One could imagine that in a state of groundlessness one could still maintain an intimate connection to the *heimat* through language, the memories one carries, and one's original community of kin and peers. In Flusser's case this is also insufficient, since long stays in different countries along the journey had forced him to 'repatriate' in at least four languages. He later discovers the core of his thinking in this constant exercise of translation, writing in different languages, translating himself over and over again, moving from English, to Portuguese, German, French back and forth. He claimed that his thinking transformed according to the language he was using, and that the same essay in two different languages could yield different results, where words shape thinking in singular ways according to the language it is performed in. His working method was similarly constructed by contaminating different discourses: philosophy, anthropology, communication theory, art, design, and zoology, to mention only a few. In *Bodenlos*, he embeds hospitality into the very act of writing his life by hosting dialogues with significant guest-Others, and uses the autobiographic text as a means to expound his thoughts about migrancy *via negativa*, that is, by calling forth his own subjectivity as an *expelled* by revealing the characteristics of the expeller through an unfurling of a dialogic text.

It is essential to understand the terms 'nation' or 'homeland' to separate the different emotions human beings can go through when being away from what they consider their homes, if we consider home indeed as a sort of place, in a process of deterritorialization and reterritorialization. At the outset, Flusser says that *heimat* can be established far from the place of birth. In *Taking up Residence in Homelessness* Flusser states that 'the homeland is an event one cannot control: one is thrust into it at birth, never by choice'.[59] One cannot choose one's origins as they are accidental and inherited, and at the same time one cannot simply escape from them-people are bound to their heimat by their birth and their childhood, their language, their earliest experiences, acquired vital affinities, and predefined cultural habits. The homeland is an interlacing of customs, beliefs, rituals, norms, laws, family ties and friendships as invisible, hidden and unconscious strings that impregnate one's existence, and this results in framing the subject within a specific cultural and identification framework. These threads also create the confidence for creating the rootedness that for many represents the condition for a settled and happy existence. More than happiness, says Flusser, being rooted to a place produces a kind of asphyxia.

The body needs to be somewhere, occupying some form of territory-it can be located somewhere, and this location creates the first identification of the self with time and place. In the most radical form of embedding of the body in a place, a strong feeling for territorial space with a given political and cultural system creates an unconditional love for it. This love for the 'homeland' becomes the parameter that defines all values and functions in a society that is an inherited system away from one's choosing. Language, race, customs, art, for instance, are intrinsic components of the self and form a 'home' which creates a nationalistic conscience and determines one's political identification. It also defines the relationships created within a society, ties which are not created according to one's will necessarily but which are equally inherited and accidental. As Edward Said would say, 'identity is the child of birth, but at the end, it's self-invention':

> What about identity? I asked. He said: It's self-defense . . . Identity is the child of birth, but at the end, it's self-invention, and not an inheritance of the past. I am multiple . . . Within me an ever-new exterior. And I belong to the question of the victim. Were I not from there, I would have trained my heart to nurture there deer of metaphor . . . So carry your homeland wherever you go, and be a narcissist if need be The outside world is exile, exile is the world inside. And what are you between the two?[60]

Flusser arrives at a certain formulation for his own philosophy where he becomes a nomadic thinker not only because he has wandered from country to country, but because he cannot locate his thinking at a precise origin nor link it to any territory that has been clearly defined for him *a priori*. In a way, his own condition as a migrant coupled with his activity as a thinker of migration shows no desire to conquer a space where solid constructions can be built. On the contrary, Flusser builds philosophical campgrounds and shifts them in certain paths often returning to the same places, yet with no intention of defining stable zones. New territories of thought can be dwelled upon temporarily for those who feel intellectually (or artistically) homeless and who can 'take up residence in this homelessness', as he phrases it.

59 Flusser, 'Exile and Creativity', p. 105.
60 Ma□mūd Darwīsh and Mona Anis, *Edward Said: A Contrapuntual Reading, Cultural Critique*, Minneapolis: University of Minnesota Press, 2016.

Flusser's notion of translation takes its strength from this intentionally precarious and nomadic theoretical construction inside a mind that allows itself to become nomadic. If the original text in a given language is the home of a particular idea, then any movement of translation will displace the origin and meaning of the text into other paths, never being able to return fully to its point of departure. This, however, does not presuppose a loss of the original meaning, but rather adds new potentialities to ideas, as different languages possess different expressive vocabularies that lead ideas into new directions. In this way, language becomes a form of hospitality that acknowledges the existence of the Other through the practice of becoming oneself – a reflexive self, nonetheless.

The act of self-translation then acquires an autophagic critical capacity that puts in check his multiple selves – constantly creating and recreating multiple versions of his own original. We can relate this gesture to several acts of translation as multiple instances of the self which acquire new potentialities from each instance of being in a new cultural and political context through successive subjective migrations-always referring to the original self, but no longer having the capacity, nor the desire to remain in that original state. Flusser takes Walter Benjamin's 'the task of the translator' and reconfigures it as 'the task of *self*-translator', where one moves away from the idea of copying, towards the idea of recreating, or, listening to the sounds of the echo coming from 'the depth of the forest', to paraprase his original metaphor. It is equally important that translation is not only possible but also desirable, as only multiple versions of the 'text' can progress towards truth:

> All suprahistorical kinship between languages consists in this: in every one of them as a whole, one and the same thing is meant. Yet this one thing is achievable not by any single language but by the totality of their intentions supplementing one another: the pure language. [...] Where the literal quality of the text takes part directly, without any mediating sense, in true language, in the Truth, or in doctrine, this text is unconditionally translatable.[61]

In the connection between translation of language to translations of the self, as connected to the migrant condition, Flusser posits in the essay *Exile and Creativity* that migration is, at least philosophically, a creative situation. It is a condition that allows for an expansion of reality and the renewal of cultures through a process that includes a series of destabilizations, allowing a new subjectivity to emerge. To speak of a migrant subjectivity necessarily needs its polar opposite: the rooted subject. The rooted subject is blinded by habit into accepting familiar surroundings as self-evident, where the homeland becomes an aesthetic experience against which everything else is deemed ugly and undesirable. This in turn feeds into a dangerous sort of nationalism led by these identifications. In her capacity to assimilate a new context, the migrant subject puts into question the inner workings of the rooted culture, and threatens its instituted norms, 'for the displaced people threaten the "character" of the natives – who are then put into question by their alienation'.[62]

61 Walter Benjamin, 'The Task of the Translator', in*The Translation Studies Reader* (ed.) Lawrence Venuti, London: Routledge, 2000, p. 18.
62 Flusser, 'Taking up Residence in Homelessness', p. 101.

The host subjects feel a violence of change by welcoming the Other who upsets the habitual balance they are accustomed to.

These threads that bind one to the accident of birth, however fixed as they may seem, can be influenced and changed as long as one becomes conscious of them. On the other hand, those who have to distance themselves from their homeland initially experience a kind of collapse of their universe. In this severance, one slowly cuts these strings one by one, and not without suffering. This slow separation from the homeland, origins and referential aspects of the signal culture also means, for Flusser, that one is thrust into freedom. Even though Flusser never used references or footnotes (because he thought they interrupted thinking), I will venture into a reference for Flusser's idea of this thrust into freedom in Lévinas's explanation of alterity and the formation of the 'I' in relation to the idea of home and belonging:

> The *way* of the I against the "other" of the world consists in *sojourning*, in *identifying oneself* by existing here *at home with oneself [chez soi].* In a world which is from the first other the I is nonetheless autochthonous. It is the very reversion of this alteration. It finds in the world a site [lieu] and a home [maison]. Dwelling is the very mode of *maintaining oneself [se tenir]*, not as the famous serpent grasping itself by biting onto its tail, but as the body that, on the earth exterior to it, holds *itself* up *[se* tient] and *can.* The "at home" [Le "chez soi"] is not a container but a site where I *can,* where, dependent on a reality that is other, I am, despite this dependence or thanks to it, free. (...) The site, a medium [Le lieu, milieu], affords means. Everything is here, everything belongs to me; everything is caught up in advance with the primordial occupying of a site, everything is comprehended.[63]

If home is indeed a choice, the question of freedom in locating one's *heimat* remains problematic. It is not the severance of familiar ties that leads to freedom – the kind of freedom characterized by the ability to create new threads alongside the existing primary threads. When a migrant arrives in a new land, she may feel relieved from the external threats to her existence and finally feel safe and secure. Yet this freedom is illusory as new threats arise in new situations.

## THE JOURNEY IN BETWEEN

The poet Abdullah Yüçel was born in 1929 in the village of Kulu, Konya province in central Turkey, and immigrated to Sweden in the 1970s as part of the Turkish guest workforce in Swedish factories. He was better known among his colleagues at the worker's union as a poet.[64]

---

63 Lévinas, *Totality and Infinity*, p. 37. Italics are from the original text where the translator chose to keep Lévinas's words from the French original. *Translator's note: 'Se tenir' involves the notion of containing oneself; it is the idea of an active identity with oneself. It also involves the notion of holding oneself up, of standing, of having a stance-which is at the same time a position and an attitude, a posture and an intention. Hence Lévinas immediately passes to the idea of the 'I can' it implicates.
** Translator's note : «...tout a l'avance est pris avec la prise originelle du lieu, tout est com-pris.»

64 Emrah Sönmez, *Abdullah Yücel: En marginell man - en diskursanalytisk studie om poesi och identitetsskapande i en svensk-turkisk migrationskontext*, Sociology Department,

In his poems about his own migrant condition, many of them written in the satellite city of Fittja, Sweden where he resided in the 1970s, he uses the terms migrant, exile, but also 'pioneer' to describe himself and others. In Yüçel's work, he reveals antagonistic identifications and how migration imprisons him between two worlds, thereby creating a split identification. These poems, written originally in Turkish, were, according to Emrah Sömnez, very well-known among the Turkish workers on the factory floors in Sweden where Yüçel became a voice that could express the individual as well as collective dilemmas of exile and their role in shaping new identifications. Yüçel's poem 'The Journey' shows how he seeks to overcome the split identification, being caught between two worlds. It is apparent in this poem, in which Yüçel constructs his persona as a 'people's poet' and where the term 'migrant' appears nuanced between the destructive identification which represents a crisis, coupled with a creative identification, where a positive representation of reality is seen in the coupling of poetry to the sense of adventure.[65] The last stanza of this poem reads:

Between Denmark and Stockholm
I was greeted by language problems
My travel adventure poem has
Left me behind in Sweden and returned[66]

Here, Yüçel reveals a sense of inbetweenness of being lost in translation in between places, in between languages, and finally using poetry as a medium for expressing his subjective identification with words, as being left behind but also returning. Yüçel lived in Fittja, a few years after it had been newly built in 1973. Built mostly in the peripheries of cities to attend to a housing shortage, this specific typology of Swedish social housing architecture called *miljonprogrammet* was meant to accommodate the working class and raise its living standards to the middle class. The objective was also to build residential areas close to city centers and to factories, thus creating satellite cities to accommodate the planned growth of these communities away from the city centers. As such, the *miljonprogrammet* accommodated both the traditional Swedish working class as well as the new guest workforce, invited to join the country's economic uprise in the golden age of social democracy.

Stockholm University, Stockholm, Sweden, 2014, http://su.diva-portal.org/smash/record.jsf?pid=diva2%3A732009&dswid=85740896. The mass emigration from Turkey to Sweden gained momentum during the second half of 1965, from Kulu, a town in central Anatolia with rurality. Since it was initially solitary adult males who emigrated, labor migration led to chain migration when families were reunited and placed to live in *Miljonprogram* areas in the early 1970s. This helped consolidate the Turkish associations and their economic organization. Author's note: Yüçel lived in Fittja as soon as it was constructed in 1973.Until today, the region of Kulu is well-represented in Fittja, and there is even a diaspora from Sweden back to Kulu in recent years.

65 Sömnez, *Abdullah Yücel: En marginell man,* p. 1.

66 Sömnez, *Abdullah Yücel: En marginell man,* p. 34. My English translation from a Swedish version of the original poem in Turkish.

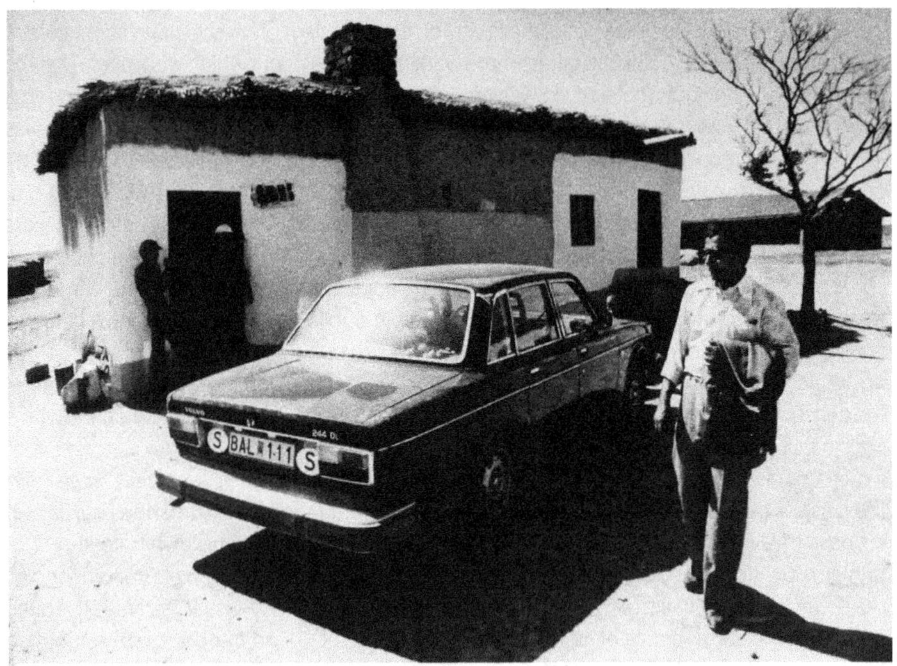

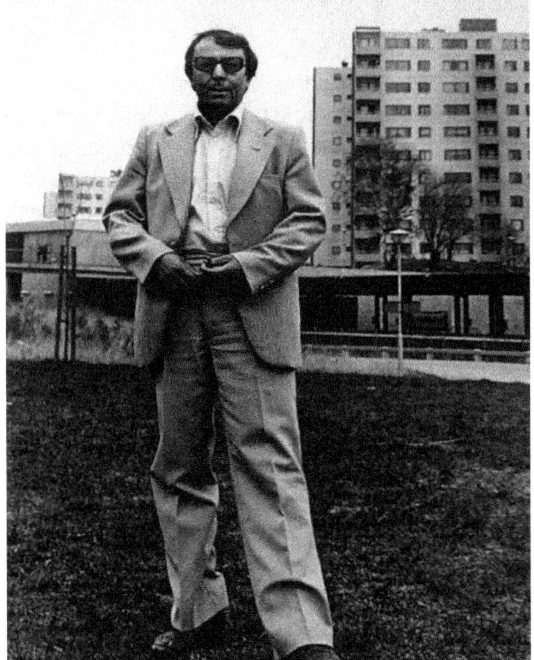

*Figure 4 and 5 – Abdullah Yüçel in Kulu, Turkey, with a Swedish Volvo, the symbol of the journey into exile (photo credit: Gösta Nyberg) and in Sweden, with Fittja in the background, presumably 1979-80. Photo: Behçet Holago. Source: https://abdullahyucelisvectebirturkoncusununhayati.wordpress.com/.*

Yüçel is one of the voices that reveal the contradictions of the migrant condition connected to these specific places – satellite cities where workers first lived, but which were already at the outset slowly emptied out of native Swedes and gradually replaced by the migrant workforce at first, and by humanitarian immigrants in later decades. At first, the guest workforce was invited on temporary contracts and an array of multicultural policies were created for this state of relative permanence, recalling Kant's 'right to sojourn'. Guest workers were expected to remain as guests and not necessarily as new settlers in society. However, as contracts were stabilized and guest workers organized in unions, more and more guest workers decided to settle permanently, also as conditions in the homelands did not improve for them. Since this time, the *miljonprogram*met has been stigmatized in public opinion with negative connotations of social chaos, urban decay, social isolation, and cultural estrangement which it was designed to eradicate. Here we also begin to see the contruction of self in exile realted to the construction of place, as per a utopian architectonic vision of social emancipation which does not always emancipate, as we shall see in the next chapter.

In Flusser's own process of identity destabilization coming from a traumatic expulsion, in his case the Holocaust, he wrestled with the meaning of freedom in his own trajectory. The primary question to understand is: freedom from what? Is the life of the exile conditioned by the phantom of that which expelled her from their 'original' place? Flusser reframes the question of freedom as a means of looking ahead: I now have acquired freedom *from* something, but freedom *for* what? As he writes,

> I experienced freedom during the first year of World War II in London, a place that seems like China to someone from the Continent. I experienced freedom while anticipating the coming horror of humanity in the concentration camps. The changing of the question "freedom from what?" into the question "freedom for what?" – this turning of one thing into another, which is characteristic of hard-won freedom – followed me like a *basso continuo* through all my future migrations. We are all like this, we nomads who have surfaced after having experienced the breakdown of a settled form of existence.[67]

If migration becomes a question of coexistence and existential belonging projected into the possibility of a future, it also has a spatial aspect and a spatial expression we must take into account. Are there spatial aspects or 'sites' that reverberate with a philosophy of difference and alterity?

## HETEROTOPIAS AND HOSPITALITY

To understand the multidimensionality of a space for hospitality, it is useful to examine Michel Foucault's idea of space in *Utopias and Heterotopias* (1967) and how it corresponds with our understanding of space over time, and also the power relations involved in the shaping of spaces and cities *of difference*. In this essay, Foucault establishes two unique sites – utopias and heterotopias – which are extensions of 'other' spaces yet are also in contradiction to other sites they are linked to. A utopia is a fundamentally unreal space, imagined:

67 Flusser, 'Taking up Residence in Homelessness', p. 93.

> Utopias are sites with no real place. They are sites that have a general relation of direct or inverted analogy with the real space of Society. They present society itself in a perfected form, or else society turned upside down, but in any case these utopias are fundamentally unreal spaces.[68]

In contrast, a heterotopia is an existing space which is simultaneously mythic and real. Neither here nor there, a heterotopia can be a Persian rug where the image and symbology of a garden is projected onto, or the space of a phone call with a loved one. In Foucault's view, all cultures are heterotopias who provides two categories and five principles to explain the concept's application in reality. The five principles are as follows: 1) all cultures constitute heterotopias; 2) heterotopias can change function within a single society; 3) they may take the form of contradictory sites, such as the representation of a sacred garden as a microcosm of the world in the patterns of a Persian rug; 4) they are linked with a break in traditional time, identifying spaces that represent either a quasi-eternity, like museums, or are temporal, like fairgrounds; 5) heterotopias are not freely accessible, they are entered either by compulsory means, such as prisons, or their entry is based on ritual or purification, like Scandinavian saunas, and Islamic *hammams*. The principle of exclusion and inclusion, 'presupposes a system of opening and closing that both isolates them and makes them penetrable', where one must have a certain permission to make certain moves or must behave in a certain way.

These principles relate to the following categories. The first category, *spaces of crisis*, refers to sacred and forbidden places, 'reserved for individuals who are, in relation to society and to the human environment in which they live, in a state of crisis: adolescents, menstruating women, pregnant women, the elderly, etc.', such as a 'young woman's deflowering [which] could take place "nowhere" and, at the moment of its occurrence in the train or honeymoon hotel becomes the place of this *nowhere* – a heterotopia without geographical markers'. The second category, *spaces of deviation*, entails those spaces in which 'individuals whose behavior is deviant in relation to the required mean or norm are placed', such as the sick in rest homes, the mentally ill in hospices or psychiatric hospitals, and convicts in prisons.

The notion of accessibility and permission is, as we have seen, one of the ways in which, in the context of hospitality, the guest and the host may interact. These interactions pertain to both categories of crisis and deviation. The permission to visit or sojourn, or to conditionally visit, is inherent to the establishment of the contract between guest and host and the transgression of which may result in conflict, which may, as we have seen through Derrida, include the destruction of the host by the guest. In defining the mechanism of inclusion and exclusion, Foucault reveals a similar paradox related to these spaces, 'we think we enter where we are, by the very fact that we enter, excluded'. The example given is of a Brazilian colonial farmhouse, where:

> (...) the famous bedrooms that existed on the great farms of Brazil and elsewhere in South America. The entry door did not lead into the central room where the family lived, and every individual or traveler who came by had the right to open this door, to

68 Foucault, 'Of Other Spaces', p. 46.

> enter into the bedroom and to sleep there for a night. Now these bedrooms were such that the individual who went into them never had access to the family's quarter, the visitor was absolutely the guest in transit, was not really the invited guest.[69]

I associate this description of the guest room disconnected and inaccessible from the space of the host as a metaphor, in a larger geographical context, for the urban zones of exclusion. In the context of urban segregation, the 'ghetto' is such a zone where the 'guest' may transit and even inhabit but may never trespass a certain boundary towards the center. This boundary may be physical such as a wall, a gate, a street, a police checkpoint, or may be an instrument like a law, such as apartheid, or immaterial and invisible boundaries.[70] According to Fanon, in terms of the geographic construction of > the colonial world is a world divided into compartments. It is probably unnecessary to recall the existence of native quarters and European quarters, of schools for natives and schools for Europeans; in the same way we need not recall apartheid in South Africa. Yet, if we examine closely this system of compartments, we will at least be able to reveal the lines of force it implies. This approach to the colonial world, its ordering and its geographical layout will allow us to mark out the lines on which a decolonized society will be reorganized.[71]

Foucault goes on to speculate on the heterotopic quality of a space of a much larger and temporal scale, the space of the colony as *Other*, where the colonizer saw their role in creating a 'space that is other, another real space, as perfect, as meticulous, as well arranged as ours is messy, ill constructed, and jumbled'. Foucault calls this type a heterotopia of *compensation*, which could also be a form of utopia turned into reality.

The author wonders if some colonies have not functioned somewhat in this manner:

> I am thinking, for example, of the first wave of colonization in the seventeenth century, of the Puritan societies that the English had founded in America and that were absolutely perfect other places. I am also thinking of those extraordinary Jesuit colonies that were founded in South America: marvelous, absolutely regulated colonies in which human perfection was effectively achieved. The Jesuits of Paraguay established colonies in which existence was regulated at every turn. The village was laid out according to a rigorous plan around a rectangular place at the foot of which was the church; on one side, there was the school; on the other, the cemetery, and then, in front of the church, an avenue set out that another crossed at right angles; each family had its little cabin along these two axes and thus the sign of Christ was exactly

69 Foucault, 'Of Other Spaces', p. 47.

70 It can also be *a media boundary*, an immaterial barrier that constitutes a space ruled by similar principles albeit in a media context, if we understand a medium as a space. For example, the segregation of media consumption, whereby different groups consume different media but are prevented from consumption of certain media by way of language difference or difference in the technology's availability or literacy, can form media zones of exclusion, with significant consequences given the role that the media has in the nation and community building in modern societies grounding themselves in democratic ideals.

71 Fanon, *Wretched of the Earth*, p. 37.

reproduced. Christianity marked the space and geography of the American world with its fundamental sign.[72]

Indeed, the very foundation of the New World was based on a complex system of reparations from European society as well as structures of dominance, where colonies are established as a form of domination but populated by communities and subjects which were either persecuted, such as Puritans in the United States, or the sending of prisoners and social renegades as in Australia and Brazil. The metaphors of the promised or prosperous lands would resonate into an *Eldorado such as* in Voltaire's *Candide,*[73] they were partially made real by the religious missions, seeking to establish ideal worlds. This was done largely through the establishment of laws and rules in the autonomous colony, the establishment of the rights of inclusion and exclusion, the attempt to construct ideal worlds far removed from the referential world of the European metropolis. Once again, like Walter Benjamin's reading of ideology and political structuration of urban space behind Haussmann's demolition and construction project in Paris, the city functions as a medium that organizes the content of human transactions it enables.

## CAN THE EXPELLED HAVE A HOME?

And here we return to the kind of programmatic hospitality, the duty of hospitality and the right to hospitality, as reflected in spaces of urban coexistence which may be both imagined and real. In the context of migration and immigration, they are spaces that host, even if temporarily, a subject that is so hard to name, but which we will provisionally call the expelled.

An architecture designed specifically for individuals with transitory status involves a specific type of building that reflects this temporariness, such as the barrack, the shack, the camp, or spaces appropriated for temporary occupation. These are spaces that form a part of a rite of passage from a proto-legal (paperless) to legal status (citizen). A quasi-citizen who lives in quasi-housing, who precedes the politics of social housing per se – an architecture of quick encampment of migrants and their 'warehousing' as Sassen called it (and sometimes their unwillingness to be housed in such conditions – with insufficient resources, heating, privacy, lack of information, lack of stimulation, long waiting times, etc.). Yet in this case, not only is the architecture the result of the politics of temporariness, it results in its normalization, preservation, and reproduction. It is not only designed for temporary occupation, it also reproduces and renders any occupation – no matter how prolonged in many cases-as temporary and endowing the inhabitants with the same temporariness (unlike the stable host populations, firmly rooted in the permanent housing as almost an outgrowth of the native soil). This creates a condition of the eternal guest who can never fully acquire the agency to be herself a host in the receiving society – unless she herself finds the means to transcend it.

72 Foucault, 'Of Other Spaces', p. 51.

73 In one passage of Voltaire's play, Candide runs away from the Jesuits in Paraguay, and joins Cacambo, a native whom he met there. Finding themselves in an escapade, they lose track of their whereabouts and, exhausted, climb onto a raft which flows downstream on the big river. By chance, they land in the Eldorado, happy to have escaped a possible death along the way. Here, Voltaire reveals the wonderful aspect of this new landscape and announces the discovery of a Utopia.

In the movement towards legal citizenship status, the politics of rental contracts and real estate politics in relation to immigrant populations in Europe come to the fore as such spaces of difference in the form of *satellite cities*. The satellite city may then also be another form of the architecture of migrancy, albeit a more permanent one, and as such, a space of difference and a heterotopia of exclusion. In Sweden, the issue of housing for newcomers, that is refugees and asylum-seekers, is contentious. Due to insufficient housing for newcomers, many properties, farms, deactivated clinics and prisons, and even former military barracks have been refurbished for the purpose of temporary housing, or as Sassen would say 'warehousing', for those newly arrived and waiting for their asylum claims or citizenship applications to be approved – a process that may take up to one year or more. Some of these places have a history of detention and serve as a temporary home for future detainees of the global migration phenomenon, creating a new geography of hospitality.

The architecture of migrancy also carries with it a particularly profitable economy. Many different kinds of 'immigration entrepreneurs' have been earning high profits in the entire supply chain of refugees, from the coyote who extorts refugees through dangerous and illegal pathways out of countries, down to the companies that sign leasing contracts of the aforementioned 'warehousing' properties to the government in host societies.

A newspaper feature story in *Dagens Nyheter*, one of Sweden's main newspapers, titled 'The Occupied Landscape: The Idyll as Hostage' from May 10, 2015, recounts a specific instance where the politics of migration and habitation, rising nationalism and multinational companies meet.[74]

In Central Sweden, near the industrial town of Ludvika, there has been an interesting, if not macabre, configuration of such spaces for newcomers that collide with two other ideological spheres of hospitality and transnationality. These three different spaces overlap each other on the shores of Lake Väsman, in the village of Sunnansjö, near Ludvika, a small industrial town whose economy depends on multinational company headquarters. First, a group of two hundred asylum-seekers from Syria, including entire families, have been temporarily quartered in a deactivated anthroposophic medical clinic. Here, the common root fo the words *host* and *hospice* becomes spatially materialized. Twenty kilometers down the road and across the lake live the leaders of the Swedish (The Nordic Resistance Front, NMR) and Norwegian Opposition Parties, considered to be the most violent extreme-right political factions in the Nordic region. Their presence in the area have attracted an array of supporters, and these have in turn elected the leaders of these parties into municipal government positions where they are beginning to exert considerable influence. On another shore of the lake are upper class villas rented temporarily by the executives of ABB, a Swedish multinational company headquartered in Ludvika, with hundreds of employees hailing from several different countries in the world.

74 Björn af Kleen, 'Det ockuperade landskapet: Idyllen som gisslan', DN Fokus, *Dagens Nyheter*, 10 May 2015, https://fokus.dn.se/det-ockuperade-landskapet/.

Each of these spheres represent vastly divergent economies, ideologies, and ways of belonging in the area. A philosophy of care of the anthroposophic lineage becomes an isolated sanctuary and hospitality amidst a landscape where nationalistic exclusionary ideology governs, supported by a local, corporate global capital-driven, economy. They are *heterotopias* in their own right, with their attendant modes of access and expected behaviors and associated cultural rituals. While the more cosmopolitan corporate workers may be able to coexist within such extreme differences in their corporate bubbles, the remaining two represent antagonistic forces in a polarized public sphere.

These situations where extreme nationalism and its opposition to immigration meet the politics of asylum and hospitality, and crosses with globalization, may serve to illustrate the potential sources of conflicts that emerge from these clashing worlds. Here, an ethics of hospitality becomes a fundamental instrument to understand the forces at play. I keep imagining how the city of Ludvika functions in everyday life according to the performative interactions between these groups. What happens when the newly arrived asylum seeker, the extreme nationalist, and the corporate worker all meet in line at the local supermarket? What happens when they meet face-to-face?[75] What kinds of gazes and greetings are exchanged? Does the face-to-face encounter in line to buy milk become a courteous everyday situation able to suspend differences, or does it ignite more tension? Who becomes more vulnerable or more empowered in this encounter, or do they choose to simply ignore each other and carry on? It is worth noting that the supermarket becomes a medium for human encounters conditioning such interactions and potential confrontations. After all, Jean Baudrillard noted the shift from factory (production) to supermarket (consumption) as a central and organizing element in postmodern urban community.[76]

If the characters in this situation choose to greet each other with respect in line at the supermarket, the supermarket becomes an extension of public space where dialogue could be possible. If they choose to confront each other, the supermarket becomes a space of confrontation, a dangerous place for the most vulnerable ones. If they ignore each other, then the logic of alienating consumption and the passive flattening of all differences comes to the fore. Who is host, who is hostage? Who is the temporary guest, who is the permanent visitor? Who is entitled to the space, who is not?

In this hypothesis, 19th century industrial town of Ludvika, formerly a site of industrial production, has become a site of corporate capital, and the supermarket becomes a representative of the experience economy as the site of antagonistic global forces at play (migration, nationalism, corporate capital), which are nonetheless co-dependent. The nationalist depends on the existence of the migrant as 'the other' to confirm his national identity and his right to the land predetermined by birth and race, from which all 'others' are excluded. The newcomers, a very small minority, who have been expelled from their homeland, need the host society to ensure their own survival, unable to return to their home and living in temporary 'warehousing' solutions that maintain them in marginality and as eternal guests, and not always

75 'Det ockuperade landskapet'.
76 See Jean Baudrillard, *Simulacra and Simulation*, Ann Arbor: University of Michigan Press, 1994, p. 77

welcome. The corporate worker and expatriate community fuel the local economy and gentrify the area, polarizing local society into distinct socio-economic classes even further. In this sense, the small microcosm of Sunnansjö and Ludvika takes the contours of the dynamics of the global city, which can be defined as a space where the forces of globalization exert considerable external influence in the dynamics and interactions between its inhabitants. Even though the extent of media globalization has been demonstrated, for example in Kai Hafez's well-founded critique,[77] to be much less significant than one tends to think, the city emphasizes the importance of globalized deterritorialization by virtue of its inherent spatiality.[78]

In these circumstances, media representations and practices (such as satellite television or media reports on migration) create an extension or an extra layer of a physical, territorial space.

Moreover, the global city, with its realities of segregation and opportunities of interaction, becomes a medium for examining shifting boundaries and territories, which allows us to explore the spatial and temporal dimensions of hospitality, and its performative qualities. The city and the media are bound with each other, amplifying and complementing each other's consequences. As Myria Georgiou writes,

> On the one hand, the intensification of mediation and urbanization advances proximity to one another. Close encounters with difference, when rubbing shoulders with others in the street or when being reminded of their proximity in the media, forces urban subjects to become more aware of the challenges and opportunities difference presents. On the other hand, those close encounters with difference become necessary ingredients for the media and the city to sustain their symbolic power [...].[79]

## CITIES OF REFUGE

The most basic form of cosmopolitanism, a political theory closely related to the philosophy of hospitality as we have seen, maintains that there are moral obligations owed to all human beings based solely on their humanity alone, without reference to communal specificities such as race, gender, religion, ethnicity, culture, political affiliation, etc. Cosmopolitanism is based on the acknowledgement of some notion of common humanity that ethically translates into an idea of shared or common moral duties, in contrast to the conventional paradigm of international relations that focuses on states, nationality and power balances between states. When the primary units of moral concern are individual human beings and not states or other forms of political association, there are universal commitments that should be equally applied *among* human beings, in spite of the place of birth and community of belonging. The universal notions contained in cosmopolitanism apply to all persons *as if we are* all citizens of the world. To place the individual as equal and universal beyond state borders also insists

77 Kai Hafez, *The Myth of Media Globalization*, Cambridge: Polity, 2007.

78 Jan Aart Scholte, *Globalization: A Critical Introduction*, New York: Palgrave, 2005.

79 Myria Georgiou, *Media and the City: Cosmopolitanism and Difference*, Cambridge: Polity, 2013, p. 4.

that these moral features act as key regulative features in reforming global structures.[80] On the same token, *I* welcome the *Other* into my home, and *I* welcome the *Other* in myself *as if we are* equal *while also* acknowledging difference.

This welcoming becomes a means of an ethical relationship between these interconnected yet distinct entities, and this leads us to think of what interconnectedness means: a sort of 'global cohabitation', and the accompanying profound contradictions and paradoxes this entails. If we consider modernity as being based on nation-state societies, where social relations, networks and communities are essentially understood in a territorial sense, there are distinct processes that have been superseded by a later form of modernity based on an entirely different frame of reference.

Ulrich Beck, in his *Cosmopolitan Manifesto*, lists five interlinked processes in the current phase of modernity that he calls 'second modernity': namely 'globalization (whereby we can inscribe the current processes of migration), individualization, gender revolution, unemployment and global risks (as ecological crisis and the crash of global financial markets)'. The challenge today is that we need to deal with all these problems all at once. These five interlinked processes are unforeseen consequences of a 'first modernity' where simple, linear, industrial modernization based on the national state (which has been the focus of classical sociology from Marx and Durkheim to Luhmann) lead to a 'radicalized modernization that undermines the first modernity (...) often in a way that is neither desired nor anticipated'.[81]

In this scenario, the idea of controllability, certainty and security so fundamental in the first modernity collapses and gives way to a new form of social, political, global and personal order that comes into being into the second modernity. This second modernity, according to Beck, calls for a new framework, a 'reflexive modernization' that opens possibilities for models of different modernities that are able to coexist in different parts of the world. In a reflexive mode, a new system of risk and guarantees, what I have termed 'technologies of life support', needs to be in place in a globalized world where state structures are weakened, and the autonomy of power and the state are diminished. This leaves the ground open for other powers to take control. He writes,

> We live in an age of risk that is global, individualistic and more moral than we suppose. The ethic of individual self-fulfillment and achievement is the most powerful current in Western modern society. Choosing, deciding, shaping individuals who aspire to be authors of their lives, the creators of their identities, are the central characters of our time.[82]

---

80 Garrett Wallace Brown and David Held (eds) *The Cosmopolitanism Reader*, Cambridge: Polity Press, 2010, p. 1-4.

81 Ulrich Beck, 'The Cosmopolitan Manifesto', in *The Cosmopolitanism Reader*, Cambridge: Polity Press, 2010, p. 217.

82 Beck, p. 94.

Beck claims that this new generation of 'me-first' subjects, are more moral and more political about issues that were not of concern to previous generations such as environment, gender equality, race and human rights. In a world where ideals of human rights have moved center-stage, both politically and ethically, the 'circulating concepts do not fundamentally challenge hegemonic liberal and neoliberal market logics. We live in a world in which the rights of private property and the profit rate trump all other notions of rights.'

David Harvey explores another form of 'right': the right to the city, in other words, the right that each citizen (and non-citizen) can claim in relationship to the urban environment she lives in, and the 'right to change ourselves by changing the city. It is (...) a common rather than an individual right since this transformation inevitably depends upon the exercise of a collective power to reshape the process of urbanization'.[83] In the current media environment, characterized by participatory culture and prosumption, the modern concept of citizenship is supplanted by do-it-yourself citizenship[84] identification with ad-hoc deterritorialized groupings and imagined communities oftentimes based on common interests, (sub)cultures, activities etc, and most often facilitated by the participation-driven matrix of social media.

Beck believes that this provides the basis for a 'new form of cosmopolitanism that places globalism at the heart of political imagination, action and organization'.[85] If the basis for a cosmopolitan political theory, and its relationship to hospitality, is the individual, Beck stresses that what is meant is individualization as a structural concept. All structures are related to the individual, in a form of institutionalized individualism, as in a welfare state where rights and benefits are directed towards the individual rather than families. In order to become an individual in the structural sense, one must be employed, to be employed one must have some sort of education, and both combined constitute social and economic mobility.

Mobility is often associated with dynamics of political freedom that together with citizenship and civil society propose a definition of modernity. In the first modernity, Beck continues, 'the issue of who has and who has not a right to freedom was answered through recourse to such matters as the 'nature' of gender and ethnicity: contradictions between universal claims and particular realities were settled by an ontology of *difference*'.[86] The difference is that now, as modernities overlap each other across the world and as the bias whereby 'contemporary societies are relegated to the category of 'traditional' or 'pre-modern' (...) as the absence of modernity' is replaced by a 'pluralization of modernity', there is a possibility now to stress the aspects of sameness, and not otherness, between interconnected entities (communities, structures, individuals, networks, etc.) in this globalized constellation. With the speed, intensity and significance of processes of transnational interdependence, Beck suggests that what we call *non-Western* societies need to be included in the discourse of globalization and examined in its different sites. In fact, any analysis of this reflexive modernity thus needs to

83 David Harvey, *Rebel Cities: From the Right to the City to the Urban Revolution*, New York: Verso, 2012, p. 9.

84 John Hartley, 'Silly Citizenship', *Critical Discourse Studies,* 4.7 (2010), p. 128..

85 Beck,'The Cosmopolitan Manifesto', p. 222.

86 Beck,'The Cosmopolitan Manifesto', p. 221.

take into account the means by which different worlds are connecting. It is the matter of an ethics of hospitality as an ethics of becoming.

If Marx's *Communist Manifesto* was about class conflict, Beck's *Cosmopolitan Manifesto* is about 'transnational-national conflict and dialogue' with the aim to study the possibility of democracy in a global age. Then we must ask, who will raise this question? Is it the vagabond, burdened with low education, skills and status, or the tourist, 'light' thanks to their high economic and educational status, as the ideal types found by Zygmunt Bauman in the liquid modernity, those who freely choose to travel because they can afford to and those who are forced to do so due to security, political or economic reasons – because they cannot stay where they are? Is it the 'me-first' generation, the individual as a structural element in society? Are they personified in the apartisan and newly empowered mass of individuals that manifest in the streets of Brazilian metropolises claiming investments in health and education, or the *New Swedes* demanding non-discriminatory measures and equal rights in a society of widening social gaps?[87]

A corollary to this concern is, how are the spaces where these questions are raised being conceived? Are they the civic spaces of the city designed for political gathering (main squares, centra, streets, markets), are they the obsolescent vehicles of mass media (print and television, etc.) or are they ever more the spaces of intensive personal exchange (through social media or 'pop-up' social movements such as Occupy and flash mobs) acting on a global level parallel to, and in defiance of, national politics? Is there a particular space within the hospitable city for a new notion of the 'public' to develop?

Beck's infrastructural retooling can be related here to Derrida's call to action for the formation of 'cities of refuge.' In *On Cosmopolitanism*, Derrida expounds his reasoning in search for an autonomy, both for the exiled subject and for a spatial politics. Here, Derrida begins by challenging the reader into a 'genuine innovation of the right of asylum or the duty to hospitality', and opening a discussion of a cosmopolitics that outlines a place for the cosmopolitan, as 'the proclamation and institution of numerous and, above all, autonomous 'cities of refuge', each as independent from the other and from the state as possible, but nevertheless, allied to each other according to forms of solidarity yet to be invented'.[88]

Derrida created a vision for establishing a group of cities of refuge/asylum where people could come from anywhere and be well-treated, recalling 'his invocation and development of an unconditional law of hospitality, a law always constructed as a non-utopian guide for what is often viewed as a utopian politics, as the guiding mode of solidarity for the cities'.[89] He describes the support necessary for imagining such a city of refuge and

87 From 2011 to the present date, more and more youth from suburban areas around Stockholm and other large Swedish cities have been organizing into citizen movements against discrimination, intolerance and segregation. The criticism against the visibility of such activities, coupled with a generous refugee and asylum policy, has caused more voters to vote in nationalistic parties and normalizing intolerance and segregation, and thus polarizing society further.

88 Derrida, *On Cosmopolitanism and Forgiveness,* p. 410.

89 This refers in part to the Biblical six Levite cities of asylum, but more importantly, to Derrida's effort in

making the connection of architecture and cities to the laws of hospitality, to the imagination of a space where the Other may have the right to inhabit. Derrida looks upon the city, and not the state, for such a task: 'If we look to the city, rather than to the State, it is because we have given up hope that the State might create a new image for the city'.[90]

Moreover, the city, the media and the individualistic and fluid social media spaces have the possibility of hosting the cosmopolitan question of transnational conflict/dialogue, as Beck suggests, that denote both territorial and extra-territorial aspects. One wonders, then, where a collective aspect of cosmopolitanism could reside. An ethics of hospitality applied to urban form could be the degree in which these spaces are able to accommodate the conflicts inherent in the interconnectedness of individuals, communities, and shared risks.

This cosmopolitan subject, if we may call her so, as a world citizen and operating in a transnational context, is constantly wavering between a concern for the global and the expression of a 'cosmopolitan common sense', and the concern of the citizen as a member of a national state. As with all research, the most interesting question is always related to the exception: the refugee or the asylum-seeker – a person who stands outside from a global system of world citizenry and from belonging to a national state, albeit temporarily, and is simultaneously the effect and victim of an interconnected transnational context of conflict. For this exception to be used as the cause of a national dilemma between welcoming the Other, or turning our backs to the Other, or worse, being indifferent to the Other, ignoring the Other, we might ask: is world citizenry even possible? For Beck, cosmopolitanism may remain a democratic utopia. One hypothesis to think about is if this necessary utopian thinking is what could save democracies from the impending rise of the nationalistic discourse which crystallizes all differences and similarities into one direction towards hyper-territoriality, just as we might still be living in the illusion that with the information revolution borders may have been dissolved, or simply shifted to other dimensions.

As a space of intense communication and difference, the global city forces us to think about the challenges of living in close proximity to each other. Do we really see, hear and understand our neighbors? As city centers and suburban areas grow, merge and densify, does this proximity to the Other imply that we know, or let alone desire to relate to the Other? What are the contradictory realities of cosmopolitanization as these emerge in the shape of the city as a site of antagonisms, empathies and co-existing particularities?

However, we still live in the concept of the city as a 'machine to live in'[91] as Le Corbusier postulated in the early history of modernism, which has today been converted to the city as

---

creating vision for the International Parliament of Writers' (IPW) cities of asylum within the context of his political philosophy of a democracy to come, and asks to reassess how the political act of hospitality toward acts of free speech is approached. See: Sean Kelly, 'Derrida's cities of refuge: toward a non‐utopian utopia', Contemporary Justice Review 7(4):421-439, December 2004; see also: ICORN - International Cities of Refuge Network, https://www.icorn.org/

90 Derrida, *The Cosmopolitan Manifesto*, p. 414.

91 See also Le Corbusier (Charles-Edouard Jeanneret), *Towards an Architecture,* transl. John Goodman, Los Angeles: Getty Research Institute, 2007 (1923).

*an image to live in* in the transition from an industrial to an experience economy. Le Corbusier had created an architecture built on principles of universalism that reflected the industrial age, within the logic of mass production and as 'signal expressions that are at once pragmatic, utopian and ideological in force'.[92] Though universalist in intention, even the most utopian modernist city had principles of exclusion, including aesthetic exclusion, embedded in its own design. Today, exclusion by design uses covert tools advanced by subtler methods of real estate markets and housing policies such as privatization, gentrification, etc. which render habitation precarious for those marginalized from these systems. This leads us to ask not how we can lead a good, moral life, but how we can have a good, trendy lifestyle – but inaccessible to many. Modernism, even though modernist buildings still exist to be visited, needs to also be seen in the context of modernity. As sociologist Ulrich Beck has argued, modernity has become reflexive, concerned to retool its own infrastructure.[93] Architecture could very well be this reflexive image – a hospitable image, an image designed as welcoming. And yet, is it possible to inhabit an image? I will recall Agamben briefly here, where the hospitable city as a Möbius-shaped space,

> (...) would not coincide with any homogeneous national territory, nor with their topographical sum, but would act on these territories, making holes in them and dividing them topologically like in a Leiden jar or in a Moebius strip, where exterior and interior are indeterminate. In this new space, the European cities, entering into a relationship of reciprocal extraterritoriality, would rediscover their ancient vocation as cities of the world.[94]

To end this chapter, we can now say that the idea of hospitality beyond the law works independently of the legal field that regulates the rights of others and operates within the realm of physical materialities and the experience of the human. This kind of cosmopolitan hospitality is attached to a full, radical diversity. If we return to Lévinas briefly, he elects the idea of the feminine[95] as the infinite potential of hosting the radical Other, and I would like to link this to an examination of the urban space of the suburb as assuming a similar 'female' role in our subsequent discussion of hospitality and urban form. In other words, the suburb and the satellite city exposes more radically the alternations between reflexivity and hospitality than other parts of the city and as such has the potential of hosting the radical Other. Perhaps it is the 'systemic edge' of the city, to use Sassen's spatial concept[96], embodied in the suburb/satellite city, together with the radical Other, incarnated in the notion of the female, that may lead to the innovation Derrida calls for, as mediums for refuge in a new dimension of solidarity, to be devised in the future, as elusive as the future may be.

---

92 Hal Foster, *The Art-Architecture Complex*, London: Verso, 2011, p. 7.

93 Foster, *The Art-Architecture Complex*, p. 3-4., see also Ulrich Beck, *Risk Society: Towards a New Modernity,* Polity Press, 2008.

94 Agamben, 'We Refugees', p. 117.

95 Lévinas, *Totality and Infinity, p.* 99.

96 Sassen, 'At the Systemic Edge: Expulsions', *European Review, 24.*1 (2016), p.90.

# CHAPTER 2: THE CITY AS AN ACT OF HOSPITALITY

# CHAPTER 2: THE CITY AS AN ACT OF HOSPITALITY

> (...) from the number of imaginable cities we must exclude those whose elements are assembled without a connecting thread, an inner rule, a perspective, a discourse. With cities, it is as with dreams: everything imaginable can be dreamed, but even the most unexpected dream is a rebus that conceals a desire or, its reverse, a fear. Cities, like dreams, are made of desires and fears, even if the thread of their discourse is secret, their rules are absurd, their perspectives deceitful, and everything conceals something else.[1]
>
> – Italo Calvino

## Writing the City from the Beyond

One of the ways in which we may define hospitality is the initial process of allowing or opening oneself to become inhabited by the Other. In so doing one gives life, form, and an environment to the subjectivity of the Other through oneself. In the words of Jeremy Fernando in the afterword of the book *Poetry Beyond the Grave*, by Brazilian psychic Chico Xavier, 'What does it mean to inhabit another's voice? Perhaps the more appropriate question is: what does it mean to allow another to inhabit oneself?'[2]

I call forth the Brazilian psychic Chico Xavier[3] in order to describe a city of spirits written 'from the beyond' called *Our Home*, which reflects the notion of the city as an imagined entity in which the human condition is mirrored. The first city plan drawn up in 1944 consists of a psychographically transcribed book written by him entitled *Nosso Lar: Life in the Spirit World*[4] (known as 'Our Home' or 'Astral City' in English) dictated by the spirit of a deceased Brazilian physicist referred to as Mr. André Luiz in continuous sessions of psychographic trance.[5] During these sessions, which any surrealist artist would have recognized as an experiment of *écriture automatique*, or automatic writing, Xavier kept his eyes closed or partially

---

1 Italo Calvino, *Invisible Cities*, New York: Harcourt Brace Jovanovich, 1974, p. 44.

2 Francisco Cândido Xavier, *Poetry from Beyond the Grave (Afterword by Jeremy Fernando)*, trans. Vitor Pequeno, Uitgeverij, 2013, p. 195.

3 Xavier claimed to be contacted by spirits since he was a boy growing up in a poor family of nine children in the rural area of Minas Gerais, a state in Southeastern Brazil. After having lost his mother at a young age and enduring torture by his godmother's physical abuse, he claims to have been chosen by the spirit world to pursue a career as a professional psychic. Besides healing many people from ailments, Xavier has psychographed 485 books, of which more than fifty million copies have been sold. Xavier was responsible for funding approximately 2,000 spiritist centers all over Brazil, which were in charge of disseminating knowledge transferred by himself as well as functioning as social centers for the poor. Two million people watched his first live television broadcast performing a healing session in 1971. Jonas Staal, *Nosso Lar/Brasília*, Capacete/JAP SAM Books, Rio de Janeiro, 2014, p. 11.

4 Xavier, *Nosso Lar,* Brasília: International Spiritist Council, 2006 (1944).

5 The English language version of this book is Francisco Cândido Xavier and André Luiz (Spirit), *Nosso Lar/The Astral City: The Story of a Doctor's Odyssey in the Spirit World*, Christian Spirit Center, 1986.

covered, having new sheets of paper placed in front of him while his pencil scribbled nonstop for seven hundred days.

Xavier himself never claimed authorship for any of his books, but rather said that he was committing his body to a hospitable act in allowing a spirit to write through him. Xavier, the *medium*[6] or psychic, is both host as he allows himself to be inhabited, but also a guest in a work he does not claim to be his own. The psychic is able to relay meaning but not to create it; his body is available for the message to occupy it. As such, his body becomes the definition of a medium in and of itself, as a form of mediated and embodied hospitality, as his body is merely a tool for the spirit – the body *becomes* the communicative device he claims himself to be.[7] As Fernando describes, Xavier is 'the home to the messages even as they might well remain unhomely in, and through, him: he is their haunt, even as they haunt him, haunt us through him'.[8] In other words, Xavier claims himself to be able to relay meaning but not create it, he is merely available to the message as a body to become occupied by it, which gives *life* to the voice of the spirit, or, to the Other. In the case of *Our Home*, to the vision of a city, a spiritual colony, where the intricacies of afterlife and reincarnation can be observed.

## Our Home

We can read hospitality into the very subject of the book *Our Home,* which describes the creation of a temporary spiritual home as an allegory of a city with a spatial configuration suited for both hosting and excluding or expelling specific subjects. But first, we should not fail to notice that *Our Home* is the name of a city that begins with a pronoun – *our* – which presupposes a *We*, and therefore, the Other as well. *Our Home* is therefore not for everyone. It is only for those spirits who, in their migrant route from earthly life towards a higher stage of spiritual evolution, are allowed to inhabit it according to specific laws and conditions, that is, according to certain laws of conditional hospitality. As a blueprint for a religion, *Our Home* becomes, as the spirit André Luiz intended, a meta-city much like Thomas More's *Utopia,* about the political system of an imaginary ideal island nation, as a satire about tumultuous English politics published in 1516.[9] In narrative terms, More and Xavier transmitted their cities to us by using frame narrative devices for engendering alternative stories within stories told by a guide who speaks directly to us. In both instances, the city appears as a medium for describing ideologies of worlds-out-of-this-world, establishing visions and possibilities that offer an escape from, a mirror of, or a sanitation from an imperfectly lived reality. The relationship between hosts and guests and the space inhabited by and created from this relationship also acts, in both cases, as both an affirmation and critique of current politics.[10]

6 'Médium' in Portuguese means 'psychic'. Here, a wordplay between 'médium' in Portuguese and 'medium' in English would be in place.

7 In Spiritism, the set of teachings contained in the works of Allan Kardec (1804–1869), has organized and spread the interchange of news among the incarnate and the discarnate. For the Spiritists, there is no death, life as we call it is only an intermediary stage in a longer span of evolution.

8 Xavier, *Poetry from Beyond the Grave*, p. 207.

9 Thomas More, *Utopia*, transl. Paul Turner (ed.) Penguin Classics, 2003 (1516).

10 As we shall see later, there is a hypothesis that sustains the fact that *Nosso Lar* is a simulacrum of religious and political conditions in Brazil at the time it was written, in such a way that it puts forward

In *Our Home*, the spirit André Luiz hosted by Chico Xavier describes his journey from the moment of his death to the moment of arrival in the city of spirit, following the model of ascent into Dante's *Inferno*. He is guided from the darkest circles of hell towards reaching the places of light. In contrast to Dante's protagonist, he is not simply a visitor, he has also subjected himself to each of these stages of punishment and forgiveness in the journey towards the city. The author (Xavier? Or Luiz?) discloses a spiritual society, a colony of work located near the Earth's surface, where one finds the happy or sad results of one's acts after reaching *the other side* of life. In this way, we realize that we are only guests in our earthly lives, and what happens between birth and death is a journey from and between worlds of permanence, where the 'final homeland' is the eternal world of the spirits.

The form of the narrative is also akin to an odyssey presenting several obstacles and trials before reaching the end destination of spiritual evolution beyond the city, recalling the grand narrative of travel, the epic journey of the hero, and the trajectory as a form of migration from one stage to the next. André Luiz is guided by several citizens by means of walks and flights on special air buses through the futuristic colony. In this 'guided tour' he learns of its government, its economy, its arts and culture, its infrastructure, the highly developed science-fiction-like technology and how one can gain access to a higher level of spiritual development after several stages of reincarnation.

According to Luiz, the colony's essential purpose is for labor and production. Labor leads to the correct spiritual mentality of selfless dedication, while benefitting the spiritual regeneration colony both culturally and technologically. In the large city blocks, Luiz describes its workers as 'one hundred thousand individuals who enlighten and regenerate themselves while working.'[11] In addition, this regeneration colony takes control over the fertilization of humans to engineer and monitor the exact spiritual developments of its subjects on Earth, an idea very closely related to the narratives of biopolitical science fiction thrillers like *The Matrix*,[12] and which can also be connected to the biopolitics of social engineering as they have been applied and developed by way of visionary architectonic visions in the 20th century, such as the modernistic Brazilian capital city of Brasília. A planned and 'invented' city like Brasília also included the project of a new and ideal subject to inhabit it and fulfill the promise of progress and modernity.

---

a Spiritist point of view by assimilating the forms and principles of the Catholic church and the Vargas dictatorship in Brazil (1930–1945) while at the same time critiquing them. In a similar way, Thomas More's *Utopia* is a satire of monarchy, the dominant political system in the 17th century England, and puts forward a new moral philosophy by assimilating aspects of monarchy into the outline of a perfect society, only to denounce the vicissitudes of the system in allegorical form.

11 Xavier, *Nosso Lar*, p. 59.

12 This narrative reminds us of the basic premise for *The Matrix* series (dir. Wachowsky Brothers, 1999–2003) as well as aspects of Aldous Huxley's novel *The Island* (1962), both of which deal with dystopian biopolitics of the future taking shape within specifically designed environments/cities.

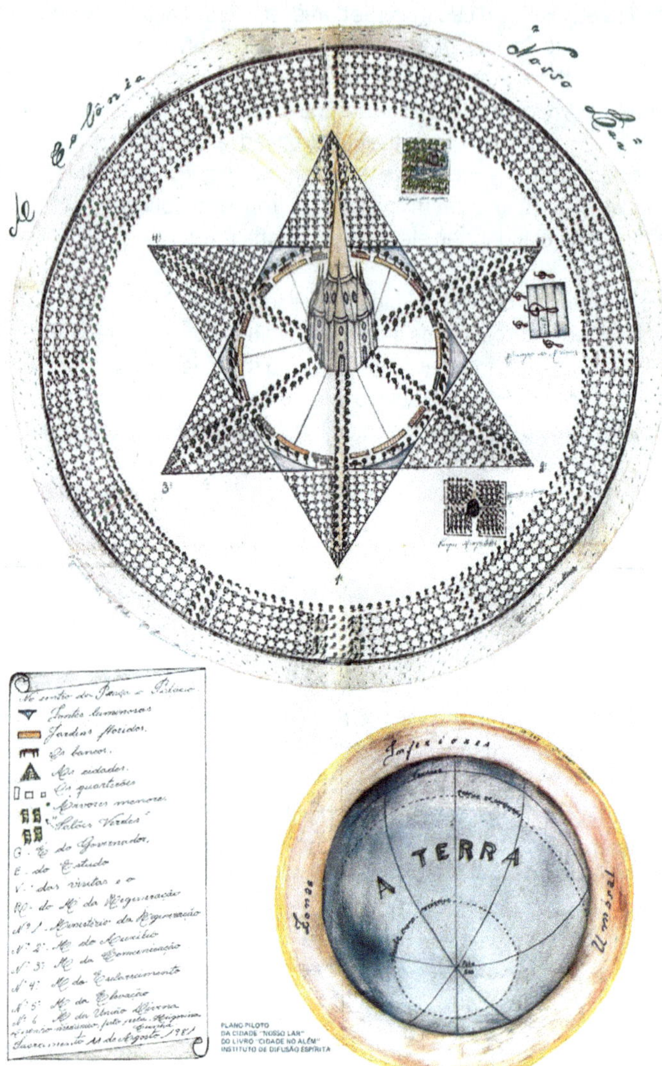


*Figure 6 – A plan of Nosso Lar, as psychographed by the psychic Heigorina Cunha, Sacramento, Minas Gerais, on January 12, 1980. Source: Mensagens espíritas,* ***https://mensagensespiritasapp.wordpress.com/2012/12/14/mapas-de-nosso-lar/****.*

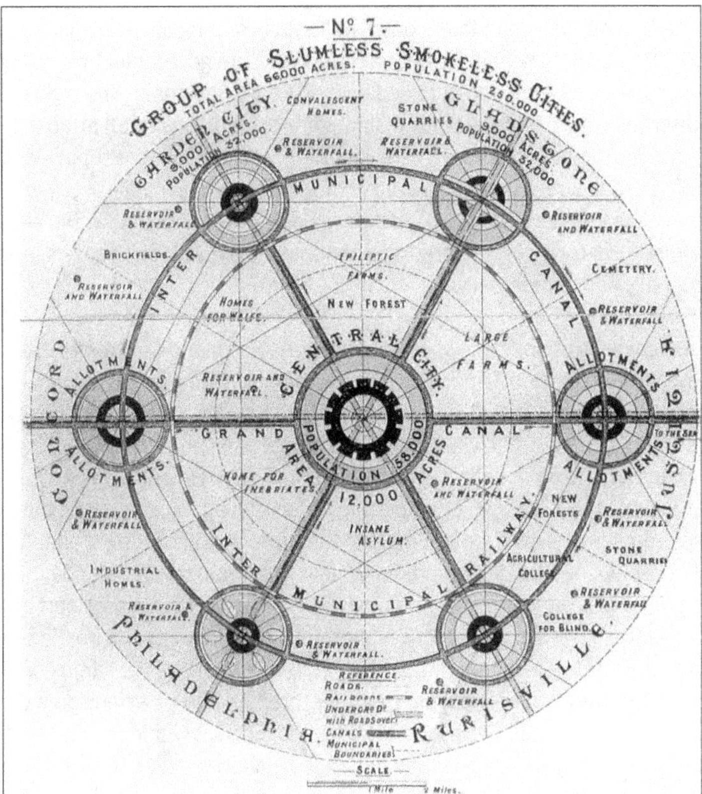


*Figure 7 – The original Garden City concept by Ebenezer Howard, 1902. Ebenezer Howard's garden cities are also based on a radial plan with defined areas for different functions arranged in concentric circles connected to different nodes by access routes within an overall circular plan, in contrast to visions of cities based on the rationality of the square grid. Source: Data Cities,* **https://data-cities.net/from-garden-cities-to-data-cities/.**

*Our Home* is not only a city on clouds, a planned city, but also a city of history. It is said to hover above the Earth dating back to the 16th century when it was founded by 'a group of distinguished Portuguese', with a clear reference to the first European colonizers of Brazil, expanding their colonial enterprise long after their death into the spiritual realm, attempting to finish what they started on Earth in the spirit world. *Our Home* appears as a para-modern futuristic colonial fantasy of liberation. A utopia, no less. Perhaps.

Physically, *Our Home* takes the form of a city for over one million people, shaped like a six-pointed star with a fixed central point where the Government House and its pan-optical structure is located, and from which all other living areas radiate in concentric circles. A central power led by the Governor rules from this central point, and the city radiates outwards divided into six equal modules, each one assigned to a branch of public administration with compelling names: the ministries of Regeneration, Assistance, Communication, Elucidation, Elevation, and Divine Union. Surrounding the administrative centers is a large square followed by triangularly shaped residential areas, each one housing employees of the respective ministries. The most spiritually developed citizens live closer to the centre while the less developed live closer to the outer wall, thus creating a spatial hierarchy connected to status. The zones between residential areas and the government center are occupied by green spaces for leisure and service facilities for the residents. The big star is protected by an outer wall where batteries of projectors are placed to ward off attacks from invading 'inferior' spirits, and outside the wall are vegetable plantations that supply food for the residents.[13] This urban structure reminds me of the structure of a medieval city which still forms the historical core of several European cities, albeit now encrusted within several layers of modern infra-structures, even though the concept of city walls still persists in several cases, both materially and immaterially.

On the vertical dimension, in the space between the Earth and *Our Home*, lies the limbo-like region under the city called 'Umbral' where Luiz begins his journey. This intermediary zone is described as an enormous slum inhabited by the discarnate souls. The only way in which the discarnate souls in the Umbral can be granted citizenship into *Our Home* and ascend onto the hovering city is to demonstrate genuine remorse for their faulty life and the reassurance that they will not rebel against its autocratic order; elevation can only be attained through repentant obedience. However, the majority of humankind is deemed unable to reach this stage of consciousness and thus remains within this limbo for eternity, becoming mentally ill to the point of no return, and eternally revolving in a world that they can neither escape from nor change.[14] Besides hospitality, in the sense of welcoming and hosting, including and excluding, *Our Home* also functions as a hospital, which shares the same etymological root as *hospitality*, in the sense of healing, treatment, repair, and by extension a Catholic sense of purgatory and redemption – a kind of heterotopic space within the meta-city. Culture in *Nosso Lar*, in all forms of art, theatre and music, is a 'joyful incentive' meant to reward all those who are in the 'good path' towards spiritual elevation, and thus, the sensible also becomes a device of purification.

Access into *Our Home* is very strict. The laws of hospitality are tightly enforced and follow strict rules to achieve access into all levels of the system, each with specific spiritual criteria. So, besides the uncertainty as to which level of spiritual development is fit for entry, additional criteria of entry reflect characteristics of the dominant elite which trace back to the very first group of colonizers of who had indeed built it in the first place, a meritocracy no less. It is the world as we know it, with striking resemblance to the immigration and citizenship laws of the real world: which groups are granted entry, and which are left out? On what grounds? What is the ultimate objective of the laws of hospitality in this city?

---

13 In this respect, *Our Home* is very much shaped like a medieval walled city, and we can infer that *Nosso Lar* is more based on a European city plan than an American city plan which is not based on the centrality of the temple but rather on the grid. The idea of projectors as surveillance devices reminds one of watchtowers surrounding walled cities.

14 This description is remarkably accurate in the context of segregation and the city, as it metaphorically describes the 'floating' condition of migrants, paperless and stateless peoples, as they equally 'hover' in conditions of para-legality, which we shall see later in Chapter 3.

## Inevitable Histories

*Our Home* is thus continuation of the dominant order of colonization, or rather, a 'corrected' version of the current order of the materialist, statist and colonial project, including the necessary violence to maintain it, either as gate-keeping through bureaucracy or in the enforcement of a disciplinarian order without which the colony cannot function. The outlines of the Governor's project of social engineering, discipline, and punishment, for instance, become clear through his monopoly on state violence. No matter how educated or elevated the spirits are, they cannot be fully trusted to uphold the order as only a single ruler can guarantee it. From a visual and architectural standpoint, everything in this dwelling place for spirits is dedicated to sustaining the ruler's central power and overseeing every stage of transformation from the raw spiritual nature of the 'primitive' spirit to the recently spiritually enlightened or 'civilized' person. This is made manifest by the concentric circles of the city and the projectors that protect it from outside invaders: a pan-optical structure that reminds of Jeremy Bentham's panoptical prison design,[15] an example exhaustively used to signify the surveillance apparatuses in modern societies.

According to Dutch artist Jonas Staal's appraisal in his project *Nosso Lar/Brasília*, *Our Home* is a *mediated city*, as it is psychographed by Xavier while the spirit André Luiz mediates political figures and the Catholic Church from the beyond into the present. It is a socially engineered city, where its citizens become ideal subjects for a model spiritual person. It is also a colonial project, as it consciously tells of its own history of appropriation, destruction, and cultural overcoming of indigenous people's land and resources. Moreover, it is a gated community because of its closed structure with strict policies of inclusion and exclusion of its members on a meritocratic basis. Lastly, it is a hierarchic model that organizes its citizens in classes and different partitioned segments under different administrators, as well as segregates them in different parts of the city, closer or farther from the prestigious center. Finally, it is a statist society where the means of production, social resources and monopoly of violence are in the hands of an autocratic regime.[16]

I bring *Nosso Lar* into this book *via* Jonas Staal's book *Nosso Lar/Brasília*[17] as it draws up a hypothesis that the creation of the Spiritist city and the construction of Brazil's modernist new capital city Brasília, inaugurated in 1960, both present visions for cities that are innovative and modern but cannot escape the contradictions of a history they cannot do away with. It is as if the land on which a city is built is already impregnated with a past that is inescapable and contaminates it sooner or later. In this sense, we could say that all visionary, utopian projects are doomed to a destiny that precedes them – history catches up. However, this fatalism can only be procured on hindsight. *Our Home* is an allegory of a city in a radical form with all its contradictions revealed and systematized. The city

15 Jeremy Bentham, *The Panopticon Writings*, Radical Writing Series, Verso Books, 2005 (1791).

16 Jonas Staal, '*Nosso Lar/Brasília*', Capacete/JAP SAM Books, Rio de Janeiro, 2014, p. 32.

17 Artifacts related to this research were exhibited at the 31st São Paulo Biennial, 2014, São Paulo, Brazil. 'Nosso Lar, Brasília', *31a. Bienal - How to Become Things that Don't Exist,* 14 September, 2014, http://www.31bienal.org.br/en/post/1520.

subjects are defined according to a predetermined plan of spiritual elevation, ultimately creating the blueprint of a religion.

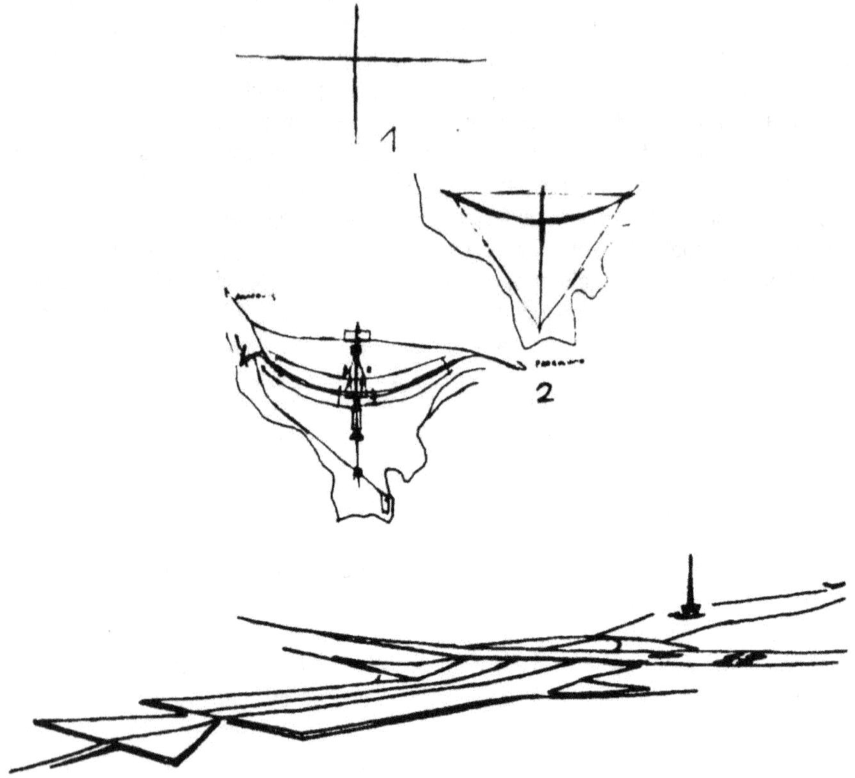


*Figure 8 – Brasília's Pilot Plan, winning entry for competition, sketch by Lúcio Costa, 1956.*

On the same token, Brasília, a capital city that was declared a monument at the moment it is born, and conceived and brought to life in the shape of an airplane, also represents the channeling of a 'spirit' and is a blueprint of a modern society in a country touted as 'the land of the future'.[18] This time it is the spirit of nationhood, a national spirit, a point of identification and orientation. The city is, as mentioned before, the medium through which this spirit is embodied. Both cities are also typical of the 20th century that has seen many urban grand schemes aiming to improve the human condition, especially after the mass destruction in Europe caused by two consecutive wars, not to mention other conflicts, or as moves towards territorial expansion and occupation. Brasília was grounded on a historical vision and represents a possibility for achieving the ideals of 'modern man' and thus fully inhabiting modernity. As Bauman elucidates,

18 This term was coined by the Austrian émigré writer Stefan Zweig in the book *Brazil: Land of the Future*, first published in 1941. It is a historical account of Brazil as a modern, utopian society.

> the desire of better life focused on the search for the model of good society – a setting for human life more solid, reliable and resistant to corruption than any model could provide. Utopian blueprints were the findings of that search.[19]

These references are important in understanding the articulation of architecture and politics of modernization and exclusion that helps us in understanding current politics of spatial hospitality, and how we can imagine exceptions as heterotopian moments of hospitality. According to Nikolaus Hirsch, 'a plan designs an object, unifies diverse, often contradicting, factors into one language and establishes control towards the future. The planned project becomes a projection thrown into the future: a predictive model.'[20] In these two examples, the realization of ideal cities serves to reify, rather than challenge, existing power structures that reify the exclusion apparatus from which we cannot seem to escape. In other words, we are not able to envision a world that we cannot yet experience. Does this mean that we cannot envision the future, that we are not able to imagine what the 'coming community' will be like?

## Empty Plateaus

In addressing the failures of ideal cities, James C. Scott identifies four conditions common to them all: the state's attempt to impose administrative order on nature and society; a high-modernist ideology that believes scientific intervention can improve every aspect of human life; a willingness to use authoritarian state power to effect large-scale innovations; and a prostrate civil society that cannot effectively resist such plans and succumbs to the higher order.[21] Brasília is one such planned, invented city that could be used to exemplify what Scott means by the traps and failure of planning, with the difference that Brasília was indeed created in a time of democratic expansion in Brazil and had democratic aspirations. The authority, in this case, can be said to be the authority of the author of the plan over the empty landscape on which the new city is to be built on. However, for us to speculate about some its failures as well as its innovations, we need to first understand how this city was engendered.

Different from the imagining a spiritual city psychographed by a psychic, the design of Brasília followed a far more conventional approach. The new design for the city was the result of a national competition won by urbanist Lúcio Costa and the architect Oscar Niemeyer in the early 1950s and inaugurated in 1960. Its location in the geographic center of Brazil became the fulfillment of a 'manifest destiny' vision inherited from the 19th century Imperial era, as a strategy to occupy the scarcely populated hinterlands of the country, in the empty central plateaus.

19 Zygmunt Bauman, 'Utopia with no topos', *History of the Human Sciences*, Vol. 16 ,No. 1, 2003, p. 17.
20 Nikolaus Hirsch, 'A Model World', in Andrea Phillips and Fulya Erdemci (eds) *Social Housing-Housing the Social: Art, Property and Spatial Justice*, Amsterdam/Berlin: SKOR/Sternberg Press, June 2012, p. 44.
21 James C. Scott, *Seeing Like a State: How Certain Schemes to Improve the Human Condition Have Failed*, New Haven: Yale University Press, 1998, p. 104.

In 1956, with the democratic election of President Juscelino Kubitschek, this vision became true as part of a national development plan that became known by the slogan '50 years in 5', which helped create a cult of progressivism and modernism as a force of the future.[22] Inspired by previous projects of complete urban reform such as Haussmann's plan for Paris,[23] Kubitschek was able to quickly generate enough capital to build Brasília in the record time of forty-one months by redistributing enough surplus commodities from raw material exports, by expanding the industrial sector to attract foreign investors, by establishing multinational companies, and chiefly by creating a system of debt – financed infrastructural urban improvements. The difference here was that building a new capital city with the latest technology and the most innovative aesthetics and social programs was not the case of *urban reform* as in Haussman's plan, but of *urban generation*[24] – of creating a city directly from a blueprint on empty land, without the interference of history. Brasília was literally built from ground zero, on a virtual no man's land with no preexisting infrastructure. Its urban plan therefore also required building roads in all directions to connect it to the rest of the country.

The shape of Brasília has a practical but above all an imaginative and symbolic dimension: a cross-shaped master plan of the city resembled the shape of an airplane. This shape was, at the time, not only symbolic of a utopian movement through time and space, it was also the only means of transportation available to transport materials and workers to the site during the first year of construction in the absence of land roads leading to the city-to-be. The incredible speed of construction was certainly accelerated by the airplane; rather than repeating the history of extending terrestrial paths towards new locations, this project sought to rewrite history by building a city that had everything to do with air.[25] In the 1950s, airplane technology was considered highly advanced and a symbol of progress and forward-thinking. The replacement of land by air represents a reversal of urban genealogy according to the French philosopher Paul Virilio's theory of acceleration, for example, where the intersection of air strips and runways replaced ancient caravan tracks, thus establishing an infrastructure based on the paradigm of speed.[26]

---

22 It was a golden era for the Brazilian economy and for its culture, with the new beats of *bossa nova*, the football star Pelé, and, of course, Brasília channeling the new 'Brazilian spirit' and charting the country's course as a promise for the future in a global perspective and emancipated from history.

23 According to David Harvey, in order to implement his design for a new Paris in the 1850s, Haussmann needed to create new financial institutions and debt instruments to help resolve the capital-surplus disposal system for financing Paris urban reform by setting up a 'proto-Keynesian system of debt-financed infrastructural urban improvements.' David Harvey, 'The Right to the City' in Andrea Phillips and Fulya Erdemci (eds) *Social Housing-Housing the Social: Art, Property and Spatial Justice*, Amsterdam/Berlin: SKOR/Sternberg Press, June 2012, p. 77.

24 Here it is necessary to disambiguate this term. It is altogether more common to hear about urban regeneration and renewal which can be defined as the integrated local redevelopment of deprived areas (neighborhood, city, metropolitan area). It covers many aspects of city life: physical, social and environmental. Approaches depend on a city's history, and therefore policies must be integrated and contextualized. However, the term 'urban generation' as it is used here refers to the engendering of a new city, of generation in the root definition of the word of engendering, of bringing into being. Here we are talking about the creation of a city as if painting on a blank canvas, devoid of previous marks.

25 'Como nasce uma cidade', Correio Braziliense, 13 April 2012.

26 Paul Virilio, *Speed and Politics*, NY: Semi(o)texte, 2006.

It is possible to relate the techno-politics of Brasília with Ebenezer Howard's *Garden City of Tomorrow*[27] (see Figure 7) and Xavier's *Our Home* and their relationship to transportation technology. Howard included elevated train tracks around the nodes of his city, while Xavier's spirits were led in sorts of airbuses through the city of spirits. If we look at the design of Brasília and its scale, it is one of those cities that are designed from the perspective of an airplane, or bird's eye view – the same vantage point of the architect standing up and looking down at a model on a drafting table. The architectural model, then, becomes the projective surface on which both the envisioning of the future and the realization of the city become unified under a single vantage point, which inaugurates a new way of seeing, a new way of building, and a new way of living at the time.

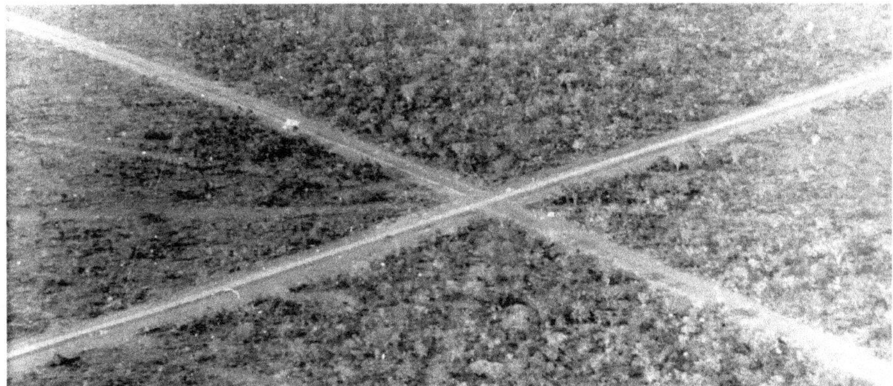

*Figure 9 – Aerial photograph of Brasília's point zero. The opening of the first two roads of Brasília on the central plateau of Brazil, demarcating the main axis of the Pilot Plan. The point zero was not a result of an existing system of roads but stems from the existing placement of a cross on the plateau's highest point, from which the main squares of the pilot plan were placed, and from which the main axes were built.*

Kubitschek determined that the construction of the new capital would actually begin at the intersection of the airplane runways, and the first construction should be the airport, followed by the Presidential Palace, then Congress and other government buildings.[28] Later, the axial airplane-shaped plan would include innovative proposals that would substitute the European colonial legacy of Brazil's historical cities with something completely new – with something about the future. Additionally, a revision of Brazil's relationship to Europe, Costa and Niemeyer would bring to Brazil the European architectural avant-garde. They planned the city to its smallest detail, largely inspired by European modernism and functionalism, namely the CIAM principles largely based on Le Corbusier's ideas for the modernist ahistorical city and the city as a 'machine to live in',[29] with rigorous division of functions, rationalization of living

27 Ebenezer Howard, *Garden Cities of To-Morrow,* London: Faber and Faber, 1946 (1902). http://urbanplanning.library.cornell.edu/DOCS/howard.htm.

28 Gabrielle Hecht, *Entangled Geographies: Empire and Technopolitics in the Global Cold War,* Cambridge: MIT Press, 2011, p. 196.

29 'Congrès International d'Architecture Moderne (1928–1959), a hugely influential organization engaged in formalizing the architectural principles of the Modern Movement. It saw architecture as an economic and political tool that could be used to improve the world through the design of buildings and through urban planning. In 1933, the group concentrated on principles of 'The Functional City,' which

spaces, preservation of natural areas for recreation, the elimination of narrow, convoluted plans in favor of open boulevards built according to the machine logic as cars and collective transport that cuts through the monumental architecture.

This relationship between architectural avant-gardes of the early 20th century is not coincidental. Both Costa and Niemeyer had assisted Le Corbusier in the late 1920s in designing a government building in Rio de Janeiro, and learned the foundations for what later became the emblematic style of Brazilian modernism.[30] In its tropical version, pure geometrical shapes also embodied modernist principles inspired by postwar architecture with the use of modular and structural elements, this time with the extensive use of the circle and the curve requiring engineering feats with reinforced concrete, whose plasticity lends form to extraordinary shapes while at the same time being rigid and durable. However, Costa and Niemeyer did not abandon history to the same radical extent proposed by Corbusier's *tabula rasa*, and rather chose to re-interpret several historical elements into new textures and spatial possibilities within a new architectural vocabulary – a vocabulary based on the reinvention of forms from a variety of sources.

The most important connection to Le Corbusier, however, is that Brasília brings to life the unrealized urban masterplan of Le Corbusier's *Ville Radieuse/Radiant City* (published in 1935) and the *Plan Voisin* from 1924 (and published in 1933), with wide open spaces and grand gestures imagined by Le Corbusier in reaction to the 'atrocious narrowness of [European medieval] streets and spaces'. Le Corbusier's city of the future would provide a better lifestyle and contribute to a better society embodied in radical, strict and nearly totalitarian order of symmetry and standardization, being highly influential in modern urban planning, especially in the development of new high-density housing typologies based on the concept of zoning. Le Corbusier was never fully able to build the *Radiant City* as conceived.[31] Brasília, however, was the perfect tabula rasa for Le Corbusier's ideas

broadened CIAM's scope from architecture into urban planning. Considering an analysis of thirty-three cities, CIAM proposed that the social problems faced by cities could be resolved by strict functional segregation, and the distribution of the population into tall apartment blocks at widely spaced intervals.' Per Eric Paul Mumford, *The CIAM Discourse on Urbanism - 1928-1960*, Cambridge: MIT Press, 2002. http://designtheory.fiu.edu/readings/mumford_CIAM_discourse.pdf.

30 Le Corbusier designed a master plan for downtown Rio de Janeiro in 1928 that included razing entire traditional neighborhoods and opening up boulevards. While his full plan was never realized, subsequent administrations incorporated some of his demolitions into creating main throroughfares, including a perimetral viaduct along 10km of coastline which has recently been demolished to give way to a program o urban renewal of its port area (like Puerto Madero in Buenos Aires, and South Street Seaport in New York City). Corbusier did design the then Ministry of Culture and Education, the Palácio Gustavo Capanema, which brought the innovation of building on pilotis, thus allowing for air circulation at pedestrian level, and light control by the system of brise-soleil, which gives the building an ever-changing façade as these sorts of venetian blinds can be manipulated from the inside out and control the amount of light. This would also later be echoed in the façades of the residential units in Brasíla. Critics contend that the Brazilian architects were not only inspired by Corbusier's aesthetic ideas, but also inherited his contempt for history that fit the bill of modernism as a means to overcome the colonial past.

31 His ideas influenced smaller projects and later materialized in the architecture of the administrative center in Chandigarh, the Indian capital of Punjab.

that had been shelved decades earlier, and which provided Costa and Niemeyer the opportunity to create a city that embodied the future, materialized equality and justice all the while being the country's site of administrative power.

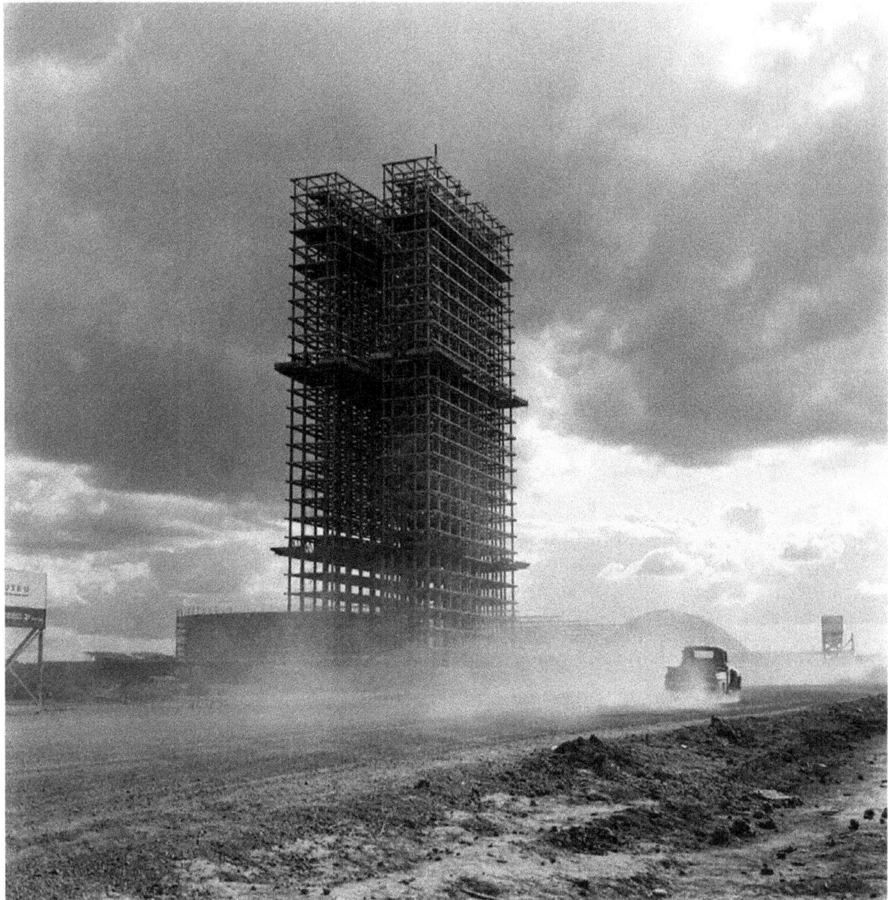

*Figure 10 – Construction of Brasília in 1956. Photo by Marcel Gautherot.*

Brasília was originally designed for a population of 750,000 inhabitants,[32] included an artificial lake and was divided into 'sectors' dividing it into two main axes: the monumental power axis north and south, and the residential axis east and west. Government buildings lined a central, monumental axis while residential and service areas radiated from the center, each functioning into its own allotted space in the overall scheme with very few overlaps. Connecting all these sectors were six-lane highways between which cars, mounted in Brazil's then new Volkswagen plants, would flow seamlessly. Traffic jams would become a thing of the past: the absence of traffic lights and the use of roundabouts to direct flow glorify the car

32 The city's current population in 2020 is estimated at 3 million inhabitants. *Instituto Brasileiro de Geografia e Estatística - IBGE*, https://cidades.ibge.gov.br/brasil/df/brasilia/panorama.

driver as the essential unit connecting the city. These endless boulevards were seemingly inspired by the scale of Baroque urbanism, with endless perspective planes that can be seen from several vantage points, giving a sensation of infinity and grandeur. Ideas about collective living in *superquadras*, or super blocks, where a range of services and residential units could be united into housing blocks that contained all services required for residents without having to depend on a fixed city center.[33]

If cars and airplanes determined the main mode of circulation to and within Brasília, interestingly pedestrian access was limited to the residential areas and within compounds and buildings. There are no streets, street names or street corners in Brasília in our understanding of what a street is, and sidewalks are few.[34] The naming of streets is particular: the ungridded Brasília required a naming system that resembled an algorithm code on a software more than a coordinate on a flat plane, like Manhattan. A typical address is a combination of codes: SQN-E-214, (meaning Superquadra Norte Block E, apartment 214). The Super Blocks encompassed the residential units. Lúcio Costa describes his ideas behind the Super Block:

> I believe that this conception was very wise: all the buildings were freestanding, resting on pilotis, with the average proportions of traditional European cities, (...) harmonious, human, with everything connected to everyday life; children playing at ease and within reach of the mother's call, with schools located inside the block; every four buildings contains an access point where 'neighborhood stores' are located, and in the remaining courtyards, secondary schools, churches, clubs, cinema and supermarkets alternate.[35]

Unlike traditional urban planning where commerce appears intermingled in the very fabric of the street, commerce in Brasília would not allow to turn its face outward onto the boulevard – because there was no boulevard to face onto. Instead, the pulverization of the city square into small units spread commerce inwards in each housing zone, in such a way that commerce would face inner courtyards, in the guise of galleries or passageways contained within the service blocks in the *superquadras*. The elimination of the street corner was also a strategy intended to take 'dangerous' elements, such as prostitution and petty crime, out of pedestrian life. In a way, Benjamin's *Arcades Project* would find a futuristic modernist manifestation here. The *flâneur*, the typical subject of the Parisian urban reform in the 19th century and the enabler of poetic reveries in Belle Époque Paris, or even the Parisian 1960s Situationist *dérive*,[36] is not

---

33 Super Quadra means 'super city block' in Portuguese. Each superquadra consisted of 360 apartments housing between 1,500-2,000 residents, with its own nursery and elementary school, and each grouping of four superquadras had a secondary school, a cinema, a social club, sports facilities and a retail sector. See also Scott, *Seeing Like a State*, p. 125.

34 This is an interesting irony of modernity. Whereas Corbusier advocates the sovereignty of the car and the obsolescence of the pedestrian, Jane Jacobs in the United States creates in the very same 1960s a very different view, and no influential view, of the city. She writes about something which is apparently, by plan, abolished from Brasília, namely 'the ballet of the good city sidewalk never repeats itself from place to place, and in any one place is always replete with new improvisations (...)'. Jane Jacobs, *The Death and Life of Great American Cities*, New York: Vintage Books, 1992 (1961), p. 25.

35 Lúcio Costa, *Registro de uma vivência*, São Paulo: Empresa das Artes, 1995, p. 98. [Author's translation].

36 The Situationist's engagement with the city life included many performative practices, one of them

possible in Brasília, as the subject that lives in such a planned city cannot grasp its totality by foot. In Brasília, everything is intentional, programmed, rational, emancipated from the erraticness of the labyrinthine city which entraps its citizens in historical time. The street, the *flâneur*'s medium, is substituted by the freeway, the walker is substituted by the driver, speed is the mode of perception, and the mode of orientation is to execute a predetermined code. Yet to affirm that there is no urban life in Brasília would be an exaggeration. Life in the super blocks is in fact akin to villages or enclaves encrusted in the larger pattern of the capital city, between freeways, and other neighborhoods with more individualized, albeit planned houses are similar to suburban life in most cities.

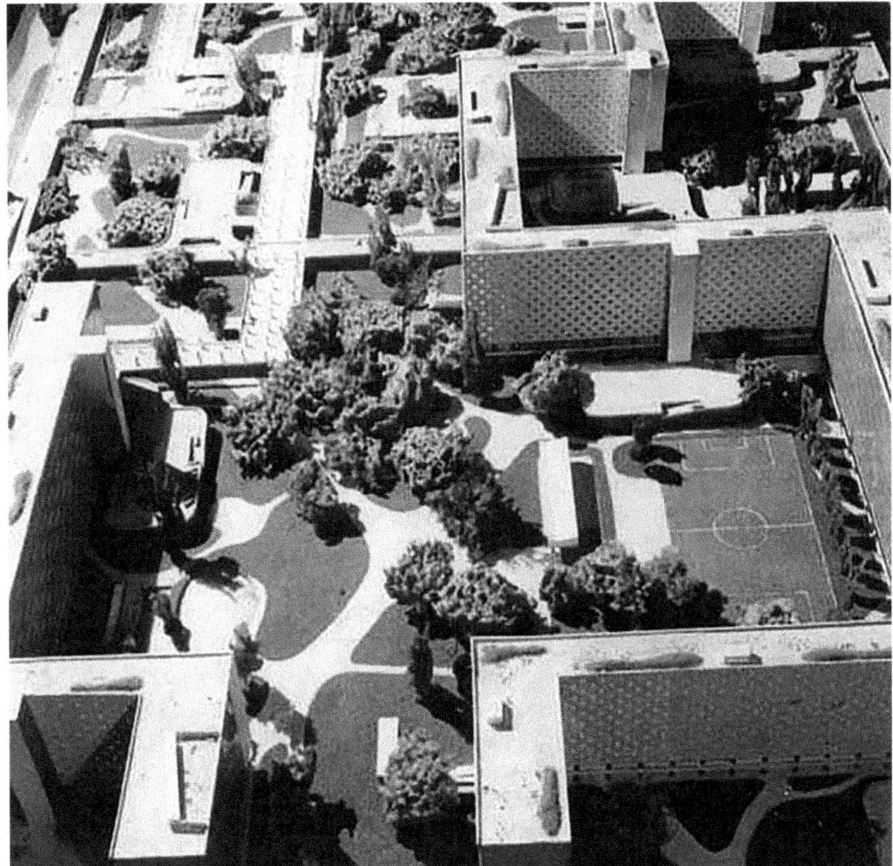

*Figure 11 – Photograph of the model of the Ville Radieuse/Radiant City, Le Corbusier, 1935. © FLC-ADAGP. Source: Fondation Le Corbusier.*

being the *dérive*, or the act of drifting along the empty and undefined spaces of the city in order to reveal and experience the free flow of life away from the axes of commercial and bureaucratic control in the city. The Situationists would defend the city against the spectacularization and commodification of urban space, trying to safeguard the zones, both physical as well as psychological that would resist social relationships that were mediated by the culture of spectacle. See also Debord, *The Society of the Spectacle.*

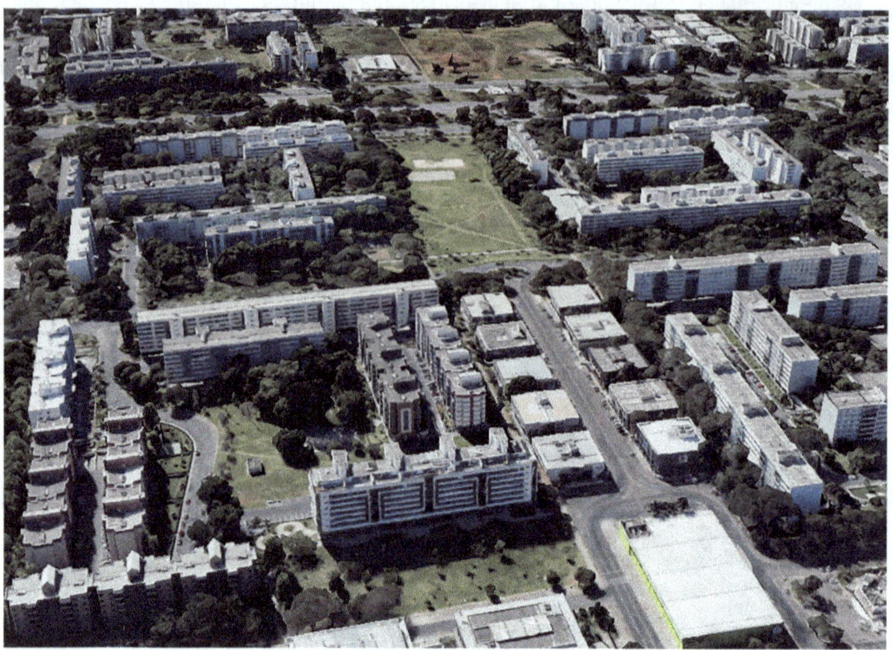

*Figure 12 – Digital image of Brasília, today, with the 'super blocks' in the foreground. Source: Google Earth, https://www.google.com/earth/.*

In *The Urban Revolution*, philosopher and sociologist Henri Lefebvre lays out a criticism of the cold and modernist visions of the city, especially of those embodied by architects and urban planners like Le Corbusier, and against what the Brazilian planners believed in for Brasília – the promise of the modernist utopia as a rupture from the past. A major critic of Le Corbusier's style of urbanism, Lefebvre was thrilled that the *Radiant City* was never built. He had previously attacked the visions of the utopian modernists for designing carceral cities in which the poor are locked up and thrust into a strangely narrow utopia of light and space but removed from a social life in the streets. Lefebvre instead proposes that the life of the city and the lived experience of individuals are the basis for an urban utopia characterized by self-determination, individual creativity, and authentic social relationships. 'The invasion of the automobile', Lefebvre says, 'and the pressure of this industry and its lobbyists (...) have destroyed all social and urban life. When you eliminate the street, there are consequences: the extinction of all life, the reduction of the city to a dormitory, to an aberrant functionalization of existence.' The street, he believes, contains qualities ignored by Le Corbusier:

> (...) there is an informative, symbolic, and ludic function. In the street, you play and learn stuff. Sure, the street is full of uncertainty. All the elements of urban life, elsewhere congealed in a fixed and redundant order, liberate themselves and gush onto the street and flow towards the center, where they meet and interact, freed from fixed moorings.

In the street, there is a degree of disorder of a superior level – a disorder that informs and surprises, a disorder capable of engendering another order. The street for Lefebvre is also the site of disruption, and therefore the site for revolution.[37] The reaction against the ideal city plans and Le Corbusier's ideas was also expressed in the Situationist movement, mainly through the fictional city of *New Babylon* in 1950 as a refusal to then existing models of planned cities. According to Lefebvre, who was very much involved with the Situationists during the 1960s, the pivotal figure was Constant Nieuwenhuys, the utopian architect who designed a utopian city, a *New Babylon* – a provocative name, since in the Protestant tradition Babylon is a figure of evil. *New Babylon* was to be the figure of good that took the name of the cursed city and transformed itself into the city of the future. Constant's *New Babylon*, and his 1953 work *For an Architecture of Situat*ion, were based on the idea that architecture itself would allow and instigate a transformation of daily reality. Lefebvre writes,

> While in utilitarian society one strives by every means towards an optimal orientation in space, the guarantee of temporal efficiency and economy, in *New Babylon* the disorientation that furthers adventure, play and creative change is privileged. The space of *New Babylon* has all the characteristics of a labyrinthine space, within which movement no longer submits to the constraints of given spatial or temporal organization. The labyrinthine form of New Babylonian social space is the direct expression of social independence.[38]

This was the conception with Lefevbre's *Critique of Everyday Life:* to create an architecture that would itself instigate the creation of new situations.[39]

## The City Before the City

The intention behind the design and construction of Brasília has, like *Our Home*,[40] on a pragmatic and ideological basis, is above all embodied in a plan and conceived as a model, which are interesting elements to set against the background of history and experience. All models represent ideals, which are by definition unattainable because something will always remain in the gap between the ideal and its manifestation in reality. To make his ideas more convincing, Le Corbusier built a detailed model of *The Radiant City* and commissioned a photographic essay which would frame the model in such a way that it *appeared* real. The construction of this model, rigorous in its smallest elements, requiring five months of work and resulting in a series of photographic documents, could express eloquently the new conditions of the

37 Henri Lefebvre, *The Urban Revolution*, trans. Robert Bononno, Minneapolis: University of Minnesota Press, 2003, p 18-19.

38 Lefebvre, *The Urban Revolution*, p. 30.

39 Kristin Ross, 'Henri Lefebvre on the Situationist International', *October*, 79 (Winter 1997). Available at: http://www.notbored.org/lefebvre-interview.html. See also Constant *New Babylon,* Written by Constant, for the exhibition catalogue published by the Haags Gemeetenmuseum, The Hague, 1974. https://stichtingconstant.nl/system/files/1974_new_babylon.pdf.

40 Canberra, Australia and Pondicherry, India are also examples of generated/invented modernist cities, however, Brasília is the largest 'invented' city in the Western Hemisphere in the 20th century.

dwelling in the cities of the 'Radiant City' type,[41] but we may wonder to what extent a model, *any* model, is able to reproduce actual experiences of inhabitation.

Even though we may live and act in the present, inside the planned city our movements and behaviors are in large part influenced by the shape of the environment which has been decided *a priori*. To live in a planned city means to be trapped in the rationality and norms predetermined by the *plan*. In Brasília and *Our Home* (and in any modernist planned environment whose design includes an urban, cultural and social reform and the creation of a new subject to sustain them) the form of the new city, whether a six-pointed star or an airplane, paradoxically reflects previous forms of social organization and affects the future relations of those who will inhabit those cities. In his acid critique of Brasília, writer Benjamin Moser writes,

> (...) the architecture itself gives you the sensation that you are very small. It crushes you and gives you the sense that you don't matter in the landscape. As if entering a gigantic temple of some foreign religion, as if you are there to adore some god you don't know anything about. In Brasília, I felt this very strongly, 'who am I here?' 'what am I doing here?'[42]

While criticizing the oppressive monumentality of planned cities, we may fail to realize that what is important in rational and modernist cities like Brasília is the same principle that applies to modernist abstract painting: it is the empty spaces that count. And yet there is no empty space that is not eventually inhabited in some way, even if it is inhabited by emptiness itself.

As in *Our Home*, Brasília also carries with it the pain of its own birth, and the burden of its own history. Its quick construction in less than five years from conception to inhabitation required the mobilization of an enormous workforce that precipitated the temporary migration of thousands of workers who saw the promise for a new life in this massive construction effort. However, the workers that erected its towers and opened its boulevards needed to live somewhere themselves during construction.

Hailing from all parts of the country, these pioneers[43] later called 'candangos' formed a precarious mass of workers hired to build the utopian forms of the government buildings or

---

41 *Fondation Le Corbusier*, http://fondationlecorbusier.fr/.

42 In *Cemitério da Esperança,* Moser presents a critique of Brasília. In this book, he presents a thesis that there is a tendency in Brazil to erase social problems in public space by razing it to ground zero and constructing new cities following imported models. He maintains that there is a pervasive pattern in Brazilian urban history to use architecture and urbanism as a political tool to hide the people from view and in so doing revealing a compulsion to despise the national, the vernacular and the existingarchitecture. See Benjamin Moser. *Cemitério da Esperança*, São Paulo: Editora Cesárea, 2014.

43 For every form of migration in Brazil, there is a specific name that identifies both the origin and the purpose of migration. The figure of the pioneer takes many guises: the 'bandeirante,' is the one who opened the footpaths in the landscape establishing commercial routes and connecting cities and villages during colonial times, especially in the eighteenth century. In the early twentieth century, the populations migrating from the droughts in the northeastern states to the large cities in the south were called 'retirantes,' literally meaning 'those who leave' or 'the leavers.' The migrant population of Brasília, egressed from adjoining states called themselves the 'candangos.' Today, anyone born in Brasília is called a 'candango.'

lured to the construction site from mainly the dry Northeastern parts of Brazil as a promised land. Temporary shacks and encampments in the outskirts of the construction site were built organically to accommodate this growing mass of guest-workers. The government assumed the workers would leave after the job was completed. However, as was to be expected, many decided to stay and became the area's first *de facto* settlers, long before the political class moved to the new capital.[44] These settlements were first established as 'free cities' where anyone had permission to build an establishment or a house made of wood, precarious enough to discourage its permanence, agreeing to destroy it when the construction of the capital was concluded.[45] When it became apparent that migrant workers remained permanently, these free settlements became known as *satellite cities*.[46] Thus, even before the planned modernist futuristic city was even built, the encampments for guest-workers were already established as a permanent condition of that city, marking the birth of the city *before* the city.

The first such satellite city was named after Kubitschek's spouse, Sara, making it very difficult, if not symbolically impossible, for the government to evict its residents. *Vila Sara Kubitschek* was inaugurated even before Brasília itself was made official. How could a brand-new city planned in every detail include in its very inception the paradox of the informal city like the shantytown? Rather, how could its designers not have accounted for this in their overall urban plan in which social engineering was so heavily embedded?

---

44 The migration begins in 1956 with the arrival of 256 workers, mostly male, the first 'candangos' as they were called. In January 1957 the population rose to 2,500 workers. A population count in July of the same year indicated 12,283 candangos. In March 1958 this figure rose to 28,000 workers, with an average monthly growth of 2,100 people every month. The male to female ratio during the years of construction was 192 to 100, whereas the national level was 99.3 to 100.Gilberto Costa, 'Censo populacional de 1959 revela quem eram os candangos que construiram Brasilia', Agência Brasil, 21 April 2010, http://memoria.ebc.com.br/agenciabrasil/noticia/2010-04-21/censo-populacional-de-1959-revela-quem-eram-os-candangos-que-construiram-brasilia.

45 'Como nasce uma cidade: com quantos goianos se faz uma utopia', *Correio Braziliense*, 18 June 2011, https://www.correiobraziliense.com.br/app/noticia/cidades/2011/06/18/interna_cidadesdf,257450/como-nasce-uma-cidade-com-quantos-goianos-se-faz-uma-utopia.shtml.

46 By definition, a satellite town or satellite city is a concept in urban planning that refers essentially to smaller metropolitan areas which are located somewhat near to, but are mostly independent of, larger metropolitan areas. Each city and country may use the same term to describe a variety of similar urban formations adjacent to or dependent on larger metropolitan areas. In the case of Brasília, satellite cities are more like shanty towns than fully urbanized suburbs in most large cities. In Sweden, a satellite city is usually an autonomous suburb, usually planned and built from scratch and linked to the downtown by subway. This term is often used interchangeably with suburb, although the differences between a suburb in the American sense (a rich area) and in the European sense (a poor area) also vary widely.

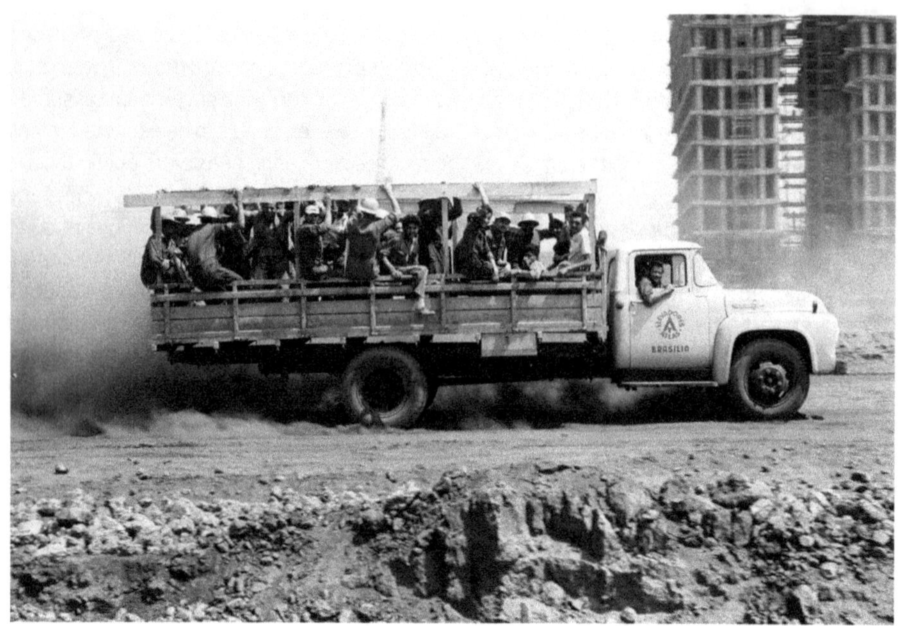


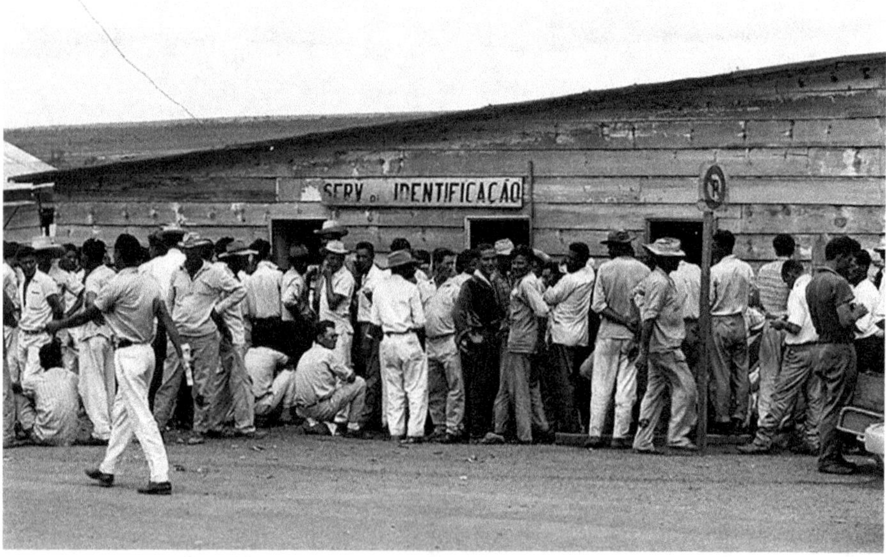


*Figures 13 and 14 – Top: Guest-workers, or 'candangos', transported to the construction site, late 1950s, Credit: Mário Fontenelle/Arquivo Público do DF. Bottom: The supposed incentive of recognition for migrant laborers as citizens through national labor identification cards quickly became a means of greater state surveillance. Credit: Arquivo Público do DF. Source: Memorial da Democracia.* **http://www.memorialdademocracia.com.br/card/construcao-de-brasilia/5.**

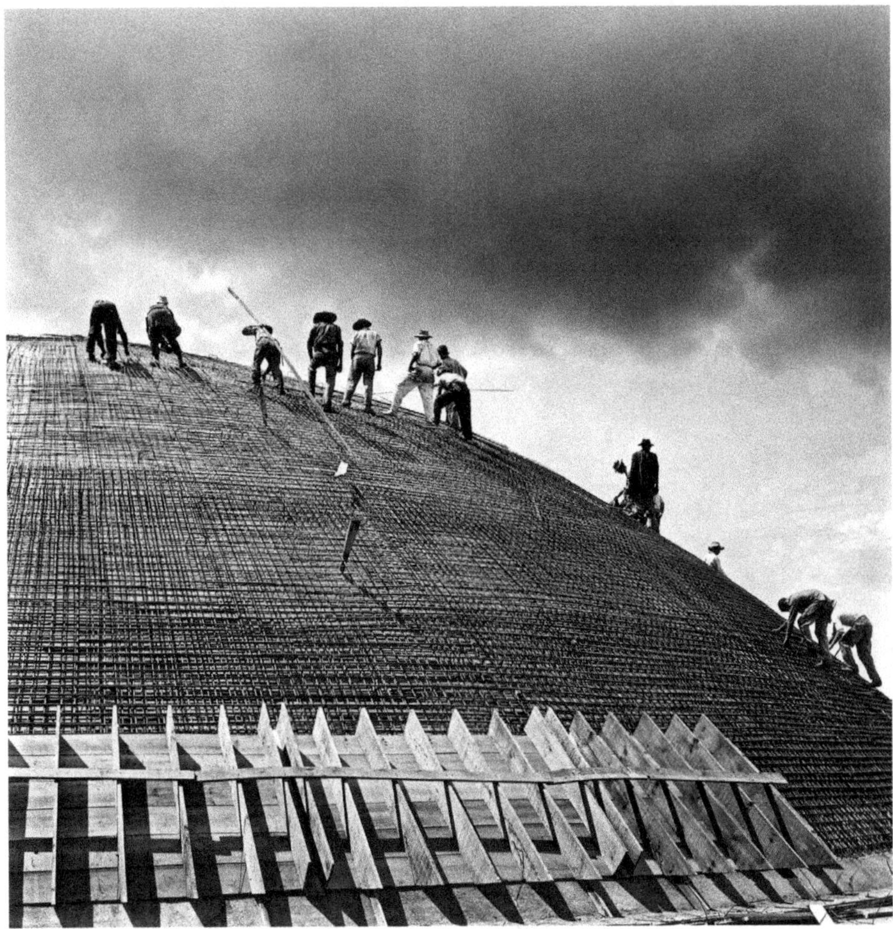

*Figure 15 – Guest-workers in Brasília and the monumental curves made possible by reinforced concrete.*

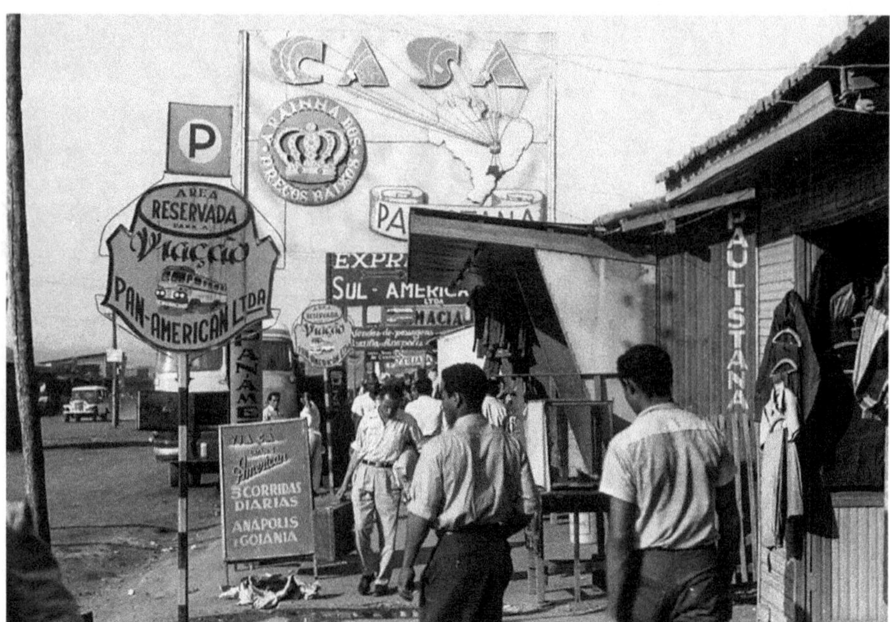


*Figure 16 – The 'free city' of guest-workers during the construction of Brasília, late 1950s. Credit: Arquivo Público de Brasília. Source: Memorial da Democracia,* ***http://www.memorialdademocracia.com.br/card/construcao-de-brasilia/5****.*

In Brazil, the term 'satellite city' refers specifically to the unplanned parts of Brasília that developed from the first guest-worker settlements even before the official city was inaugurated. Eventually, these temporary encampments would become cities of their own. The satellite city is the anti-Brasília, the 'other' to the utopia. It was everything the modernist vision of the future was not supposed to be: organic, historical, spontaneous, sprawling, and a reflection and continuity of what the rest of Brazil already was. There was no room for poverty in the modernist plan because, if we follow Hirsch's logic that a plan is a prediction of the future, in this very future there would be no poverty – it would either be a feature of the 'historical' city or it would be mitigated by the design of the new city to the point where it would cease to be called poverty. How could the guest-worker be refused the possibility to inhabit the city he has helped to erect? Instead of the city of *refugees*, we could say that Brasília is surrounded by cities of the *refused* – those not only needing to seek refuge from the plan, but also being refused by the plan.

Is this refusal an endemic part of the Brazilian history of social inequality alone, or is this a side effect of modernity in a more general sense? Should the guest-worker reside in a permanent state of homelessness? In the outskirts of the yet unpopulated city-to-be, the only residents are temporary guests who are formally denied the right to inhabit it officially. The guest-worker becomes the permanent nomad in this constellation, relegated to the empty spaces of the architectural drawing. He inhabits these empty spaces with his self-determination – one of the few instances where the guest-worker would, as Flusser posited, reside in homelessness. We wonder then, how are the first guest-workers valued and remembered in the making of

Brasília? I return briefly to the names given to migrants, and there is, in Brasília's identities the figure of the pioneer, as the first guest-workers and settlers were called, who acquired a singular identity and signifier as 'candangos'. To call oneself a 'candango', however, is more than being pioneer – it's a way of remembering the thousands of workers who built the capital, and who were beat, jailed and humiliated by police in a few insurrections, and the countless men who died during construction.

Concerned with the lack of agency of the workers in the construction of the capital city as the future of the nation, Brazilian artist Athos Bulcão (1918-2008) decided to address the aspect of the workers when he was commissioned to create artworks integrated to the new archictecture of Brasília.[47] Bulcão executed ceramic murals in Brasília both using the labor and the participation of the migrant construction workers in creating them. The aesthetics of ceramic tiles and urban walls has a long tradition in Brazilian architecture, inherited by the Portuguese, but here the notion of the combinatory tile was used to create aesthetic patterns that follow more closely the logic of programming, in the sense of using bits of code that could be laid out on a surface in infinite combinations, like a visual algorithm.

Bulcão designed the tiles himself in modular geometric and colorful patterns, but it was up to the workers to place the tiles on the wall surfaces in whatever way they saw fit. There is a performative element in their making that follows a process of co-generation with the workers and artist together. This is one of the few such instances at the time where a participatory process occurs in large-scale commissioned projects where there is a sense of inclusion and visibility of the hand of the laborer in the expression of the city. Participation, in the case of Bulcão, did not have at the time the same discourse of art institutional critique that it has today and which we will address later in this book, but was entirely articulated by the artist as a way of bridging the gap between the artist, the monumental architecture, and the workers – and giving way to a popular expression to an architecture otherwise entirely determined by the plan and the model.

## Lost Narratives in the New City

Whereas the medium that best expressed the ideology of Brasília was architecture, film is a medium which lends itself to expressing critical voices about the construction of the new city and reveal hidden aspects beyond the official narratives regarding its design. Film appears here both as a medium and a site where these contested histories regarding the modernist city and patterns of segregation become evident, and where claims for social justice and reparations for the casualties of the construction of the new capital can be made, where the voices that have been ignored, silenced, or exploited by planners, politicians and mainstream media are allowed to speak. At the same time, while potent in presenting personal stories and challenging the established narratives, film as a medium has fewer opportunities to represent the true scope of suffering as it depends heavily on the availability of archival materials and

47 Athos Bulcão was part of the design team of Brasília since 1955, working closely with Oscar Niemeyer in conceiving ceramic murals and stained-glass windows in dozens of locations in Brasília through fifty years. *Fundação Athos Bulcão*, https://www.fundathos.org.br/.

the memory of survivors to tell these stories. Furthermore, the fluctuating, emotional, and subjective nature of film stands in stark opposition to the very medium of the city which is durable and rationally planned.

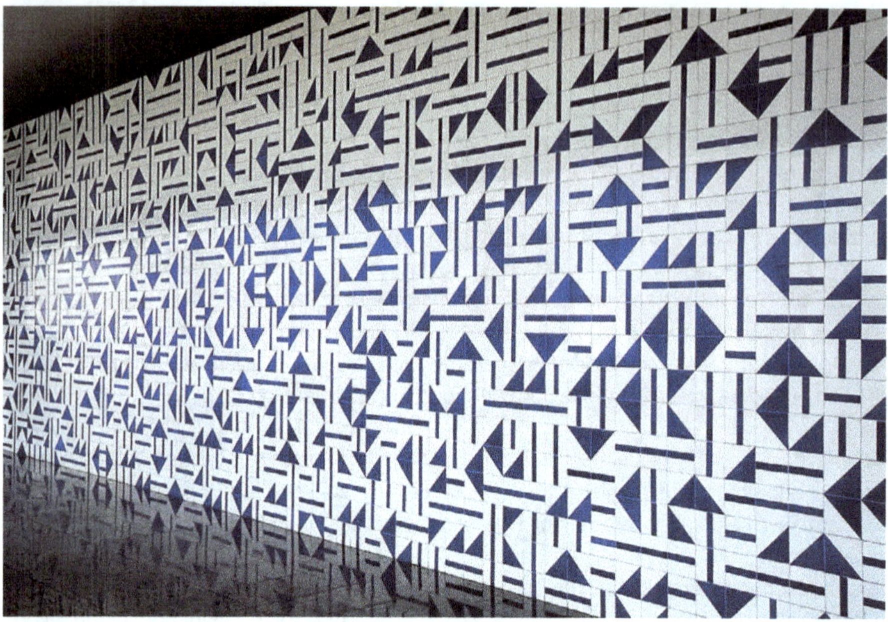

*Figure 17 – Ceramic Mural, TV tower, Brasília, 1966 (left), Foreign Ministry, Brasília, 1968. Photo: Edgar César Filho. Source: Fundação Athos Bulcão,* ***https://www.fundathos.org.br/.***

In one of the last scenes of the feature film *Bye Bye, Brazil* by Carlos Diegues,[48] a young family formed by the film's main supporting characters migrates to Brasília from distant northern regions of the country in an attempt to remedy their previous lives as poor wandering circus artists in a caravan theatre, in a symbolic journey towards the sanitizing effect of modern architecture and the big city, thus exposing the challenges and contradictions of the modern project against a Brazilian reality of poverty and inequality. Upon arrival at the bus station in Brasília, they are greeted by a social worker who is in charge of driving them in a Volkswagen bus through the modernist city to their final destination. We see the tall concrete buildings passing by the car windows and we understand Brasília as a city of speed. With the arrogance of a proud state employee, she says:

> One and half million inhabitants and we hardly have any more space for anyone, and yet new people keep arriving everyday. We, from the social service, will take care of you. We will guide you in your new life and give shelter to your whole family. But it can't be here in the center of town.

Jump cut to a street in a distant township, we see boys playing football barefoot on the cracked pavement and stray dogs barking in the distance. The Volkswagen bus stops in front of a row

48 *Bye Bye Brasil* (dir. Carlos Diegues, 1980).

of wooden houses. The family steps out and is left there, looking lost, staring blankly at their new home. They look at each other as they enter the house, the baby in tow representing the new life they now begin in a wooden shack outside the white city of concrete. This young family in many ways represents the typical subject that went to Brasília as their *Eldorado* in the emblematic 20th century narrative of internal migration from countryside to city in search for work and better conditions of living. The desire and necessity to emancipate the population out of poverty is embodied in the dream of the big city as the dream of the future, where a new life can begin. The film ends with this uncertain promise.

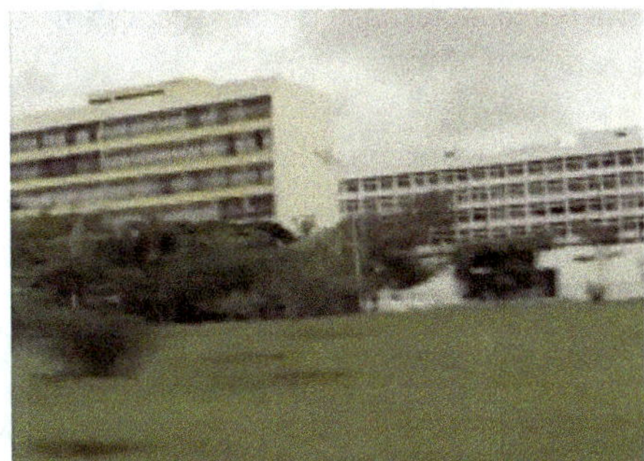

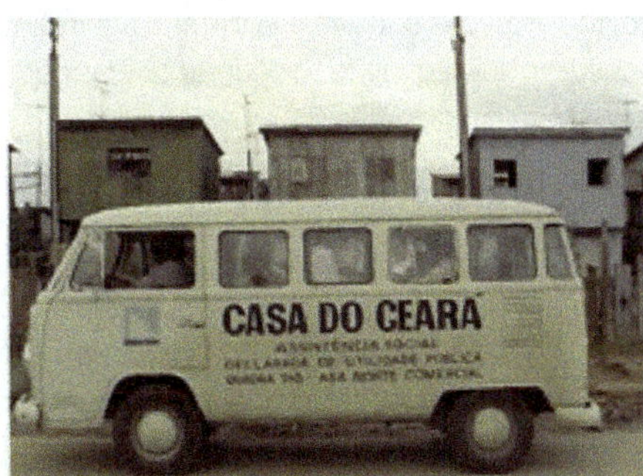


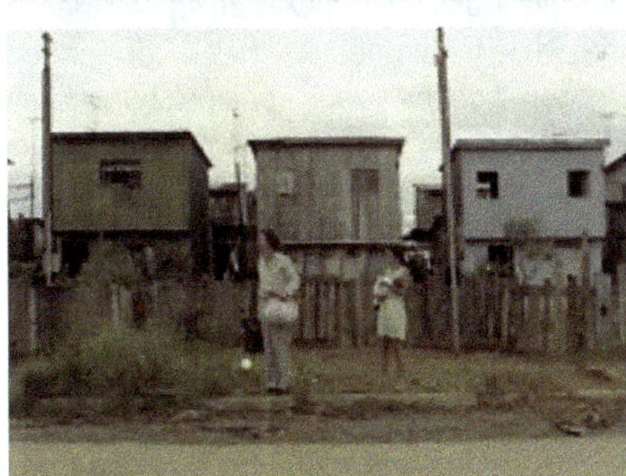

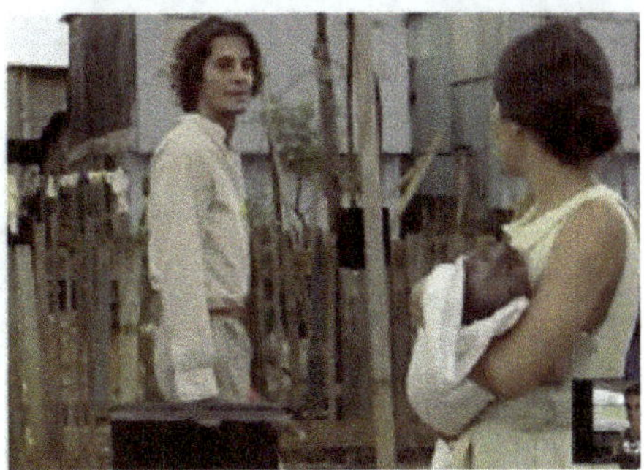

*Figure 18 – Scenes from Bye Bye, Brasil (dir. Carlos Diegues, 1980). A migrant couple arrives in Brasília, we see them drive by the Super blocks on a Volkswagen Bus with the social assistants until they reach the wooden barracks built for migrant workers.*

In the documentary *Conterrâneos Velhos de Guerra*, or 'Old Countrymen of War', director Vladimir Carvalho shows us the backstage stories of guest workers of the construction of the city of Brasília, and the abuses and humiliation they suffered during the construction of the city, after being lured to the great promise of a democratic future in the empty plateau. The film shows several testimonials of the first guest-workers and the realities they faced during the extraordinary construction effort, their working conditions and how these realities were not necessarily made visible at the time. In the film, workers reveal that newspaper articles denouncing the death and disappearance of migrant construction workers are few and far between, and it becomes clear that the mediatized success story of the construction of the city supersedes the narratives of those who actually built the city. Among the vast archival material are shown rare newspaper headlines such as 'Twenty thousand slaves build the adventure of the New Babylon',[49] revealing the precarity of working conditions. Also, the film provides a contrasting account of the official communications and the propaganda of the government against real-life stories of the workers.

The film also tells of the successive evictions in Brasília's satellite cities once the main city was formally established, as a continuous effort of sanitizing the city, of pushing the people out of view, demolitions, and relocations to unsatisfactory temporary housing solutions, and other means of urban, social, and mediatic disappearance. As a way of contrasting the inhumanity of the evictions and Brasília's grand aspirations, we see tractors toppling down shacks amidst children screaming to the sound of Wagner's *Ride of the Valkyries*.

In the film, architect Oscar Niemeyer, who claims to have been inspired by socialist ideas in constructing the city, is confronted with the human cost of the construction. Whereas Brasília's master planner Lúcio Costa, also interviewed, expresses a puzzled bafflement at the 'extravaganza and folly' in realizing his own plan, denouncing the grandiosity of the State and the debt incurred during construction, Niemeyer rather arrogantly denies that there had been any deaths among the workers. He says, 'we hear of construction workers being killed everyday, I had no idea about this at the time [of Brasília's construction] (...) Here in this country, the people in the peripheries and the *favela* look at the city as an enemy area'.[50] Niemeyer dismissed them as 'collateral damage' while in another interview a former construction worker gives his testimony of the plight of construction having personally witnessed the dangers of the undertaking. Further in the interview, while reflecting on the treatment granted to workers after the inauguration of the city and having passed the initial phase of optimism, Niemeyer admits that they made a mistake in thinking that the city would create an equality among its citizens, and says:

> We thought these relations were going to be transformed, but they didn't. A wall was built between 'us and them'. We realized after the inauguration that Brasília would never be a city of the future, and it ended up being like any other city. We regret that the workers, our brothers from all over the country who came to help us, who built the palaces, the apartments and the schools didn't enjoy the fruits of their labor and left the city even poorer than when they came, moving out of the city only to look at the city they built from a distance, like a frustrated dream. This is the negative aspect of Brasília which we should have considered at the outset. So Brasília is not the city of the future we had envisioned, a city where all would be equal.[51]

49 *Conterrâneos Velhos de Guerra* (dir. Vladimir Carvalho, 1991). Available at: https://youtu.be/wWRmY-2rxD4.

50 Carvalho, *Conterrâneos Velhos de Guerra*.

51 Carvalho, *Conterrâneos Velhos de Guerra*.

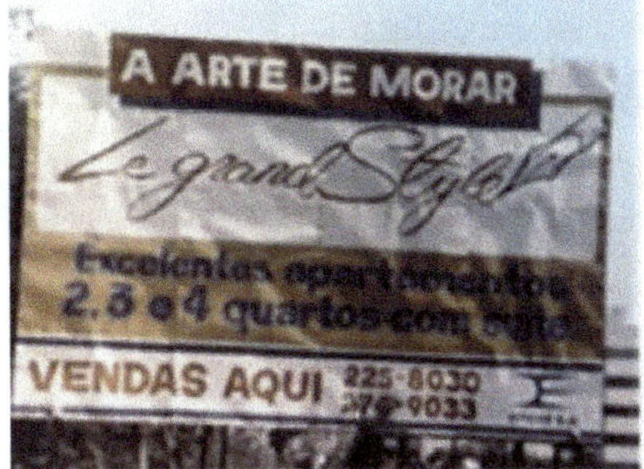


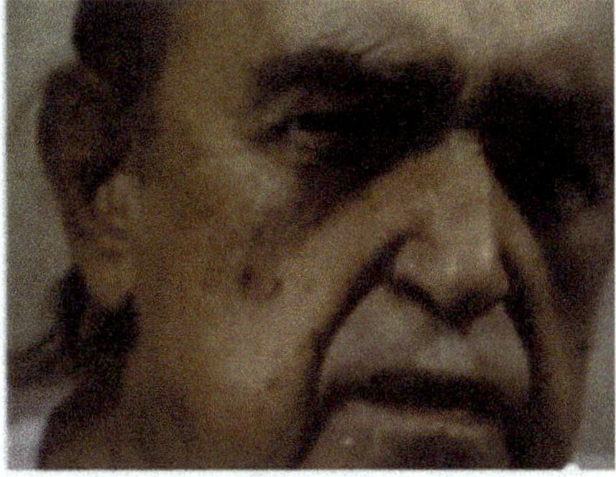

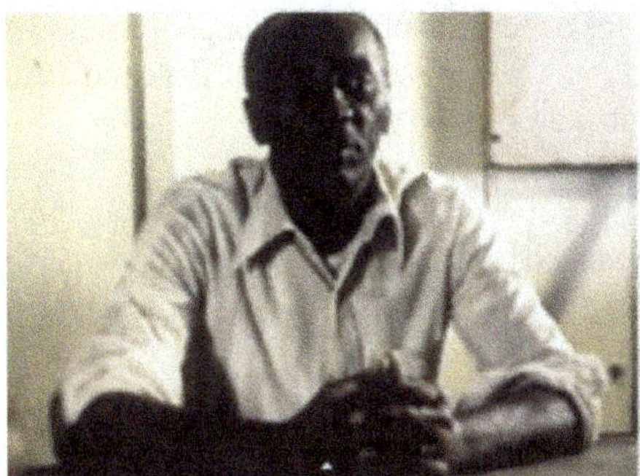

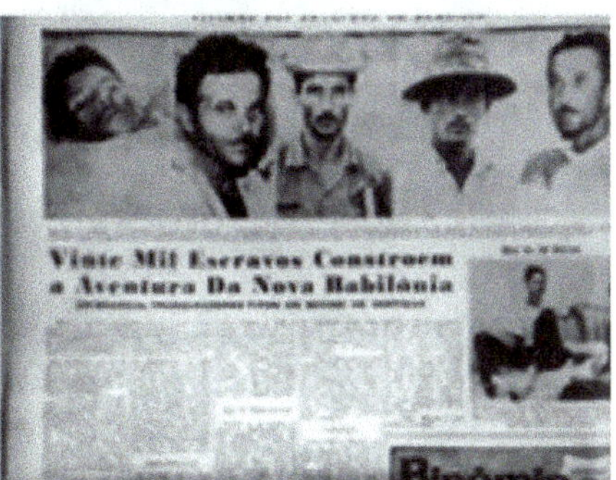

*Fig. 19 – Clockwise from top left: A billboard announcing a new development in Brasília, the sign reads 'The art of living: Le Grand Style, Excellent apartments 2, 3, and 4 bedrooms ensuite'; Oscar Niemeyer; Albino de Souza, a former construction worker; and a newspaper article with the headline 'Twenty thousand slaves build the adventure of the New Babylon'. Film stills: Conterrâneos Velhos de Guerra (dir. Vladimir Carvalho, 1991).*

## The Satellite City Talks Back

Sixty years after its founding, Brasília's satellite cities have matured their own aesthetic voice and are able to talk back to this history. In 2011, Adirley Queiroz, a former football player turned filmmaker born in Ceilândia in 1970, one of the satellite cities of Brasília, made the documentary film *A Cidade é Uma Só?* ('Is the city only one?')[52] about the city's haunted past of settlement, evictions, and real estate speculation. Besides Brasília appearing as a character itself, five main characters reveal different aspects of the city's persistent specter of construction and destruction, occupation and expulsion.

One of the characters, Nancy, a middle-aged woman from Ceilândia, narrates a past that repeats itself since the city's origin, and remembers the purposeful division of the people and the government marked by media campaigns supporting evictions and re-settlements for the working class. Another character, Dandara, lives in the countryside and dreams about moving to Brasília, to the downtown glamorous areas, where the diplomats live. Running for local elections, Dildu lives in Ceilândia and is anxious about election results, always counting with support from Marquim, an ex-rapper turned political marketing specialist. The last character,

52 *A Cidade é Uma Só?* (dir. Adirley Queiroz, 2011). Available at: https://youtu.be/vVlqCVKdlxA.

Zé Antônio, sells irregular plots of land in the periphery of the capital. Recalling her childhood in one of the first satellite cities of Brasília, Nancy says in an interview:

> Their [the government's] discourse was that they would remove us into a legal situation, where we would have allotments, with all the necessary infrastructure, and at the end, this was not what happened. When we arrived here [at Ceilândia], there was nothing. What they really wanted was a place to throw that bunch of poor people, to remove the ugliness from Brasília, and bring them to a place as far away as possible. When we arrived here, we had another shock. The place was a bush, with lots of mud, dust and no infrastructure. Where the poor people lived before was right at the crossroads where politicians, diplomats and others would have to drive through on their way in and out of the airport. They didn't want to see crowds of poor people. The poor people uglified Brasília, and the result was not to remove, it was to really expel, with no dialogue, nothing. Once they took us away, we were completely on our own.[53]

Here, Nancy uses the term expulsion to signify the state in which they were exiled away from the built capital, and out of view. Ceilândia was created by the government in the early 1970s to keep people from moving into downtown Brasília and setting up shanty towns near the government buildings. The political class, whom the main city was designed for, was meant to be separated from the working class that helped to build it. The naming of the satellite city of Ceilândia is all the more ironic. The root of the name *Ceilândia* is 'CEI' which is the acronym of *Centro de Erradicação de Invasões*, or, 'Invasion Eradication Center,' created to solve the housing crisis involving poor people and illegal land occupations. In 1969, before Brasília completed its first decade of existence, the poor population mostly living in shacks in 'favelas' (slums) numbered almost 80,000 out of a total population of 500,000 in Brasília's metropolitan area. The solution was to create small allotments at subsidized prices where poor people could be transferred to. Due to the urgency of the matter, precarious houses were built in only nine months, and people were transferred even before the necessary infrastructure of sewage, electricity, and transportation were laid out; in fact, they have never been fully completed, as Nancy tells us.

Even though she was a child at the time of the 'removal', Nancy remembers vividly her appearance on radio and television singing the propaganda jingle promoting the transference of families like hers to Ceilândia.[54] The television campaign recruited future residents of the settlements to advocate for the promise of a better life and a better future.[55] In the

---

53 Queiroz, *A Cidade é Uma Só?*.

54 Television in Brazil was inaugurated in 1950 and was never a public affair. Rather, it was always privately owned and therefore followed a commercial model. The country's television network started as a network of regional and local networks which were successively bought and incorporated by Globo corporation, led by the media tycoon Roberto Marinho Jr. For the history of television in Brazil, see *Globo: Beyond Citizen Kane* (dir. Simon Hartog, 1993). Available at: https://youtu.be/-bR8AkMaG1g. Produced by the BBC and exhibited on Channel 4 in 1993. The documentary shows the relationship between media and power and was censored in Brazil upon release by a court decision.

55 It is important to note that Brasília also inaugurates another fundamental technological feature as part of its planning: television. The inauguration of the city also saw the inauguration of its television channel,

documentary, Nancy is seen singing the 'removal song' on television as a child, part of a media campaign in the recently inaugurated *TV Brasília* channel in 1969, a channel affiliated with TV Globo, to this day one of the largest private media conglomerates in the world, which expanded television coverage to connect even the most remote areas of a country of continental proportions. It's important to note that Brasília was inaugurated in 1960 by a democratically elected president, but in 1964 a military coup inaugurated a 21-year long military dictatorship relying heavily on televised propaganda to maintain its power. The campaign jingle reads 'The City is Only One' as an attempt to create an ideology of togetherness to gloss over the actual segregation in the city. On television, the child Nancy sings the jingle together with a dozen other children, as follows:

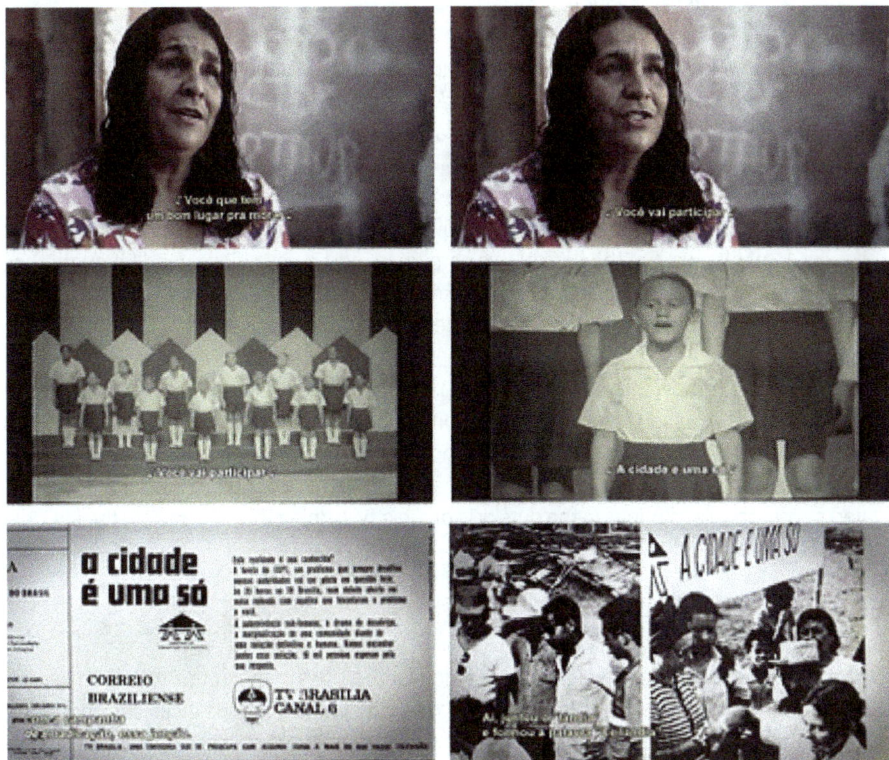


*Fig. 20 – Top row: Nancy recalling the 'removal' jingle in still images from A Cidade é Uma Só? Middle row: Archival television footage from broadcast television showing her as a child participating in the campaign in 1969. Bottom:*

*TV Brasília*, later called *TV Nacional*. In a country where a considerable part of its population had restricted access to basic infrastructure such as electricity, and basic services as education, television was then and now a fundamental part of Brazilian everyday life and national identity, and still plays a pivotal role in its political life. Its impact on the elections have only recently been surpassed by the digital platformization of politics and social media following the evolution of communicative capitalism in the 21st century, as seen in the presidential election of 2018, when Jair Bolsonaro came to power. During the election, he never came to television debates, and campaigned almost exclusively on social media.

56 Queiroz, *A Cidade é Uma Só?*.

*Campaign leaflet 'The city is only one' commissioned by the government to the newspaper Correio Braziliense and TV Brasília; Images of the eviction in 1969. Still images from the film.*

The campaign leaflets shown in the film were commissioned by the government to the newspaper *Correio Braziliense* and *TV Brasília*, with the following text:

> *The City is Only One. Do you know this reality? The favela of IAPI, a problem which has always challenged the authorities will be discussed at 11am. in TV Brasília, in an open debate between those who can respond to this issue, and you. The subhuman survival, the drama of homelessness, the marginalization of a community will be discussed in light of a definitive and humane solution. Let's find this solution together! Ten thousand people are waiting for your response.*[57]

Here, the media and the government are using participatory tactics in a variety of media to convince people that they are actually working together to make a better city, under the rubric of unification. And Nancy was herself drawn to participate in the campaign along these premises, as she says,

> So it was fantastic, we really thought we were helping out. It didn't really turn out that way. I wasn't aware at the time of this campaign, and in my child's mind I thought they were taking us from where we lived to somewhere even better, I was a very happy child and I thought we would go somewhere decent.[58]

These campaigns show the extent of citizen participation as pure media play in this forced removal of the poor aimed to maintain the rationality of the plan that supported the aesthetics of power, a model society, and the birth of a modern nation ridded of its social ills.[59] Pushing the migrant or the worker out of view is then part, intentionally or not, of this rationality, mitigated by temporary solutions in the outskirts of the city, turning the migrant into the invisible and the expelled.

## Europe's Brasília

Nonetheless, Brasília has been touted as a vision for the cities of the future, with wide international recognition. In the early 1960s a group of urban planners and politicians from Gothenburg, Sweden went on a study trip to the recently inaugurated Brazilian capital and became impressed with its modern and futuristic design. This is the starting point for the documentary

57 Queiroz, *A Cidade é Uma Só?*.

58 Queiroz, *A Cidade é Uma Só?*.

59 See also a fiction feature by Adirley Queiroz, *White Out, Black In* (2014) which is a sci-fi docudrama played out in Ceilândia and recounts a massacre in a bar where the police entered asking the white people to leave while asking the Black to remain and be killed. See also Once There was Brasilia (2017), where the synopsis reads 'In 1959, disgraced intergalactic agent WA4 receives a mission: to come to the Earth and kill the president Juscelino Kubitschek on the day of Brasília's inauguration. But his ship is lost in time and lands in 2016 in Ceilândia-a Black suburb of Brasília-on the verge of Dilma Rousseff's impeachment.'

film *A Perfect New World/Europe's Brasília* (2017)[60] by Carl-Pontus Hjortén that reveals a genealogy of the vision for Swedish modernist suburb of the *miljonprogram* (known as the Million Program) typology in the design and visionary architecture of Brasília. Today, one quarter of the Swedish population lives in satellite towns from the 1960s and 1970s, inspired by Brasília.

The film focuses on a specific area outside of Gothenburg, Hjällbo, and its description reads, 'Due to an acute housing shortage in 1960s, the city planners in Gothenburg [Sweden] were affected by lofty ideals. Inspired by [Corbusier's ideas of the city as a machine], and Brazil's new capital, Brasília, they wanted to build a new city for 200,000 residents in the middle of a forest. Nothing went as they had planned'. The new city of Hjällbo, completed in 1969, and located 30 kilometers northeast of Gothenburg's city center would be 'Europe's Brasília' as its architects had envisioned. Here, it was not a matter of creating a monumental architecture for a new seat of power as in Brazil, but it was meant to create a modern standard of living for the working class.

In the film, we follow 17-year old Sagal Hussein, a student and young boxer born in Sweden to Somali parents, as she tells about her lifestory in Hjällbo. She interviews architecture historians and architects from the academic white middle class, who in different ways try to convince her why the suburb she grew up in is an eyesore and a failure from the very start, coupling social ills to the architectural design of the modernist suburb which has been, since its inception, considered a synonym of urban blight despite its modernizing aspirations. When confronted with the history of her neighborhood and its socioeconomic profile through the architect's perspectives, she is perplexed. Hjällbo is considered today one of Sweden's most segregated suburbs in a city where there is an abismal contrast between all-Swedish areas in city centers and mainly immigrant suburbs, or satellite cities, in the outskirts. Yet Sagal cannot imagine a better place to grow up in. Like Adirley Queiroz in *A Cidade é Uma Só?*, director Carl-Pontus Hjorthén combines archival material and contemporary narratives that make this disparity between the perception of a place from the outside and the experience of a place from the inside even more apparent. This leads us back to a discussion of the notion hospitality in the city, and the different ways in which definitions of home and belonging differ widely between residents of satellite towns and its critics.

60 *A Perfect New World/Europe's Brasília* (dir. Carl Pontus Hjorthén, 2017). Available at: https://youtu.be/UDhuA4efq0A.

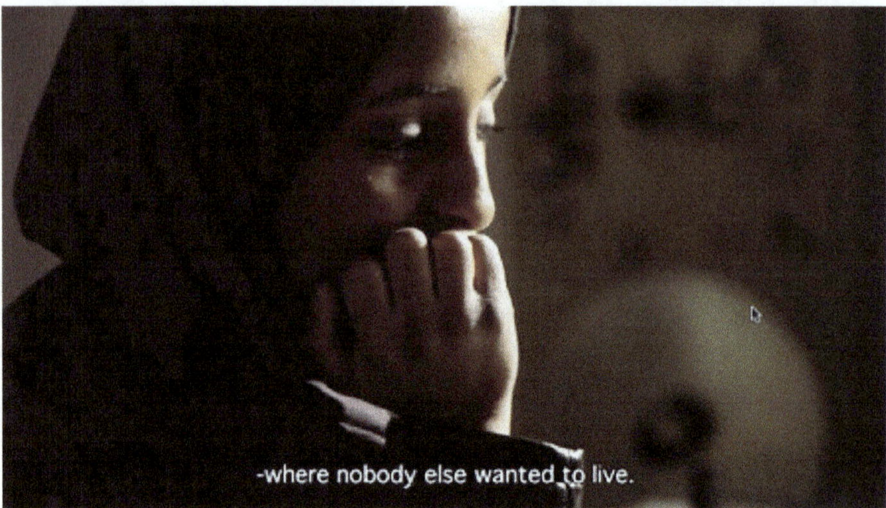


*Figure 21 – Sagal reflects on the perceptions of her neighborhood Still images from the film A Perfect New World/ Europe's Brasília (dir. Carl-Pontus Hjortén, 2017).*

The industrial crisis that hit Gothenburg in the early 1970s, and its long history with worker's movements engaged in city planning, shattered the politician's vision of a successful Europe's Brasília. The modernist suburbs erected on rural land were never fully built due to a sharp decline in jobs which halted the growth and the expansion of the city as had been previously imagined. The satellite towns never really fully connected with the main city as was envisioned because the commutes from the shipyards where its residents worked in were too long. Workers chose to move to detached homes closer to their jobs rather than the planned suburbs. As a result, the expected demographic growth of the city did not happen as expected – they became instead isolated islands in the middle of the forest and former pastures far from the city center. Furthermore, the plans for the consolidation of a forward-looking Swedish society connected to a radically innovative new Swedish technology of living also went awry. Shortly after the inauguration of the satellite towns in the early 1970s, the occupation shifted gradually from the intended growing working and middle classes to the lower income and marginalized populations, giving these areas a negative reputation, especially in the media. The press put forward an image of these areas being unfit for children to grow up in and pointed to design failures in the plans. In the film, we see Sagal watching archival films and saying: 'It isn't fun to know that you grew up in a place where nobody else wanted to live'.[61]

Sagal tells us that she was actually born in another building complex in nearby Hammarkullen that was torn down in the early 1990s shortly after her birth due to its low occupation rates.[62] Her family was then relocated to Hjällbo which needed more residents to occupy its empty apartments. Only in the beginning of the 2010s, politicians decided to give Hjällbo a

61 Hjorthén, *A Perfect New World/Europe's Brasília*.

62 According to the film, the parts and modules of this building after demolition were offered to the shipyards in Gothenburg who did not want them, and later offered to the city of Kaliningrad to build housing complexes there, which were also denied by that city.

facelift and make it more colorful, arguing that more attractive environments could, to some degree, improve the social conditions. Here we see color playing a cosmetic role in social transformation. In the film, a local politician exclaims, 'is it because 8 out of 10 residents in Hjällbo are immigrants that renovations took so long to take place?' Sagal interviews children on the street whose families come from Somalia, Bosnia, Iran, Iraq-Kurdistan, Lebanon, Syria about their opinions on their own neighborhood. Their origins reflect the recent geography of conflict in those regions and explain the immigration patterns based on the humanitarian asylum policies in Sweden. Sagal struggles to find Swedish residents in her neighborhood and finds only two pensioners who have been living there since the satellite town was first built. While one seems to be fine about the changing character of the neighborhood with more residents with immigrant background gradually moving there since the 1970s, and believes that cultural diversity is positive. By contrast, the other one says, 'I feel like an immigrant in my own neighborhood'. She inverts the guest-host equation where she feels like a guest in her own home country and city, and feels isolated in her guesthood. She doesn't dare to go out claiming the area's reputation of gang criminality and drugs in schools causes no one to want to come visit her.

In a scene of a conversation between friends, Sagal asks them, 'When did you first become aware that this was a segregated area?' They respond, 'When the teachers asked them to behave on school trips, and when people from the outside said they would never set foot there'. To counter this image, they say they need to be ten times better than anyone to ward off the stigma. 'No one expects anything from us,' says a friend in resignation, 'if you come from here, you represent the entire suburb. They think we are all the same.' Another one says, 'Who are the ones who are segregated? If we who come from all corners of the world are considered segregated, what are the others considered as? Who is segregated then?'[63]

When Sagal interviews an architecture critic who is very negative about *miljonprogrammet*, she looks at images of the building where she was born, now demolished. 'It looks like a dystopia, where children have no one to play with, and it's empty and isolated. But when I go to the store in Hjällbo, there are lots of people I meet on the way that I know well'. She feels that there is surely a need for more investments in the suburbs to fill the gaps in terms of stores and social spaces, but she disagrees that the architecture is to blame. She asks, why should people who fled hunger, war and poverty be criticized for wanting to build a new life? Here, the hope of a better future for the resident population is eclipsed by the common assumption and also mediatized perception of the planned suburb as a place of social failure. What is then the foundation of this critique? Is the issue at hand a critique towards a modernist vision with its aftermath of inequality and segregation? Or is it a fear of the Other regardless of the architecture the Other now occupies?

63 Hjorthén, *A Perfect New World/Europe's Brasília*.

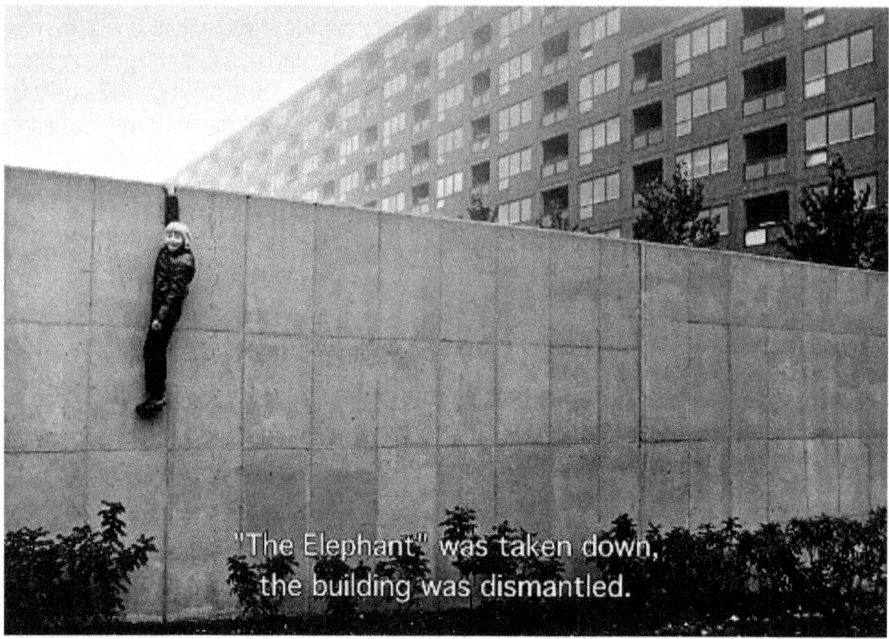


*Figure 22 – Film still of a photograph of the building where Sagal was born in before its demolition, known as 'The Elephant' for its large scale.*

Having myself visited many apartments in Brasília and also in *miljonprogram* neighborhoods across Sweden, one must recognize that the design standard, from a formal point of view, can be considered very high. Individual apartments are well planned with good orientation for maximal sunlight in countries with either extreme or contrasting seasons, and the apartments are large and well equipped. From a design perspective, the planning in *miljonprogrammet* is considered by architect Erik Stenberg[64] (one of the architects Sagal interviews and an expert in this type of housing architecture), as a great improvement on average living standards in Sweden until the 1970s. They are more similar to the apartments planned in the center of Brasília meant for the political and middle classes, than the satellite towns like Ceilândia that sprouted outside the Brazilian capital, showing the complexity of modernity and its architectural projects as well as the utopian societies that were envisioned. Furthermore, Ceilândia and Hjällbo, specifically, are satellite cities with widely different characters: the former is informal while the latter is fully rationally planned. However, both cities, even considering the differences in their design and geographical and political contexts, are stigmatized and discriminated against as the other to what a city should be. The stigma is beyond a matter of architectural taste, it is in fact, an overt expression of social, class, ethnic, and racial discrimination.

In the film, Stenberg is the only one able to mirror Sagal's experience and questions regarding the critique of her own neighborhood and to offer a plausible reasoning behind the historical

64 See a lecture by Erik Stenberg, *Miljonprogrammet - framtidens stad*, Stockholm, 12 September 2012, https://youtu.be/pxplKifguLA. Stenberg was an early advisor for the art project *Satellitstaden*.

stigma that has puzzled her throughout the entire film. Stenberg states that the critiques towards these planned neighborhoods play out negatively against those who live in these neigborhoods and lead perfectly good lives there. The criticism towards the design itself, argues Stenberg, is unfounded, for if we were to look at the design aspects alone, they represent a step forward in building construction and living innovation. In fact, the criticism, he argues, is more towards modernism which brought about a big social change, from living in smaller-scale units to more large-scale industrial economies which requires a new form of mass architecture and new forms of living. 'What is it that people don't like about these neighborhoods', he reflects, and who is the criticism targeted to – those who live there, or someone else? Sagal reflects that the criticism that the housing blocks being too large or too tall, a clear improvement from previous constructions, feels like ingratitude. That perhaps it is a matter of taste, where concrete housing blocks can be beautiful for some and that the underlying democratic ideals of better conditions for all is worth respecting and valuing. 'Hjällbo will always be my home, regardless of what people think, where my family lives. It is a place and a starting point for people from all over the world who have fled poverty and war to build a new life. Is that really so bad?'[65]

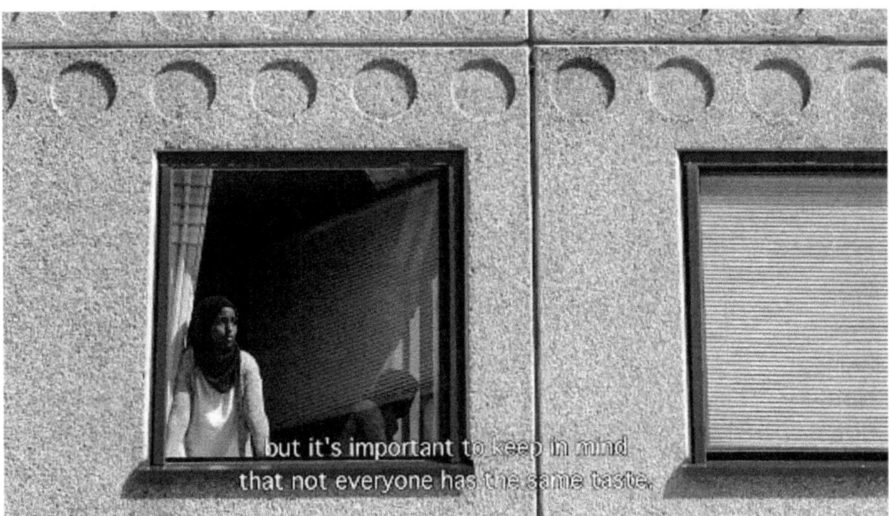


*Figure 23a – Still image from the film A Perfect New World/Europe's Brasília (dir. Carl-Pontus Hjortén, 2017). Courtesy of the author.*

65 Hjorthén, *A Perfect New World/Europe's Brasília.*

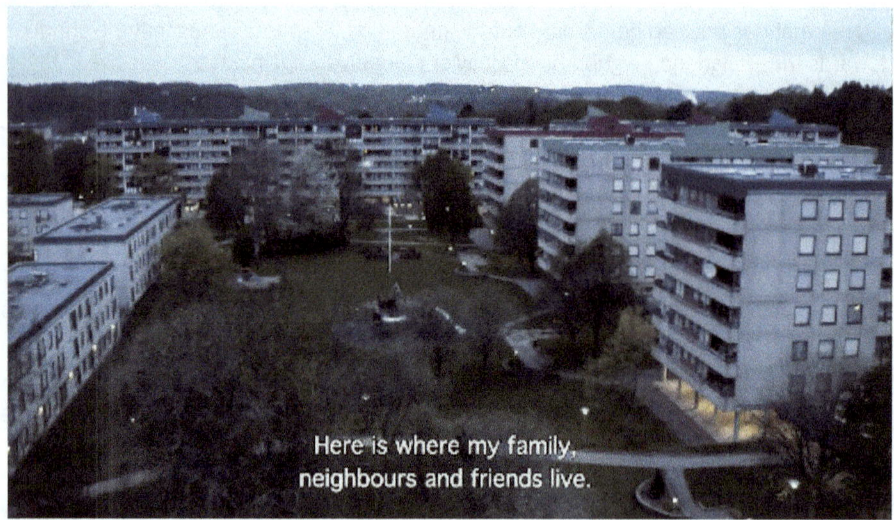


*Figure 23b – Still image from the film A Perfect New World/Europe's Brasília (dir. Carl-Pontus Hjortén, 2017). Courtesy of the author.*

## Cities of the Expelled

The phenomenon of precarity in global cities has been discussed by many theorists, covering a wide range of precarious urban typologies from satellite towns to more informal parts of cities like slums. In *Planet of Slums*, Mike Davis' perspective that the slum is the blueprint for the future instead of the city of steel and concrete, finds an echo in what he contends is seemingly permanent state of urban informality and precarity. In his study of several world metropolises and their patterns of 'swelling', Davis announces that for the first time in history the slum is becoming the new normal.[66] A vast majority of the world's population are housed within deteriorating cities with deep class divides which push most people into the slums and informal economies. Added to the fact that in recent years most displaced persons find refuge in cities rather than in camps, the phenomenon of migration needs also to be considered in light of urban design and urban studies. Just like the design of Brasília and Hjällbo, as revolutionary as they could have been at the time of their construction, their initially design already contained issues of segregation which cannot be pushed away, denied or undone. Both cities present an interesting dilemma: how do we deal with the present inside yesterday's plan for the future? How do we live with a plan for the future that, in its inception, has never happened?

Indeed, the suburban zones of so many cities across the world are now so vast that Davis urges us to rethink the term *peripherality*. If we consider the genealogy of social housing, for instance, this building type that is emblematic of the 20th century and its social revolutions across the whole world, Hirsch allows us to understand that due to the extent of the 'planning' involved in creating a social housing plan,

66 Mike Davis, *Planet of Slums*, London: Verso, 2006, p. 15.

> almost everywhere, inhabitants of social housing experiments were – and still are – unable to alter the built environments they live in. Without the money to leave, the inhabitants have to deal with architecture that tells them, with every concrete staircase, that they are powerless to change anything. Every iron gate shows them that this architecture was built for people who generally cannot be trusted to change something for the better. (...) They are powerless up to the point where they can't even argue against the destruction of their self-made living arrangements within the strict planning system that was superimposed on them in the first place.[67]

However, as Davis elucidates:

> Housing choice is a hard calculus of confusing tradeoffs. (...) The urban poor have to solve a complex equation as they try to optimize housing cost, tenure security, quality of shelter, journey to work, and sometimes, personal safety. For some people, including many pavement-dwellers, a location near a job – say, in a produce market or train station – is even more important than a roof. For others, free or nearly free land is worth epic commutes from the edge to the center. And for everyone the worst situation is a bad, expensive location without municipal services or security of tenure.[68]

As architecture is a slow medium, today we still live amidst these plans from yesterday and their promises of a better tomorrow. To 'design' is to plan, but also to model; which also means that there will always be a gap between what is conceptualized and what is put on paper, written; and yet another gap between what is built and what is lived upon. Social housing, for example, is specifically an aspect of urban planning and architecture filled with good intentions, and yet there are many promises for a good life inside ambitious plans that have only partially solved the problem of poverty and segregation in urban centers. In cities like Brasília, rationally built housing reached only the select few from the political elite and an upper middle class, for instance. For the rest of the population in large urban centers, proper housing is the exception, if existent at all. The informal and improvised settlements in the peripheries, as we have seen, can thus be considered as the cities of the expelled. Whether these peripheral dwellings are temporary dwellings or permanent constructions, they attest to the fact that the task of achieving equality by design lies within the realm of a coming community. Perhaps, the greatest unknown of the city planner is the unforeseeable subject, the one that escapes the 'programming' of the city. Or the ones that escape themselves from being programmed by the city – unprogrammable subjects – whose behavior we cannot predict, the ones who will challenge the capacity of the city to play itself out and become more than it was intended to be, and allow the process of an urban ethics of hospitality to unfold.

67 Hirsch, A Model World', p. 73.
68 Davis, *Planet of Slums*, p. 27 - 29.

# CHAPTER 3: HOSPITALITY, MODERNITY AND THE SUBJECT

# CHAPTER 3: HOSPITALITY, MODERNITY AND THE SUBJECT

> Utopian imagination was essentially architectural and urbanistic. Most attention of the model builders was devoted to plotting and mapping, leaving the job of projection of the map over the territory (or more to the point the job of remaking reality to the likeness of a map) to the rulers of the *topos*. The purpose was to design a spatial arrangement in which there would be a right and proper place for everyone, for whom a proper place would be designed.
>
> – Zygmunt Bauman[1]

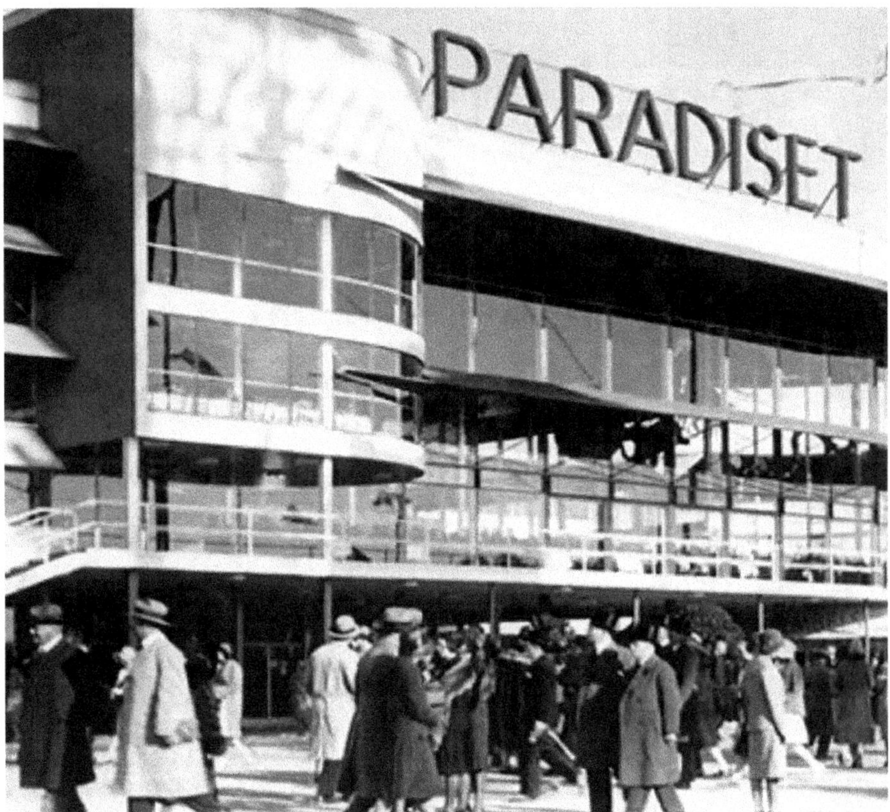


*Figure 24 – 'Paradise' Image from the Stockholm Fair 1930, when modernism and functionalism were established as the expression of social democracy.*

1 Bauman, 'Utopia with No Topos', p.16.

The modernist utopia of Brasília set a template for Gothenburg's suburb Hjällbo in the 1960s after a group of Swedish urbanists went on a study trip to Brazil. There was also a more systematic effort in Sweden to harness modernist architectural thinking in order to solve housing problems, inspired by the growing popularity of the architectural style and bold experiments in Brazil and other rapidly developing nations. The results of this effort became entangled with migration in a peculiar way. The period of increased labor immigration in the 1960s coincided with the government's massive housing overhaul that generated the rapid construction of one million homes mostly in suburban constellations, called *Miljonprogrammet,* where many guest-workers were employed. This was the crystallization of social democratic principles in urban form reflecting the values of the working class and the flagship achievement of Prime Minister Olof Palme.[2]

As in many other European countries, Sweden has experienced a rapid growth of its foreign-born population over the last few decades. While Sweden has steadily received influxes of Europeans and Scandinavians across the centuries up to the Second World War, non-European immigration is a fairly recent phenomenon. The impact of its short-lived colonial history has had marginal effect on contemporary migration patterns when compared to countries who are former global colonial powers such as Great Britain, France or the Netherlands, but this does not mean that Sweden can claim any form of colonial innocence. While it shares a colonial history that overlaps with that of continental Europe, it is altogether brief and mostly marked by trade rather than settlement outside the Balticum.[3]

Despite historical differences with the rest of Europe and other Nordic countries, migration in Sweden today follows patterns and policies similar to most countries in the European Union: migrations based on labor politics, demographic adjustments, and humanitarian reasons. It is the result of diplomatic and humanitarian conventions abroad where the largest incoming populations are refugees, asylum seekers, and family members, coming mostly from zones of conflict around the world. Immigration has not only become a demographic issue but also addresses a deeper moral problem that includes a humanistic stance of 'aid' and hospitality to the victims of worldwide conflict as dictated by Sweden's state policy.

2 Born in 1927 and murdered in 1986, in Stockholm, Sweden. Swedish Prime Minister from 1969-76, and 1982–86, leader of the Social Democratic Party 1969–1982.

3 Swedish colonies consisted of five possessions, four of which were very brief. The colonies were located in North America, Africa and Asia. Possessions were mainly focused on trade. New Sweden was the only attempt at a real colony with a focus on settlements. The island of Saint-Barthelemy in the Caribbean is the only colony that was under Swedish administration for a longer time, 93 years, the colony of New Sweden was Swedish for seventeen years, trading station Cabo Corso for eleven years, the island of Guadeloupe for only fourteen months, and a factory in Porto Novo for less than one year. It should be noted that a colonial mentality can be said to exist as exemplified by the Swedish Race Purity department which was shut down only in 1976 and by the assimilationist policies applied to two of Sweden's ethnic minorities, the Sami and the Finns, for over a century and still considered highly discriminatory. Sweden has also participated in the Berlin Congress of 1884 and 1885 where it participated in the Scramble for Africa by signing trade agreements with King Leopold's International Congo Association. David Nilsson, 'Sweden- Norway at the Berlin Conference 1884–85: History, national identity- making and Sweden's relations with Africa', *Current African Issues*, 53, Series 2013.

This state policy of openness, a praxis of Sweden's social democratic tradition and what it saw as its responsibility in terms of international solidarity is now being put into question by the current political landscape. As is the case in the rest of Europe, the extreme-right minority will oppose any ruling party that does not accept to decrease the number of asylum seekers and refugees in favor of more exclusionary policies based on rising nationalistic trends. The recent riots in the suburbs however have been caused by increasing poverty, and immigration being identified with poverty, also becomes the cause.

When a country positions itself as the paradigm of hospitality for the victims of global conflicts what are the effects on the host society? Does a population reflect the goodwill of its foreign policy in everyday proceedings? Where are the friction points? Does the current upswing of extreme right anti-immigration supporters reflect a malaise regarding immigration that more open governments failed to take into consideration? What happens to the migrant upon arrival when hospitality policies have failed? Is the welfare model sufficient to accommodate the gaps of hospitality?

While neighboring Denmark has taken a more restrictive approach towards immigration in the past decade, Sweden has, until 2014, taken a liberal approach which, as preconized by David Goodhart years before, would 'provide a social laboratory for the solidarity/diversity tradeoff in the years to come'[4] The 'solidarity/diversity tradeoff' Goodhart refers to is based on the assumption that immigration renews the host culture by bringing difference into it. The effect of aid and solidarity politics to the victims of conflict zones around the world yields a demographic adjustment that begins in a gesture of international solidarity and has the additional benefit of diversifying the population, reversing birth rates and increasing the labor force. The arrival of different groups with different backgrounds also helps to destabilize existing structures and bring self-awareness to the host culture and its institutions. With new demographics, new policies of 'diversity management' come into play, such as multiculturalism and integrationist approaches that regulate the processes of adjustment of individuals and groups into the new system.

All of this can be seen as positive ways of looking at migration. However, Turkish theorist Mayda Yegenoglu would argue that a 'closer examination of the judicial-political regulations developed in response to these demands [the recognition of cultural, racial, and ethnic differences] reveals a troubling tendency: cultural/racial difference is translated into an understanding of cultural diversity that treats minorities (...) as 'add-ons' to the existing nation form.' Yegenoglu asks whether diversity, as a solution for a demographic crisis or need for internationalization of its native population, would be capable of inducing a radical transformation in the idea of the sovereign position of the national self. In other words, does the arrival of the immigrant automatically signify a transformation of the host? Along her essay, Yegenoglu argues that a liberal imperative to tolerate and respect cultural difference is 'far from displacing the sovereignty of the host society in question'.[5]

---

4 David Goodhardt, 'Too Diverse?', *Prospect*, 20 February 2004, https://www.prospectmagazine.co.uk/magazine/too-diverse-david-goodhart-multiculturalism-britain-immigration-globalisation.

5 Meyda Yegenoglu, 'Liberal Multiculturalism and the Ethics of Hospitality in the Age of

What happens instead is the crystallization of the host culture as the main superior culture around which all other cultures become 'satellite cultures' orbiting around a constructed idea of the 'national'.[6]

This gives way to fictive constructions of the national subject to create exclusionary politics, often by claiming that the national sovereign state can no longer afford to take care of everyone and therefore creates new rules of engagement in the system. In this case, the myth of a national self becomes a way for neoliberal politics to practice selective welfare. With evidence in electoral politics and a rising xenophobia in Europe, and in Sweden, as a political issue immigration is too often used to crystallize the host culture even further and make it more resistant to change, the result of which is a radicalization of the host culture that leads towards the systematic exclusion of the 'other.' According to the American philosopher Nancy Fraser, it is the politics of redistribution (welfare) set against the politics of recognition (multiculturalism). Fraser reminds us that,

> In these "post-socialist" conflicts, group identification supplants class interest as the chief medium of political mobilization. Cultural domination supplants exploitation as the fundamental injustice. Cultural recognition displaces socioeconomic redistribution as the remedy for injustice and the goal of political struggle.[7]

Fraser's comment points to a critique of a selective welfare politics today. I would like to keep her analysis in mind while uncovering the historical basis that relies mostly on very specific guidelines for the 'welfare subject' which provides the basic building block for a social democratic society in Sweden, and the attendant building forms as lifeworlds and mechanisms of support that encapsulate an ethics of hospitality, as discussed in previous chapters.

## Welfare and Hospitality

The welfare subject, at least within the 'Swedish model',[8] can be said to have originated from a comprehensive response to an earlier demographic crisis in the 20th century, a crisis of falling birth rates in the 1930s. The solution for this crisis was presented in the book *Crisis in the Population Question* (1934), in which sociologist Alva Myrdal and economist Gunnar

---

Globalization', *Postmodern Culture*, 13.2 (2003), https://search-proquest-com.till.biblextern.sh.se/docview/1428990315?accountid=13936.

6 Yenegoglu, 'Liberal Multiculturalism and the Ethics of Hospitality in the Age of Globalization'.

7 Nancy Fraser, 'From Redistribution to Recognition? Dilemmas of Justice in a 'Post-Socialist' Age', *New Left Review,* I.212, (July-August 1995).

8 'The central feature of the so-called 'Swedish model' was the historical compromise between a social democratic ruled state and a privately owned industrial sector. The compromise constituted a middle way between unrestricted capitalism and centrally planned economy. The ownership of most of the large companies, except for the state-owned monopolies, stayed private and expanded side by side with the public sector. The 'Swedish model' can be summarized as follows: 1) a large, privately owned industrial sector, 2) a large public sector financed by taxes, 3) a large trade union movement, 4) the state plays an active role in labour market policies, and 5) the ambition is to achieve an even distribution of income and wealth. Over the next three decades, the terms 'The Middle Way' and 'The Swedish model' came to be well-known trademarks for the Swedish economy.' Source: http://ekonomifakta.se.

Myrdal argue that one way of averting a demographic crisis was by increasing birth rate by way of social reforms that provided the basis for the benefits, or rather rights, of the citizen by ways of a universal welfare state.[9]

These reforms included social support for families by making women more economically independent, increased social services (daycare, laundry rooms, etc.), and economic incentives for better schooling and housing which aimed to radically improve living conditions. This would also facilitate conditions for healthier and more rational living which, at the end, would favor increasing birth rates and ensure a 'better life'. The universal access to welfare made no *a priori* differentiation between individuals based on class or income-every Swede has the same right to welfare as any other. For example, the rich as well as the poor get the same child allowance as a matter of principle, not only as a matter of need. These social benefits largely persist today and still form part of the egalitarian backbone of Swedish society.[10]

While birth rates did not dramatically increase with these reforms in the 1930s, they did however establish radically new 'technologies of living'.[11] The Myrdals would be a lasting influence in the formation of the social democratic state, under which a government regulation of the economy would make sure that the state would prevent over-speculation while safeguarding social guarantees. At the same time where the government would also become a partner and an actor in an expanding economy: 'the state is increasingly involved in coordinating and regulating the national economy (...) and to try to modify its policies for commerce, finance, development, and social reform in the light of what these forecasts show'.[12]

---

9 Brochmann, *Immigration policy and the Scandinavian welfare state*, p.10.

10 There is a darker side to the issue of social reform and the ideas laid forth by the Myrdals in the 1930s. It is a well-known fact that Gunnar and Alva Myrdal were eager proponents of applied eugenics, and their eugenic ideas had an enormous impact in their ideas about community formation. In their book 'Crisis of Demography' of 1934, the Myrdals advocated forced sterilization of those who they considered highly 'unfit' individuals. What is less known today is that several laws were enacted to that end between 1934 and 1941 and abolished as late as in 1974. The knowledge that thousands of Swedes were forcibly sterilized by eugenic reasons – most of them unskilled women from the working class and minority groups, has been made public in the last decade or so. A rather notable fact is that these laws coincide with the Social Democrats' 44-year-long permanence in power between 1932 and 1976, an argument often used by those who oppose the ideas of the welfare state. The Swedish coercive sterilization is a good example of social engineering and supports the idea that welfare may not have initially been motivated not with only equality in mind, but with racial homogeneity as well. It is also interesting to note that The Race Biological Institute (Rasbiologiska Institutet), which supplied much data for the ends of eugenic research, was created in 1922, and renamed the Institute for Genetic Medicine of Uppsala University in 1956. See also 'Agne, ett av alla offer för svensk rasbiologi', *Dagens Nyheter*, 30 March 2010.

11 A term I use to signify all the systems and apparatuses that sustain life in the biopolitical sense. These include social benefits which help sustain life, such as i.e. maternity leave, as well as the use of the 'technology' as *techné*, in our everyday understanding of technology as instrumentality, as a way of getting things done, a technique. It can also be understood in the context of Heidegger's pursuit of the essence of technology, where he argues that technology is a kind of *poeisis*, a way of bringing forth or revealing.

12 This was later interpreted by critics that the economy would also be adjusted according to individuals who were fit to receive benefits, according to the Myrdals' eugenics principles, in such a way that the state would only invest in those 'welfare subjects' who would be worthy of carrying out the overall social

After the Second World War, immigration, as part of a populational issue was seen as one of the forms in which this crisis could be handled. However, immigration cannot only be seen as a solution for a demographic crisis without realizing the impact on the welfare state and of the transformation of social contexts as a result of increased mobility. According to Gunnar Myrdal's theory of cumulative causation of migration, 'each act of migration alters the social context within which subsequent migration decisions are made, thus increasing the likelihood of additional movement. Once the number of network connections in a community reaches a critical threshold, migration becomes self-perpetuating because each act of migration creates the social structure needed to sustain it'.[13] By initiating small social networks of migration, chain migration becomes a larger mass movement alone. Whereas today there are many issues regarding immigration and the welfare model, in the 1960s and 1970s, when immigration was characterized by labor migration, guest workers such as Youssel coming from Turkey, were seen as a positive impact on the welfare model.

Since the 1960s when a series of cooperation agreements stimulated the free exchange of workers across Nordic countries, migration to Sweden has increased steadily, but changing in character in each subsequent decade. As most other countries in Europe, Sweden did not regard guest workers as permanent residents and created policies related to their temporary status, until the influx of arrivals exceeded demand for labor in the late 1960s and early 1970s – at which point the expectation was still that many would return to their homelands. In 1967, the liberal approach to labor migration began to change due to pressure from labor unions. Interest in the Swedish labor market among immigrant countries decreased markedly during the 1970s due to a recession, following a decline in the manufacturing sector and a reduced need for labor force which restricted entry policies for new arrivals. Because of this, immigration between 1969 and 1970 was temporarily put to a halt. This development was prompted, among other factors, by intensified criticism from trade unions fearing that increased competition from outside would affect the domestic labor force negatively, thus reversing the trend that prompted the migration of foreign labor ten years earlier.

Until the mid-1970s, migration was jointly handled by the labor and migration boards that sought the rapid integration of newcomers into the welfare state. Becoming a citizen was relatively easy, with few obstacles and the right to vote in national elections was obtained in less than three years. This, of course, was favorable to the Social Democratic party as the immigrants strengthened their voter base in the working class. At that point, immigration did not rank as a contentious political issue as today, when compared to the attention given to labor rights and the strength of the labor unions, for example. Immigrants were rather seen as part of the labor force and not as a separate or ethnic class per se, even though legally they might have had differentiated status.[14] At the end of the 1970s, virtually all labor force recruitment ended due to a change in immigration policy and outsourcing of manufacturing

project. Myrdal, Alva, and Gunnar Myrdal. *Kris i befolkningsfrågan.* Bokförlaget Nya Dox, 1997 (1934). (Transl. *Crisis in the Population Question.*)

13 Gunnar Myrdal, *Rich Lands and Poor*, New York: Harper and Row, 1957.

14 This scenario differs dramatically from today's scenario where immigration, as stated above, almost constitutes a social class in and of itself, and has become a polarizing issue in electoral debate. *Swedish Migration Authority*, http://www.migrationsverket.se.

and production to other parts of the world. Since the 1980s, immigration to Sweden became dominated by refugee and family reunification, and this model based on humanitarian aid persists until today.

From the 1980s onwards, the pattern of immigration began to shift. Sweden's approach to labor migration reverted to being more liberal and is now considered to have the most liberal system among OECD countries. If one looks at the current immigration patterns, one can sense a direct correlation of the patterns of war and conflict around the globe and the arrival of refugees and asylum-seekers. In fact, the overall pattern of immigration in Sweden today reveals a geography of global conflict. The point is not that migrants come to Sweden because it is a good place *per se*, the point is that often Sweden is the one of the few places that will accept migrants in certain quantities from certain regions by placing fewer restrictions than other countries. A contentious issue in the immigration debate in many high-income countries such as Sweden is immigrants' actual or potential use of the host country's welfare systems. A common argument often expressed in public opining and in the media in favor of restricting immigration is the perception that the risk of immigrants benefiting disproportionately from welfare systems is draining public finances.[15]

This position is best illustrated by Slavoj Zizek's analysis of the senseless violence targeted towards immigrants, from a psychoanalytic perspective. He writes, 'what bothers us in the Other (...) is that he appears to entertain a privileged relationship to the object. The Other either possesses the object-treasure [like welfare], having snatched it away from us (which is why we don't have it), or poses a threat to our possession of the object'.[16]

A point in case must be noted since so much of the Swedish immigration debate depends on certain technicalities of the migration system and the process of welcoming upon arrival – the conditions of hospitality. Since the EU expansion in 2004, when the original fifteen member countries with high and relatively similar income levels were joined by another ten countries with substantially lower income levels on average, Sweden was the only member country that did not impose restrictions on access of the new EU citizens to its welfare system.[17] These new members, mostly countries in Eastern Europe, had on average lower income levels and higher unemployment rates than the original member countries. With free movement across the European continent, the debate about the possible consequences of free labor mobility across asymmetrical economic situations came to the fore. The UK and Ireland imposed very few restrictions on free labor movement whereas Sweden exceptionally did not impose any restrictions on free labor movement, and provided access to all welfare benefits provided that the EU citizen was actively looking for employment.

---

15 Joakim Ruist, 'Free Immigration and Welfare Access: The Swedish Experience', *Fiscal Studies*, 35.1, (March 2014), p. 20.

16 Slavoj Žižek, *The Metastases of Enjoyment: Six essays on Woman and Causality*, New York, 1994, p. 71.

17 Žižek, *The Metastases of Enjoyment*, p. 3.

The conclusion of an economic analysis of free immigration on public finances states the following:

> 'Immigrants' use of basic social welfare is not significantly different from the total population on average, also when differences in age structures are controlled for. (...) Yet even with quite conservative assumptions about income assimilation and the difference between marginal and average costs the predicted discounted net contribution is positive. The results of this study indicate that the fears that lead all other *EU-15* countries to restrict A-10 immigrants' access to their welfare systems may have been ill-founded.[18]

The entry of new EU citizens who no longer need a permit to work in Sweden, especially from Eastern Europe, and labor reforms in 2008 are the cornerstones of current Swedish orientation. Today they are joined by mainly Somali, Afghan, Eritrean, Palestinian, Iraqi, and Syrian refugees, many of whom are denied resident status in other European countries as a result of an open-door policy based on human rights solidarity. At this very moment, faced with mass exile, all Syrians arriving in Sweden are granted permanent resident status.

Since the industrial mid-1970s, perceptions about immigration have changed radically, as multiculturalism became the main ideological direction in Sweden's immigration policies. 'Multicultural' refers to a characteristic of society that consists of persons with a diversity of cultural, ethnic and religious affiliations, while 'multiculturalism' refers to the normative response to this, whereby the state makes certain provisions that recognize and protect cultural minorities and distinct groups tolerated within a nation-state, based on the idea of freedom of cultural belonging. Some of these protections include the maintenance of cultural norms, language and social conduct in ethnic/national groups as a form of institutionalized tolerance.[19] On the other hand, because immigration in the 70s was based on labor migration, the assumption was that some immigrants would eventually move back to their native lands once their work contracts were concluded, something which happened to a very small degree since Sweden's economic success provided good conditions for many immigrants to remain in the country and settle permanently. When immigration later became more focused on receiving refugees and asylum-seekers in the 1980s and early 1990s, this policy changed, and Swedish language training is currently

18 Žižek, *The Metastases of Enjoyment,* p. 15.

19 At the time, the policy was directed to facilitating immigrants' adaptation to Swedish society through a variety of measures that supported the newcomers in keeping their native culture, customs and language. This included teaching Turkish for Kurdish immigrants or Spanish to Chilean immigrants as their first language in school, with Swedish as a second language, for example. The 1970s policy, led by Olof Palme, was later criticized for not focusing enough on cultural adaptation and integration into mainstream society because those who studied Swedish as a second language never mastered it well enough in order to be able to function in society like native Swedes. The policy which embraced a more cosmopolitan stance and defended the immigrant's mother tongue before Swedish proved to be good in the short-term but not in the long-term. Since language is one the main cultural signifier and divider between guests and natives, those who never learned Swedish as a first language remained in a disadvantage. It also did not take into account the need to change society alongside immigration, partly because 'keeping one's own culture' is built on an interpretation of culture as something static and not as something dynamic.

compulsory and a condition to stay in the country in many cases. This time, some immigrants were in the country to stay, many without a choice of turning back. Even though there are efforts for public services to be translated into several languages, the weight given to Swedish language proficiency in the job market is still very high and a defining factor for who gets which jobs.

This is an important distinction because while a society may be composed of several different groups, *multi*cultural as in containing multiple cultures, it does not presuppose that other groups are recognized and acknowledged by policies of multiculturalism per se, but perhaps by other normative modes of 'diversity management', such as in assimilation and cosmopolitan models.

In Sweden, multiculturalism in practice includes the facilitation of bureaucratic matters, basic language training and a grace period of two years between acquiring official residence status and the first job. Integration has been viewed as a chronic problem in the past 40 years and figures very prominently in current political debates, with discussions on structural racism, cultural integration and the failure of a multicultural agenda. 'The foreigner whose [political] status is never properly 'regulated',' explains Slavoj Zizek, 'is the indivisible remainder of the transformation of democratic political struggle into the post-political procedure of negotiation and multiculturalist policing'.[20]

One of the reasons leading to this is the transformation from an industry-based society to a service and knowledge-based society which organizes production in a different way. Whereas earlier anyone could have a factory job regardless of cultural background, the consequence of this structural change is the demand for social competency where the ability to communicate as well as more specialized skills has increased significantly. If most jobs in a service economy require social competency of language skills and behavioral codes, for example, there are groups that perform the same jobs better than others in different contexts. If this is true, immigrant populations, especially those newly arrived, begin their professional lives at a disadvantage from more established populations. In addition, many refugees arrive at an early age in need of further education, may not be skilled into a profession upon arrival, or even illiterate in extreme cases. Many questions that define policy sound like: How can one operate in a knowledge economy without the requisite knowledge? What if the knowledge one has or comes with is not the knowledge that is needed? What are the possibilities of retooling knowledge and education in a way that quickly prepares newcomers for the job market, provided there is a job market they can get into?

It follows that fewer industry placements coupled with low-skilled immigration of refugees and political asylees are the cause of high unemployment among newly arrived populations. Many live on some form of social welfare as their base income, especially upon arrival, and while the government gives a two-year window for each new citizen to find a job in the country, less than half have permanent employment after this period. Even though only a minority of immigrants live entirely on social welfare, the fact remains that unemployment

20 Žižek, 'A Leftist Plea for 'Eurocentrism', *Critical Inquiry*, 24.4 (Summer 1998), p. 997.

among immigrants, especially those upon arrival and living in typically 'immigrant' neighborhoods, is the highest amongst any group in the country, followed by young people. Both these groups are the 'new entrants,' which says more about the impermeability of the job market than about the identities of the groups themselves.

There are other possible explanations for the current situation of segregation in Swedish society and in Swedish cities. The first has to do with structural changes in the demand for labor, and social discrimination in the workplace. The status of 'foreign-born' citizens in the labor market has declined politically and economically. In the 1970s, immigrants had the same salaries and employment opportunities as national Swedes as they were considered part of the labor force and therefore belonging to the working class. Another possibility is that creating an 'immigrant class' defined by multicultural belonging before working status gives a smaller chance for adequate political representation and participation, meaning, the very right to be heard and recognized as an equal participant in the public debate. In Zizek's words, 'Instead of the political subject 'working class' demanding its universal rights, we get, on the one hand, the multiplicity of particular social strata or groups, each with its problems [the dwindling need for manual workers, and so forth), and, on the other hand, the immigrant increasingly prevented from politicizing his predicament of exclusion'.[21]

A third possibility of explaining segregation is cultural discrimination as the main cause for immigrant populations' lessened status in the job market, and therefore less general economic status, creating not only a racial and economic segregation but also a *media segregation*. Just as migrant and host populations are confined to specific territories and social fields, many of them are likewise often segregated in terms of media use on the one hand (thanks to cultural, linguistic and technological specificities, receiving relevant information from channels different from host societies, and thus acquiring bonds necessary for identification to different imagined communities), and in terms of media representation, with limited agency in determining how the media portrays or gives space to immigrant voices.

## Undoing Welfare, Undoing Hospitality

On a more structural level, we can speculate that immigrant unemployment could be part of the neoliberal strategy to 'undo' social democracy. Replacing the social democratic class compromise with new class relations would require a felicitous economic structure (such as the ability of Swedish capital to invest outside Sweden), political organization, and, where those falter, crisis and shock. The ability of Swedish capital to invest outside Sweden was facilitated by the rise of the European Union. While the economic crisis raged throughout Sweden in the 1990s, unemployment among New Swedes (those with immigrant origins, including immigrants and their non-naturalized descendants) began to rise faster than unemployment among ethnic Swedes. There is, in addition, an 'invisible' black market for low-paid jobs which are taken mostly by illegal migrants or those waiting for asylum approvals. They are cleaners, warehouse workers, who work in odd hours for low pay, usually not in sight of the customers in supermarkets, but who perform the services that no one else will.

21 Žižek, 'A Leftist Plea for 'Eurocentrism', p. 998.

In *A Critique of Postcolonial Reason*, Gayatri Spivak reflects on Swedish exceptionality: 'Sweden is a generally 'enlightened' donor country, responsible in the context of globality and global post-colonialism. It is in its domestic treatment of the great waves of migration generated by the so-called end of the Cold War that its enlightenment begins to crumble: postcolonial migrancy'.[22] Is welfare enough of a guarantee for the postcolonial migrant, is the benevolent state the only solution for those, as Spivak calls it, the 'detritus of globalism'? She continues:

> (...) in the New World Order – or hot peace – the hyphen between nation and state comes looser than usual; and in that trap fundamentalisms fester. Even Sweden could offer an example. In that dreadful winter of mosque-breaking (...) the Swedish protest against the outrage of November 30, 1992 (when a group of young Swedish racists marched under the banner of the King), was strong. Yet, unless one believed (and many do) that faith in human equality is simply a natural characteristic of the Swedish nation (it is against such convictions that underclass multiculturalism fights) (...) Although we must work to elect public officials who must soldier to shore up the benefits of the Welfare State, that alone is not the kingpin of the global future.[23]

The Myrdals were one part of a larger political project of creating a society that was homogeneous and equal. If we ignore for a moment the initial implications of what was meant by homogeneity, the genius of the welfare state until then was that it intende to produce a society with a collective subjectivity. There were institutions within the society that interpolated, for lack of a better term, people as a collective entity. Yet, with the erosion of welfare services, that is, with the application of Milton Friedman's models since the 1990s, investments in the public services are diminished to the point where these services become insufficient. When public services are perceived as bad, clients begin to consider other alternatives. This means that the welfare state is eroded from within, with privatization and a consumer model in public services coupled to the principles of 'new public management',[24] when people begin to become neoliberal economic subjects and therefore lose this sense of collectivity in favor of the ideal of individual pursuits. The economic subject's biggest advocacy is having the freedom to choose rather than having things chosen for her and willingly paying the price for this freedom. And yet, Zygmunt Bauman summarizes the paradox of this age: 'Never have we been so free. Never have we felt so powerless'. Our presumed freedom is tied to one central condition: we must be successful – that is, to 'make' something of ourselves. If we become nothing, it is our own fault – there are no life support mechanisms or immunological systems besides the ones you managed to create yourself. In this case, welfare is no longer a public good but only a private matter.

---

22 Gayatri Chakravorty Spivak, *A Critique of Postcolonial Reason: Toward a History of the Vanishing Past*, Cambridge, Massachusetts: Harvard University Press, 1999, p. 373.

23 Spivak, *A Critique of Postcolonial Reason*, p. 374.

24 The ideas of New Public Management have become the gold standard for many administrative reforms around the world. Most of these ideas for reform are based implicitly on the assumption that government will function better if it is managed more as if it were a private-sector organization guided by the market. To achieve better results in the public sectors, governments should be run like businesses. See also M. Shamsul Haque, 'New Public Management: Origins, Dimensions, and Critical Implications', *Public Administration and Public Policy*, vol.I (2013): 13–27.

Similar to the erosion of the welfare state, another institution strongly associated to social democracy is public service broadcasting (PSB), which has been in decline for a long time.[25] With the neoliberal turn in the 1980s and 1990s, new commercial channels were introduced, and the resulting competition led to the relative decline of public service broadcasting (even though it remains relatively strong in Scandinavia where it played a major role as an institution ensuring democracy and national cohesion[26]). But it is ironic that satellite television became an early nemesis to PSB, contributing to the weakening of its monopoly and the fragmentation of the audience. Its status has declined further with the advent of social media, even though public service broadcasters in many cases are trying to mobilize the new possibilities for their purposes.[27]

Yet, all in all, the breaking of the near monopolies of public service broadcasters all over Europe in the 1980s despite their struggle and the spread of the more North American commercial television model across the world has changed the television landscape for the past two decades and allowed for an analysis of the field that goes beyond the function of television in nation-building. Cross-border television channels, with the help of satellite and the Internet, have opened up television into the global sphere and causing temporal and culturals shifts that have somehow accompanied the flow of populations across the world.[28]

Researchers specializing in race studies in Sweden today have begun to reassess this period critically. Tobias Hübinette, a researcher of race studies in Sweden has proposed a renaming of these moments in Swedish migration politics through the lens of 'whiteness studies'. He names the era of progressive antiracism between 1968–2001 the 'white solidarity period' characterized by Third World solidarity, international adoptions, interracial intimate relationships, and a radical, idealistic, utopian and millenarian colorblindness. The 'white melancholy period' from 2001 and onwards, is our time of white regressive mourning characterized by retro aesthetics, colonial amnesia and cultural nostalgia.[29] He claims that 'Sweden is currently undergoing a double crisis of Swedish whiteness. "Old Sweden", i.e. Sweden as a homogeneous society, and "Good Sweden", i.e. Sweden as a progressive society, are both perceived to be threatened by the presence of non-white migrants and their descendants. Both the reactionary and racist camp and the progressive and antiracist camp are mourning the loss of this double-edged Swedish whiteness'.[30]

---

25 Håkon Larsen, 'The Legitimacy of Public Service Broadcasting in the 21st Century: The Case of Scandinavia', *Nordicom Review*, 35.2 (2015), p. 66.

26 Larsen, p. 67

27 José Van Dijck and Thomas Poell, 'Making Public Television Social? Public Service Broadcasting and the Challenges of Social Media', *Television & New Media*, 16.2 (2015), p. 154.

28 See also Andreas Fickers and Catherine Johnson (eds)*Transnational Television History: a Comparative Approach.* London: Routledge, 2012. We will go into more detail into this aspect in Chapter 5.

29 Tobias Hübinette and Catrin Lundström, 'White Melancholia: Mourning the Loss of 'Good Old Sweden'', *Eurozine*, 18 October 2011. https://www.eurozine.com/white-melancholia/.

30 Hübinette, ' White Melancholia: Mourning the Loss of 'Good Old Sweden''.

## Terms of Urban Engagement

> They say power, we say potency. They say integration, we say open code.
>
> – Paul B. Preciado[31]

How easy or difficult is the integration process for a newly arrived person in Swedish society? At this moment, the current policy enforces a welcome package called 'the Establishment Plan', a series of social benefits that help in the introduction phase of arriving.[32] Even if citizenship status takes a certain amount of time to become official, those newly arrived are housed temporarily, or, as Saskia Sassen has stated, 'warehoused', sometimes in precarious conditions since the beginning. Some individuals are granted the possibility of family reunification, something that is becoming increasingly uncommon as in France, for example. While there is an certain openness from the government and high tolerance among the general population, the receptivity of Swedes to immigrants in everyday life – in the face-to-face encounter – is generally more reserved, making social and cultural integration a challenging process in the long-term. Why? One possibility is that there is no trust and legitimacy from the people about immigration policies, and a silent disapproval of immigration is never said outwardly expressed in everyday encounters between Swedes and immigrants, but only indirectly through social exclusion, job discrimination, urban segregation (often voluntary), to name a few othe factors.

The elections of 2014 with a marked increase in voters shifting to the extreme right marks this dissatisfaction. What could be the terms of engagement for making coexistence possible between the host society and the newcomers or guests? Further, when one does mention 'integration', what is meant by this term and who is meant to integrate to what and with whom? Very often, integration is meant as something that the host society provides tools for (such as language training) and the newcomer is responsible for assimilating and putting into practice. This implies that the only subject that undergoes change is the guest, who inevitably must adapt in order to survive in the host's environment. What often remains untheorized in this equation, are the processes related to the extent in which the host also needs to change and adapt in order to make this integration work. This means that integration requires both sides of the relationality of hospitality at work, hosts receives guests who integrate to hosts who also adapt and change according to the guests and begin to evolve together in a common co-existence.

---

31 Paul B. Preciado, 'Nós dizemos revolução', Universidade Nômade do Brasil, 24 March 2013, http://uninomade.net/tenda/nos-dizemos-revolucao/.

32 According to legislation, 'The establishment plan shall be designed together with the newly arrived and in collaboration with concerned municipalities, authorities, companies and organizations. The plan shall cover a maximum of 24 months and contain at least 1 Swedish language course for immigrants to the person entitled to attend such training under the Education Act; 2. 60 hours of social orientation, and 3. activities to facilitate and accelerate the new arrival's establishment in working life.' This establishment plan is for adults ages 20–65 years. Orphaned minors who come as refugees and elderly have special programs. Source: *Swedish government*, http://regeringen.se.

The often-cited interpretive scheme from John Berry describes four possible strategies of acculturation for migrants in the host society and may serve as a model to understand and the problems associated with the notion of integration.[33]

## Strategies of acculturation

| Degrees of Identification | Identification with the home culture: high | Identification with the home culture: low |
|---|---|---|
| Identification with the host culture: high | Bi/Multi-cultural integration | Assimilation |
| Identification with the host culture: low | Separation | Marginalization |

*Figure 25 – Modelling acculturation strategies (after John Berry, 1997).*

Depending on the level of acceptance of the host culture and the maintaining ties with the home culture, there can be different reactions to the situation. Some are trying to avoid the home culture and people from the same migrant background and to dissolve in the new culture, learning the new language and relying on it heavily for all information and interactions. This is called assimilation strategy. The opposite would be avoiding the host culture and trying to live a life as close as possible to the one led at home – the separation strategy. There are also migrants who either cannot or do not want to acquire the new identification but are unable to maintain the ties with the home culture either, and thus become isolated from both. This is marginalization. Finally, the strategy that is arguably characteristic of the most successful migrants is bicultural integration, whereby they maintain close contact with the home culture and manage to develop a likewise close contact with the host country.

What would this diagram be like from the host's perspective, and why didn't John Berry design a similar diagram for degrees of identification of host cultures with guests? Does the position of power that hosts maintain exempt them being categorized in different degrees of *hostness?*

While there is no question that democracy still remains the founding principle of Swedish society just like most other European countries and the West, the overvaluing of individual autonomy culturally and economically stands in sharp contrast with other cultures entering Swedish society. As most incoming cultures come from places where social interdependency may be the norm and family values are more important than the individual (I am referring here mainly to cultures from South America, the Middle East and Northern Africa) and where religious beliefs and values may differ, there needs to be a stance of tolerance and solidarity for different modes of living, believing and making choices, in consonance with democratic values. Prioritizing bicultural integration could present a more just and effective approach to managing migration in Sweden, but it would require more openness from the host society

33 John W. Berry, 'Immigration, Acculturation, and Adaptation', *Applied Psychology*, 46.1 (1997), p. 9.

to generate a higher degree of identification with newcomers. The issue at hand is understanding how this can be achieved without shattering necessary identifications for both hosts and guests, but rather finding a common ground for identifications to be able to coexist and evolve together. Among many aspects, architecture and city planning could become a key factor in this process.

However, in my observation the neutralizing architecture of the Swedish suburb – the functionalist 'box' whose design is based on universalist principles pertaining to the modernist styles which were once believed to emancipate humanity – as we have seen, has proved to be insufficient as an aesthetic or social equalizer able to act as a common denominator for all. As Hübinette notes, 'When it comes to the discrimination of migrants and their descendants, particularly non-white and non-European groups, Sweden barely differs from any other Western country today. Particularly when it comes to housing, Sweden stands out for its highly racialized patterns of residential segregation'.[34] In addition, the subject produced within and by the concrete suburbs today is no longer the social-democratic subject that the Myrdals or Palme had once imagined, and yet, newcomers' integration depends, in the public imagination, on them somehow entering this hegemonic model, which urgently needs to be reimagined.

In the 1940s, Antonio Gramsci resignified the concept of 'hegemony' as the ideological domination of one social class over others in order to deny their political voices. Those classes that suffer from the brunt of this hegemony are the subaltern classes, according to him. Years later, Spivak wrote an article whose title asks a fundamental question: 'Can the subaltern speak?'[35] What are the limits and possibilities of speech for the subalterns of hegemonic domination? The field of subaltern studies seeks to address these issues. Therefore, when one refers to 'subaltern identities' or 'subaltern subjects,' it is not a criticism or a curse or a qualitative assessment of these subjects, but rather a recognition of the fact that these identities were placed in a subordinate position by a white (or its hegemonic equivalent), colonialist, patriarchal, society. The subaltern is the one who is the victim of 'otherphobia',[36] precisely belonging to the groups that Gramsci identified.

---

34 Hübinette, 'White Melancholia: Mourning the Loss of 'Good Old Sweden''.

35 In this essay, Spivak wonders how the third world subject can be studied without cooperation with the colonial project. Spivak points to the fact that research is in a way always colonial, in defining the 'other', the 'over there' subject as the object of study and as something that knowledge should be extracted from and brought back 'here'. See Gayatri Chakravorthy Spivak, 'Can the Subaltern Speak?', in Cary Nelson and Lawrence Grossberg (eds) *Marxism and the Interpretation of Culture,* Basingstoke: Macmillan, 1988, p. 271–313.

36 'Otherphobia' is a term coined by the Brazilian novelist and historian Alex Castro. It refers to the fear of the Other, a notion which encompasses not only fear of the stranger or foreigner as in xenophobia, but the fear of that which is considered not normative. See Alex Castro, *Outrofobia*, Rio de Janeiro: Editora Publisher Brasil, 2015. (It is worth noting there has also been some discussion of xenophilia, or desire of otherness, sometimes typical of disempowered communities in the face of assertive others but not limited to this case. P.A. Owens, 'Xenophilia, Gender, and Sentimental Humanitarianism', *Alternatives*, 29.3 (2004): 285–304, for a more positive discussion.)

The welfare subject that was once the building block of an egalitarian society as envisioned by the Myrdals, for example, was supported in large part by the socio-immunological mechanisms of the welfare state within the framework of a universal welfare.[37] In a welfare state, all persons are in principle regarded as equal and therefore have the same rights over the welfare benefits, yet this presupposes citizenship to a national state. How, then, does the welfare subject change with globalization and increased displacement? How do welfare and mobility go together? How does the migrant condition change the way in which we perceive national welfare systems and could there be such a thing as global welfare? Does globalization depend on the balance of inequality between those who have welfare and those who do not? The subaltern, in this case in the figure of the migrant, is usually the one who suffers the brunt of the precarity of falling through the cracks of national welfare systems. This question is a concern for moral philosophy as it is an ethical question, often disguised by corporate pragmatism where one needs to be a part of the system in order to reap its benefits. Perhaps welfare and mobility do not go together because welfare benefits will benefit those who are inside the system, who are rooted, settled citizens. Can the migrant ever become a citizen? When you settle into a system do you cease to be a migrant?[38]

The reason why I compare the welfare subject to the subaltern is because the urban typology of the suburb, the shanty town, and the edges of the city are the home of the subaltern in large cities. But this does not mean that the subaltern cannot live everywhere. The welfare subject is no longer the universal emancipated subject – it has become the state of the subaltern. In the neo-liberal régime, to be a welfare subject is to be the victim of state dependency and not the receiver of equal rights. To recall Agamben briefly, how can one transcend subaltern status and become more than the 'avant-garde of society' and more than a 'border concept' that puts all other subjectivities into check?

---

37 Welfare, whether our own or that of others, is not merely a practical concern, it is also a prominent feature of our common-sense morality where a due concern for others and for ourselves governs virtually all aspects of our lives and leads us to make decisions in the best interest of all those affected with the least possible harm inflicted. The welfare subject receives the benevolence of the state, justice and equality among all citizens and benefits from collective support systems whether by receiving benefits in the form of direct money subsidies or in-kind in the form of childcare, healthcare, and other services. These welfare benefits are guaranteed for every citizen, as a right from birth or acquired via legal alien or naturalization status.

38 A possible expansion on this question could be illustrated with the phenomenon of welfare tourism within the European Union, where citizens from one country relocate and become guests in another in order to earn the benefits of the host country. Where the system of life support fails in one country (i.e., the Roma beggars traveling throughout the Schengen region), the benefits can be reaped elsewhere if one understands how to work the system. Just as EU countries have restricted multiculturalism policies, they are also restricting welfare benefits within the EU, where Europe moves towards a continent with open borders, but diminishing benefits. See also 'Benefits Tourism Not OK', *The Economist*, 15 November 2014.

## The Swedish Dream: Welfare and Collective (Dis)Contentment

> We love it! We lived before in an old house. One room and kitchen with a wood stove. Now we have a living room and our own television set. A refrigerator with icebox and electric range in a kitchen that has its own balcony.[39]

This statement is from an old couple that had recently moved into a 'new suburb' in the greater Stockholm region in 1968, not too far from Fittja. It shows the difference between the state of housing in most Swedish metropolitan areas which, until the early 1960s and despite a previous housing overhaul in the 1930s, had one of the lowest overall living standards in Europe. From the 1950s onwards, Stockholm and the rest of the country began a construction overhaul of modern housing to raise the overall standard of living.

The 1920s were a turning point in Swedish urban development, in part triggered, as we have seen, by a political project based on a homogeneous and equal society, aided in large part by the Myrdal couple's ideas for the 'The People's Home', or *folkhemmet.*[40] Emerging from a rather quick growth after the First World War, Sweden's prosperity was left unmatched by its housing situation. The urban population at the time lived in one of the worst conditions in Europe: numerous families living in old buildings and cramped apartments with poor services, insufficient sanitation, often with no electricity and therefore no proper heating. Since Sweden did not participate in the Second World War due to its neutrality, it did not suffer any destruction in its territory which would have precipitated a reconstruction overhaul as in France or Germany. Despite this, by the 1960s much of Swedish housing standards remained lower than in most of Europe even though the initial welfare housing construction boom had begun in the 1930s.

Internal migration and growth of industrial towns beckoned a housing overhaul that would modernize existing housing and increase the offer of apartments tenfold between 1964–1975. Prime Minister Olof Palme promised to deliver one million homes in ten years and called this massive overhaul the *miljonprogrammet*, or 'Million Program'. These new suburbs followed the general guidelines of welfare housing from the 1930s in a larger scale, with satellite towns radiating from city centers to ease urban density and to provide residents with access to wide open green areas. To finance this enterprise, the government subsidized construction and encouraged banks to open credit lines to facilitate ownership and transferred the task of building worker's quarters from the industry owners, for example, to the government.

During the decade of the *miljonprogrammet*, the city of Stockholm expanded very quickly and doubled its population with the construction of suburban districts such as Rinkeby, Tensta to the north and Fittja and Alby to the south. Many of these areas have been criticized since their construction for being 'concrete suburbs', dull, grey, low-status areas built mainly out

---

39 Author's translation. Klas Ramberg, *Allmännyttan: Välfärdsbygge 1850–2000*, Stockholm: Byggförlaget, 2000, p. 169.

40 Today, the same *folkhemmet* and the Myrdals biopolitical project are touted as symbols of a 'national identity' by extreme-right parties. Myrdal and Myrdal, *Kris i* befolkningsfrågan.

of prefabricated concrete slabs in record time, without particular attention given to details or to the creation of public life. Today, the most common complaints are about the high crime rate and the high racial and social segregation in these areas. As mentioned earlier, these suburbs radiating from city centers create urban, social and political 'border situations' and beckon an investigation of the relationship between the typology of these suburbs and the reasons behind social and ethnic segregation in contemporary Swedish society.

The location for our case study described in the next chapter, Fittja, located south of Stockholm, is such a 'new suburb' of 2,500 units built between 1972–1973. As we have seen in the previous section, the period during Fittja's construction in 1973 coincides with a generation of intensified labor migration to Sweden, followed in the 1980s and 90s to humanitarian purposes and politics of foreign aid related to the victims of global conflict and protection of political dissidents as a result of political transformations around the world.[41]

In order to locate the historical significance of the *miljonprogrammet* and its relationship to welfare and migration, it would be useful to track back to the origins of this urban and ideological project in the 1930s. Like its modernist precursor, miljonprogrammet continued the tradition of modernist welfare housing with social aims to create 'good democratic citizens' by building at high quality with a good range of local services including schools, nurseries, churches, public spaces, libraries, and meeting places for a cluster of households. This represented an update of Alva and Gunnar Myrdals' overall plan of universal welfare resulting in new 'technologies of living' in the 1930s, as mentioned previously, accompanied by parallel events in the technologies of dwelling and in considering the city as a site of historical and demographic change. As formulated by social-democratic leader, and later Prime Minister Per Albin Hansson in 1928,

> The foundation of the home is the feeling of togetherness and cohesion (...) In the good home equality prevails, as do attention, cooperation, helpfulness. Applied to the people's and the citizen's home at large, this would mean a tearing down of all social and economic barriers now dividing the citizens into privileged and deprived, rulers and dependents, rich and poor, propertied and pauperized, plunderers and plundered.[42]

In the 1930s, the materialization of welfare in urban form was the *folkhem*, the 'people's home'. Combined with Hansson's suggestion, many of the ideas behind the *folkhem* stem from the manifesto *acceptera!* ('Accept!') from 1931 by a group of young architects seeking to formalize their avant-garde architectural ideas against architectural traditionalism and historicism and setting the path for a new way of thinking about architecture, the city and society. The members of this group were the already famous modernist architect Gunnar Asplund, together with Wolter Gahn, Sven Markelius, Gregor Paulsson, Eskil Sundahl and Uno Åhrén who would all exert considerable influence in the Swedish built environment in the decades to follow, culminating in the *miljonprogrammet*.

---

41 As of May 2015, over 20,000 asylum applications have been processed. *Swedish Migration Authority*, http://www.migrationsverket.se.

42 Ramberg, *Allmännyttan*, p. 90.

*Acceptera!* is a modernist manifesto that leaned on national identification and historical continuity based on ideals of progress, in line with contemporary architectural thinking of the time. The title of the manifesto was a cry for people to 'accept' that the times have changed and that 'we can no longer live trapped in history or traditions that prevent the improvement of our condition'.[43] The manifesto also served as a pedagogical project that addressed politics through aesthetics, representing a compromise between capital and labor, crafted by avant-garde designers. It also became the starting point for key issues of the modern project of the city: the possibility of freedom in the political era, the relationship between aesthetics, consumption, and labor, and what is more important, the role of architecture in the construction of a subjectivity that would be necessary to create and uphold a budding welfare state.

This subjectivity would be translated into what architect Uno Åhren called the 'good democratic citizen-type',[44] led by the belief that material improvements that translated democratic values into built form would also result in an improved and more democratic social being. This subject was socially conscious and for whom freedom and social responsibility become the foundations for good citizenry.[45] Not only would this idea of citizenry become the forefront of a national integration project, it was later declared to be the very expression of Swedish identity and the cornerstone of social democracy. In fact, functionalism moved beyond the radical and the avant-garde as it became state policy from the 1930s onwards.[46] If modernism can be said to be a pivotal point in the construction of the social-democratic welfare state where such democratic subjects exist and operate, touching this foundation would mean to touch the very roots of the core identification of Swedish society and its belief in modernity as social progress.

A concrete example of these ideas was Alva Myrdal's design for a cooperative *kollektivhus* (collective house) in 1937 (in collaboration with architect Sven Markelius[47]) intended to create more freedom for individuals, especially women, and helped set the guidelines for future construction around the social-democratic subject. This rather experimental construction offered communal amenities like childcare facilities, shared kitchens and meeting spaces in each building (as opposed to in every city block) that allowed adults to provide basic care for children on a rotation basis, thus freeing up time for work and other activities. This demonstrated a strong commitment to early ideas of feminism and to the emancipatory potential of social housing, influenced by previous German architectural avant-garde and Soviet socialist models. While the first *kollektivhus* was experimental in character, many of its features such as collective laundry facilities and the importance of meeting places and social spaces in defining sociability were eventually adjusted and applied into the development of standards which are still operative as the technical and sociological basis of Swedish social design until today.[48]

43 Gunnar Asplund, Wolter Gahn, Sven Markelius, Gregor Paulsson, Eskil Sundahl, and Uno Åhrén, *Acceptera*. Stockholm: Tidens förlag, 1931, p. 13.

44 'Interview with Per Hasselberg', no date, http://perhasselberg.wordpress.com/konsthall-c/.

45 Compare to Kant's theory of cosmopolitanism based on the freedom of the individual.

46 Helena Mattson and Sven-Olov Wallenstein, *Swedish Modernism: Architecture, Consumption and the Welfare State*, London: Black Dog Architecture, 2010, p. 65.

47 Eva Rudberg, *Sven Markelius Architect*, Stockholm: Arkitektur Förlag, 1989, p. 79.

48 These standards are a set of measurements and dimensions based on an 'average' person and for

In 1945, however, Uno Åhrén publishes an assessment report where he exposes a self-critical view on the ideals of functionalism he had set forth years earlier. Functionalism had failed in many important respects: it provided material and technical improvements in society, but no direct social benefits as the Myrdals or Hansson had expected. Åhrén's initial democratic ideas were carried out by building meeting places in the *folkhem* suburbs, that would have both very clearly defined practical and social functions in its design, if only life could be planned beforehand. According to Swedish artist Per Hasselberg, 'some people believe in this social engineering and still try today to create social contexts and behaviors that improve people's general disposition into this defined and universal subject',[49] that is part of the social-democratic mythology from that time. One such meeting place would be communal laundry houses which Hasselberg adapted into the arts center Konsthall C in 2009, located in a southern periphery of Stockholm. These laundry houses were managed as cooperatives and became an essential part of the social-democratic 'Swedish Model' where residents would book times to do their laundry and lead activities such as reading groups or collective leisure activities while waiting for the washing cycle to finish. These services also freed up both the home from these tasks and made time more effective, especially for women, on the outset. Hasselberg explains, 'later, these meeting places became places of conflict and disagreement corrected by electronic booking systems to avoid confrontation between people'.[50] But as these corrective measures were implemented, a truly democratic subject was already not possible, claims Hasselberg, and what follows after this 'failure' is the myth of the good solidary citizen to which every Swede, native or otherwise, somehow feels the need to live up to.

In a contemporary philosophical critique of *acceptera!*, Swedish philosopher Sven-Olov Wallenstein and architect Helena Mattson expose the political relevance of Swedish modernism as a crucial part of its national identification, deeply embedded in the national psyche that it has become synonymous to Swedish core values, leaving few other alternatives to a Swedish modern identity. Yet this symbiosis between building and culture, politics and aesthetics also has international significance in that it gave architecture a political, and according to

---

a family composed of parents and two children to determine specific characteristics of an 'average' apartment. The extent to which these socially determined measurements collide with or complement the lifestyles of other cultures, as seen in Fittja, is interesting to note. A Swedish 'shell' with Turkish decoration, for example, an apartment for a nuclear family of two children adapted for a family of 6, 7 or 8 people, rooms with adapted functions, etc. IKEA has taken many of these principles and applied it to their products which are now sold worldwide, with Swedish names and standards applied to a global scale.

49 'Interview with Per Hasselberg'.

50 Laundry houses are typical of Swedish housing units where collective laundry rooms were meant to free up space in the apartments, save water and energy, while at the same time creating opportunities for people in a community to meet. Often, these laundry houses had a functional part with machines and also leisure rooms where people could hold association meetings, hold activities, have coffee, etc. This theme inspired the exhibition 'Washed Out' which I co-curated in 2011 in this arts centre and its laundry room. The central theme of democratic ideals which are in way of disappearance from contemporary political culture in Sweden. More about this exhibition: *Washed Out* (Curated by Isabel Löfgren, Corina Oprea, Judith Souriau, Valerio del Baglivo, Milena Placentile, *Konsthall C*, 2011), http://apexart.org/exhibitions/washedout.htm.

Wallenstein and Mattson, a '*bio*political function that marks a critical moment in international modernism, and placed architecture on par with political and social reform'.[51] The *accep-tera!* manifesto put an already existing thrust of construction and a modern philosophy of living to the forefront, moving beyond the radical and the international avant-garde and was adopted as State policy after the manifesto became widely spread and accepted. Manfredo Tafuri, a well-known critic of modernism,[52] believes that the modernist project fails when it is appropriated by the State.

Similar to the modernist manifesto of the 1930s, at the time of conceptualization and construction, the *miljonprogrammet* also belonged to the architectural avant-garde of its time. It was a 1960s-70s concrete-brutalist version of the modernistic *folkhem*, with the most efficient and innovative prefabricated building techniques that could be afforded at the time.[53] In its revised form, the suburb evolved from a modernist village of the 1930s to a large-scale architectonic sculptural ensemble in the landscape, to be perceived in speed from a moving vehicle or from the railroad tracks. It would additionally contribute to the overall project of closing the gaps between income groups and social classes by creating living solutions based on the average person's living standards and its attending lifestyle techniques, affordable to all. These standards, based on universal values of democracy and equality, reflected a sophisticated level of the rationalization of life. It included, by design, the optimal planning for the nuclear family of two children, with two working adults, with a 'garden city' surrounding the estates and with necessary commerce in the vicinities and transportation access to the workplace in the city or in nearby industry complexes.

Inside the homes, kitchens and bathrooms were designed based on extensive user studies on the best ways to store and prepare food, at least according to the technology and cultural norms of the time. The first beneficiaries of these new estates were young working-class families who lived in cramped inner-city apartments that had become unsuitable for living and would soon be demolished. Other tenants included those migrating from the countryside who would take up industrial jobs in or near the city. A third group, much smaller at this time, included the immigrant workforce, who, at the time, was viewed from an economic class perspective, rather than the ethnical background perspective. With easy credit and large offer of units, many families moved into these new estates even before they were completed.

51 Mattson, *Swedish Modernism*, p. 67.

52 Manfredo Tafuri stirred up controversy by criticising modern architecture's alliance with capitalism. See also Manfredo Tafuri and Francesco Co, *Modern Architecture*, New York: H. N. Abrams, 1979, and Manfredo Tafuri, *Architecture and Utopia: Design and Capitalist Development*. Cambridge, Mass.: MIT Press, 1976.

53 *1930/80 ARKITEKTUR-FORM-KONST*, Kulturhuset, Stockholm, Sweden, 6 May–24 October 1980, p. 43.

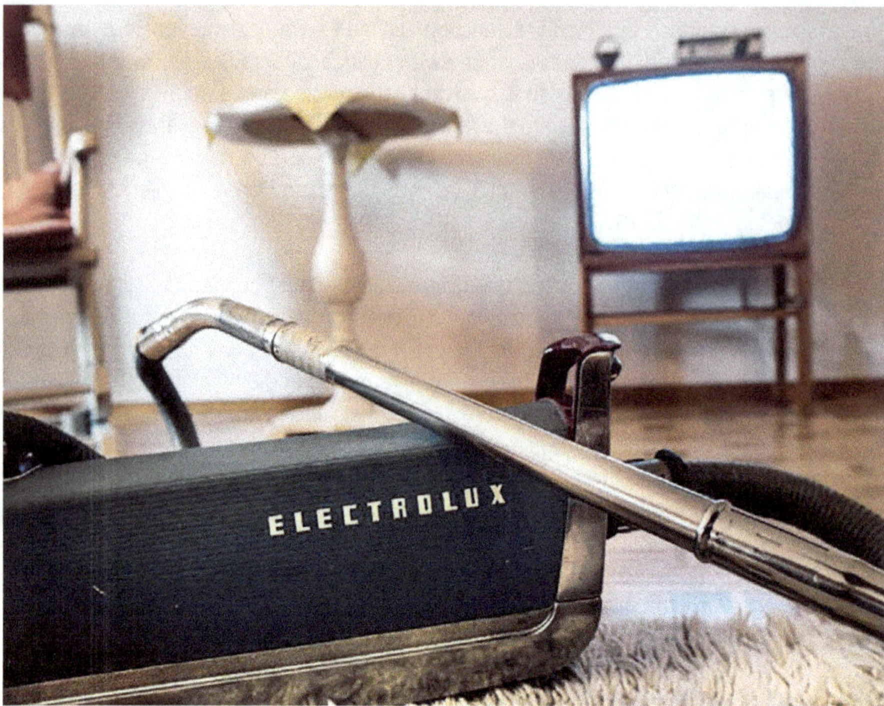


*Figure 25 – The interior of a miljonprogram apartment, preserved with household appliances and decoration from 1969 at Tensta Museum, northern Stockholm. Source: Stadsmuseet,* ***https://stadsmuseet.stockholm.se/****.*

As with the *folkhemmet* project in the 1930s which caused a largely rural population to flock to cities and suburban centers under the banner of modernist efficiency and rationalization of space and life, *miljonprogrammet* also had a philosophical dimension. Moreover, many engineering and financial breakthroughs were needed to make this happen. Ready cash, cheap loans and a thriving national industrial sector made possible quick construction at a reasonable quality standard. Like a war effort, industry needed to mobilize quickly within the ten-year timeframe between 1964 and 1975 to build one million homes. Empty terrains were more favorable because they required less time of preparation, and construction would occur at an even faster pace. Within this period, one-fourth of the Swedish built landscape had been transformed by housing blocks of pre-cast concrete, and a massive migration from countryside to city, and from city centre to suburb ensued. Subway lines and fast trains connected residential areas to the workplace. Basic amenities were located close to home, and jobs were created in these new areas. It was even intended that some of the areas would become autonomous, independent townships that could evolve into cities over time, as embryos of satellite cities.

## The Morphology of the Satellite City

A satellite city is a concept in urban planning that refers to smaller, self-contained metropolitan areas located near to a town or city. They are built to house and employ those who would otherwise not be able to afford living in the city center and who are usually dependent on the parent city for major services. The definition of a satellite city may also vary according to the image of the city in the mind of the reader and may easily be confounded with the notion of suburb since a satellite city is usually located between the city and the countryside. Whereas a suburb for an American signifies a wealthy area in relation to an impoverished downtown, for a Brazilian a suburb is conversely a poor area in relation to a wealthy downtown. In its European form, the suburb may, in fact, be both a poor or a wealthy area, but the founding idea of suburbs in Europe comes from the city in the industrial era where it was necessary to locate the working-class closer to workplaces, whether factories or offices. Already in the 1920s, Le Corbusier created *The Contemporary City* where he envisioned satellite cities built for the working class, away from the central core (which he wanted to raze to the ground) and living in dwellings much more modest than those of their elite counterparts in the city centers. This idea of a city with different areas separated by class was later substituted by the plans for *The Radiant City*, where the city would be organized according to function and not social class. Whereas the *Radiant City* was never built in Europe, it has been very influential in the design of 'modernist' cities since, with as many praises as criticism.[54]

In Stockholm, satellite cities were grown out of a need to settle the outskirts of a city at a particular density that neither characterized it as a neighborhood (which many suburbs are prone to be) and neither as an autonomous city. They are designed as self-contained, multi-functional clusters of housing, commerce, and public services that are connected to the city and to other satellite cities by direct subway line. Stockholm is a city that grew from the edges: one satellite city was built at the end of each subway line, and smaller city-suburbs grew over time around the stations along the subway lines. Instead of relying on the modernist suburb for defining democracy, Hasselberg rather states that it is the subway lines radiating from center and connecting the suburbs like a 'pearl necklace' that became the largest democratic project of the time, because 'speed helped create the city'.[55] The modern towers were not only the ideal solution to the problem of housing provision, but also as the vehicle of modern life.

By no means is this a uniquely Swedish phenomenon. The basis of modernity and its ideology of universal democracy were inspiring the design of satellite cities, suburbs and monumental housing schemes all over the world. The integration of transportation modes with cutting highways through city centers and digging tunnels for the expansion of subway lines was reconfiguring the urban landscape at full speed. Brasília and the *superquadras* inaugurated in 1960 (but as a result of the 1950s design) would largely determine the adequate proportions for the use of space and time in the modernist ideology and would be perceived as monolithic blocks from the wide axial roads of this planned city, mainly reachable by car.

---

54 Henri Lefebvre was one of the main critics of Le Corbusier's ideas, see Chapter 2. See Lefebvre, *The Urban Revolution*.

55 'Interview with Per Hasselberg'. See also Virilio, *Speed and Politics*.

Also, the Parisian suburbs of the 1950s and 1960s known as *Grands Ensembles*, equally square, mono-functional and surrounded by open spaces, are the first view foreign visitors get from Paris as they arrive from the airports.

Updating the ideology of sheer functionality of modernism meant revisiting the capacity of mass construction at a reasonable cost with unique details only possible through standardized mass production. Here, the monumental scale of the constructions as sculptural elements in the landscape provided the opportunity for volumetric exercises in spaces of large dimensions, with larger densities than the *folkhem*'s smaller scale. The proposed alternatives embraced the possibility of creating complete design systems that encompassed the architecture of the buildings, its social spaces, urban furniture, lighting schemes and each area having unique characteristics. This can be seen from curving façades, large systems of identical blocks over an area, 'Venetian' pedestrian bridges/viaducts connecting parts of neighborhoods above motorways, and the commissioning of site-specific artworks that would function as aesthetic landmarks within the grand scheme of a particular region. These suburbs from the 1970s would never attain the level of historical citation and ornamentation than French counterparts at the *grands ensembles* at the time, and the 1980s in Sweden would see a halt in social housing. It seems like the *miljonprogrammet* would be the last housing overhaul in the span of one generation, moving the debate from building a modern society to renovating older constructions with a highly mediatized debate about the historical value of these constructions based on an assumption that these projects have failed to address the social ills they tried to avoid by design. Until today, there has not been a unified replacement movement of social housing in the same scale, but rather fragmented initiatives by private realtors to gentrify areas and increase density in existing neighborhoods, with the new generation of technologies with smart homes and the Internet of Things. As with the *folkhemmet* project, *miljonprogrammet* also had a philosophical dimension, and the ambition to create a 'good democratic citizen' persisted. In the hopes of the government, this would signify the ultimate expression of the socialist welfare ideology which would eventually be crystallized into a contemporary version of the 'The Swedish Model'.

Unlike Brasília and the Parisian *grand ensemble* suburbs which are monuments to modernism, *miljonprogrammet* was the next generation at the cusp of modernism and postmodernism in the late 1960s and 1970s. I choose to mark this transition by the implosion of the Pruitt-Igoe complex in St. Louis, USA, in 1972, a social housing complex built by Japanese architect Minoru Yamasaki in 1956.[56] Pruitt-Igoe was built in the mid-1950s to put a stop to the slummification and overcrowding process of St. Louis and offer high-density areas and better living standards for the poor people of the city as a process of 'urban renewal'. Within a few years of completion, the complex had become internationally famous for crime, poverty and segregation and became a symbol for the failure of public policy and urban

56 Ironically, this is the same architect of the World Trade Center in New York City, another complex of buildings that went to the ground through an implosion. While Pruitt-Igoe crumbled from the inside through its almost instant decay after construction, the WTC would crumble from the inside when hijacked airplanes crashed into its façades on 11 September 2001. Has this architect built anything that is still standing, one may wonder?

planning. American architect and urban theorist Oscar Newman, a thinker of sociophysical aspects of community building, claims that the buildings were so large and the areas so wide that 'when the number of residents per public space rose above a certain level, none would identify with these 'no man's land[s]' – places where it was 'impossible to feel ... to tell resident from intruder'.[57]

## Other People in the 'People's Home': Architecture and Hospitality

Many theorists and commentators point to a double genealogy of the *miljonprogrammet* from the outset: as both the most modern and desirable technique for living, and socially and economically segregative – hospitable in theory, inhospitable in practice. Decades later and still caught in the double bind of its myth of origin: with all the best intentions behind such a revolutionary project, how could it have failed so miserably? The debatability of its failure came to rest upon the definition of the *miljonprogram* as a social and economic separation from the rest of society, especially when demographically these areas came to become increasingly identified with immigration. Is it a programmatic, political, or aesthetic failure? Or, as Sagal Hussein reveals to us in her search for understanding her hometown of Hjällbo, is the *miljonprogram* a failure, and if so for whom? Even though Sweden is known for its generous immigration policies, social and economic segregation is a fact of contemporary Swedish urban life.

Who were these housing estates aimed at first? In the late 1960s and 1970s, the first occupants were the working class, those tired of living in the cramped city center, those who needed to move closer to their factory jobs, and those only able to afford to buy apartments there. With easy credit, many Swedes eventually moved out and those with weak financial resources, often from rural, immigrant or socially excluded backgrounds, moved in. 'Every summer we would realize that one more family had moved out, and we never knew where they had moved to or why', says Ozman Gül, 38 years, born and raised in Fittja in an interview for this book. Into the 1980s, however, the suburb became increasingly 'different' from the rest of society, no longer as peaceful havens of upward social mobility for the white working class, but as synonymous with a 'white flight'. With increased immigration, an economic crisis and growing racism in the 1990s,[58] suburbs began to be associated with everything negative – crime, drug abuse, ethnic conflicts, isolation, segregation and social alienation. This is when the press helped create the image of the 'violent' suburb which has stigmatized the satellite cities up to now, as opposed to the 'safe' and controllable areas of the inner cities. It is as if the monotypical architecture, large-scale buildings and barren outdoor environment, often mentioned as typical features that make the areas unattractive, make them by default naturally prone to marginalization. The suburbs eventually have become zones of exception, and, more recently, zones of exclusion.

---

57 Oscar Newman, *Creating Defensible Space*, Collingdale: DIANE Publishing, 1972, p. 11.

58 The mid-90s saw a rise in neo-nazi movements and race 'riots' in central Stockholm and Gothenburg reaching a peak in 1993.

Several mass media representations of life in large cities and their inhabitant's less affluent suburban areas are linked to an image where the poor and excluded are regarded as, in some sense, abnormal. The main reason for their existence in the fringes of society is blamed on the communities themselves for their own lack of commitment, capabilities or knowledge to transcend their own condition. We can also read between the lines of the public debate in newspaper articles, media articles and in informal conversations, the undertones of a typically conservative Western dialectic discourse between civilization and barbarism, normality and abnormality, pretty versus ugly, culture versus nature, us and them. Between the polarities, the power structures underlying these arguments are clear, where the second term is subsumed by the first. This dialectic distancing only serves to uncover what Flusser had so cleverly exposed: that the concept of the migrant is not the opposite to the concept of the host, but its distorted mirror image, or better, the host pushes the migrant to the opposite pole in order to distance herself from having to confront the fact that it is the migrant that allows her to be the host.[59] This is a system of mutual dependency that defines both poles, but that doesn't solve the riddle of coexistence between these two poles. If the migrant is viewed as a constituent part of the host, then there would no longer be the need for this distinction.

If we look closely at the dominant representation of the suburb in Sweden, or in any European country for that matter, we begin to see that much of the negative and prejudiced image comes from early depictions of city life from as far back as the late 1800s. 'The dangerous underclass' and 'slummification' of the developing urban metropolis is a common way of addressing those fringe areas which have escaped, or have been purposefully left out of, the master plan of major cities. The 'slum' was the cause of a series of social phenomena, the origin of crime, alcoholism, prostitution, the degeneration of the people, lack of hygiene, general disorderliness, and political instability. In short, the slum is the representation of chaos. If unconfined, these ills would spread to other parts of the city. Under this reading, the typical slum dweller, as a subject, was the symbol of the lowest in a society, and by consequence one who can potentially become the perpetrator of social disorder. The slum environment determines a certain type of 'othered' behavior which the slum dweller may not be able to overcome. Moreover, the designation of the slum as a 'jungle' has a clear colonialist undertone. Because the slum is typically inhabited by subjects who are not from dominant society, and in our specific case, foreigners coming from countries that have been decolonized, the 'barbaric' and dangerous metaphor finds echo in the 'otherness' embodied in the African migrant, the Middle Eastern refugee, and the Latin American exile, for example. Unfortunately, this colonist's 'gaze' is also existent in postcolonial societies and is by no means exclusive of Europe as a remnant of its once world dominance. And where the question is not of racial hegemony alone, it is one of class.

These othered urban areas, teeming with foreignness, are usually considered to be less developed than the main city, and therefore need to be educated, redesigned and disciplined in order to reach the same level as the 'civilized' part of the city. In short, the discourse is that the suburb needs to be 'normalized'. The jungle metaphor is equally used in the media as a

59 Flusser, 'Making a home out of homelessness', p. 125.

place far away from the safe, ordered and civilized world, and paradoxically this very image of disorder is what establishes the advanced status of the center in relationship to the peripheries. It can be said that the media language, as well as the logic of representation, used in the description of these 'disorderly' urban areas are identical to colonial descriptions of faraway places. In practice, journalists make expeditions to these areas as a form of colonial journey where, after a few hours, they return to their downtown desks and write narratives about sad concrete blocks, heartless shopping malls, alienation, poverty and crime or else exotic food stores, ethnic dances, football and gang violence.

In 'The Spectacle of Others', Stuart Hall looked closely at precisely such Othering and its functioning. He proposed that the construction of difference (racial difference first and foremost, by extension any other representation of Other as well) is governed by 'the set of representational practices known as stereotyping'. It leads to effects like essentializing, reduction and naturalizing.[60] Othering is related to type-ing as simplification and reduction of real phenomena – it helps grasp and construe the world – as well as stereotyping as difference's simplification and affixing, deeply rooted in power relations, in such a way that 'the racialized discourse is structured as a set of binary oppositions'.[61] Suburbs are 'foreign' and 'problematic' while at the same time they represent an opportunity to learn more about the world as a cosmopolitan place where cultures coexist without the intrusion of the dominant culture. This kind of narrative also establishes the center as the prevailing view for what a 'good city' should be and reflects the normative mentality. We know these narratives all too well, as they only serve to confirm existing prejudices. What do the suburbs say about themselves?

*Miljonprogram* estates are now nearing 50 years in completion, and like many similar housing projects in the world need renovation. Are we talking about an architectural renovation or a cultural renovation? What are some of the ways in which we can begin to transform these suburbs and give these concrete 'utopias' a second life? What are ways in which we can embed complexity, flexibility and shifting notions of lifestyle and culture within a bygone modernist housing ideology? How can we work together with the State and realtors to create spaces that residents can call their own? Is a collaboration even possible or desirable?

## The Efficient City

Fittja is one of the few public housing estates in Sweden still under public administration, and a neighborhood that is still entirely composed of rental apartments. Half of its area was privatized one decade ago, and the income from this sale was used to renovate the other half. It is claimed that the state can no longer afford urban renewal. Populations in this neighborhood are highly mobile, making the neighborhood socially very dynamic. Today, many suburbs are occupied by immigrants, along with students and young families – those with the weakest incomes. The adjoining suburbs are slowly being sold to generate revenue for renovations of the rental apartments that remain there. Due to this, populations in this neighborhood are

60 Stuart Hall, 'The Spectacle of the Other', in Stuart Hall (ed.) *Representation: Cultural Representations and Signifying Practices*, London: Sage, 1997, p. 260.

61 Hall, 'The Spectacle of the Other', p. 243.

highly mobile, making it socially very dynamic and internationally diverse. Many say this is also the cause of insecurity in the area as more permanent community relations do not persist under conditions of high mobility.

Municipalities are charged by the government to take care of a certain number of 'prospective citizens', in other words, asylum seekers and refugees newly arrived in the country. As public housing properties become privatized according to neoliberal policies of systematic rationalization, social housing is slowly being eroded of public ownership to private administrators. In practice, this means that those unable to get mortgages to buy their apartments will have very few options of rental or temporary housing in the future. Among those are immigrants, those who have just gained citizenship status, students, the unemployed and others who have little or no credit history in the country. The result is these populations are being pushed further away into the outskirts into less valued areas, away from visibility and in neighborhoods with worse living conditions and with less chance of renewal and investment.

Under the logic of privatization and effectivization of the suburb, these small *centrum* are considered not so profitable. What follows is the relocation of several public services such as schools and health clinics and establishments such as banks and pharmacies to large-scale shopping malls in a central location in the region where the concentration of public and commercial services into massive shopping arenas erodes a neighborhood's local economy and makes the accessibility of basic services more difficult. Relocating services is backed up by decisions to build shopping mall concepts with aggregated services in more central locations, making neighborhoods less autonomous. This way, Stockholm not only becomes further divided between higher income residents in the center of the city and lower and temporary income holders in the outskirts, but there also occurs a segregation of services and diminishing local economies, which serves to further disaggregate local communities. In a 'neighbor hour' meeting in Husby, a suburb north of Stockholm, residents complained that the preschool and the pharmacy had moved to adjoining neighborhoods one or two subway stops away, adding the pressure of a commute for parents, and diminishing children's mobility and safety in the city-small details that make a difference in everyday life.

> After the Right came into power in 2006, suburbs like Husby were set aside and forgotten. Local administrative services were moved to other neighborhoods, which further fueled frustrations. Many Swedes are victims of where they live. They are trapped in their suburbs, without much hope of being able to leave one day.[62]

As a result, diminishing jobs in the local economies, rising unemployment and the social effect of dwindling social support structures result in fragmented social relations. For example, by relocating schools farther away from where the child lives, the social life the school provides for children and families becomes less tightly knit. With less movement in the neighborhood, the business opportunities decrease as well. This condition of increased local poverty and

62 Olivier Truc, 'Sweden Pays the High Price of Segregation', *Le Monde*, 3 June 2013, https://worldcrunch.com/culture-society/sweden-pays-the-price-of-segregation.

service precarity reflects negatively on the immigrants themselves who become stigmatized by an image of decaying neighborhoods and disappearing local economies. Zygmunt Bauman believes that what creates this sense of insecurity is the vulnerability to these unpredictable market forces. Political power does not need to make the social effects of the market any worse. The state builds its power by taking care of a certain level of uncertainty. This is done in order to limit the damage done by the forces that it, the State, cannot control, and at the same time minimize the risks of the free market, providing certain 'inalienable' rights based on citizenship, etc.[63]

This kind of legitimation expresses itself in the modern management definition of *état providence,* a kind of unity that takes up, through its administration and leadership, duties and obligations which before were in the divine powers 'to protect the believers against radical changes, to help them in the case of personal accident, and to relieve them in their sorrows and worries.' And yet, it seems like the State's 'protective' powers are directed towards containing certain 'target groups', certain minorities, whose unemployment and dwindling welfare become precedents for potential criminality. If unemployment and job insecurity was one side-effect of capitalism and the struggle of worker's movements and unions, today's unemployment leaves one vulnerable to risk destiny at the hand of unpredictable market forces. Failing to overcome market uncertainties leads one to the next stage of exclusion where one is more prone to be suspected of criminal activity. Insecurity becomes the breeding ground of potential criminality. The state then is left to take care of the collateral damage, ignorance, and insecurity of the free market logic (or lack thereof), sort of like 'cleaning up the mess', which entails more investment in police forces, and less investment in citizen services. How did things become this way in a country famous for being one of the most egalitarian and developed societies in the world?

Under the previous conservative government (1996–2010) the relationship between social welfare and individual investment has shifted considerably from social democracy's golden age under Olof Palme in the 1970s towards neo-liberalism. The current rhetorical focus is divested from social welfare and invested on the individuals' economic autonomy through the means of free enterprise and competition, where one is free to choose one's support structure from a variety of choices available. The focus shifts from universal social welfare to conditional welfare by means of privatization through the rhetorics of overvaluing the role of the individual and by placing value on private ownership. As the grassroots activists from the organization *Megafonen*[64] exclaimed in 2013 in a protest against privatization in Alby, a southern Stockholm suburb, 'Thirty to fourty years ago, the state could afford to BUILD one million flats in ten years, now it's too poor to even RENOVATE them'.[65]

---

63 Bauman, *Collateral Damage*, p. 84.

64 Megafonen is a grassroots organisation working for social justice founded by young residents in the suburb of Husby in northern Stockholm in 2008, with initiatives and actions around the principles of democracy, welfare, community, work and education. Megafonen, https://www.facebook.com/Megafonenorten/.

65 *Megafonen, Alby är inte till Salu!,* http://megafonen.com/alby-ar-inte-till-salu/.

What sustains a neighborhood structure when public services have moved elsewhere? As Saskia Sassen points out in her description of the global street,[66] one possibility is that residents can 'collectively make neighborhood upgrading – even if they are very selfish and did not intend to do something for the neighborhood, but just for themselves. They open a little store to make a living for their family, but collectively they make a neighborhood economy'.[67] In her view, this very small-scale economy provides the 'making of a collective project (...) as urban capabilities [that] arise out of these processes and interactions'.[68] Another solution is for self-organized groups to create strategies of dialogue-building with the authorities to voice out opinions and work collaboratively in elaborating solutions that benefit the communities. However, none of this occurs always under peaceful conditions. For the small shop-owner to avoid being exploited for higher rents, and for the urban movements to be able to implement the changes they require, it requires an everyday struggle.

Preventing urban deterioration and thinking about urban renewal requires, among other factors, a cultural change. A participatory process could lead to bottom-up movements where residents and citizens take ownership of the changes and become responsible for the process of change. An open-source citizenship, a crowd-sourced effort that pools the needs and desires of residents and citizens and their capacity of self-affirmation in confrontation with the structures of local power. This much seems to be obvious in the cultural logic of participatory social media where the micro-politics of certain groups, rather than the macro-politics of the elites, become agents in promoting social change. Experts are drawn in at certain execution stages, but everyone is allowed to participate in the planning. What kind of subjectivity does this emancipatory struggle require? In other words, who are the agents for change?

In the past decade, youth groups made up of first- and second-generation Swedes have begun to self-organize in citizen movements and enabling new networked cultures aiming to create spaces and opportunities to voice out a growing situation of uncertainty among the communities in the suburbs. Megafonen is one such movement started in northern Stockholm in 2008; Pantrarna, or 'The Panthers', in Western Gothenburg, inspired by the American civil rights movement started in 2011 and created networks across several suburbs in Gothenburg, Stockholm, Malmö and other cities. Megafonen and Pantrarna have begun to delineate new political strategies and increase media visibility to local struggles. On their website, under Megafonen's slogan 'a united suburb can never be conquered',[69] their mission statement reads,

66 A concept Sassen uses to describe different urban and social movements. 'When I bring in the global street I am trying to capture a space that really takes many different forms and shapes, from Occupy movements and Tahrir Square to urban agriculture and squatting buildings to make a cultural center.' Nick Holdstock, ''Artisans for incorporation' – An interview with Saskia Sassen', *Citizenship in Southeast Europe*, 17 December 2012, http://citsee.eu/interview/%E2%80%98artisans-incorporation%E2%80%99-interview-saskia-sassen.

67 Holdstock, ' 'Artisans for incorporation' – An interview with Saskia Sassen'.

68 Holdstock, ' 'Artisans for incorporation' – An interview with Saskia Sassen'.

69 *Megafonen*, https://www.facebook.com/Megafonenorten/.

> Getting organized is the most effective way to influence society. *Megafonen* works for social justice in Sweden. We organize young people in the suburbs to create a society where everyone has equal opportunities and where the people themselves are in charge of public policy, not vice versa.

Many design strategists would call this need of self-organization in marginalized strata of society as 'innovative' and 'creative' but this undermines important movements as ephemeral and short-lived. Instead, social movements are strategies for claiming social justice when the given solutions to those living outside hegemony are oppressive and insufficient. To use our hospitality vocabulary, it is not enough if only the 'guests' do an uprising, and yet things don't change unless there is strong bottom-up mobilization. There also needs to be some willingness from the host community to listen to and fulfill the demands of the minority groups. Saskia Sassen frames this host-guest 'collaboration' by naming those in the host community who build bridges of collaboration as 'artisans of incorporation':

> When I speak of artisans for incorporation I am referring to the fact that any period in the turbulent history of migrations in our diverse countries, there were always some members of the host community who believed in the project of incorporating the outsider. This was not just for charity but mostly to make membership more expansive. And whenever the outsiders were included, the host community benefited (...) I argue that you *add* to the notion of membership when you support incorporation of the outsider. But note that the outsider here is not just any outsider, but one who has already participated in the rituals and the practices of the daily life of a society. Allowing them in is not a zero sum (...) but a mechanism that expands the rights of everyone.[70]

I have previously discussed the necessity for a vocabulary that gives the 'expelled' a proper name as it includes the expeller in the same equation. I had mentioned about the terms of engagement of guests into host societies but had failed to address at that point the notion of 'membership', that is, the terms through which one becomes a part of something. Then, Sassen uses the expression 'artisans of incorporation' which signals a productive relationship between the hosts and guests. First, it is interesting that she uses the word incorporation instead of integration. To incorporate is to embody. To incorporate means to take in, in a more fundamental level than just 'inviting' or giving the permission to pass through, as Kant would advocate the 'right of temporary sojourn'. It involves a fundamental change in form and not just in content, and not just of temporality: a sort of anthropophagy where the hosts and guests 'devours' each other, not to eliminate her, but to extract her better qualities as nourishment for the new body (another body) to come and add new qualities to the existing *corpus*, and therefore change it at its core.

When we talk about the guest-host relationship, I have kept this distinction fairly dialectic in terms of personae (the guest and then the host) and also in spatial terms (the center and the periphery) when we have identified the thresholds that are crossed by the guest into the space of the host, and the obligations of the host not to harm the space of the guest,

70 Holdstock, ' 'Artisans for incorporation' – An interview with Saskia Sassen'.

for instance. We have seen that the guest and the host are separate bodies which meet in a specific space that regulates their relationship reciprocally, or, in the examples of segregated satellite cities, we have seen how the bodies of guests are instead kept at bay from the hosts in a relationship of inequality and subordination. When we speak of an in*corpo*ration, we are no longer dealing with separate bodies, but rather with the potential (and also willingness, even desire) of separate bodies capable of merging together so that new entities can be created: a new body that is neither same or Other but is just *another.*

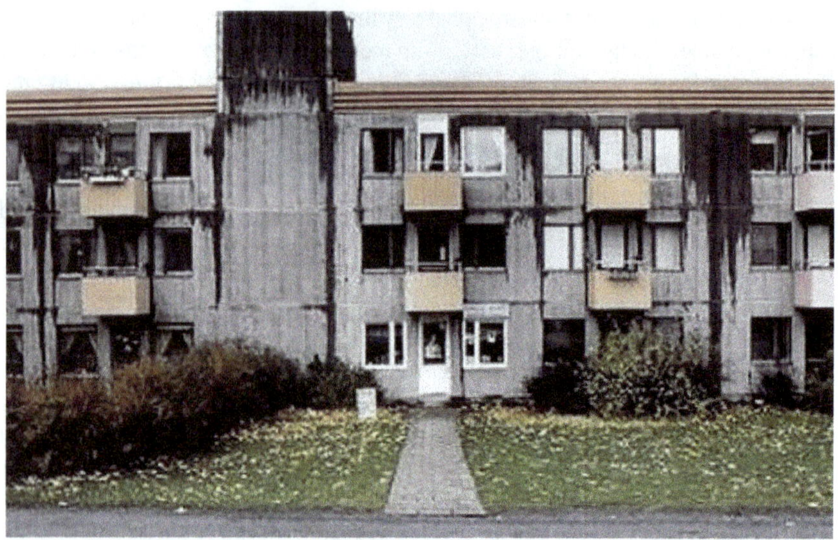

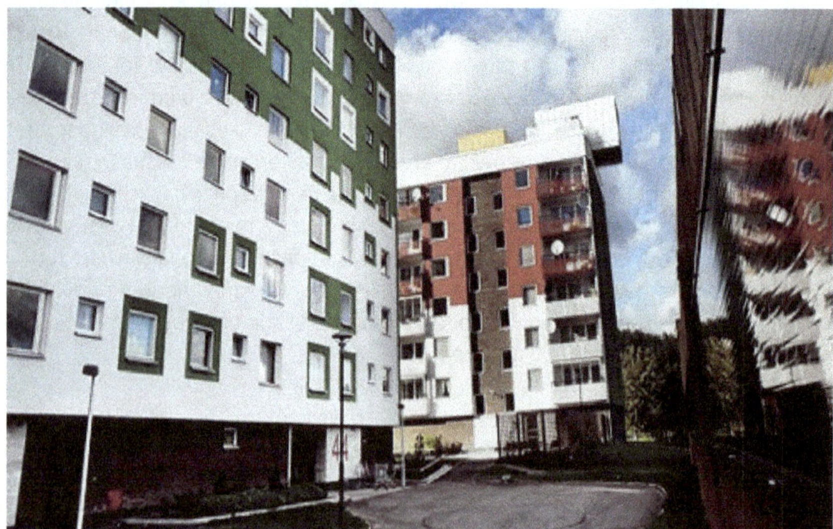

*Figures 26a and b – From decaying concrete Brutalism in 2001, to gentrified 'multi-colorism' in 2015-urban renewal programs in Stockholm today, before and after (Husby, northern Stockholm).*

# CHAPTER 4: SATELLITE CITY: ART AND HOSPITALITY

# CHAPTER 4: SATELLITE CITY: ART AND HOSPITALITY

> There is a voodoo character in every image. The image has a purpose to orient people from outside in the world in which they are thrown. An image is a possibility for me to step out of the world and see it from outside. They are sorts of maps, they are mediations, they mean the world. And by meaning the world, they also hide it. This is an inner dialectic for every mediation. *(...)* Images are meant for people to orient themselves in the world. But when they become very strong, they use their experience of the world to orient themselves in the image. The image becomes the concrete reality, and the world is only a pretext.
>
> – Vilém Flusser[1]

According to Franco 'Bifo' Berardi, Europe is lamenting the loss of its centrality in terms of world power, where the problem may not be necessarily one of nostalgia for the past or its decline in the world stage, but an exhaustion of its models. This exhaustion may not be all negative – it may, in turn, be an opportunity to consider new points of view.[2] In addition, instead of fixating on identification and culture, two European obsessions, Berardi's suggestion is that perhaps a post-identitarian aspect of Europe could lead to thinking of new modes of aggregation, of 'being together', if we are able to engage in processes of de-crystallizing certain life processes, to use his biological metaphors. But what is meant by 'life processes'?

At a media arts conference in 2011, Franco Berardi's lecture 'Life at Work' begins by asking 'what is life?' in an attempt to situate his thoughts and strategies for overcoming current digital, financial and political realities at the wake of the protests in the Middle East and the crisis in Greece and Italy.[3] He responds to this question in two directions. First, 'life' is defined as a machine and a crystal, and secondly, 'life' as resulting from a cycle of disruptions that

1 *We Shall Survive in the Memory of Others, featuring Vilém Flusser*. (dir. Center for Culture and Communication Foundation, Budapest in cooperation with the Vilém Flusser Archiv Universität der Künste Berlin, 2011).

2 Franco Berardi, 'Life at Work', *Transmediale 2011*, Berlin, 30 January–2 February 2011.

3 In early 2011, the world had just seen the uprisings in Tahrir Square, in Egypt and the recession hitting an all-time low in Mediterranean Europe, Spain, Italy, Portugal and Greece adopting austerity packages at the same time when nationalistic movements begin to garner more and more popular support in Nothern Europe. Three years into the financial recession, when this chapter was taking shape, there had begun a consensus that the crisis was no longer temporary but would have lasting effects in increasing the levels of poverty in Europe. Later in 2012, the United States would also join the discontentment in the form of Occupy movements by denouncing the growing class and economic inequality and taking to the streets with new forms of political debate. The 2014 Euromaidan protest movement in Ukraine tried to rekindle European solidarity, and Hong Kong's umbrella movement showed way to challenge even a truly oppressive state. The Anonymous movement and other forms of protest, and their attendant aesthetics, also took sway of public debate. In the culture and art world, the debates about the neo-liberalization of the public sphere and other topics were generating a lot of new thining and knowledge about these issues. By 2020, when this text has been concluded, the situation in Europe has become further aggravated with the healthcare crisis provoked by covid-19, and poverty is growing.

yield the creation of new forms. He uses the term 'crystallization' as an image, and refers to Schrödinger's ideas about life having the structure of an aperiodic crystal, stable and clearly defined, – a crystal as the 'the germ of a solid'. He mentions several processes of crystallizations of life today such as debt-based economy ('the future transformed into a crystal of debt'), capitalism as a crystallization of economic processes, digital absorption of affective life as a crystallization process and so forth. Given these examples, he claims that the riots and uprisings in Egypt,[4] for example, are attempts to return to life processes that have become too crystallized.

Can we de-crystallize? If so, how? Is there a method we can follow? He suggests taking control of the human will on social reality, on the possibility of producing form according to our intentions. On the contrary, reality is based on functionality and automatism, which, he claims, is of crystal constitution. Politics as the ability of shaping reality within a finality is over, he claims. In a crystallized world, the construction of further automatism is what remains – and perhaps this is what he thinks of Europe and its exhausted models. If we look at the morphogenesis of the crystal, we find that it was formed from the beginning by a disruption, the second given definition of 'life.' After a disruption, new life forms begin to enter the process of crystallization anew, this time different from before. He concludes that the problem today is not in inventing new forms per se, but the challenge lies in how to de-crystallize current realities, digital, financial, political, so that new forms may *emerge* from this phenomenon.

This image from mineral forms could be used to describe different cultural processes as well. If within the discourse of multiculturalism difference is considered as the 'absolute other', it relies upon an understanding of 'difference' that sees racial and ethnic identities as fixed, historical, and discrete categories as preexisting crystallizations from other territories and other historical conjectures. What happens when these are displaced? A de-crystallization, or disruption, of this understanding of difference would instead help to articulate how identifications can shift and bind subjects together provisionally so that they may work towards shared projects which could become the basis for new modes of aggregations.

## Uncanny Textures: Migration, Culture and the City

In reference to the French context, in 'Postcolonial Hospitality' theorist Mireille Rosello, who works with concepts such as *border aesthetics*[5], where 'borders become meaningful through

4 At the time of the lecture in 2011, the riots in Cairo had just happened and had become a topic of discussion during the conference.

5 'The contemporary geopolitical context to the border aesthetics field, and its focus on cultural encounters, has removed it from the Kantian division between aesthetics and politics in line with Rancière's concept of 'political aesthetics' (2004). This form of *aisthesis* focuses on the central role the senses have in our political systems, as well as the specific forms of political *aisthesis* in art. Rancière defined politics as the *partage du sensible*, the 'division/sharing of that which can be sensed' through which people can be made visible as political subjects and given an (audible) voice with which to share their concerns. The *partage* can also make people invisible and inaudible, or visible in non-empowering ways. Recent work in border aesthetics has developed on the notion of 'in/visibility' (Brambilla, Pötzsch 2017), especially of migrants, inspired by Arendt's political thought. Read in terms of border aesthetics, Rancière's definition in itself designates a bordering process, since the *partage du sensible* is activity

sensory perception, and can only be legible, understandable via forms of aesthetic sensitivity',[6] notes that a new cultural phenomenon seems to have altered the course of the politicization of immigration issues such as the involvement of cultural agents, intellectuals, philosophers, artists, architects, and social scientists who are taking 'strong and visible positions, using the media's willingness to relay their voices as a way of intervening in the [immigration] debate'.[7] The same could be said of the current Swedish media and cultural context in the past decade, when articles on various aspects of immigration are written about on a daily basis, where, for instance, new cultural institutions are established in the suburbs, some of them traditionally immigrant areas, which offset them from more central and conventional arts institutions that cater to a mainstream audience.[8]

On the other hand, grassroots cultural movements have been gaining strength in the peripheries of the larger cities in the country thus addressing the deficit in democratic participation and representation of these 'new' groups in society. The use of the word 'new' here can be seen as an alternative to the word 'Other'. Perhaps it is within these 'new' groups where Berardi's new modes of aggregation can be possible. Yet how are these aggregations being formed in practice?

To establish arts institutions in the peripheries of large cities by definition involves programmatic considerations as well as a discussion on how relevant and how integrated the institution is to the community around it, notwithstanding the consideration of what culture means in low-income areas defined by social, economic and cultural segregation. Paradoxically, cultural institutions operating in border situations also acquire a more experimental nature, and as such contribute to notions of border aesthetics and poetics, that is, an aesthetics that brings border situations into the régime of the sensible and of the visible.

---

of dividing – and in the ambivalent fashion of borders, also of sharing. Rancière makes clear that this *partage* is connected to 'style' in the literary and artistic sense. Different aesthetic categories and ways of bordering aesthetic forms will produce different variants of political aesthetics.' *International Lexicon of Aesthetics,* https://lexicon.mimesisjournals.com/international_lexicon_of_aesthetics_item_detail.php?item_id=70.

6 Johan Schimanski and Stephen F. Wolfe (eds) *Border Aesthetics: Concepts and Intersections.* Berghan, 2018, p. 5.

7 Mireille Rosello, *Postcolonial Hospitality: The Immigrant as Guest,* Palo Alto: Stanford University Press, 2002, p. 24.

8 I am referring specifically to art institutions established in the suburbs since the late 1990s, such as Tensta Konsthall in northern Stockholm, Botkyrka Konsthall, and Konsthall C in southern Stockholm, each one located at the end of one of the subway lines, in different kinds of social housing projects and neighborhoods resulting from modernist planning such as the *miljonprogram*, and dealing with the question of the suburb and migration; each one with a different business model (Botkyrka Konsthall is funded by the municipality, Konsthall C with cultural grants and Tensta Konsthall by a mixed model of foundation and cultural grants). All are directed by leading curators in the field and have discursive ambitions beyond the exhibition format, i.e., residencies, publications, debates, seminars. etc. This research has benefitted greatly from Tensta konsthall curator Maria Lind's seminar series about suburban architecture and society at Tensta Konsthall from 2012 to the present, for example; and was executed entirely with the support of Residency Botkyrka, a residency initiative by Botkyrka konsthall. http://www.botkyrkakonsthall.se, http://www.tenstakonsthall.se, http://www.konsthallc.se.

It is interesting to point out the connection between artists and migrants through specific projects, and within specific institutional conditions. One such instance could be local politics and a supposed instrumentalization of culture under a shared project of 'creative economies' which signals a process neo-liberalization of culture. As theorized by Terry Flew ('creative industries') or David Hesmondhalgh ('cultural industries')[9], this neo-liberalization increases revenues in the culture sector and fragments the market into niche audiences, but commodifies artistic and cultural work, increases exploitation of the creative professionals and extorts from them what often amounts to free labor. John Howkins', who first proposed the terms 'creative economies' as a creativity-based model that includes all kinds of creativity, whether expressed in art or innovation and which straddles specific industries, has more recently written on the 'invisible work' where work is moving from observable public spheres into the private and unseen and how we may approach the changing notions of labor and power as a 'creative class'.[10] Other definitions are Martha Rosler's 'taste class' or 'culture class', understood as large social groups differentiated by their choices of products and lifestyles, expressed in a critical description of 'the creative class' as a 'motley group of self-actualizing people who are mostly university-based and float free of the demands of social codes of dress and behavior, pleasing only themselves'.[11]

I refer here to Richard Florida's term 'creative class' to denote artists like myself, architects, writers and researchers, and technology innovators, who have done artistic and cultural as part of Botkyrka municipality's strategy for innovation and culture, where the project *Satellitstaden*, which will be described in detail in this chapter is inscribed: 'The [Botkyrka] municipality is most known as one of the main spots in Sweden for international migration and also as one of the creative clusters in the Stockholm region with the greatest arena for new circus, film making and creative entrepeneurship'. According to Nima Sanandaji, 'Florida's theories have become rather popular in Sweden, the country which tops the list of his creativity index. (...) In Sweden, Florida's ideas have been used by those who wish to argue that public funding of cultural events, rather than a competitive business climate, is the way to achieve economic growth'.[12] Some of these creative clusters includes a contemporary art institution, Botkyrka konsthall, with a program that includes art, art publications and art education, and an international artist's residency, Residency Botkyrka, I collaborated with between 2010 until 2012.

---

9 Terry Flew, *The Creative Industries*, Sage, 2011; and David Hesmondhalgh, *The Cultural Industries,* 4th ed, Sage, 2018.

10 John Howkins, *The creative economy: How people make money from ideas*. Penguin Books, 2001; *Invisible Work: The Hidden Ingredient of True Creativity, Purpose and Power.* September Publishing, 2020.

11 Martha Rosler, 'Culture Class: Art, Creativity, Urbanism, Part I', *e-flux*, 21, https://www.e-flux.com/journal/21/67676/culture-class-art-creativity-urbanism-part-i/.

12 Nima Sanandaji, 'Influence of 'creative class' ideas in Sweden', *New Geography*, 11 November 2008, https://www.newgeography.com/content/00389-influence-creative-class-ideas-sweden. See also Richard Florida, *Cities and the Creative Class*. Routledge, 2004; and *Sweden in the Creative Age*. Irene Tinagli, Richard Florida, Patrik Ström, Evelina Wahlqvist (eds) School of Business, Economics and Law, Göteborg University & Creativitygroupeurope, June 2007. Available at: http://www.creativeclass.com/rfcgdb/articles/Sweden%20in%20the%20Creative%20Age.pdf

The shape of the city and globalization processes become very important in forming the basis for these new aggregations in the sense that cosmopolitan urban space offers a critical site for the formation of new and divergent subjectivities. As Homi K. Bhabha notes, 'It is to the city that the migrants, the minorities, the diasporic come to change the history of the nation... (...) in the West, and increasingly elsewhere, it is the city which provides the space in which emergent identifications and new social movements of the people are played out.'[13] Similarly, Sassen claims that a global civil society is being shaped at the grassroots level by the daily conditions that link people's lives in cities, in the 'micro-spaces of daily life'.[14] In an urban environment of dissent and coalition, in the rioting masses of Tahrir Square, or the burning cars in Stockholm suburbs,[15] street-level politics make possible the formation of 'new types of political subjects' that do not necessarily have to go through the formal political system'.[16]

If we consider that European suburbs are often identified by the media, and also the authorities, as segregated zones,[17] this image then becomes the crystallization of *difference* as the absolute Other in the public imagination. In my view, in Sweden the suburb may stand for the possible cosmopolitan space that overlaps its status as a zone of segregation, but it fails to be perceived as such both in the public eye and in the urban imaginary. When inhabited by a heterogeneous group of immigrants, refugees and asylum seekers, this cosmopolitan space marks the most intense points of transnational collisions of culture and demography at a local level resulting from changes in global politics. In turn, these locally generated movements begin to affect global politics and even influence the paths of transnational capital. Here it becomes important to redefine what 'cosmopolitan' means.

Contrary to public perception and opposed to the crystallizing processes of the status of immigrants as 'historical objects' within a national narrative, but rather as *products* resulting from specific cultures instead of *producers* of alterity, Bhabha suggests that we focus on the fault lines, border situations, and thresholds as the sites where various identities are performed and contested. The suburb in the European context may be such a fault line, where a process of de-crystallization of fixed notions may occur. I have chosen a specific fault-line inside the suburb with which to work, where several forces converge: the force of urban planning, the reality of social housing, media and information, and culture.

What I refer to as new types of political subjects in the context of this chapter are constituted by the 'new' citizens in Sweden where a growing foreign-born population is increasing as a

---

13 Bhabha, *The Location of Culture*. London: Routledge, 1994, p. 169.

14 Sassen, *Cities in a World Economy*. 3rd edition, London: Sage, 2006, p. 72.

15 In late June 2013, the killing of an old man by the police in the suburb of Husby, in northern Stockholm, provoked riots and burning cars in several suburbs of the city. The movement was led by youth groups like *Megafonen* against police brutality.

16 Sassen, *Cities in a World Economy*, p. 76–78.

17 As we have seen in previous chapters, 'European' suburbs refer to a particular kind of suburban area that results from a planned building effort and conforms to a particular kind of state-subsidized housing areas. These are different than American suburbs that were built for private ownsership, or suburban areas in South American or Asian mega-cities that are combinations of planned and unplanned extensions of the city as a result of urban sprawl. (Author's definition.)

result of migration policies that are changing the demographic constitution of a 'national' Swedish society and challenging some of its most fundamental social, legal, political, religious, and urban structures as we have seen in Chapter 3. In the case of Swedish urban movements, these 'new types of political subjects' are formed by confronting formal political structures at the root and claiming legitimacy in terms of political representation, often in confrontation with political and market forces. Here we see a distinction between the notions of local, national and global. Whereas one could think of a structure where the local is embedded within the national, and the national within the global, one containing the other, in reality this is not so. As a result from the field research, it became clear that the local and the global are more closely aligned to each other establishing a formation we can call the 'transnational', but not without contradictions, as Sassen points out:

> Global capital and immigrants are two major instances of transnationalised actors that have cross-border unifying properties internally and find themselves in conflict with each other inside global cities. The leading sectors of corporate capital are now global in their organisation and operations. And many of the disadvantaged workers in global cities are women, immigrants, people of color – men and women whose sense of membership is not necessarily adequately captured in terms of the national, and indeed often evince cross-border solidarities around issues of substance.[18]

These 'new types of political subjects,' I argue, are being shaped by identifications that cut across the axes of inherited ethnic, cultural and crystallized social identities, and are seen not as a means at tracing back origins, but rather as a means of looking forward. These may come closer to Berardi's idea of a post-identitarian situation making new social and political aggregations – and media textures, saturated in a specific way[19] – possible. To turn this image from *segregation* to *aggregation*, I contend that different forms of shared projects are able to affect how the city is shaped in the future in varying degrees. I have briefly mentioned urban movements as one form of such a shared project. Arts projects, according to Rosello's position, may also give the possibility to engage communities in joint actions and create common experiences and common grounds. This would further enhance the public debate on migration and its collateral issues such as working possibilities, living conditions, and hospitality – the basic requirements to lead a 'good life' and create a sense of home and/or strengthening a feeling of belonging.

This of course, does not mean that art and culture in and of themselves have this task or should become instrumentalized for this function but that these kinds of actions may become important agents within already existing social processes. To put this into a critical light, in her essay 'Culture Class, Part II: Creativity and its Discontents', Martha Rosler cites George Yúdice's consideration of a broad issue of 'culturalization' of politics and the uses and counter-uses of culture, where his concern is with explicating how culture has been transformed into a public resource, available to both governmental entities and to population groups. He cites Fredric Jameson's work on the cultural turn of the early 1990s, which claims that

18 Sassen, 'Local actors in global politics', *Current Sociology,* 52(4), 2004, p. 652.
19 Jansson, 'Indispensable Things', p. 290.

'throughout the social realm, to the point at which everything in our social life – from economic value and state power to social and political practices and the very structure of the psyche itself – can be said to have become 'cultural'.[20]

Aesthetic production may result in either identifiable artworks or simply as modifications in our lived experience through a sensorial experience. Culture is central to the development of what Paul Gilroy called a 'planetary consciousness'.[21] It echoes an earlier idea of *noosphere*, developed by the Ukrainian scientist and thinker Volodymyr Vernadsky, as the next evolutionary step in the development of biosphere, a global sphere of knowledge or consciousness.[22] For Gilroy, the planetary is one of the possible homes we can inhabit – it bypasses the notions of local, national, the racial, the colonial and the fictions made around these notions, and makes a stronger case for the connection of aesthetics and politics to human survival – to 'bare life'. A multicultural 'conviviality', as Gilroy calls it, requires a metropolis 'in which cultures, histories, and structures of feeling previously separated by enormous distances could be found in the same place, the same time: school, bus, café, cell, waiting room, or traffic jam'. A multicultural democracy, it follows, can only be bred in spaces which allow for this conviviality. Gilroy calls for a planetary humanism that is tolerant, humane, pluralistic, and cosmopolitan in outlook. This is not the direction the current metropolis is moving towards, and Swedish cities are certainly following this trend where people of different backgrounds do not meet symmetrically in a café, if there is even a café where they meet.

I appropriate Gilroy's use of the *planetary* here as a poetic dimension of the word 'satellite' and the triad I will work with from this point forward is: satellite cities, satellite dishes, and satellite transmissions. From this, I will sketch an outline of a *satellite subjectivity* that is produced, where a planetary conscience meets the cosmic scale of the satellital in its political, cultural and aesthetic implications. This leads me also to think about the potential of a *satellite consciousness*, one that orbits around the planetary consciousness reflexively – an updating of Beck's reflexive cosmopolitanism in relation to Gilroy's multicultural metropolitanism.

Hospitality, in a planetary scale, may have to do with the act of guests (smaller planets) orbiting around hosts (larger planets), like the moon is to the Earth. These satellites may remain in orbit or may spin out of control and hit the surface of the Earth like a meteorite – disrupting 'life' by collision, causing, in the words of Berardi, new life-forms to emerge. As in Eames' short films 'Powers of 10',[23] I invite the reader to make the journey back from cosmic space (and the space of theory) down to Earth with a camera zooming in to a small place which most people travelling by subway in Stockholm would hardly notice up close: Fittja, Sweden, 59'N 17'E.

20 Rosler, *Culture Class*, Berlin: Sternberg Press, 2013, p. 108–109.
21 Paul Gilroy, *After Empire: Melancholia or Convivial Culture? Multiculture or Postcolonial Melancholia*. London: Routledge, 2004.
22 Volodymyr I. Vernadsky, 'The Biosphere and the Noosphere', *American Scientist*, 33(1), 1945: 1–12.
23 *Powers of 10*, (dir. Charles Eames, 1970). Available at: https://youtu.be/0fKBhvDjuy0.

## Fittja: Media Texture, Social Assemblage

Between 2010 and 2012, I was dedicated full-time to the practical part of my PhD degree, which centered on the creation and execution of *Satellitstaden*, an artistic project conceived as a research device for the dissertation. I have briefly stated my motivations for doing this project in the Introduction and have described the urban and political context in which the project is situated in previous chapters, having highlighted the possibility of thinking of cities in terms of host-guest relationships which define the notion of hospitality in segregated or divided cities. *Satellitstaden* is, in many ways, hospitality put into practice in the form of an art project that entailed many dimensions of host and guest relationships, inside and outside, nationals and foreigners, strange and familiar, center and periphery. Let me try to phrase these relationships in terms of the language of hospitality which we have outlined in Chapter 1.

First, the urban context where *Satellitstaden* occurs is in an immigrant community, Fittja, a satellite city south of Stockholm. In the urban context alone, as we have seen, the community lives in a social housing *miljonprogram* project meant to originally accommodate the working class, but now turned into areas that house 'ethnic enclaves', constituted of the 'expelled' (according to Sassen's and Flusser's terminology of the migrant subject as put forth in Chapter 2) that determine Stockholm's status as a segregated area. Fittja is an area that is 'outside', populated by 'foreigners' who are 'strangers' to what is considered a 'national' culture. We have also seen how the master plans of well-intentioned social housing projects in peripheral areas, which in turn are the embodiments of certain political visions and ideologies, have failed to include (in the case of the Hjällbo), and sometimes have purposefully excluded (as in the satellite cities of Brasília) migrant and immigrant populations in their initial plans. I refer to the plan as both an abstract projection of something, but also as a course of action, as a procedure to be followed and maintained. This exclusion creates a space of friction between that which is 'living' and which animates the urban as inspired by Henri Lefevbre, including people and their ways of living, their things, behaviors and customs; and that which is built and inanimate, the concrete structures, the bureaucratic structures, etc.

In Sweden, urban segregated areas tend to get renovated in the guise of gentrification that in reality pushes its residents further out into invisibility. Inversely, when urban grassroots movements succeed, they can strengthen local identities and sense of belonging that transform into local commitments for urban revitalization through formal or informal channels, and are therefore able raise the self-esteem of the citizens in a satellite city. In psychology, individuals suffering from low self-esteem live haunted by the belief that their lives are not valuable and meaningful. Likewise, peripheral areas of the city with low urban self-esteem may be perceived as areas that are not desirable and not worth visiting, whose residents are ashamed of saying where they live, perceived by media discourses and reproduction of prejudices as dead ends or stigmatized, and as breeding grounds for social woes. Who wants to be identified with that? As these areas are not considered valuable to the city, they decrease the entire city's value in the public's perception.

Gentrification of so-called blighted peripheral neighborhoods, in some cases, can be sold to the local population like a therapeutic drug that boosts confidence on the short term, but which only creates more problems once its calming effects have subsided with higher rents and expensive services which communities cannot afford. In the film *Push (2019)* about the financialization of real estate and the ensuing housing crisis in several cities in the world, by Swedish director Fredrik Gertten[24] shows how a private realtor offered mindfulness sessions to residents threatened by eviction in the UK to mitigate the psychological process of imminent eviction, thus showing how the process of gentrification and speculation offers absurd palliative measures for residents who are unable to afford their own housing and offered no way out. In light of this, residents are forced to move elsewhere, into precarity and marginalization while buildings are refurbished to standards that invite new residents, or worse, as the film shows, leaves the buildings empty as a way to increase property's value of speculative financial capital. This, the film shows, leads also to a social death of the city as speculation empties the areas of its community life by way of expelling its lower income residents. The work of urban justice movements is to see through this urban *pharmakon* (meaning, remedy-as-poison) and work on a more structural level in the re-habilitation of their urban psyche. Their mechanism is not to flee from the suburbs in a sort of denial mechanism. On the contrary, their strategy is to confront their problems and bring them into conscience (perhaps a form of urban mindfulness?) while creating tools capable of lifting the areas from their impoverished or depressed state. One of these tools is fostering a rhetoric of 'pride of place' and 'pride of collective self' in the struggle for urban and social justice.

Culture, art and artists may be helpful in the process of meaning-making and operate in these mechanisms of self-esteem albeit sometimes only remedially. I refer to 'meaning' in the sense of creating and making sense by way of the sensible, by creating symbolic value, even if ephemeral, and perhaps by allowing something to be perceived in a slightly different way than the usual or the familiar. In sum, as Flusser suggests, to break from the habitual and enter something new. As such, aesthetics, which is the science and ethics of the senses, is somehow always strange, different, Other, uncanny (which in German is the *unheimlich* – the unhomely). It is by way of aesthetic production that I entered the Fittja community by means of an art project, *Satellitstaden*, as a framing device for a broader field research for investigating the notion of home and belonging through the community's use of satellite television transmitted by satellite dishes dotting all the neighborhood's building façades. It was also here that I entertained the hypothesis of a philosophy and language of hospitality as a theoretical perspective for reading the divided city which would guide my own plan throughout. This language entails rephrasing all relationships in the vocabulary of hospitality: guest and host, welcoming or trespassing, temporariness and permanence, nomadic and settled, the expelled and expeller, inclusion and exclusion, home and homeland, and so on. Within this syntax, we can say that in Fittja, as a resident artist I was a guest in a community of immigrants who were themselves guests within a host society. Inversely, they were themselves hosts in this community where native Swedes are notoriously absent or largely underrepresented. In the same sense, the participatory artwork acted as a host for participants as guests, while the satellite dishes themselves, which are the objects of artistic intervention, are considered intruders in the rigorously planned architecture whose façades are hosts to these objects.

24 *Push*, (dir. Fredrik Gertten, 2019). Available at: https://vimeo.com/ondemand/pushthefilm.

## Fittja and its Self-image

Historically, when Fittja appears in the newspapers, it can only be bad news, or at least this is how its residents are used to being treated by mainstream media which is reflected by a perceived aversion to journalists coming to the area. Fittja's negative media portrayals are those of an impoverished and crime-ridden zone, which some may believe embodies everything that Sweden is not meant to be: poor, disorderly, violent, foreign. Consequently, many Fittja residents, regardless of their socioeconomic or geopolitical background, claim to have experienced some kind of discrimination in the workplace or in social life outside the area due to this negative portrayal. During an interview with a Lebanese participant, she stated that 'the image of Fittja may be negative, but life here is not negative. Come visit us and we will receive you with open arms'. Her statement shows the importance of the inside perspective and an invitation for hospitality, which is considered lacking in the host society on a social level. This awareness of the community's inner being is what unites residents in creating awareness campaigns such as 'Fittja is Peace' that continuously try to work on the self-esteem of the area while also promoting a better media image and curbing the effects of segregation and stereotyping promoted by the media.[25] The local population is resentful of this negative media portrayal which they feel does not adequately reflect the actual living conditions in the neighborhood they call home.

It is important to briefly describe this neighborhood so that we understand local specificities. Fittja's local economy is an important feature of this small community of 7,500 residents. In 2011 and 2012, I attended the yearly meeting organized by the Citizen's Office where local organizations present their annual reports in response to the question 'How are people actually doing in Fittja?'. A portrait of Fittja is usually presented in numbers, statistics and discussions with social and political representatives in the area and in the municipality. Here are some of the points combining information from the reports with my additions based on further research from observations and formal as well as informal interviews with residents.

a) *Overview*: According to Fittja's community leaders, the general view says culture could be a way to improve the collective health of the community. Culture could motivate young people to gain new skills especially in the case of those dropping out of school early, given that this group has insufficient skills for jobs and insufficient job coaching.[26] The situation is especially challenging for young men suffering from alcoholism, and idle time and lack of facilities and opportunities for organized social life are the main causes for involvement in gang crimes. Women appear as the group most vulnerable to violence, especially domestic violence mostly perpetrated by family members. Children's health was seen to be mostly affected by lack of stimulus in education and showing recurrent cases of child obesity. Forty-seven percent of men are involved in gambling of some sort, calling the area 'Lucky Fittja'.

25 The Youth Center's (Ungdomens Hus) satellite dish had this slogan on its satellite dish cover. *Ungdomens Hus Fittja*, https://www.facebook.com/ungdomens.

26 This is in addition to the fact that unemployment between ages 16 and 25 in Sweden is at 23%, with the highest percentages in the minority population, i.e. first- or second-generation Swedes. *Ekonomifakta*, https://www.ekonomifakta.se/fakta/arbetsmarknad/arbetsloshet/ungdomsarbetsloshet-per-manad/.

The education level of adults is low on average, with fewer having completed their studies but the heterogeneous profile of the area is also represented by a rising number of young people enrolling in universities or technical colleges; discussing cultural backgrounds is often taboo in association meetings.

b) *Gender*: A special report on women showed that most of them would like to work but are not allowed to for cultural or practical reasons. Even if they are skilled and have held jobs before coming to Sweden, upon arrival they are no longer active and find themselves relegated to domestic chores, leading to personal frustration that in turn affects the health of the family and the community. When employed, most women of Middle Eastern background are said to suffer workplace discrimination and feel that they are questioned about their families and culture too often, especially in regard to wearing the *hijab*. In the lower income levels, they often earn too little to afford local transportation and require that the workplace is closer to home, something which is difficult in Fittja since it has a very small economy and too few local job placements. Even if they do speak fluent Swedish, one of the greatest advantages for successful integration, they felt discriminated against based on their cultural background. They feel like they are not seen as individuals and typecast in their role within the family or within other cultural conjectures. This is especially true for Muslim women. 'How well do I need to know Swedish to be able to clean someone else's house or office?' asks Zaliha, a Satellitstaden participant.

Differently than mainstream Swedish society, which considers itself as one of the most egalitarian societies in the world, Fittja presented a very genderized use of public space and genderized perceptions of roles in society. According to the research, most women felt stigmatized in their prescribed familial and societal female roles. As a result, women feel isolated as a group without proper support structures. The gender division of urban space is a factor which caused me to relate almost exclusively to women during the research. The networks I identified were largely the effect of women's socialization in the area, followed by the children who used the city space in a very specific way for play and social interaction.

*c) Employment*: Fittja's most recent statistics show improvements in employment rates in the past ten years, but unemployment is still very high.[27] Many of the participants in Satellitstaden, generally women, agreed to participate because they were available at home due to unemployment. This happens for several reasons: some women with young children have long maternity leaves; those who have been in Sweden for less than two years are still in a probation period for learning the language; others are on medical leave for sickness, work-related injuries, or taking care of elders; others remain unemployed at their husband's determination; and a small minority depend on welfare alone. Of the women who were employed, most of them worked in public services or in commerce. Most of those who had job

27 In 2019, the unemployment rate in Botkyrka municipality where Fittja is located is 10.3%, compared to the national average of 7% and neighboring Stockholm municipality's average of 5%. If we compare Botkyrka to Stockholm, the unemployment rate in Botkyrka is twice as much, denoting the socio-economic gap between the capital and its satellite cities. *Valmyndigheten*, http://www.valmyndigheten.se

placements had internships, with no guarantee of long-term employment. It was observed that the level of unemployment was related both to the time spent in Sweden and the education level. Within the first year of arrival, only 18% have jobs, rising to 50% in the second year. This number remains stationary until after 10 years stay in the country. After 10 years residency, 66% have regular job placements. On average, 70% of Fittja's population completed high school or higher.

*d) Public spaces:* Meeting places are mostly active at daytime and revolve around activities related to children and youth. Of note are the central shopping mall, leisure centers for youth such as Ungdomens Hus (Youth Center), and Fittja gården (a club for teenagers), *Verdandi* (a meeting place that includes a café and community activities for children and unemployed women), and the public library. With the Multicultural Center (MKC), a research center dedicated to multicultural studies, and the relocation of *Botkyrka konsthall* to Fittja, the area now has two high-profile cultural outlets. Other available spaces comprise a few eateries and national associations. National associations are part of a long-standing multicultural policy that includes the creation of private associations functioning as meeting places for special interest groups. In this case, national associations, for example the Turkish or Kurdish national associations, meant as cultural meeting places to add to Fittja's cultural life, most often function as gentlemen's clubs of a certain group, yet they also promote cultural activities for wider audiences.[28] There are few meeting places or forms of entertainment after business hours. Of the few options that exist, bars that serve alcohol are not well accepted in the community because of Fittja's large Muslim population. There is a general complaint of too few meeting places which shows the fragility of the public sphere and the dominance of private spaces as the main places of socialization, and hence the dominance of television in such spaces.

*e) Self-image*: What do people in Fittja say about Fittja? Statistically, 57% of Fittja residents said they liked living there, 66% enjoyed the varied cultural offerings, 44% were satisfied with the local facilities and conditions of the buildings, while unemployment had risen among young people. A Lebanese woman I interviewed was very clear about the self-perception/perception of Fittja. She said to me 'The image is negative, but life here is not negative. Those who live in Fittja enjoy it. It is only the people outside who do not like it', she continued. Juan, who came to Sweden from Chile in the early 1970s as a political dissident, is one of Fittja's oldest residents and believes the stigmatization of Fittja as a 'ghetto' comes strictly from the outside and he does not accept the negative mediatization of Fittja, and defends its cosmopolitan character. 'We come from many countries here, and we are not all poor. My son is an accomplished filmmaker and writer. I live here because I am loyal to this community.

28 My interaction with these national associations was very double. As a white woman, and usually walking alone in Fittja, I remember feeling uncomfortable entering the male-dominated clubs. Originally meant as cultural gathering places, these clubs have an exclusive social function. The origin of these clubs comes from a multicultural policy from the 1970s where the government provided funding for the establishment of a network of national associations where people from the same country or culture could meet and conduct cultural activities. These clubs were also used to organize worker's associations. The social life of many suburbs in Sweden revolves around these associations that are still government funded and operate on a membership basis. In Fittja, there are several such associations, notably the Turkish, Kurdish, and Pakistani assiociations are especially visible.

This is not a ghetto!' he said in a community meeting. Juan made me understand that the loyalty to a community cannot be constructed artificially and requires time and dedication. He told me he identified strongly with the community and had always been a strong voice in local organizations, following his experience in the student revolts in Chile prior to 1973 when he was deported to Sweden as a political refugee. He tells me that Fittja keeps alive his revolutionary spirit, the same spirit that caused the Pinochet régime to expel him and thousands of other Chileans to Sweden.[29]

And yet, it was stated that people were constantly making comparisons with their situation in the homeland and claimed that living in Sweden gives them high status vis-á-vis their compatriates. Some groups, especially Iraqis, experience effects of trauma long after arrival and children need special attention in schools, which they do not often get. It was generally felt that the community lacks role models to increase the career possibilities for young people. Due to its small size, the community has the sensation of feeling isolated from the rest of the city. In terms of public space, street life could become a catalyst for cultural meetings, but the panel presenting this data was unsure how this could occur beyond providing the residents with new landscaping that would at least soften up the very hard appearance of bare concrete on the streets.

*f) Cultural integration*: On a resident survey from 2013 about the main issues faced by the community, the top issue identified by the residents was the lack of contact with native Swedes. Both men and women complain that they do not relate especially well to Swedish society because there are too few contact zones, ethnic groups occupy different spaces and rarely cross-over. 'Swedishness' was felt like a norm hard to break through, and extra assistance was needed for people to learn how to present themselves in society, especially important regarding language discrimination in the workplace. In a recent study conducted in similar areas in Gothenburg, Sweden, 20-25% of respondents spoke Swedish poorly. One of the conclusions of the annual reports mentioned earlier was that Fittja needed more respect from outsiders as its self-esteem improves internally. This was especially relevant in terms of security and trying to keep crime statistics low, but also in terms of Fittja's image in the media. The main idea behind this assertion is that when people respect their environment and their neighbors, there is a greater chance that people will protect each other and as a result feel proud of where they live. In addition, there is an opacity between areas of the city, and between cultures which signifies the fragility of host-guest relationships. While the bonds to the host country are fragile at best, by contrast the ties within the community, and between immigrant populations and their homelands is quite strong, in part thanks to the access to a wide ecology of telecommunications such as the viability of satellite television, in combination with digital media, travel, which create multiple connections between communities and homelands, but also across other communities and localities within each diaspora.

---

29 Following Pinochet's coup in 1973, the Swedish ambassador Harald Edelstam openly supported Salvador Allende's government and offered asylum to 1,300 Chilean opposition activists, mainly academics, professionals and students. Many more followed this first group over the years and today Chileans are the largest Latin American minority group with 50,000 nationals and their descendants.

*g) Security*: Security measures implemented by the local authorities create a resistance towards the police, who are mainly ethnic Swedes. Citizen organizations are mobilizing to promote police work as a career option for young immigrant kids. Other modes of self-organization include community night watches, a neighbor-to-neighbor network based on the familiar contact and loyalty residents have to one another. Fittja has been affected by violence in the past years, with few murders resulting from personal vendettas rather than organized crime, but also drug dealing and speed driving, among others. Nonetheless, Fittja appears in the news mostly when crime occurs in the area, something which residents resent. Fittja is still considered a 'especially disadvantaged area' according to the police classification, which means that there is more investment in the area in terms of surveillance. But local building administrators are investing in physical improvements in public areas in order to destigmatize the area and create ways to get better data in order to better understand how to tackle security issues.[30] In fact, statistics show that Fittja has improved in recent years, and residents suggest investments in social sustainability with measures such as investing more in schools, employment and improving living conditions.[31]

*h) Political profile:* It is not surprising that an area with immigrant overrepresentation votes mainly for the center-left or leftist parties that support the continuation of openness towards immigration policies and emphasis on social, rather than economic issues. In the election of 2018, nearly 70% of Fittja residents in the street where *Satellitstaden* took shape voted for Social Democrats and the Left parties, while only 7.5% voted for the extreme-right Swedish Democrats, compared to the national average of 36% for the former, and 17.5% for the latter.[32] In other areas of the same municipality with higher socio-economic profile, the extreme-right has garnered more supporters, despite a municipal effort to invest as much as possible in intercultural policies and cultural activities as a platform for innovation and cultural integration. Furthermore, satellite television plays an important role in this political life as news and programs from the homelands and diaspora television provide residents with information otherwise unavailable in Swedish public television, which has very low viewership.

As a case in point, the political history of Fittja residents outside of Sweden is worthy of note. If one recounts the most salient global conflicts or in the past 40 years, one would find a representative of most of those events in Fittja.[33] In fact, some residents have a political past

30 'Polisen: Positiva tecken i utsatta områden', *Aftonbladet*, 3 June 2019. https://www.aftonbladet.se/nyheter/a/zG9E49/polisen-positiva-tecken-i-utsatta-omraden.

31 'Efter rapport om utsatta områden: Polisen: Fittja har faktiskt blivit tryggare', *Stockholm Direkt,* 30 June 2017, https://www.stockholmdirekt.se/nyheter/efter-rapport-om-utsatta-omraden-polisen-fittja-har-faktiskt-blivit-tryggare/repqfv!NE8msk9Ps@PfmmqSbpYkkQ/.

32 For more 2018 election statistics, see *Valmyndigheten*, https://data.val.se/val/val2018/slutresultat/R/rike/index.html.

33 Asylum in Sweden has followed some of these historical events in the past 40 years: after Pinochet's coup in 1973, thousands of Chileans were given asylum; after the 1979 cultural revolution in Iran, its dissidents were granted protection; Cuban dissidents arrived following several purges in the 1980s; Kurdish and Assyrian refugees fled mass purge in the 80s and 90s, Iraqi (especially Christian Iraqis) and Afghans fleeing the American war; Muslim Chinese fleeing Western China after the riots in Urumqi in 2009; Muslim Uzbeqis fleeing persecution in the 2000s; Serbs, Bosnians, Montenegrans following Sweden's diplomatic role in the Balkan war; Sri Lankan Tamil dissidents, refugees from conflicts

and maintain active political ties with their respective diasporic communities. In most cases, the residents of Fittja are the exceptions in their own societies, having sought asylum in the country due to persecution and war: in other words, they are the *expelled* from their homeland societies. Here, micro-histories of faraway places meet, intersect and influence one another in everyday life. For example, by looking at the faces from Kurdistan, Turkey, Syria, Lebanon, Armenia and Assyria, one understands, from a historical perspective, the ethnic conflicts that resulted from the dissolution of the Ottoman Empire almost one century ago and that are manifested in the Fittja microcosm. Whereas Turks and Kurds would normally live farther from each other in their native Turkey, in exile they live side by side. Bosnians and Serbs, who once fought against each other, now cooperate as neighbors. Bangladeshis and Malians, who come from places and continents so far apart with no direct historical link between each other, now share the responsibility for taking care of hallways and common spaces.

Lastly, if she could say something about Fittja to the world, Fatimah, another participant in the project, would say 'Please come and visit us, this is not a slum, there are wonderful people, and much to learn. Welcome!' And this is what the project *Satellitstaden* addressed: a turn-around of the representation of the area by bringing forth the voices that constitute it through the lens of the ethics and practice of hospitality. Even though this was useful background information about the territory where *Satellitstaden* would take place, my interest was not to approach Fittja from a top-down perspective, but rather to address its human relations by working and living in the neighborhood for a limited time.

in Banda Aceh, Indonesia, along with Finns and Latvians escaping poverty in an earlier wave of immigration, strong Turkish contingent as part of the Turkish diaspora; Syrian refugees are arriving daily as we speak.

## Satellitstaden: The City of Satellites

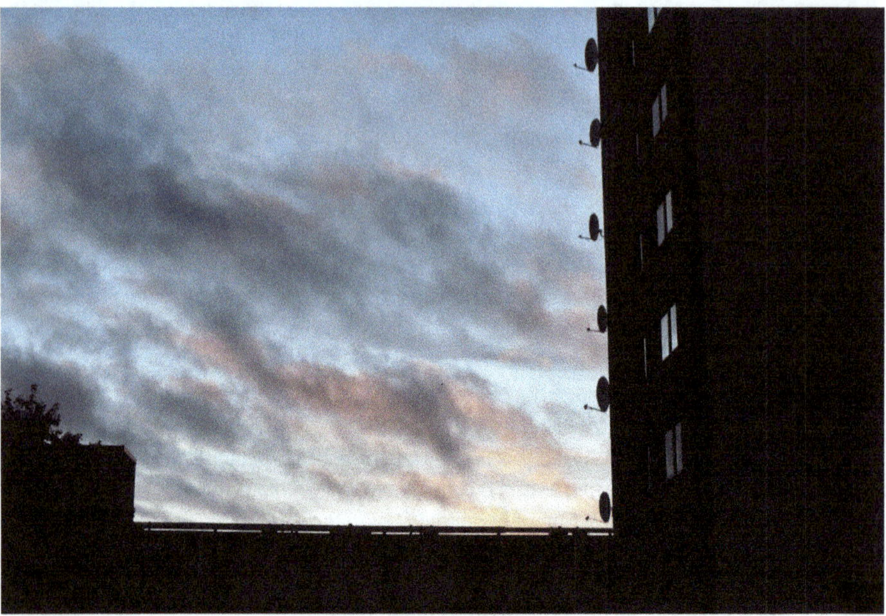

*Figure 27 – Image of Fittja's satellite landscape. Image by the author.*

On my first visit to Fittja in September 2010, I write:

> We are 30 minutes from city center. Outside, a rural landscape is cut by large roads, shopping malls and housing estates that look out of synch with the surrounding pastures. A subway line strings together these 'islands' of buildings. The subway stations are busy and run-down. At each station the faces of the people begin to change. In the city center, I felt like I was in Sweden, but as we travel south, slowly faces from every corner of the planet get in and out of the trains at each stop. I hear languages I cannot understand, I feel I am in the world. From beginning to end of the trip, it almost feels like crossing an invisible border into another country.

For Stockholm standards, a city that is generally well maintained, Fittja's small subway station had broken glass doors, and was littered. As it was almost election day, the walls were covered with electoral campaign posters. Outside the station, one could see 360 degrees of buildings that looked exactly alike and a busy central mall. Fittja follows a single architectutal design and was built on empty land next to a beautiful large meadow bordering a lake. As a satellite city, it is not a part or an extension of the city but rather a stand-alone neighborhood with an aesthetic all its own but depends on the subway line that connects it to the center of the city.

As we were guided into the community by the curators of Botkyrka konsthall, on first impression, I felt the place cold and inhospitable, with a repetitive and monotonous architecture, predominantly grey. I wrote: 'Nothing there reminds me of a sense of home. No street markets, little street life, all seems confined to the highrise buildings which are opaque. The squares are empty. Are there any rules against residents creating their own spaces and urban expressions?', I wondered.

On a closer look, the area looked a bit run-down, but not any better or worse than similar areas in Berlin or Paris. Fittja seemed generally calm from the outside when compared to the slums of Rio where I worked for many years. In fact, by comparison it looked like any other middle-class residential area in any large Brazilian city, or like a gated community where all buildings are identical.

I am struck by the opaqueness of the concrete and how the brutalist aesthetic leaves little space for that which is human, erratic, performative, and living. The public spaces and pedestrian streets covered by asphalt from edge to edge with scant greenery were known as 'the desert'. The buildings were mainly residential with little or no commercial activity except for the central mall. As with any planned community, it *felt* as if walking inside an architectural model or a blueprint, as the original design seemed intact. As we walked past building after building, I remembered Jane Jacobs' 'sidewalk ballet' and her defense of intimacy in urban space; and Dolores Hayden's tracing of material feminism in the transformation of space and cities in the US.[34] What creates a neighborhood, according to them, is the way in which people inhabit an area and their interaction with the buildings, the relation between open areas, nature, commerce, transportation, opportunities for meeting people, communal facilities, in short, inhabiting a space as a form of relation, not only as occupation.

My mental connection to a feminist perspective urbanism was not a coincidence. In fact, In the next two years, my connection to Fittja's community would occur mainly through a network of women.[35] And yet, there was a strange attractor: it was not that which could be *seen* that attracted me, but that which could only be *sensed* at that point. Imagining that behind the concrete walls and the empty streets lived the most diverse community in Scandinavia, where more than 80 nationalities live among its 7,500 inhabitants and probably as many languages spoken, turning these highrise buildings into towers of Babel.[36]

As we reached the residency apartment recently set up by the curators in the bottom floor of a highrise at the end of Krögarvägen, they informed us that the Fittja community had been targeted by the media years before as a symbol of everything that could have gone wrong in

34 Jacobs, *The Death and Life of Great American Cities,* was one of the fiercest of Robert Moses' modernist vision and urban renewal of New York in the 1960s, and was an advocate of community-based approaches.; See also Dolores Hayden, *The Grand Domestic Revolution: A History of Feminist Designs for American Homes, Neighborhoods, and Cities*, Cambridge, Mass.: MIT Press, 1981.

35 Unemployment among women in Fittja is high that many women are available during the daytime, which was when I worked in Fittja. I worked exclusively with women for the entire length of the project. As the families are numerous, children were often present. Women were very often the heads of household, while men spent much time away at work. Also, in a community where many members are Muslim, it becomes difficult to, as a woman, to come in contact directly with men. Fittja is a gender-divided community with private and public spaces.

36 In mathematics, a strange attractor represents the 'solution' to a nonlinear equation, dynamic or chaotic system.

Sweden's utopian social democracy: decaying social housing projects, middle class (white) flight, concentration of immigrants, unruly behavior, rising criminality. If social democracy was based on an effort of bridging class difference, everything that threatened this fragile equilibrium could be found there. On the other hand, Fittja was also considered a place of tolerance as one of the largest mosques in Scandinavia had been recently inaugurated nearby, for instance. As such, the dynamic character of this small multi-ethnic enclave revealed a complexity which was singular. If Fittja was indeed as unruly as its reputation, what puzzled me was the lack of expression of this unruliness in the public spaces. They were empty yet orderly, and any materiality out of synch with the design was somewhat contrived, discrete. Had the brutalist architectural design leveled all forms of cultural expression to a neutral ground? Had the residents themselves lost their 'color' after moving to Sweden? Is this what multiculturalism in Europe looked like?

As the curator Miriam Andersson Blecher described their activities in *Residence Botkyrka* by showing the work of a Dutch artist who had collected migrants' dreams and printed them as billboards, I stopped to study the buildings and looked up to its balconies and windows one by one. It reminded me of reading George Perec's novel, *Life: A User's Manual,*[37] where he meticulously describes an apartment block in Paris by skinning the building façades. I began to see through the façades in my imagination, going through every apartment carefully like a child would explore a dollhouse. Perec's novel is composed by as many fragments as there were apartments in the building in Paris, and each fragment also contains an array of narrative meta-data such as objects, clothes, spaces, architectural elements that surround each of the characters.

As I lifted my gaze floor by floor on one of the highrises, I could begin to sense the *molecular* aspects encroached on this *vertebrate* architecture,[38] to use Félix Guattari's metaphor, as signs of singularities: a rug left to dry over a ledge, a latticed curtain blowing through a half-open window, the blue glow of a television set flickering on a ceiling. In the distance, the echo of children playing in Fittja's own dialect, and a strong wind blowing swirling leaves on the 'desert' between the buildings. Two buildings away, two old ladies wearing headscarves open a door with a basket of laundry in their hands; a young man in a leather jacket walks hastily with a cigarette on one hand and a Lidl bag on another; a young mother pushing a stroller with one hand and holding a tired child on another, on the way home from school. This could be anywhere, but not Sweden; the aesthetics of the place and the movements

37 Perec, *Life: A User's Manual*. The book is an example of postmodern fiction. The novel is a tapestry of interwoven stories and ideas as well as literary and historical allusions, based on the lives of the inhabitants of a fictitious Parisian apartment block. The book was written in 99 fragments, each fragment being one of the apartments in the house. Perec moves through the house as on a chessboard, moving methodically in L-shaped movements, like the knight moves around the board landing on every square only once, from apartment to apartment. Since, at this point in the project I knew little about Fittja and its residents, observing the material aspects of the place would become an important part of understanding what life in Fittja was like.

38 I purposefully use the terms vertebrate and molecular, inspired by Félix Guattari's formulation, as metaphors for structured, hierarchical and fixed systems for the former, and organic, self-generative, disruptive elements for the latter. See Félix Guattari and Suely Rolnik, *Molecular Revolution in Brazil,* New York: Semi(o)texte, 2007; and Félix Guattari, *The Three Ecologies*. London: Athlone Press, 2000.

of its inhabitants seemed foreign to each other, but nevertheless everyone who lived here called it home.

Before entering the art residency, which was a furnished three-bedroom apartment used to receive international artists for short stays,[39] I noticed that the façades all around had satellite dishes hanging from every apartment pointing in all directions, in different sizes, some hanging from the rails, others directly bolted onto the concrete façade, in such a manner one may wonder if a trapeze artist was needed to install them that way. They disrupted the monotonous and repetitive stacking pattern of the architecture like dots randomly cast over a grid. Months later, as a resident artist living in this 'artist's hotel' as local residents called the residency apartment, I would become that trapeze artist myself when I climbed on dozens of those same balcony ledges to put color on these satellite dishes in many apartments, in the art installation *Satellitstaden* that was created as a result from this first visit.

In the months that followed, I set out to investigate the implications of creating a project in public space involving satellite dishes and local residents, and would increasingly become more involved with the community, its history, and eventually relocating there for a few months at the art residency. It results that working inside a community required the artistic skills that allowed me to make the necessary aesthetic and production decisions and an organizational ability to create a participatory structure by making connections between different people and transiting across the different dimensions of the community. It is only then, while looking up to the satellite dishes, but still not knowing anything about them, that a philosophy of hospitality would become the main mode of action that would push the project forward in every aspect.

## Satellite Dishes as Segregation Signifiers

In the early 2000s, many newspaper articles began to highlight a specific issue in areas like Fittja which became one of the symbols for the contentious integration debates in Sweden. Satellite dishes hanging from balconies in *miljonprogram* areas, like the ones seen dotting the façades and hanging in nearly every balcony in Fittja, had become markers of these segregated areas referred to as 'ethnic enclaves'. In Sweden, since 2015 the police and the media define areas like Fittja in three levels. First, 'disadvantaged area' (*utsatt område*) is a geographically isolated area with low socio-economic status, with criminal activity exerting direct or indirect pressure on the community, and 28 such areas are currently identified with this denomination. Secondly, 22 'highly disadvantaged areas' (*särskilt utsatt område*),

39 The basic goals of residency programs, which have grown exponentially in the past decade, are used for individual artistic development and the pursuit of experimentation. Nowadays, residencies are often incorporated into the core of artistic practice, which 'allows geographical imbalances to be redressed, signalling an end to artistic discourses based on one-way traffic.' In the context of the mobility of art professionals, residencies are based on the idea of temporary relocation, the remote studio, and/or as laboratories for other types of projects that straddle the boundaries of 'the representational logic of exhibitions and the related public consumption of art.' Anna Ptak (ed.) *Re-tooling Residences: A Closer Look at the Mobility of Art Professionals*, Warsaw, Poland: Centre for Contemporary Art Ujazdowski Castle, 2011, p. 6–8.

where police work is difficult or impossible, are characterized with a general disinclination to participate in lawfulness. These include parallel social structures, the presence of extremism which curtails religious freedom, and high concentration of criminality. Thirdly, ten 'at-risk areas' (*riskområde*) fulfill the above criteria close to becoming 'highly disadvantaged areas'.[40] Notwithstanding, satellite dishes are usually more visible in these areas, usually located in the peripheries of large cities, with predominantly *miljonprogram* architecture and are therefore connected to the overall perception of low socio-economic status areas.

Aesthetically, the satellite dishes are considered by the media and outsiders as an eyesore and an intrusion that goes against architectural norms and styles and the perception of orderliness. Culturally, however, they represent the presence of the use of transnational television, and wherever they have been banned by local landlords, many families with immigrant backgrounds have protested in defense for their right of freedom of choice and expression regarding media practices. Access to communication technologies and freedom of speech may not be a given in most countries where Sweden's migrants come from, such as Iran, Iraq, or ex-Soviet republics, which are dominated by authoritarian regimes. A common assumption about Sweden is that it is a democratic state where the freedom of speech and the press are prescribed in its constitution. With democracy comes the freedom to choose which medium and which message one hears, and from this perspective there is thus no logical reason why any measures against the freedom of media usage, through whatever means should be imposed. In the debate about whether or not satellite dishes should be allowed to be hung in building façades or private balconies, the discourse of freedom of speech becomes entangled with architectural, urban planning and social policy debates and different perspectives about cultural integration.

And yet, even though these freedoms are legal, what is it that makes this piece of metal pointing to the sky so controversial for some, and so necessary for others? This was the starting point for the field research which developed into a full-fledged public arts installation on satellite dishes, seeking to further investigate the relationship between access to satellite broadcasts and the notion of home and belonging in Fittja specifically. I contend that satellite dishes may be segregation signifiers for those from outside the communities, but internally they are in fact elements of aggregation and connection. As such they facilitate several social, political and existential processes by way of media, as if extending their original life-worlds through the airwaves into the host country in a kind of media-based hospitality.

40 'Boende i utsatta områden kräver att grannarna 'skärper sig',' Lars Näslund, *Dagens Nyheter*, 8 October 2019. In 2017, 566,000 people or 5.4 percent av the overall Swedish population lived in one of these areas, being that 200,000 or 2 percent of the population live in 'highly disadvantaged areas'. See *Myndighetsgemensam lägesbild om organiserad brottslighet 2018–2019 / Diarienr A495.196/2017 (Arkiverad hos Wayback Machine).* Nationella underrättelsecentret, NUC, 2017. Pp. 2, 12, 13–14, 20

## The 'Artist's Hotel': Hospitality and Art Production

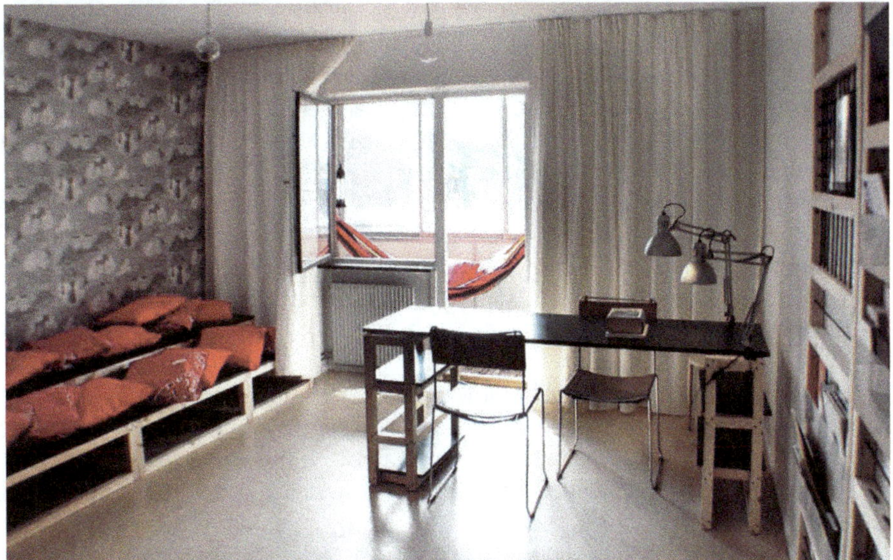

*Figure 28 – Residency Botkyrka, Krögarvägen 26, Fittja, Botkyrka Municipality, Sweden. Interior design concept by Laercio Redondo and Birger Lipinski. Image by the author.*

The only such program in a Stockholm suburb, Residence Botkyrka, or, as the local residents called it, the 'artist's hotel', would play an important role in the making of *Satellitstaden*, and provided the platform for production and permanence in the area that would support my presence in Fittja from 2010 to 2012, with the support of curator Joanna Sandell.

The aspect of hosting in the context of art residencies is important. The residency, as it was embedded inside this community, provided an interesting confluence of political forces, different subjects and many good intentions. I consider it as a place where the transnational system of the art world (as exemplified by the international artists and other members of the creative class that are invited to this residency) meets the transnational system of migrancy (as the community is composed mainly of immigrants). What brings these two subjects together is a progressive municipal political directives that consider culture as a catalyst for democracy and participation.

There is a sophisticated political apparatus behind the good intentions of bringing culture to the transnational suburbs, or to satellite cities of this character, classified by authorities as 'extremely disadvantaged areas'. According to Botkyrka's municipal secretary for culture, art and culture are seen as strategic tools of social and cultural integration across the municipality[41] and in their view, this positioning requires that cultural activities gain a differentiated character from the ones promoted by established cultural institutions in the city center.

---

41 *Botkyrka Municipality*, http://www.botkyrka.se.

With the mandate to create a context for the arts and culture in the municipality, Botkyrka konsthall's [the municipality's cultural center] strategy is to focus on high quality contemporary art and develop art's relationship to society and politics through activities beyond the traditional exhibition hall. Its main on-site activity includes an artist's residency program that supports the process and production of site-inspired works and an annual public arts festival. The residency located inside a typical 1970s family apartment is meant to host invited artists and researchers to engage in projects that use the richness of the local community and urban area as a resource for the creation and production of a variety of experimental art projects which are difficult to implement without a prolonged stay. Residence Botkyrka is also interested in the issues of co-creation and how the interaction between people can contribute to social change. As a community-based art project, *Satellitstaden* would become an example of a specific confluence of community participation, city planning, and media culture inscribed in these directives.

In Fittja, I would be the guest (she who arrives with the inherent promise of temporariness), and the Fittja community would be my host. The philosophy behind the residency apartment was to 'embed' the artist in a situation of [temporary] living that would come close to that of a normal resident in Fittja. But the apartment was in reality conceived as an extension of the cultural institution embedded in the community. This effectively makes the artist's residency a public space that is inhabited by artists, rather than a private apartment that is sometimes visited by the institution. Furthermore, the residency apartment bore no likeness to the other apartments I visited – as it was not impregnated with anything local or private, but was rather designed and re-tooled for the purpose and needs of the residency.[42] It was rather impregnated with the traces of artists and projects who had mainly come from overseas, coming from another set of transnational conditions delineated by the art system of international exchange. Since the residency apartment was a remote part of the main cultural institution moreso than a private home, the cultural institution was also my host. As a guest to two hosts I had, then, a duty to both the community and the cultural institution, and this posed interesting challenges.

As a resident artist, I would be, a representative of this art system, and, according to Jacob Racek's description of host-guest relationships in the context of art residencies, the artist-as-guest who is 'a true para-site, one who stands aloof and is never entirely here or there. As a figure on the threshold, he opens our house to the outside, giving entry to that which we sought to exclude. He intervenes, interrupts patterns of activity and thereby interferes with established rules – in short, he causes disorder. Even if we attempt not to listen to him, or drown him out, his voice is so audible as noise in our pristine channels'. And yet, Racek continues, in a 'world without parasites – today we are at risk from this totalitarian utopia than ever before – is a world that stands still. That is the particular skill of the artist; he intervenes, making action visible in is microstructures'.[43]

42 In the spring of 2011, the apartment was redesigned by the artist duo Laercio Redondo and Birger Lipinski, commissioned by curator Joanna Sandell.

43 Racek, 'Strategies of Weakness', in Ptak, *Re-tooling Residences*, p. 137–138.

I realized, during my stay, that being conscious of this position as a 'para-site' in Racek's definition, in fact inspired by Michel Serres' seminal work,[44] was fundamental in creating a project that would be closely aligned with the everyday life in Fittja. Because I would interact very closely with the community, it was essential that I define this position of the visiting artist very clearly as an active agent, and not as a passive observer or a mysterious figure that 'makes art' in the isolation of a studio.

The residency would be more than a studio: it would act as a refuge, a meeting space, and a production base. I also decided to use the apartment itself as the first site of my artistic intervention, and in doing so, I reinforced its role as a 'satellite' cultural institution by turning the balcony of the apartment where a satellite dish was hung, as the first participant of the artistic intervention. I remember Hal Foster's 'The Artist as Ethnographer?' when he mentions that while

> there is nothing intrinsically wrong with this displacement, (...) it is important to remember that the sponsor may regard these properties as just that, as sited values to develop. Of course, the institution may also exploit such site-specific work in order to expand its operations for reasons noted above (social outreach, public relations, economic development, and art tourism). In this case, the institution may displace the work that it otherwise advances: the show becomes the spectacle where cultural capital collects.[45]

In this sense, being an artist in residence has nothing radical in and of itself – it simply displaces the *konsthall* outside of the *konsthall*, and indeed amplifies its spectrum of activities. But to what point this off-sitedness amplifies the spectrum of activities available for the local community is another matter altogether.

I mentioned earlier that I had a double function regarding the residency. In March 2011, in the early stages of creating a proposal for *Satellitstaden*, I was hired by Botkyrka konsthall to set up a local council of citizens that would provide a link between the artists and the local community and as such strengthen Residency Botkyrka's local identity and also bring the residency's two funders closer together, namely Botkyrka municipality and Botkyrkabyggen, a public housing management company.

Even though art projects are usually short and intense, and its effects difficult to measure, the curators believed it was the quick nature of the art projects, the flexibility and high rotation of the residency program that could begin to form a 'cultural imaginary' in Fittja over time. Resident artists often felt displaced in the community either because of language barriers or lack of access to resources and people necessary to conduct their projects.

---

44 Michel Serres's foundational work 'The Parasite' uses fable to explore how human relations are identical to that of the parasite to the host body. Among Serres's arguments is that by being pests, minor groups can become major players in public dialogue – creating diversity and complexity vital to human life and thought. See also Michel Serres, *The Parasite*, University of Minnesota Press, 2007 (1980).

45 Hal Foster, *The Return of the Real: The Avant-garde at the End of the Century*. Cambridge, Mass.: MIT Press, 1996, p. 306.

The idea of forming the local council was that hand-picked individuals from the local community would become local ambassadors working in two directions. First, they would become reference persons for the artists during their stay, being able to guide them in the area as well as provide information, interpreters, connections and resources. Secondly, they would also be able to level with the local community about the artistic activities and projects, attending events and helping to promote the residency's activities. A more traditional type of residency is designed to offer time and space away from everyday life, and as such the focus of this activity is to provide workspace and lodging. But in more process-oriented residency programs, like the ones Botkyrka konsthall and the municipality envisioned, demanded a more active staff and more substantial support. For the artist, this type of residency allows them to develop their artistic practice by exploring new ground for upcoming projects, and in terms of the Fittja residency specifically, it encouraged the creation of new projects somehow related to the site (modernism, public housing, segregation, migration, cultural exchange, etc.). It has the practical effect of mediation in both meanings as in conflict mediation – bridging the gap between interlocutors, and as in conveying meaning through media.

Such a residency may offer opportunity for site-specific work, and further, community engagement, even though participation per se is not necessarily mandated. It also has a public component including lectures, talks, dinners, presentations, etc. The shift from a private studio to the public domain has been current since the 1960s and is the strongest argument for supporting this kind of initiative, which can be said to facilitate open-ended processes that allow 'happy failures' which may not yield any concrete results until years later. If we use the terminology of the creative economy of the early 2000s, it can be said that residencies are to the art world what incubators are to the Internet start-ups. In such a process-oriented residency, results are not necessarily manifest as exhibitions where the local community can admire a set of artworks but may take shape in terms of experiences and gatherings or temporary interventions with varying degrees of local interaction. Sometimes, results may be presented in closed doors in a format that appeals to the art world, and other times, propositions are meant to engage residents more closely. In any case, we can say that this is usually a dilemma of site-specific works and the complexity of working inside a residential community: to what extent is the community and the surroundings involved in works that are inspired by them, or are directly about them? What are the ways in a local community can become more than an object of research or artistic practice?

While there are no overtly stated obligations of the artists towards the community or vice-versa, it is important nonetheless to include a citizen perspective to the residency program, as it is publicly funded by the municipality. This can be inscribed in a larger framework of citizen movements that are put into practice in places like Fittja, that relies on multiple forms of citizen participation such as night watches and other self-organized and grassroots activities that strengthen democratic micropolitical participation. Finally, at the end, the local council was meant to close the communication gap between the artists and the surroundings and help in the cultural mediation between major forces behind the work of democracy-building in Botkyrka municipality, urban blight, creative economy, social sustainability and diversity. Setting up this small group of people was for me a way of practicing hospitality – how was art going to be welcomed, or be disruptive, inside its host community? How much transparency would be needed or even desirable?

I quote Martha Rosler's recalling of Brian Holmes sharp words, 'Brian Holmes has likened the dance between institutions and artists to a game of *Liar's Poker*. If the art world thinks the artist might be holding aces, they let him or her in, but if she turns out actually to have them, that is, to have living political content in the work – the artist is ejected. Although Chantal Mouffe exhorts artists not to abandon the museum – which I take to mean the art world proper – there is nothing to suggest we should not simultaneously occupy the terrain of the urban'.[46]

With the help of Parvaneh Sharafi from the Citizen's Office, a social worker who had arrived from Iran as an asylum-seeker after the Cultural Revolution in 1979, and who knew everything and everyone in Fittja, I could begin to trace my paths through the neighborhood and meet those individuals who later became the life support for the residency and for *Satellitstaden*. She gave me a list of ten individuals, and I set out to contact each of them and persuade them to participate in the council. The final list included a representative from the local administration company, the director of a local organization for unemployed women, and three citizen representatives. These members would create, later, a strong support network for *Satellitstaden*.

One of the council members, Björn Schenholm, was the local office manager for Botkyrkabyggen, a company that manages Fittja's rental contracts and facilities. He was a key contact to the neighborhood and to the development of the early stages of the project. Björn's job consisted of running the local administration office and coordinating the renovations in the public spaces that were supposed to take place in the following year. Through him I met Charley Malm, Fittja's area coordinator and my guide into the community. Charley knew every Fittja resident by name. He granted me access to all the buildings which helped me in distributing flyers and pinning posters, provided knowledge about the history in the area, and introduced me to key people (the football coach, the school director, the librarian, etc.). He also introduced me to his line workers who later helped me with logistics (ladders to climb over balconies, tools, access to restricted rooftop areas to take pictures, access to storage, etc.). Charley's coworker Ulf, who lived in the same building as the residency apartment, was an amateur radio expert and became my technical advisor regarding satellite dishes, as well as participating in the project.

Understanding my need to connect with residents to gather participation, Charley helped me articulate the project in the community and gave me the opportunity to present *Satellitstaden* in quarterly 'Neighbor Hour' meetings, one of the few initiatives in the neighborhood for citizen participation, so that I could begin to gather participants. Whereas the 'Neighbor Hour' meetings were designed to discuss urgent issues in the neighborhood such as crime, security and car theft, I was given the opportunity to present the project at the end and was met with delight and skepticism. Lastly, Björn's endorsement of the project led the company

46 Rosler, *Culture Class*, p. 180.

to offer in-kind sponsorship in the form of public relations service, and this explains how *Satellitstaden* got unexpected exposure in the media,[47] in the hopes that it would promote Botkyrkabyggen indirectly. Because he held a high position in the company, Björn helped me in formulating the project in its smallest details, often with more grandiose visions for it than I ever could imagine or that were impossible to put into practice with my limited budget.

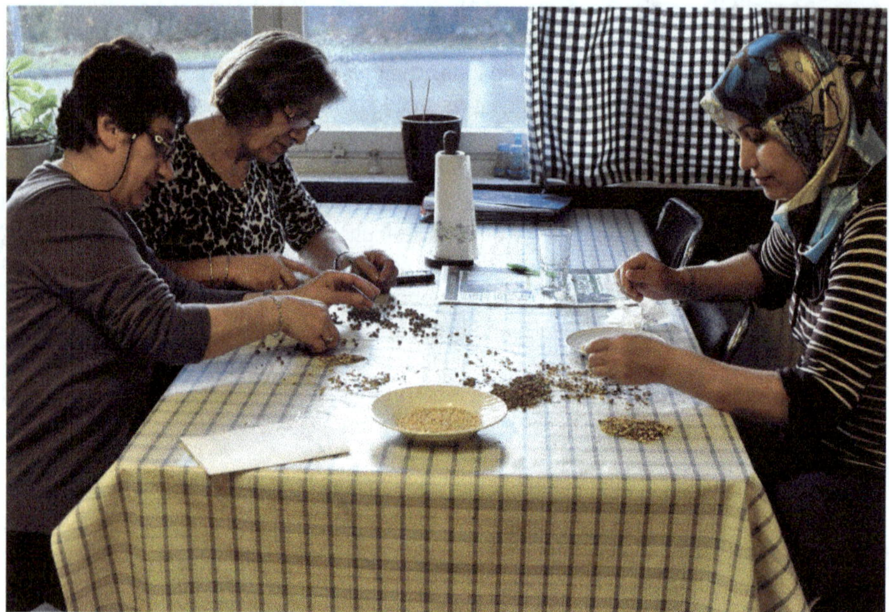

*Figure 29 – Leila Sözen and Pero Dag help a resident in preparing a community dinner at Verdandi, September 2011. Image by the author.*

Leila Sözen and Pero Dag are the directors of *Verdandi*, an organization that offers assistance to unemployed women in Fittja. The organization runs projects that give temporary employment opportunities for women, as well as workshops and further education, mainly for adults who have a long history of unemployment. One of the reasons why many older women in Fittja are not employed is because they arrived in Sweden with very little education, having dedicated their lives to raising children and caring for the home, with fragmented professional lives mostly in low-skilled labor. While most of them eventually became more educated and learned basic Swedish, their skills are still insufficient for long-term employment. *Verdandi* is an organization that takes in women with this background and offers them the opportunity to do paid work that cuts through the bureaucracy of language learning and professional certifications. Leila and Pero, the lead seamstress in the organization's sewing studio, run *Verdandi*'s activities that involve running a café, a second-hand store, a meeting space for

47 Anna Broström, 'Paraboler i Fittja blir färgglad konst', *Dagens Nyheter*, 19 April 2012, https://www.dn.se/sthlm/paraboler-i-fittja-blir-fargglad-konst/; Petter Beckman, 'Konsthögskolan kommer till Fittja', 12 April 2012, https://www.stockholmdirekt.se/sodra-sidan/konsthogskolan-kommer-till-fittja/cbbldl!9w9kgZuf2vrNPq3NXudgbA/; 'Bland satelliter och pimpade paraboler i Fittja', *Kulturradio P1*, Sveriges Radio, 11 June 2012, https://sverigesradio.se/sida/artikel.aspx?programid=3050&artikel=5143268.

classes and counseling sessions, and a sewing and carpet-weaving studios. The café, like most other organizations in Fittja, had a television connected to a satellite dish and usually turned on to a homeland channel, especially Turkish soap operas during afternoon tea. They had recently opened a weaving workshop where Kurdish women can weave their traditional hand-knot rugs with equipment imported from Turkey and rescue a craft they had almost forgotten. The space is located twenty meters from the artist's residency, and I thought it would be great to have Leila in the council, so her space could become an extension of the residency, an ideal space to hold meetings and a good place to connect with the local community, as well as her knowledge of the community from working there for more than twenty years.

During the project Leila and Pero would be my hosts at *Verdandi*, as the organization later became the production base for *Satellitstaden*. Pero would affectionately refer to the satellite dish covers that dress up the satellite dishes in Fittja as 'parabol dresses', and became an enormous source of stories, experience and confidence for me. Leila and Pero are of Chaldean Assyrian origin from Turkey, an ethnicity that, like the Armenians, underwent genocide during the First World War, something both remember hearing stories about as children. Both arrived in Sweden in the 1970s with their young children, after a long journey that began with a gradual expulsion in Turkey, through working in factories in Germany until they earned enough money to buy their free passage and reunite with their families in the affluent Assyrian diaspora in Sweden. They spoke Swedish and Turkish fluently, besides their native Aramaic. Assyrians in Sweden are more numerous in diaspora than in their homelands. They are a landless people that, unlike the Jews and the Kurds, do not lay claim to a territory. Their original homeland, Mesopotamia in Iraq, is now the site of a new genocide against the Christian populations of the Middle East, many of which also live in Fittja.

Very often, at the café, Leila and Pero would be the translators from Swedish to Turkish between the Kurdish ladies attending the café and myself. Many of the Kurdish ladies, though having arrived in the 1970s and 1980s, still did not speak Swedish fluently, some of them not at all. They came as young mothers and rarely spent time outside the community. Many of them said that there was always too much work to do at home raising several kids, and following the custom, their husbands did not allow them to study or work. They can be said to live in a triple exile: from their homelands, from the immediate world surrounding them, and also from the world of their children who are the second-generation Swedes. The language barrier is a source of painful isolation. Many of them, I learned in the several afternoons I spent at this café, were nearly illiterate upon arrival. Pero told me that as an Assyrian, she was not allowed to attend Turkish schools as a young girl and had been homeschooled by an uncle. Similarly, Kurdish girls were also not allowed to attend schools. Their life in Fittja, they told me, is similar to life back in their village in Turkey, notwithstanding the fact that all Kurds in Fittja come from the same village. Spending time with the ladies was not only tremendously beneficial to the project, but also one of the warmest experiences I have had. In time, I would have the opportunity to visit each one of them in their homes.

Shakhlo Altieva was a community representative in the council, a young woman in her early 30s, mother of two children, pregnant with her third child at the time. She immigrated from Uzbekistan to Europe, seeking refuge as a Muslim. In ex-Soviet republics, being a practicing

Muslim was seen as a detraction from a secular way of life and against the atheism in former communist states. Her husband is also Uzbeki, but of Turkish origin, a minority group in Samarkand where they both grew up. They decide to emigrate to Europe, get university education in the UK, and end up settling in Sweden. They believed Sweden would be more tolerant towards Islam. Migration for Shakhlo was both an expulsion, since her life choice as a Muslim was not tolerated in her original 'life-world,' and a choice, since she willingly chose to leave, fully conscious of the challenges of the migration journey towards Europe, where the values of individual autonomy and free choice are seen to be above the State.

As soon as she earned her Swedish citizenship, she began studies for a second university degree in sociology after having mastered the native language. She first worked together with Parvaneh at the Citizen's Office in Fittja while becoming gradually involved in community grassroots organizations, focused on minority women's rights in the suburbs. In her book *Fittjakvinnors röster!* ('The Voices of Fittja Women'), where she published nine interviews with women in Fittja, she writes:

> I moved here in 2004 and still get angry when I and other women who live here [in Fittja] are targeted as unemployed, isolated women who cannot speak Swedish, who don't want to work, who live on welfare and give birth to one child after another. There is enormous prejudice in the media against immigrant areas, places like Fittja. Especially against women with foreign background who live in these suburbs. These prejudices often reside in people who neither live or work in the suburbs, who have never been to these areas, let alone spoken to anyone who lives there.[48]

Since she speaks the native language so well and understands local political constituencies, she is able to understand, decode and transcode the core values of the several worlds she inhabits: the secular Western world and the traditions of her religion, combined with an Asian pragmatism in her manner. Today, she is a writer, public speaker, and is an active member of the local constituency of the Green Party.

As the only person in Residency Botkyrka's council who was also a Fittja resident (Björn, Leila, and others lived outside of the community even though they worked there), Shakhlo happily contributed with an insider's perspective to the group. She was also one of the first participants to *Satellitstaden* to cede her satellite dish to be colored green (in the color of Islam, according to her), which she keeps as the only means by which she can connect to her homeland culture, and especially useful when relatives come to visit. She also became an informal consultant in the project, helping with the formulation of the proposal in its initial stages and with invaluable feedback during the execution of the project.

## Satellite Dishes as Contact Zones

Before describing the art project developed with *Residence Botkyrka* in mind, let me return briefly to that moment during that first visit to Fittja, where I am standing in front of one of

48 Shakhlo Altieva, *Fittjakvinnors röster!*, Botkyrka kommun, 2014, p. 17.

these building façades, scrutinizing the 'science-fiction' element of the satellite dishes pointing to every direction. As I grew up in Rio de Janeiro, Brazil, these satellite dishes should not have stricken me as anything unusual. Rio's built landscape can be generally defined as an encounter between the formal modernist city and the historical colonial city interlaced by the informal city, in such a way that the latter engulfs the two former cities, both socially and culturally. Virtually every house or shack in a Brazilian *favela* sports a satellite dish, often with a pirated connection. These connections are constituted by many forms of transgression: electricity cables appropriated and extended into areas where formal installations are non-existent; television cables and decoders that hack into the formal communications networks; and local providers of pirate connections that distribute them to a range of local consumers at moderate rates. Satellite television is a household commodity like any other, only cheaper than in the formal city.

This eye for the unstable assemblages in urban life, or *gambiarras,*[49] which are forms of alternative engineering, allowed me to 'see' the satellite dishes in Fittja beyond mere technical fixtures that are easily overlooked. They rather resonated to me as objects that have a socioeconomic history that resonates with the life of the community.[50] Furthermore, they can be regarded, in the spirit of Bruno Latour's Actor-Network Theory (ANT), as actors in complex assemblages of networks tying together material objects, local and migrant populations, cultures, technologies, needs and experiences, and by virtue of it often influencing the balance of power in their social environments.

In her essay about the appropriation of the *gambiarra* by a few Brazilian contemporary artists, Brazilian curator Lisette Lagnado, who visited me in Fittja in October 2011, suggests that the *gambiarra* is a 'thing' that when elevated to a concept, 'involves transgression, fraud, and jiggery-pokery-though without relinquishing order, albeit a very simple one'.[51] As with all 'things,' we can translate a *gambiarra* into the art vocabulary loosely as a sculptural

49 A Brazilian expression. It means to use improvised methods and solutions to solve a given problem, with any readily available material. English equivalents would include 'mcGyverism,' 'kludge,' 'quick fix,' 'alternative engineering,' 'workaround,' and so on.

50 Many references came to mind which allowed me to sense another order of things while my thoughts persisted upon this forest of satellite dishes. I am reminded of the powerful role played by a private television network in Brazil in giving shape to the political ambition of national integration through media and thereby constructing a media empire in partnership with the dictatorship in the 1970s. A series of coincidences struck me as I felt myself surrounded by the seventies' aesthetics of the buildings and the ideas of living prevalent in architectural thinking of that time. The seventies was also the decade I was born into, coincidentally also the time when all the referential experiments in video, media and conceptual art that inspire my practice took place, it was the decade when Fittja's construction was completed. It was interesting to understand what had happened in the span of one generation, over the span of my own lifetime in the country where I was born and which I knew so little about. Later, through research, I discovered that the 1970s was also the decade when satellite television infrastructure was consolidated and regulated, and it was also the decade when multicultural policy became enforced. It was also the period when Vilém Flusser was writing about his philosophy of migration and nationalism, and also when he did a brief stint as a curator of media art in Brazil, whose failures caused him to leave the country and re-emigrate into Europe.

51 Lisette Lagnado, 'O malabarista e a gambiarra', Revista *Trópico*, (October 2003). Available at: http://www.caoguimaraes.com/wordpress/wp-content/uploads/2012/12/o-malabarista-e-a-gambiarra.pdf.

assemblage. For Lagnado, there is also a political importance beyond the aesthetic and formal emphasis on these makeshift constructions, which comes very close to the concept of 'bricolage' formulated by Claude Lévi-Strauss in *The Savage Mind*.[52] The *gambiarra* can be seen as a contraption that involves a technological recombination of new or given technologies, acting like an intervention in the social sphere in such a way that the contraption itself, often precarious, illegal and transgressive, enters a dialogue with the surrounding community and locality.[53]

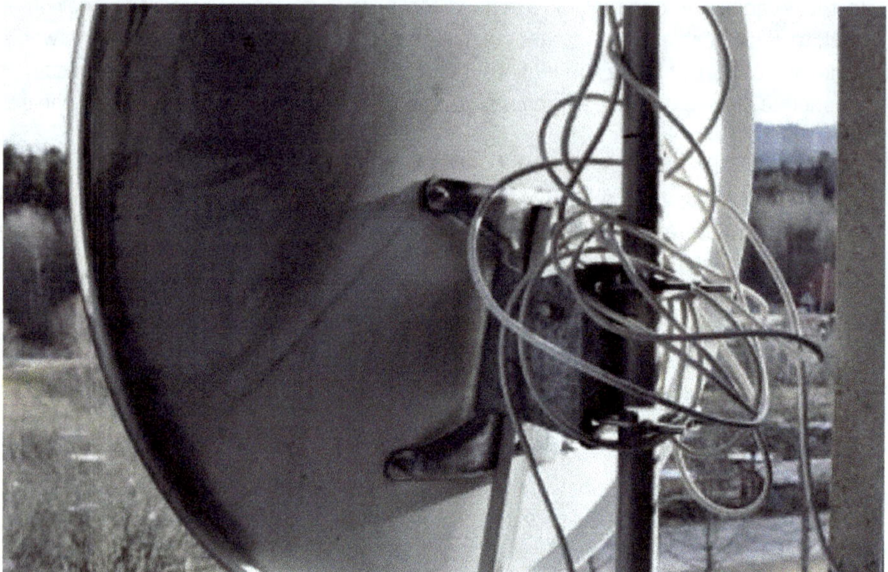

*Figure 30 – A gambiarra in Fittja, the satellite dish cabling tangled jiggery-pokery. Image by the author.*

In Fittja, I would later discover, not surprisingly, that indeed the mechanism of the *gambiarra* that I associate with the satellite dish has 'a political accent beyond the aesthetics, (...) it encompasses an entire network of subsistence that comes from an informal economy, with low-cost solutions and improvisation'.[54]

The difference from the formal-informal dichotomy in the Brazilian urban landscape[55] or

52 Claude Lévi-Strauss, *The Savage Mind*. Chicago: University of Chicago Press, 1968.

53 Ricardo Rosas, 'The Gambiarra: Considerations on a Recombinatory Technology', in Megan Boler (ed.) *Digital Media and Democracy: Tactics in Hard Times*, Cambridge, Mass.: MIT Press, 2010, p. 350.

54 Lagnado, 'O malabarista e a gambiarra'. (Author's translation).

55 In the slum areas of Rio, clandestine satellite and cable television connections are pervasive. On the one hand, they refer to a television market aimed towards the upper classes with high subscription prices which exclude those with the lowest income levels. Secondly, many poor areas have poor infrastructure and despite the large number of potential subscribers in slum areas, television companies do not invest in infrastructure to cater to these populations. Third, there is local knowledge and skill that is capable of installing these clandestine networks to such a scale that they become a pirate subscription service at an affordable price. These clandestine services are illegal and very profitable, often prone to police raids (who have also been known to earn a cut in the profits in exchange for ignoring them), often

in Southeast Asia, for instance, and the orderly, planned, and normative urban landscape in Sweden, was that no such combination or amount of satellite dishes can be seen in the downtown areas of Stockholm, or of any other city centers in the country.[56] As such, the *gambiarra* is not a 'thing' that can be readily found in a post-industrial society like Sweden, a country all too regulated to allow precarity in its urban landscape. Physical signifiers of an informal economy and haphazard technology are hard to detect, unless one travels far from the tourist gaze and away from the center of the city. What does it mean to be precarious in Sweden? In Europe? And yet, just like the agglomeration of satellite dishes in Rio would be most noticeable in the slum areas, satellite dishes in Sweden are strictly a phenomenon of the suburb, especially the *miljonprogram* suburb, which, as discussed in previous chapters, is the urban synonym for the excluded Other.

Television *per se* is interesting insofar as we consider the larger information apparatus and what is expressed and indexed by television. As receptors of satellite signals that convert into television transmissions, I saw these satellite dishes and their assemblages as 'contact zones' between a transnational media space in the air and the more intimate media space of the home. According to Mary Louise Pratt, contact zones are 'social spaces where cultures meet, clash, and grapple with each other, often in contexts of highly asymmetrical relations of power, such as colonialism, slavery, or their aftermaths as they are lived out in many parts of the world today'.[57] Lisa Parks, a media theorist specializing in satellite networks in their social, political, economic and aesthetic dimensions, states that 'no objects in the apparatus of communication technology are more architectural than antennae and satellite dishes'.[58] Ontologically, as an object encroached on architecture, the satellite dish makes explicit the relationship between the built environment and communication technology, and leads us to think of communication technology *as* architecture. If we consider the city both as an extension of technological networks[59] and as a possible response to the question 'what is it we call home?', then these satellite dishes are not merely additions to individual households, they may constitute a home in and of themselves. In the absence of social meeting places for the community (due, in part, to the stiffness of the planning that sharply divides the residential

---

leaving entire communities temporarily without television services. During research, I experienced the same phenomenon in Fittja. There is a large demand and supply chain of such clandestine satellite subscription services, suppliers and installers of satellite dishes, vendors of decoders and subscription cards often brought in from Turkey and other countries, thus creating a business sector that caters specifically to this 'household necessity' for the immigrant living in Europe.

56 I am referring specifically to urban environments. Satellite dishes are very common in the countryside, both in Sweden, Brazil and elsewhere where there is a different infrastructure altogether, and where cable television, for example, may not reach houselholds because they are remotely located. Also, in the countryside, a satellite dish does not have the same social significance as in a satellite city, the context is thus key.

57 Mary Louise Pratt, 'Arts of the Contact Zone', *Profession*, (1991): 33–40. Available at: https://www.jstor.org/stable/25595469.

58 Lisa Parks, 'Postwar Footprints: Satellite and Wireless Stories in Slovenia and Croatia', in Anselm Franke (ed.) *B-Zone: Becoming Europe and Beyond*, Barcelona: Actar, 2005, p. 306–347.

59 By 'technological networks' I refer to any network that contributes to the communication apparatus. They are information technology and communication networks, satellite, wireless, radio, cable, etc. I leave it generic in order to focus on television later on.

area from the commercial areas, but also to a sort of gender segregation in public space, and the few options of leisure available), the domestic sphere becomes the center of social life, with the television set as the centerpiece in the living room.

Satellite dishes are only a linchpin to expand on the tethering relationship between local contentions and greater transnational flows. Broadcast signals, antennae, wireless networks all contribute to the wholeness of a dwelling place, whether it be the city or the house, and have thus become inseparable. As such, it is easy to create a blindness towards them. This blindness has also been detected by Lisa Parks in terms of the absence of a discussion of satellite technology and its importance for the understanding of globalization in the field of cultural and media theory. In her words, 'In cultural theory, the satellite has been missing in action, lying at the threshold of everyday visibility and critical attention, but moving through orbit, structuring the global imaginary, the socioeconomic order, and the tissue of everyday experience across the planet. This blindness is not innocent, for it reveals that the military-industrial-information complexes of the West have been quite effective at concealing and using the most strategic technologies to assume global domination in the post-Cold War period, managing to avert the critical gaze in the process'. [60]

On a broad context, these satellite dishes are an intrinsic part of the necessary media infrastructure of contemporary living and one may even wonder why such an apparatus is not yet completely embedded into building design, to the same extent in which television is embedded inside people's lives.[61] I contend that these transnational technological networks, which respond to several political and media developments, among them the provision of new spaces for communication flows that transcend geographical borders and make exile as an existential condition more bearable, redefine the condition of the exile altogether. Whereas the notion of the exile, as *ex-ilos*, may carry with it the notion of isolation and separation from a referential home and homeland, today this geographical isolation is not necessarily a defining factor of life in exile. In fact, the idea seems more of a connected exile.

In the context of a politics of hospitality, one way of understanding host and guest relationships could be to study the effects of such transnational media on the status of guests and aliens in host societies – only to reveal to permeability of the cultural and social membranes that connect (or separate) both hosts and guests, but also to understand the intensity of

60 Lisa Parks, *Cultures in Orbit: Satellites and the Televisual*, Durham: Duke University Press, 2005, p. 7.

61 In December 2013, I gave a lecture on *Satellitstaden*, suburbs and citizen participation at the architecture course at the Royal Technical University (Kungliga Tekniska högskolan – KTH) in Stockholm, by the invitation of architect Erik Stenberg. One of the students asked if there was any recommendation I would make for architecture students in terms of how architecture could solve segregation by eliminating such physical signifiers on the façades, and perhaps, in so doing, lessening the 'branding' of difference in the suburbs, for example. Whereas the optimal response from a social standpoint would be to incorporate difference in the very conception of architecture and planning, there was another side that could be explored in terms of the incorporation of information technology and media within the architectural design. My response was to think about an architecture that incorporates information systems into the conception of architectural projects, and not only as 'encroachments' that come after construction.

relationship of immigrants to their place of origin through media during exile, as both a temporary and permanent condition.

## How Can We Live Together?

During her visit to Fittja in the fall of 2011, Lisette Lagnado asked me a few decisive questions. What is the network behind these strings of apparatuses hiding behind these satellite dishes? What are you able to discover from this object alone, from how it is hung to how it is used, to how much it costs, to what it means at the symbolic level? More importantly, she asked me over a cup of coffee at *Residence Botkyrka,* 'What is the friction? Where is the contention? For where there is contestation, there is a space for art.'

In response to Lagnado's question, the contention was that hanging the satellite dishes on the façades of many *miljonprogram* areas in Sweden was in principle prohibited, including in Fittja's buildings, which, additionally have been earmarked for preservation as historical heritage.[62] It follows that the satellite decoders and connections are mostly all pirated, many brought over from resident's homelands, in order to better access the desired channels. In 2005, a court decision determined the eviction of three families for refusing to take down their satellite dish. They were accused of disobeying security rules determined in their rental contracts in Rinkeby, a suburb in northern Stockholm, an argument frequently used in the media against this essentially suburban cultural practice. The meeting notes from a discussion in the Swedish Parliament reads,

> (...) three tenants in Rinkeby in northern Stockholm will be evicted after refusing to take down their satellite dishes. Their rental contracts will be terminated because tenants have installed satellite dishes against the landlord's will. The landlord claims that all satellite dishes must be removed due to security measures. The three tenants claim that their freedom of information is contested if they are obliged to take away their antennae.[63]

Access to communication media is indeed a very important part of everyday life experience in communities affected by exile, and it naturally follows that in areas with large immigrant populations, the satellite dish is an important part of everyday life. For many residents in the suburbs, the satellite dish, and the possibility of connecting to one's referential culture, hearing language and sounds from the homelands is essential – feeling at home far away from home. One of the evicted families defend their decision to refuse taking down their antenna, they state 'the most important is the right to access information. We live in a society where people arrive from different countries and there must be a way for these people to be informed about what happens in their country – the satellite dish offers this possibility'.[64]

62 A number of *miljonprogram* buildings in Sweden are currently considered for historical preservation due to their unique status as examples of historical approaches to design and architecture.

63 *Riksdagens protokoll 2005/06:60*, Swedish Parliament, 24 January 2005, https://www.riksdagen.se/sv/dokument-lagar/dokument/protokoll/riksdagens-protokoll-20050660-tisdagen-den-24_GT0960/html.

64 'Lättare att ha parabolantenn', *Sveriges Radio*, 25 July 2006.

Satellite dishes have been hanging in most buildings in Rinkeby or Fittja for decades, with none ever falling down. To evict tenants for such a minor issue seemed draconian at best, and not least indicative of a missing dialogue between landlords to find solutions that help tenants get access to television channels they want to see, many of which are not available in commercial packages or in public television. To get proper reception, satellite dishes need to be positioned precisely and may thus stick out of the façade. It is unclear where the jurisdictions of the tenant and the landlord begin or end – the tenant is responsible for upholding the internal space whereas the landlord is responsible for the façade and the exterior. Yet the balconies on which most satellite dishes are hung are an intermediary space between inside and outside that creates this judicial ambiguity. Both in Parliament and in the media, the discussion became a debate in ethnic and racial discrimination and the right for information, rather than an issue of architectural preservation or security.

This liminality once again draws attention to the materiality of media. Satellite television is talked about as media technology first and foremost, but it also entails a range of material objects and a certain arrangement of space, altering the look of the *miljonprogrammet* housing and is, for some, a disturbance of the aesthetic ideal of the welfare state. The very presence of a technology changes the environment where the technology is used more (is thickened, texturized and amalgamated). From Friedrich Kittler's media archeological perspective, it is the hardware, the very material and tangible expression of technology, that represents the medium, and it is this hardware which requires adaptation from human beings (not vice versa).[65] It may be worth noting that Kittler would probably also read Fittja's satellite network anachronistically, perhaps as an early expression of the new media (freedom of niche choice and resultant fragmentation, irrelevance of national borders, decentralized network that only stops short of connectivity) in a world still dominated by broadcasting.

Though forbidden, satellite dishes in Fittja are tolerated. In a 'free' country as Sweden, residents find it inconceivable that they should be barred from access to whatever media they wish and would protest if this happened.[66] My observation is that since many Fittja residents come from countries where media is heavily controlled by the government, any claims to remove satellite dishes, in their minds, can only be ideologically motivated. One of the definitions of democracy in the information age is the ability to choose your information source and distribution platform, and owning the ability to watch, emit and share your own information through whatever (free) means available. When this ownership transcends legal limits, it generally concerns file-sharing of third-party material (music, files, videos), spying on private networks, hacking into secure sites, or leaking classified documents to the public, for example. Where do we draw the line of legality when satellite signals can be obtained for free?

There are some contradictions to be considered here. While many communities of immigrants may be spatially segregated from other parts of the city and its residents excluded

65 Friedrich A. Kittler, *Gramophone, Film, Typewriter*, Palo Alto: Stanford University Press, 1999.

66 One of the Fittja residents I interviewed said that she would 'start a revolution' if the landlords decided to take them away. See Chapter 5.

from the mainstream society to varying degrees, this does not mean that they are *informationally* segregated from the world-at-large, or even from the rest of the city, and least of all within their communities. On the contrary, suburbs in Stockholm are interconnected across different parts of the city and to other suburbs in the country, both regarding the use of information technology and in shared social networks both on- and off-line. Recently, social movements begun in one suburb have found resonance in other suburbs, and the networks formed through these movements begins to strengthen and crystallize new political identities. Furthermore, the satellite lifelines to the homelands around the world are maintained through a variety of channels that creates strong international connectivity. Television, diasporic political movements, and also the flow of capital have characterized the investment of the diaspora in rebuilding hometowns and expanding local economies, signifying a flow where the regimes that have once expelled their citizens into diasporas now benefit from the expelled's investments back into the reconstruction of the homelands.[67] It is also fundamental to understand how, as foreigners, their politics of displacement has in turn influenced the future of the city, both culturally and politically.[68] As we have seen, issues related to migration are inextricably linked to globalization, whether economic globalization in the sense of populations that shift according to economic opportunities, or in the globalization of conflict, where migrations cause a displacement of a population's war traumas and also their liberation strategies.

There is a third aspect to connectivity that involves media. We have briefly addressed the possibility of media to mitigate the sense of loss and alienation of the 'expelled' while in exile. However, in the same way that the availability of information and access to television and other media keeps one connected to the homeland, this same openness also creates the possibility of more surveillance by the expellers, which may continue the persecution of the expelled remotely in diaspora. This is the double-edged sword of satellite technology as elucidated by Lisa Parks in *Cultures in Orbit*: the same technology that connects people is the same used to persecute. So, the possibility of organized activity and social movements that is geared towards the liberation of the suburb, may inversely, and undesirably so, also present the possibility of providing vital information for oppositional political groups, and so on.

The perception of simultaneous exclusion and inclusion also depends whether you are looking at these satellite cities from the inside or outside. Even if, from the outside, it may seem like living in a satellite city may be isolating, from within the 'city of satellites' it is the connectedness that counts: ties of kinship, neighbors, affinity by interests, and especially by ethnic/national groups. Whereas those living outside Fittja may consider the satellite dish to be a symbol of marginalization, within the community the satellite dish is inversely

---

67 I am referring here to the example of many Kurdish families in Fittja who have bought property in their hometowns in Central Turkey and Iraq and as such contribute to the urban and economic development of Kurdish towns now under a Turkish government that in 2012 was more tolerant towards Kurds. Also, there are many Kurdish immigrants that actively contribute to the creation of the Kurdish state conducting their activism from a distance. However, with Recep Tayyip Erdogan's administration since 2014, the emancipation and autonomy of Kurds and Kurdistan has been threatened and is a contentious issues.

68 For an account of how foreigners and exiles and their politics of displacement have affected the cultural and political life of Paris see Richard Sennett, *The Foreigner*, Notting Hill Editions, 2011.

largely considered a symbol of social status and pride (though not unanimously as we will see in the next chapter). Indeed, many residents in Fittja have purposefully chosen to live in the area because satellite dishes are allowed through a tacit agreement between administrators and tenants that allows satellite dishes to remain visible as part of the local architectural style.[69]

## Satellitstaden

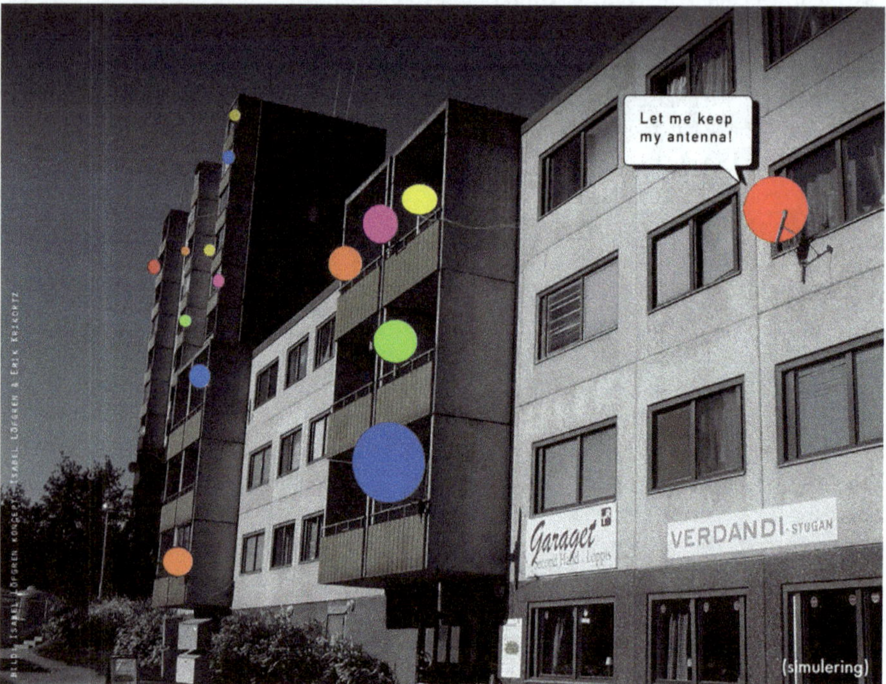


*Figure 31 – Conceptual sketch of the artistic intervention, in collaboration with Erik Krikortz. Participants were able to choose their own color for the satellite dish. The speech bubbles are statements extracted from the interview with each satellite dish owner.*

In the art project *Satellitstaden*, the intervention made directly on satellite dishes in Fittja finds its home in the grey zone between desire, longing, legality, piracy, urban segregation, relative tolerance, and the presence of the creative class. It is an artistic response to the problematic relationship between private interventions in public space, to the integration of global media in local contexts, and the limitations of the terms of engagement of the migrant, or 'guest' in the space of the host. The satellite dish can be considered to be a metaphor for such a 'guest' element, moveable and dynamic, perching on the fixed façade

69 Charlotte Brundson explored how the proliferation of satellite dishes on apartment buildings roused anxieties that involved public space, class and taste in London in the early 1990s. Charlotte Brunsdon, 'Satellite Dishes and the Landscapes of Taste', *New Formations*, 15 (winter 1991): 23-42.

of the building, its 'host'. In short, satellite dishes are an important part in the complex politics of hospitality.

Both the range of artworks created and the more ethnographic oriented research conducted as the field work for this book, would embody this positive 'parasitical' aspect which Racek described in terms of the artist as a guest[70] in several ways as it depended on the participation of the Other, in this case, the hosting community and the individuals that reside in this neighborhood, to become activated. It included three interconnected artworks: 1) *Television is a foreign country,* a 24/7 video installation displayed on the residency apartment window; 2) *Satellitstaden,* a street-wide color intervention on satellite dishes to emphasize the presence of these objects on the building façades and what they represent to the resident community; and 3) *Television is my homeland,* a series of photographs of television rooms inside the apartments I visited during interviews with residents.

These three works would involve the participation of the host community in three different ways: 1) residents meet the artwork on the street as passive viewers of a standalone artwork on a display window, as if on a gallery or museum, except that the work was visible from the street; 2) residents are actively involved in the project and even contribute to refining the proposition, that is, their participation is an intrinsic part of the artwork's realization and indeed depends entirely on it for its realization, and 3) residents give permission to have their living rooms with their television photographed, thus making the images of these intimate spaces available to the public eye.

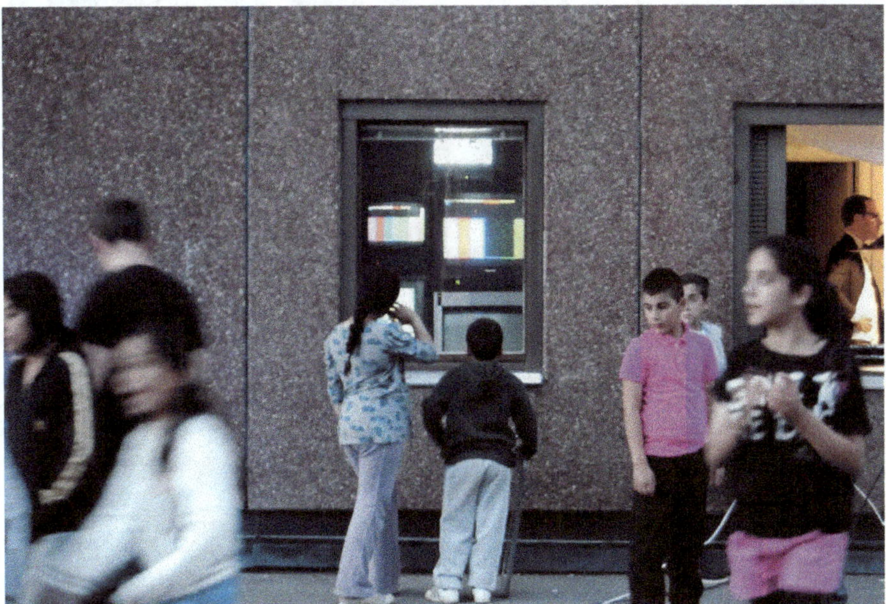

*Figure 32 –* Television is a Foreign Country, *television installation on the window of Residency Botkyrka. Five monitors show different temporalities of television, one showing white noise, another showing a still multi-colored*

70 See section '*Satellitstaden*: Media Texture, Social Assemblage' in this chapter.

*signal, a third connected to a satellite dish with a Turkish channel, a fourth showing a recording of Escrava Isaura, a Brazilian soap opera from 1979 which has been shown several times in most countries in the world, and what some residents in Fittja had watched dubbed to their language in their homelands; a fifth set turned off. Fittja Open '11, September 2011, Residency Botkyrka, https://botkyrkakonsthall.se/evenemang/fittja-open-2011/. Photo: Joanna Hüttner Lemoine.*

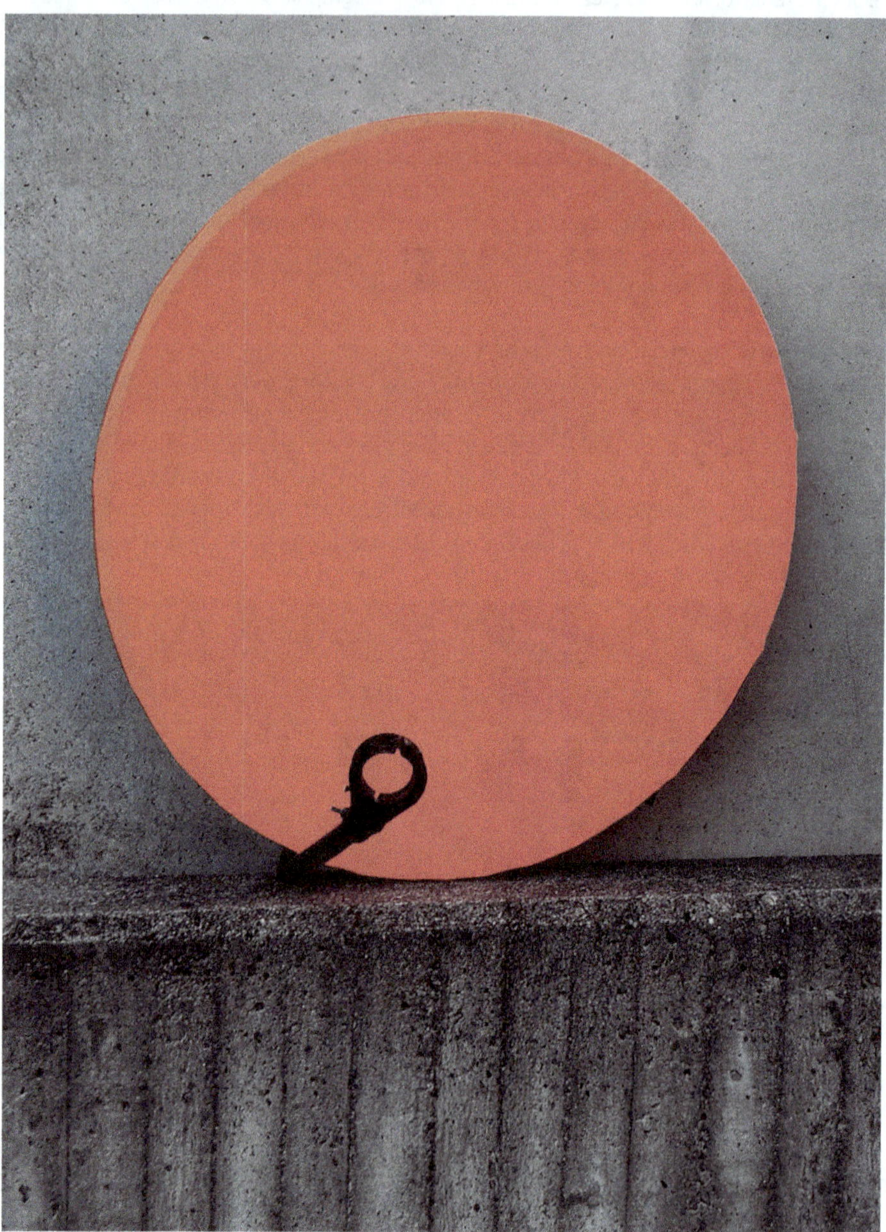

*Figure 33 –* Satellitstaden, *textile cover on satellite dish, 2011–12. Over the course of 2 years, 65 satellite dishes were covered in neon colors chosen by the residents themselves resulting in a street-wide art intervention on the building façades, following a participatory strategy. Fittja, Stockholm, Sweden. Images by the author.*

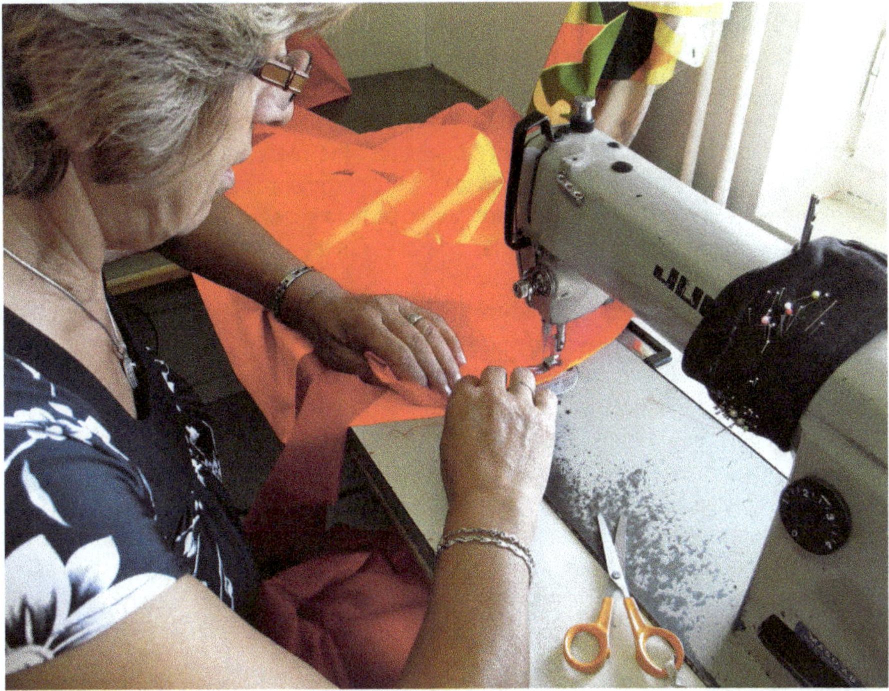

*Figure 34* – Pero Dag sews one of the "parabol dresses" in the sewing studio at Verdandi. Image by the author.

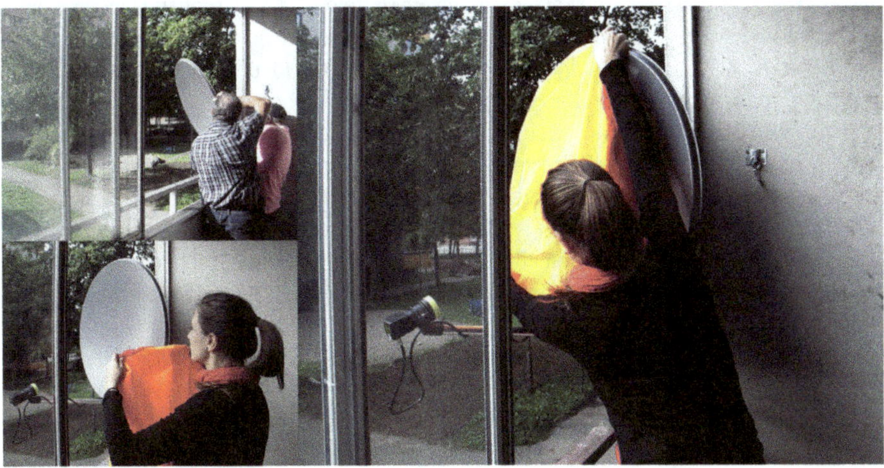

*Figure 35 – Dressing up a satellite dish. The first satellite dish was installed at Residency Botkyrka, for the public arts event Fittja Open '11. The process included, clockwise from top left: ordering the installation of a satellite dish with a local vendor; Pero Dag cutting fabric to sew the satellite dish cover; pulling the textile cover over the satellite dish; final installation view. Residency Botkyrka, September 2011. Images by the author and Lara Szabo Greisman.*

The plan for 'dressing up' satellite dishes by means of a colored textile cover entailed developing an array of strategies to get the approval and trust of organizations and individuals in the community, as well as creating tactics for contacting and engaging residents in the project. Because satellite dishes are the private property of residents, and reachable only from inside each apartment, without resident participation, the intervention would be impossible to realize. This dependency required me to visit the participant's home in order to be able to color the satellite dish. This visit, where I would be both guest and intruder in their homes, provided the opportunity to meet him/her individually in their own environment.

Many residents in the beginning asked me if they needed to pay to have their satellite dish colored. Paying for participation was completely out of the question – but I did ask for one thing in return: time for a short conversation. Usually held on the kitchen table, I would interview the participant and conduct my 'ethnographic' study based on an open-ended conversational approach. First, I asked questions about their television habits: favorite programs, favorite channels, how long ago they had acquired their satellite dish, etc. Then I moved on to more speculative questions: 'What would you do if they took down the satellite dishes? How is living in Fittja? What did you think about the election results? What is it like being an immigrant in Sweden? What do you miss most from home?', were some of the questions. Lastly, I asked that given the possibility to be heard, what would they like to tell the host society? (See Figure 58 for collected statements in response to these questions).

This way, I could gather the new data about the community, their media habits, their impressions of Fittja, and if possible, hear about their journey into exile. Spending time in their homes also allowed a glimpse into their environments, their 'things'. As a street and landscape photographer, my eye is drawn to the materials that make up one's environment and that frames one's life. For this reason, after this conversation, I would ask for one last thing: if I could take a photograph of the television room in the apartment for a photographic essay called *Television is my homeland*. This way I would make the satellite dish and the television apparatus in the home visible, one through direct intervention in the object, the other by doing what documentary photography does: to reveal spaces which the public cannot normally access.

Once inside the participant's home, the conversation started easily as it had been previously arranged, often with the presence of children by the kitchen table, where coffee and cakes lay waiting. Negotiating the photograph of the living room, on the other hand, was much more difficult. Most participants, fifty in total, did not want their home to be photographed, and most people also disapproved of recording devices during the interviews. This revealed to me that, even if local residents wished for more political visibility and representation, they still wanted to protect their own image from public scrutiny, probably for good reasons. Some potential participants were turned down because they did not want to give an interview. For the majority who consented to the interview, however, I asked if the interviews could become part of this book, which would be disclosed to a limited public. Even with their consent, most people did not want to have their images taken or voice recorded, and I would have to de-identify the material prior to publication. The satellite dish, on the other hand, was fine to use, as long as the signal was left undisturbed.

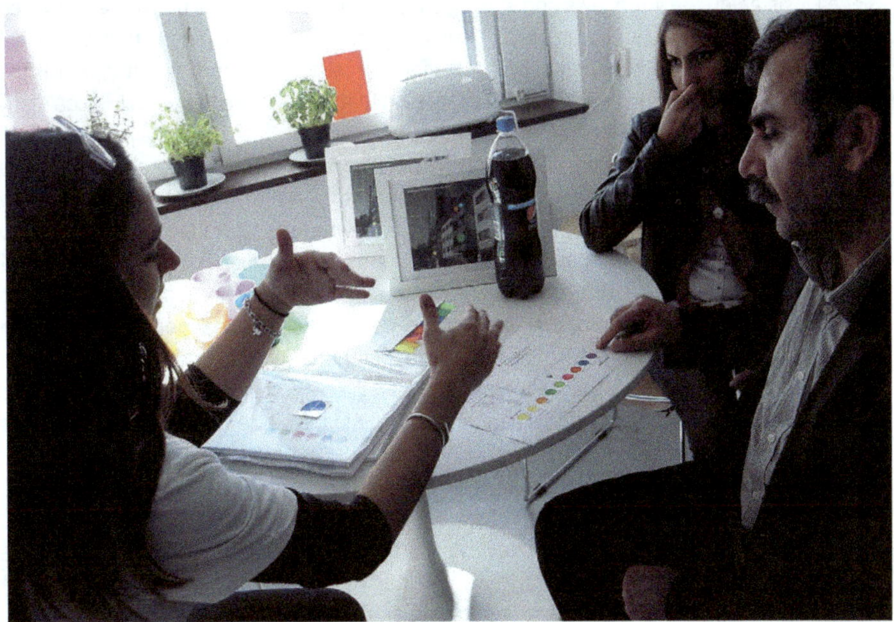

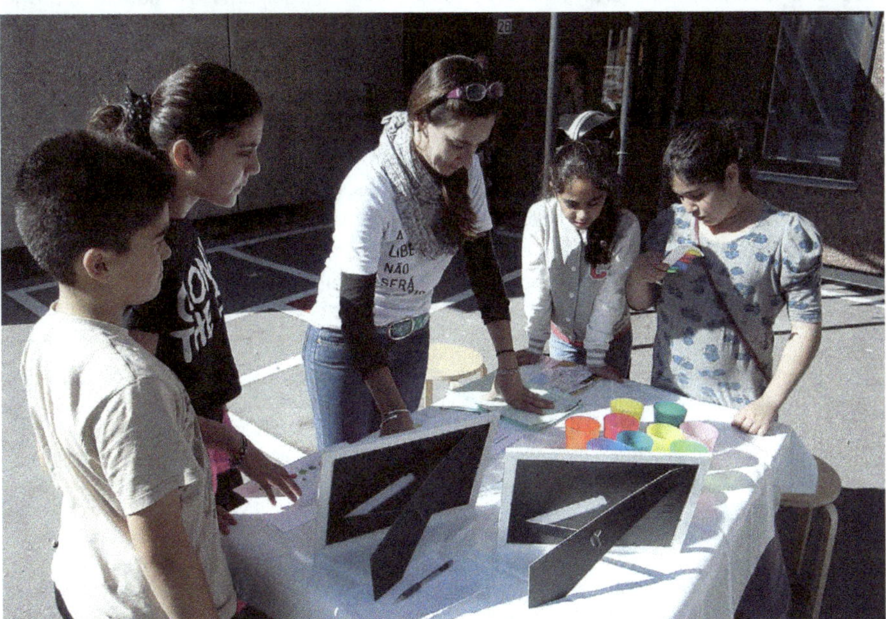


*Figure 36a and 36b – Recruiting participants for the installation of colored textile covers on satellite dishes. Residents can choose a color of their own and provide address for a later visit to their homes to install the cover. In the form, they are asked to recommend a neighbor. Residence Botkyrka, September 2011. Photo: Joanna Hüttner Lemoine.*

Since I insisted on the interviews and since I looked and sounded like a native Swede, often people mistook me for a journalist and turned away, aware that many times their words get distorted in the media, which only serves to confirm a resistance from residents towards the media. They do not need yet another article that says that Fittja is 'bad,' especially since many do not feel that way about their home. I often needed to clarify that I was not a journalist, and that the interview was part of an art project and not a newspaper article. When I said I was a free-lance artist, it led in turn led to another set of questions – what is an artist doing climbing balconies in a suburb? do you paint? who is paying you? why are you doing this? where do you live? is this art? and then more personal questions like: are you married? do you have children? who is looking after you?[71] This was not surprising since many of the people I interviewed had lived, at least for a period of their lives, under persecution, and secondly, Fittja is often in the media spotlight and an object of study by researchers. Just because they were safe in Sweden it did not mean that they were still free from their persecutors, who, many told me, could be infiltrated within their own diaspora communities. Whether this is true or not, it was not in the scope of the project nor in my ability to investigate.

The answer to the question 'where do you live' became simple to respond when I could point to the window and say, 'I live two blocks away', or, 'I am your neighbor'. Often this would be the only common denominator I would have with the participant, and it was just enough to start a conversation. Having something in common became the basis for *Satellitstaden* to become such a 'shared project'. I hardly took any photographs of participants to ensure their privacy, and will thus not be able to show as many portraits of faces as I would like (remembering the importance of the 'face' in Lévinas so valued in Chapter 1), so I will rely on the stories lived and heard as they tell of an encounter with the human. There are almost no recordings of the conversations except for my own notes and some incidental images.

As a heterogeneous community with many ethnicities, cultures, languages spoken and religions, there are many cultural codes to become aware. What may seem welcoming to one culture may be offensive to another. Hospitality is a common feature across the Muslim world, with some cultural variations. For most Muslims, hospitality lies at the heart of who they are,

---

71 These questions seem to be very intrusive of my privacy, but we need to understand the context of Fittja and my temporary place in it. I was a (white) woman living alone in an apartment in Fittja which is a family-oriented and therefore rather conservative community. I had no personal ties to the community and also did not belong to any of its ethnic groups. Since my appearance leads one to initially identify me as a Swede (or at least European) in a community where there are almost no Swedes living in, it was already reason enough to stand out. I explained that I was living in the 'artist's hotel,' which was a diffuse entity few people actually knew about. Nearly all the women my age or younger in Fittja, which made up the core of the participants of the project, were married with small or school-age children. At the time, I was not. Differently than other parts of the city, Fittja's public and private spaces are gender-defined. For example, there are many gentlemen's clubs (The Turkish association, The Kurdish association, etc.) but there are very few spaces for women. The definition of 'artist' was also diffuse – the image one has of an artist is of someone who creates an art object and exhibits them in a specific place. However, this 'myth' was easily undone since coloring the dishes created such a direct aesthetic impact on the viewer. I welcomed these private questions as a means to engage in a conversation and enrich the connections. After all, if I wanted the participants to open their homes and share their stories with me, I would naturally and reciprocally retribute with sharing a small portion of my story.

and families judge themselves and each other by their generosity to guests when they entertain. Guests are welcomed into the home and shown kindness regardless of whether they are relatives, friends, neighbors, or strangers. Islam stresses the entertainment of guests to the point where the worst kind of betrayal is by someone who has eaten with a family and then deliberately hurt them. Such a person has betrayed a sacred covenant between host and guest. Traditionally, a stranger could arrive unannounced at the door and expect three days' hospitality before being asked any questions and given enough food for a day's journey ahead.

Food is important in welcoming a guest: a lavish table is a way of bestowing esteem and affection on a guest, especially when it is their first visit. In each interview and each house visit, I was greeted into homes in a very particular way: first the slippers as it is considered rude to walk barefoot in a Muslim home, then I was offered coffee and sweets, and an invitation for a second visit. Among the Christian families, the Syrian, and Turkish-Assyrian and Iraqi-Assyrian, very similar rules applied.

Small talk and ritual greetings are normal. In many cultures, profuse greetings and inquiries about personal and family health and well-being at the beginning of a conversation may seem to take up large amounts of time or seem intrusive. However, from a South American perspective, this type of more personal introductions is important in establishing friendly relations and trust and did not seem strange at all to me. In general, I felt that entering the home of another person, and following the 'protocol' of being a guest while allowing the host to do his/her part, was decisive in determining the quality of the visit and the amount of openness obtained during the interview. In general, the rules are not necessarily strict, but I felt that a general awareness of certain social codes to be very useful during the entire recruiting and interviewing process which also made the process enjoyable and memorable.

The technical complexity of coloring the satellite dishes had to take expediency and quality control in mind. To not overstay my welcome of one hour in the participant's home, coloring the satellite dish needed to be fast and precise if I also wanted to have this conversation and take a photograph of the living room. Whereas many people thought that I would 'paint' the satellite dishes, this would be a very messy solution. Instead, I designed a textile cover in weather-proof material that would cover the satellite dish and therefore leaving it intact. The installation took no more than 10 minutes and required precision: if the satellite dish moved as much as one millimeter out of range, the television signal would be lost, which would cost time and money to reset. This installation also required a thorough inspection of how the satellite dish hung on the façade, often at odd angles and out of reach, whence I needed to calculate how I needed to position myself in order to put on the textile cover, often requiring climbing on chairs and ladders on the balconies which proved to be quite risky at times.

The essential component to the entire project, however, was manufacturing the textile covers, and I set up a local production base that involved recruiting a team of professionals to manufacture the neon-colored textile covers. The seamstresses at *Verdandi* would become my coworkers and became *Satellitstaden*'s headquarters. It was also in this café where my strongest connections to the community were formed, as much time was spent there over several months between 2011 and 2012. When the installation eventually disappeared from the landscape, with the temporary textile covers eroded by sun and wind, many of those connections also disappeared. Strong bonds remained with only very few, as in life, with the ones with whom I had the most intense connections.

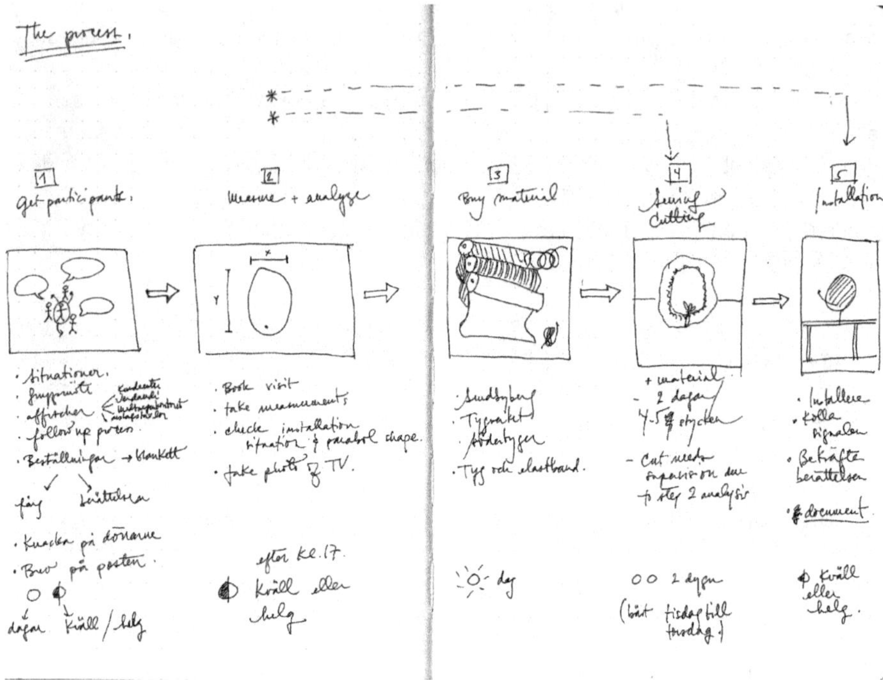


*Figure 37 – Production diagram. Each satellite dish required a custom-made solution. I visited each apartment twice, once to measure and evaluate the possibility of installing the textile cover and returning a second time for installation and interview. This process was laborious, slow. It required the management of a chain of social situations, materials, collaborators, and schedules. This process needed to become optimized so it could be stepped and repeated. Author's notes.*

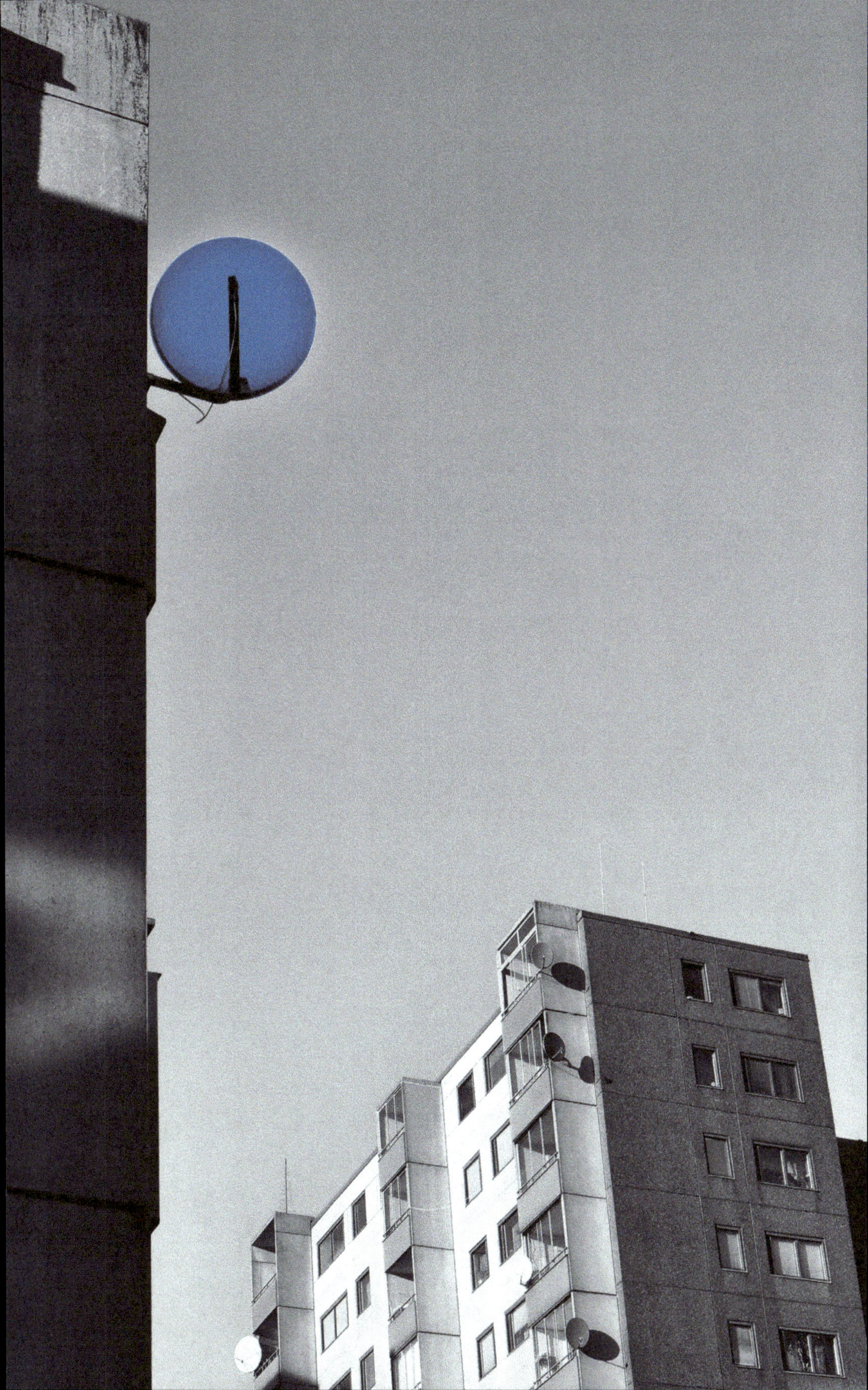

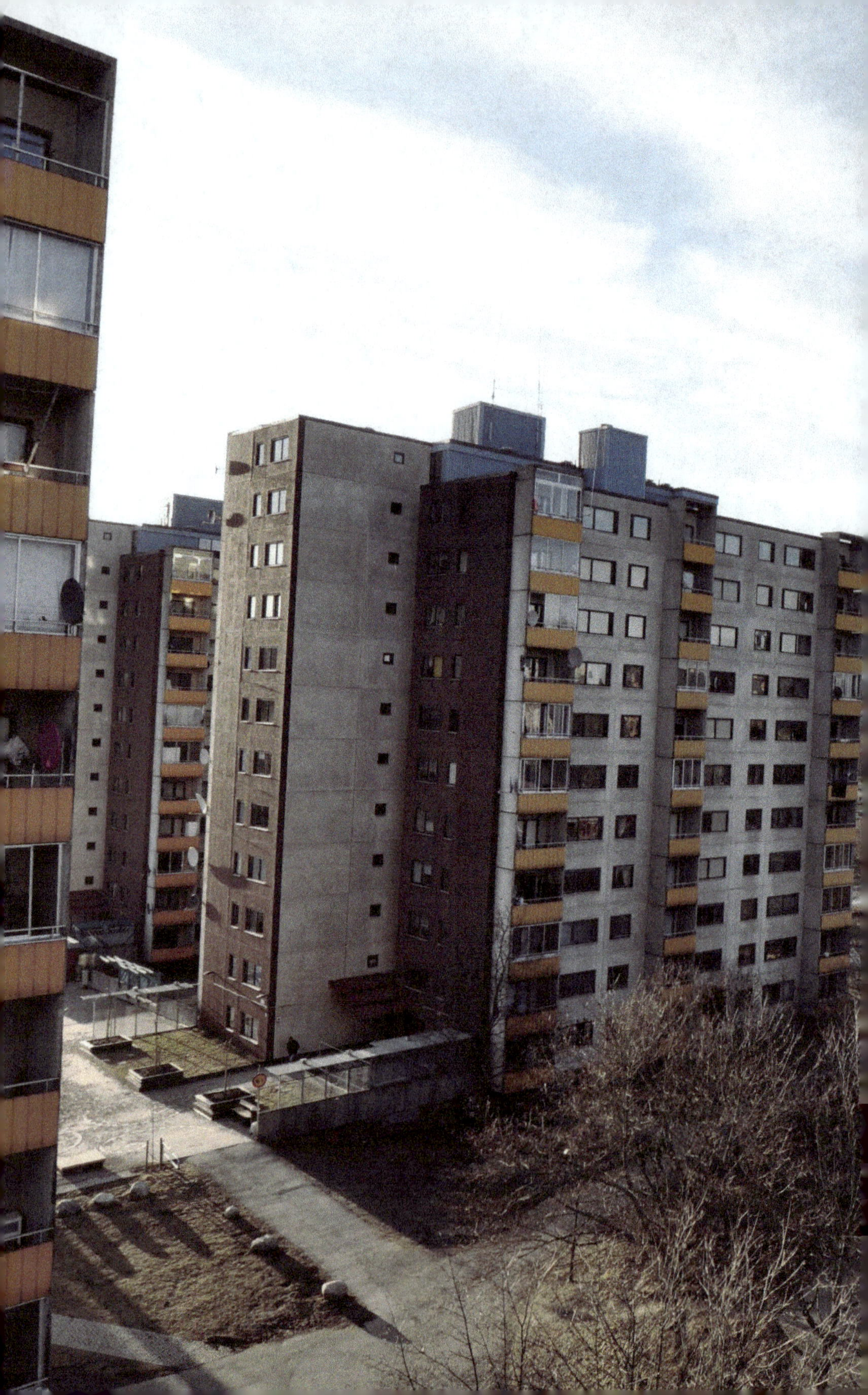

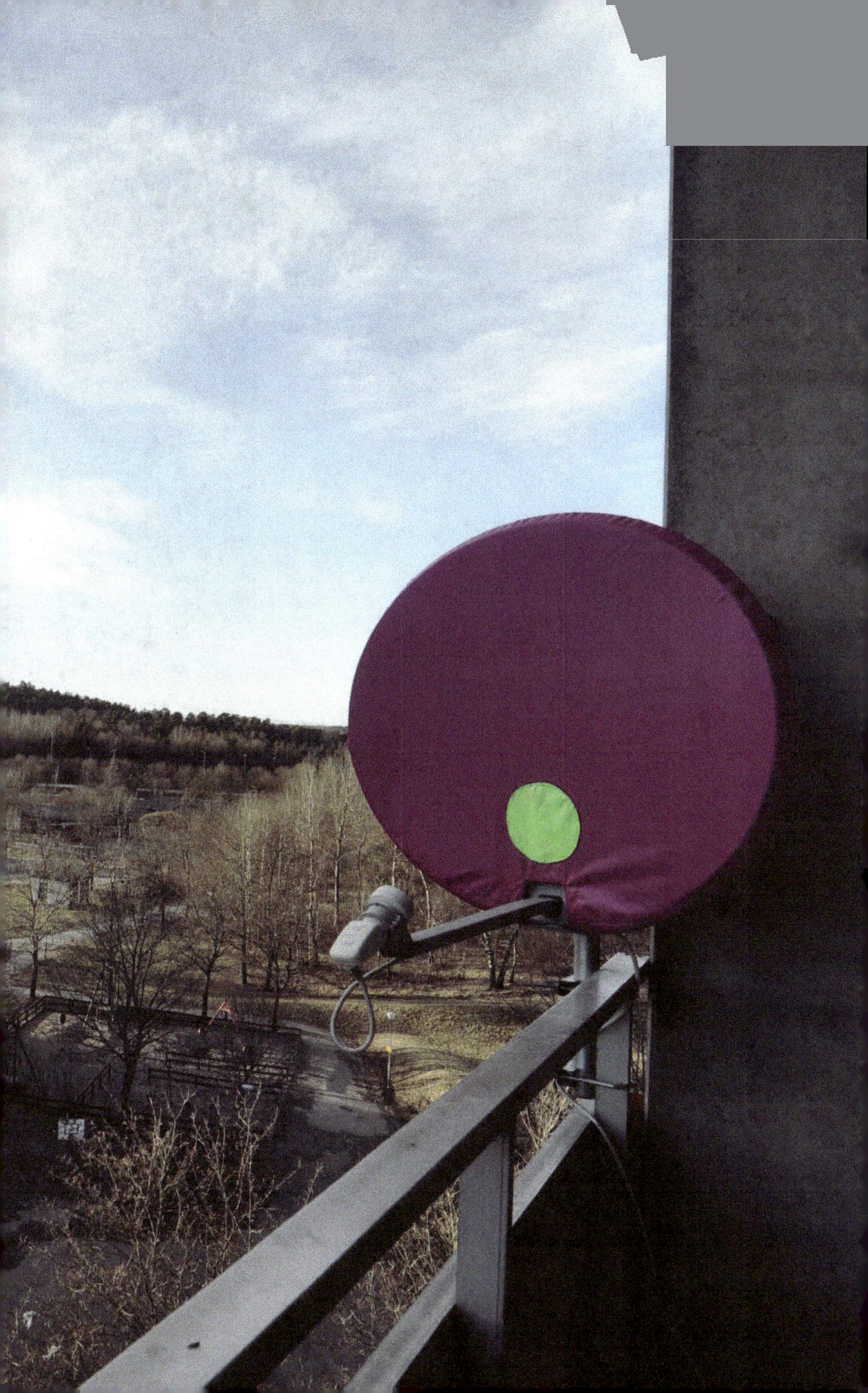

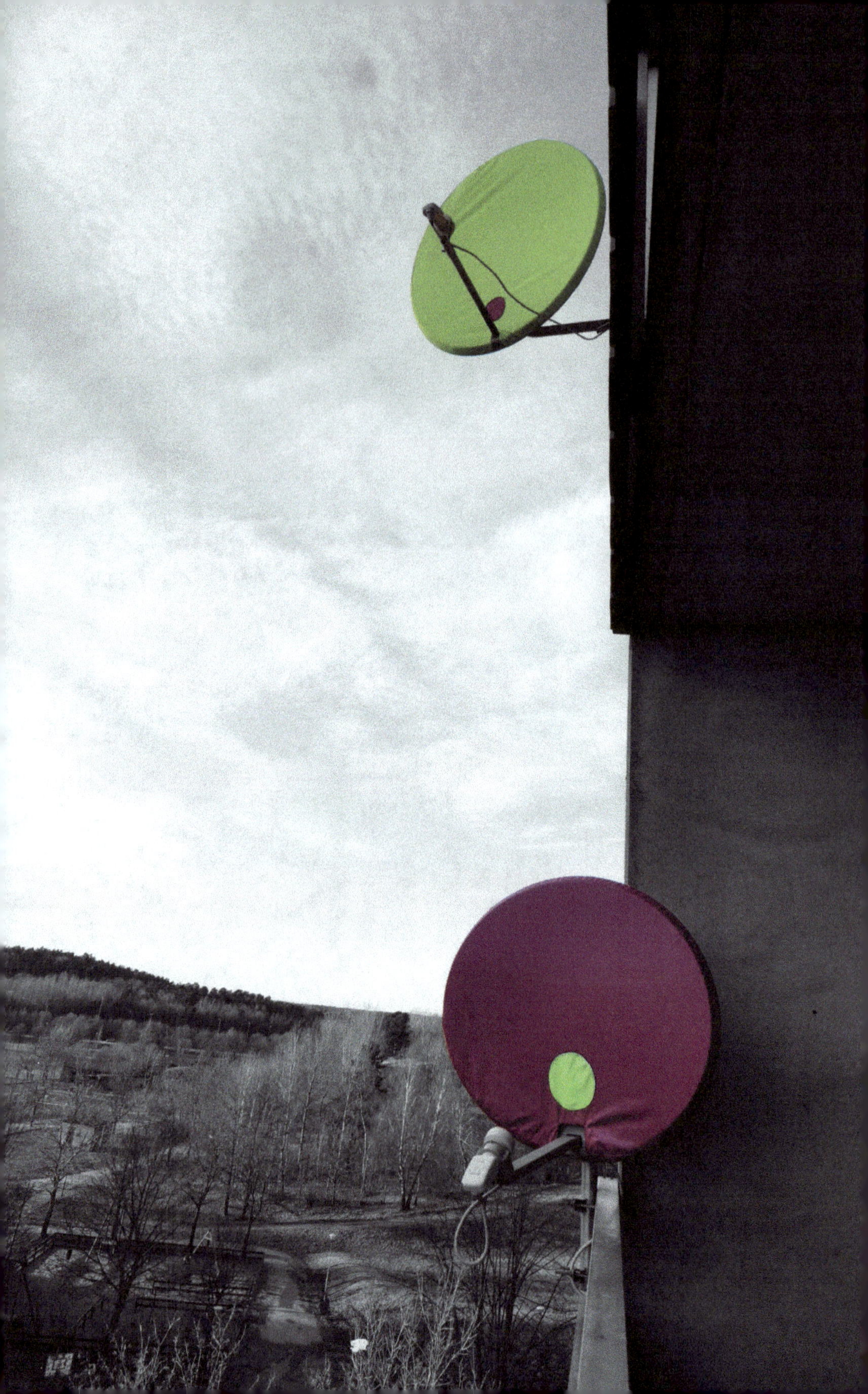

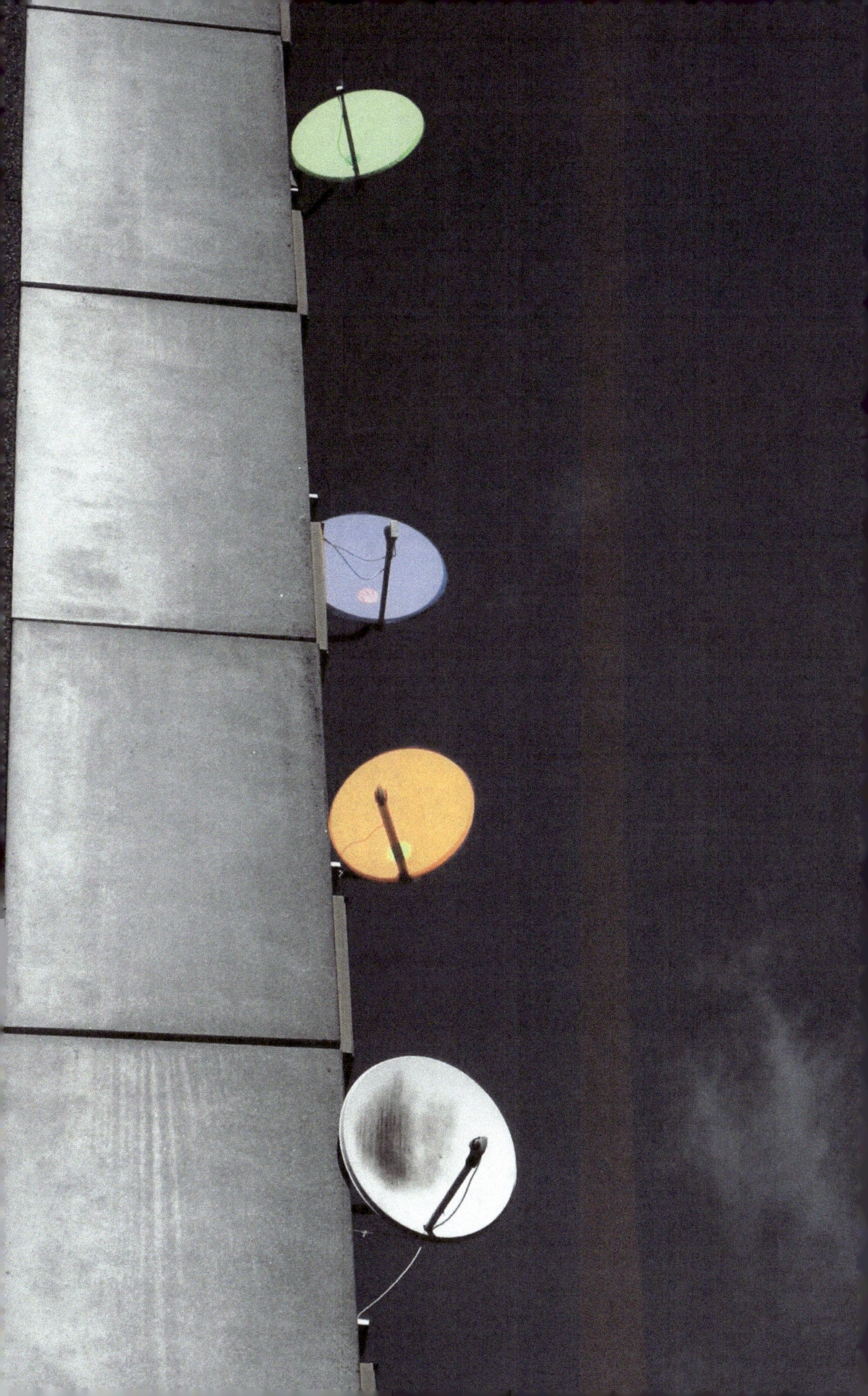

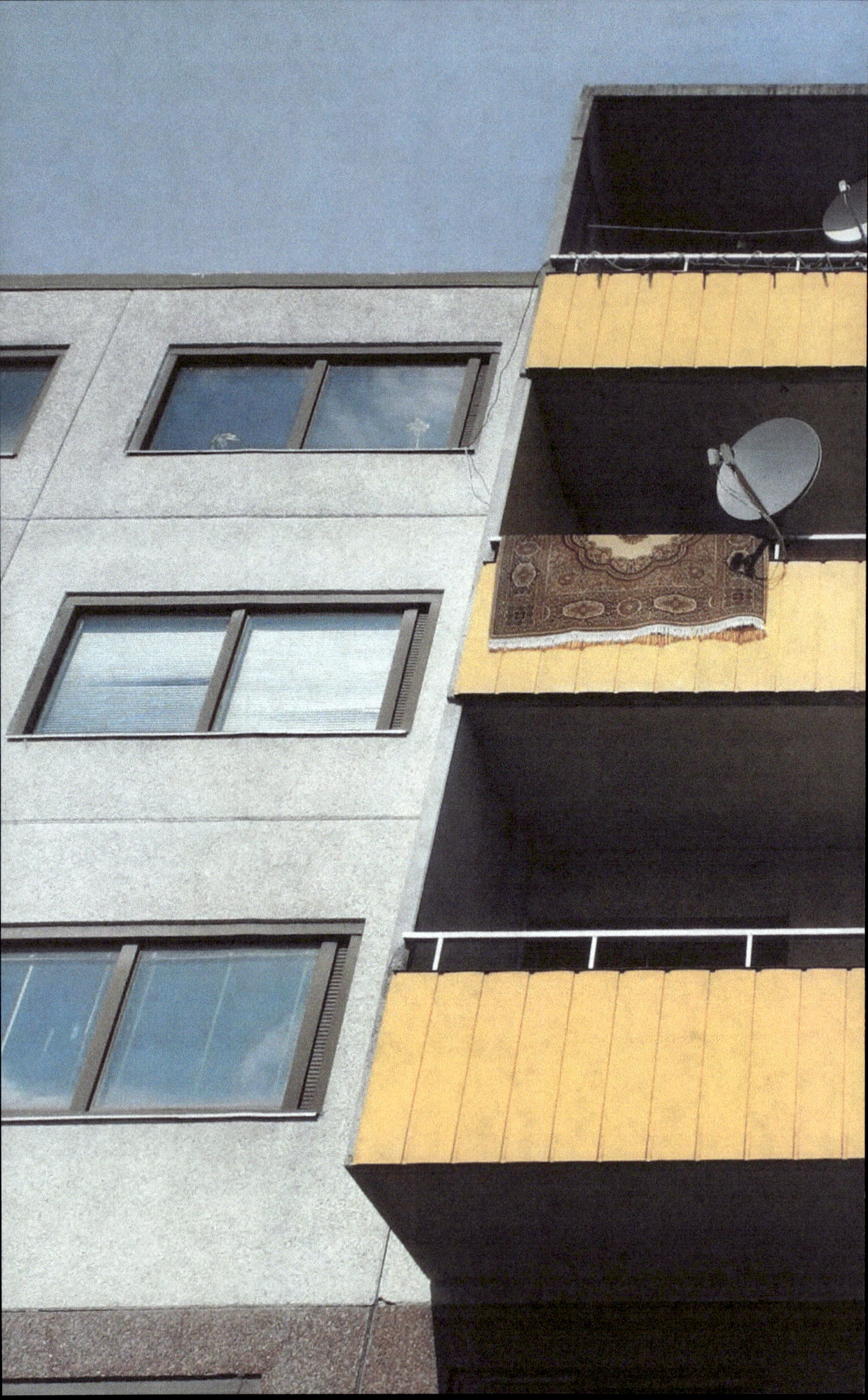

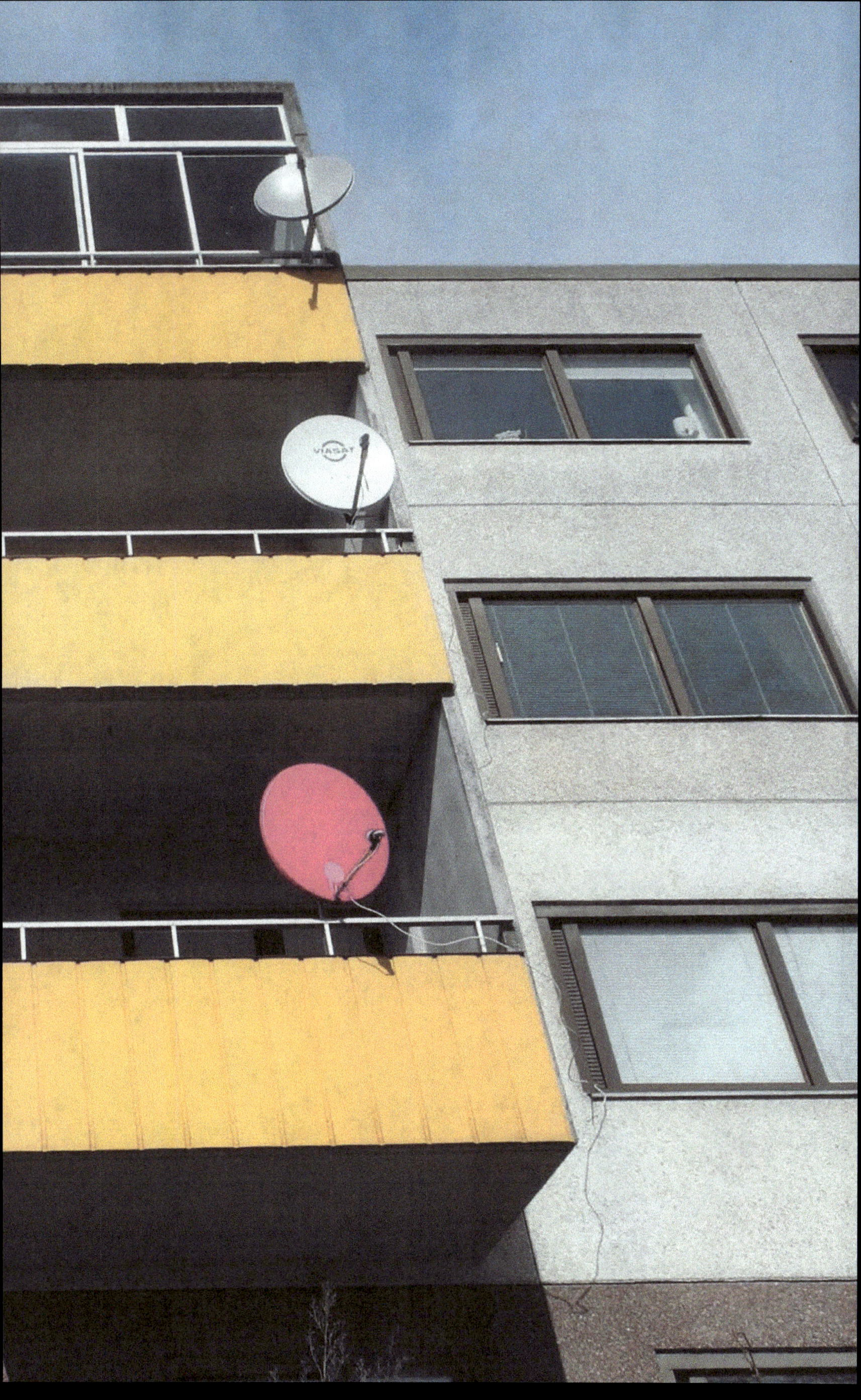
VIASAT

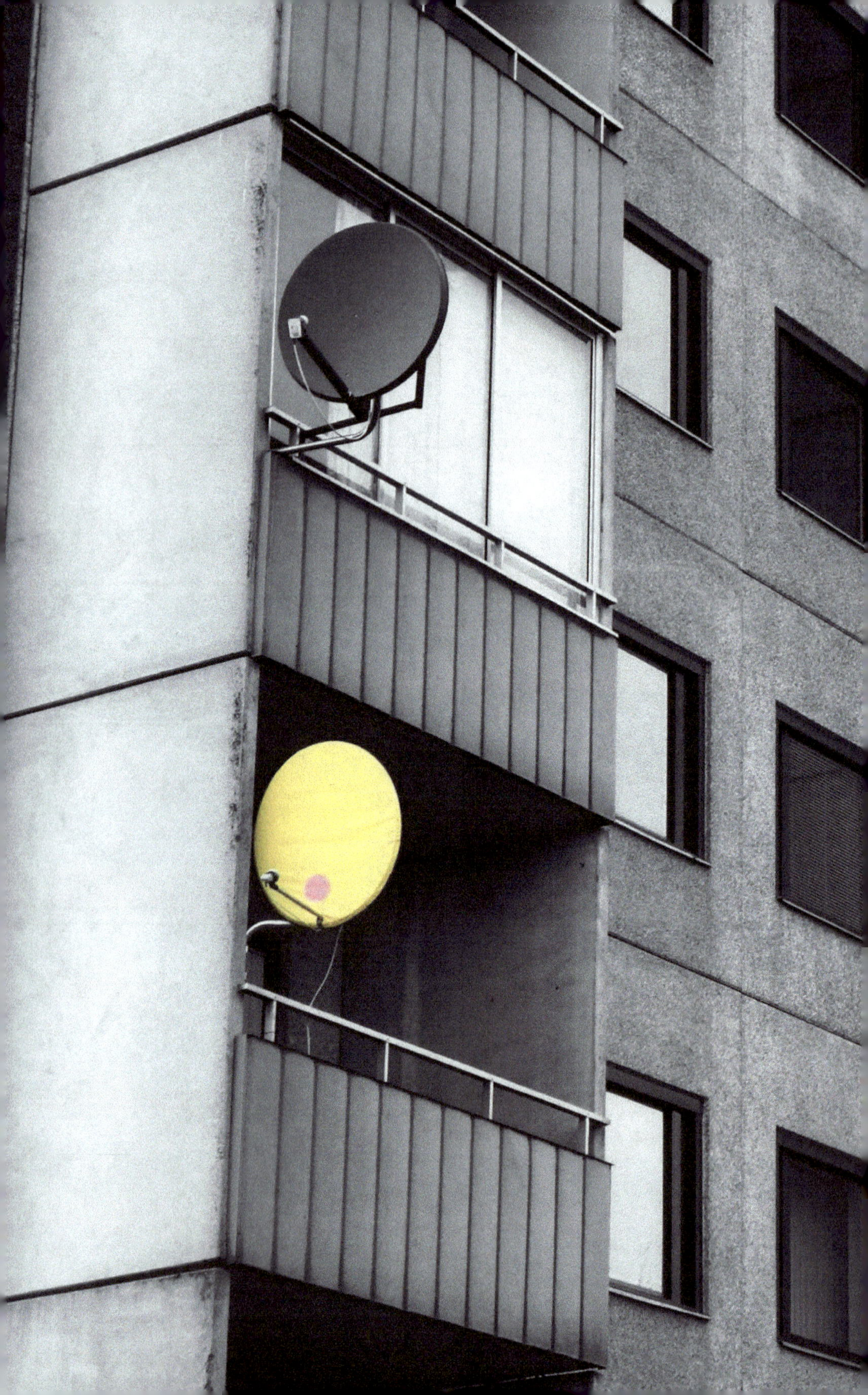

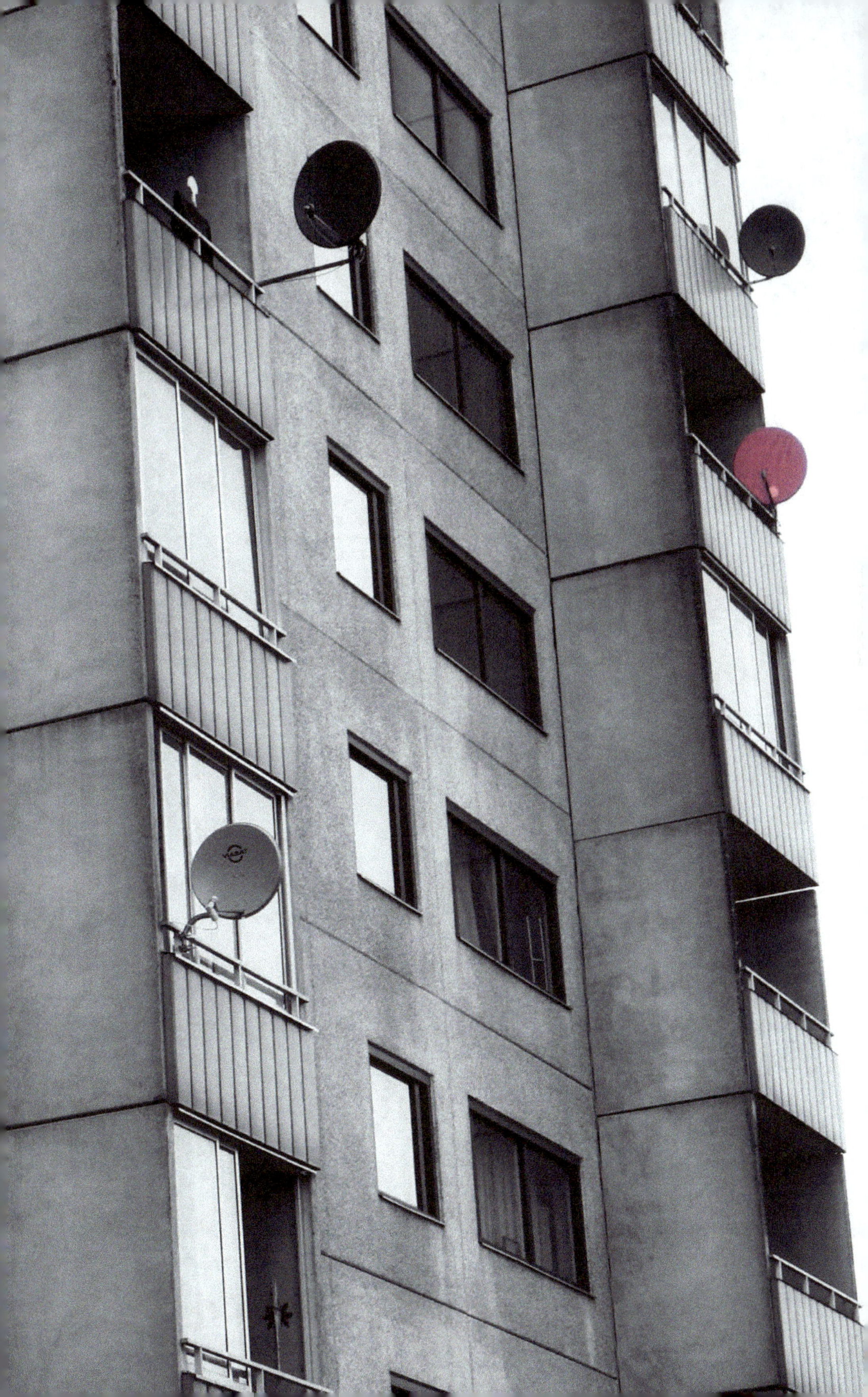

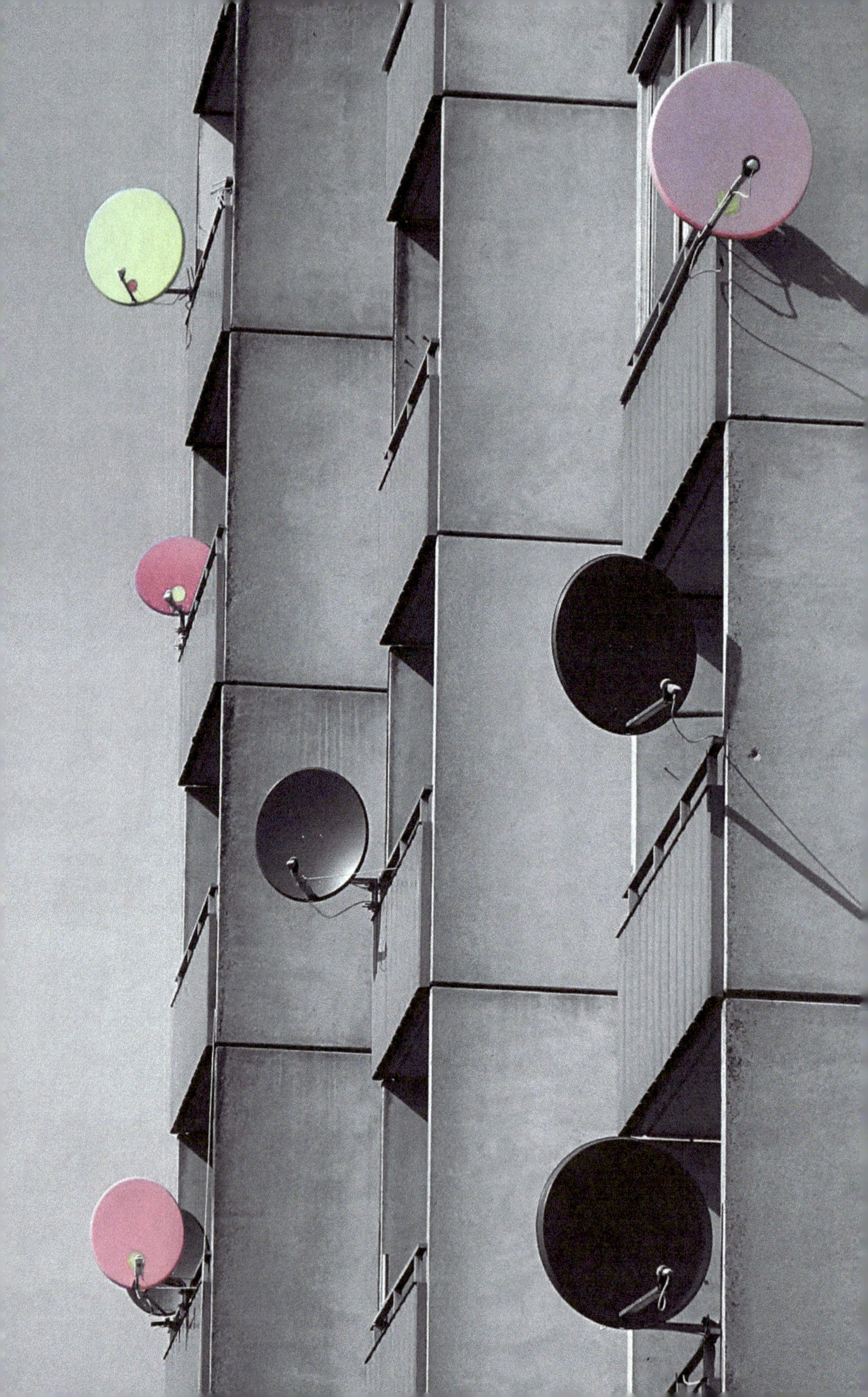

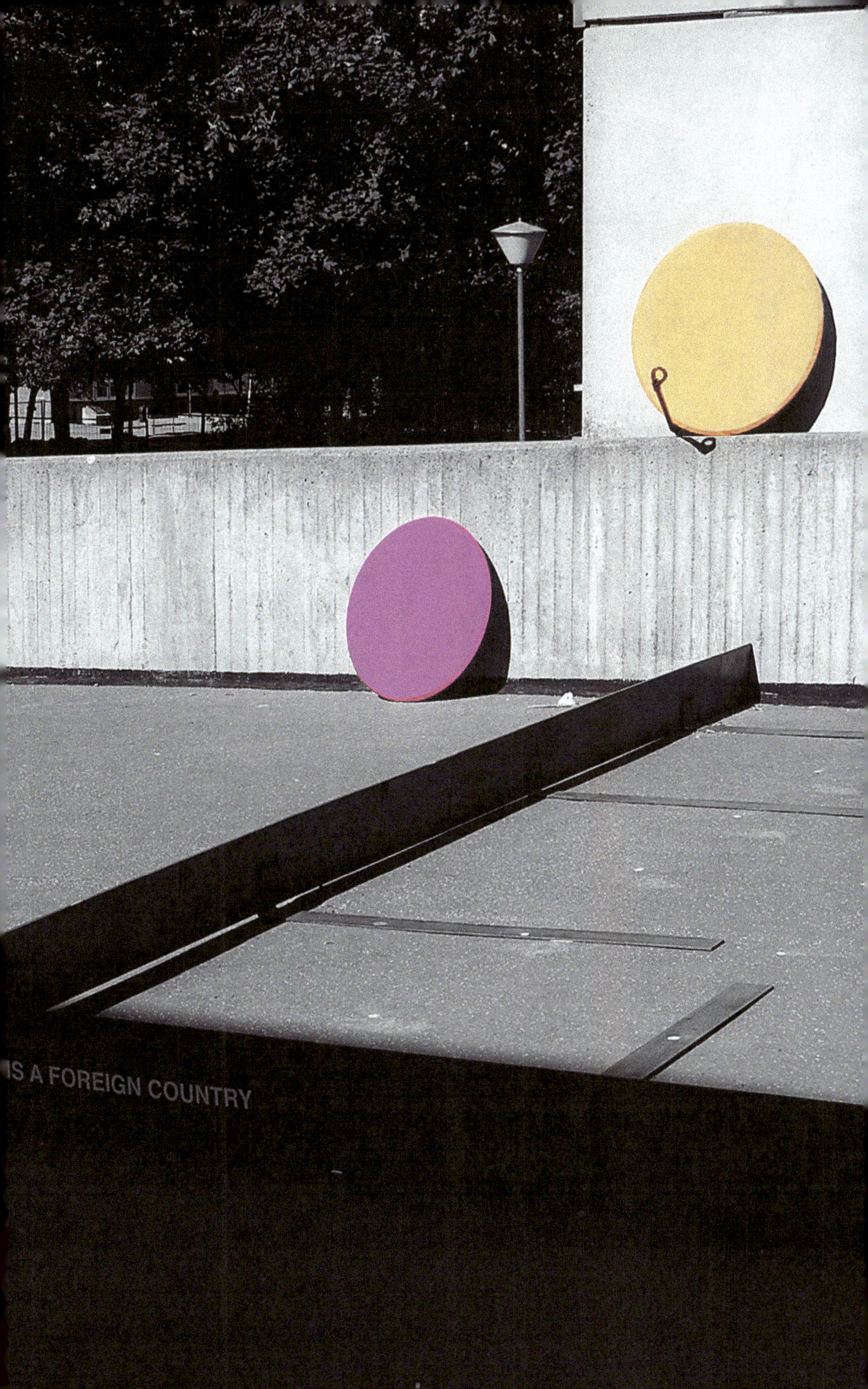
IS A FOREIGN COUNTRY

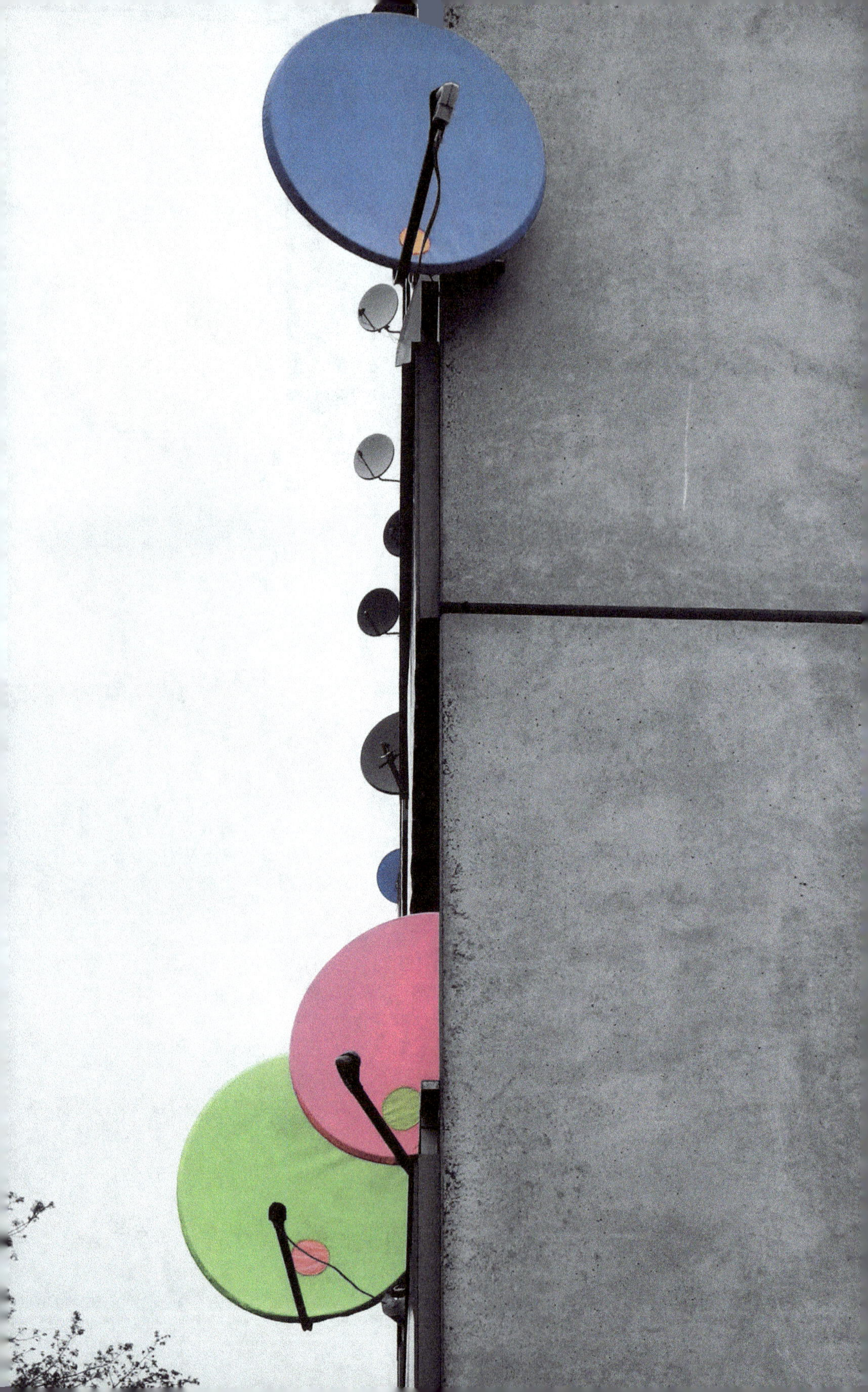

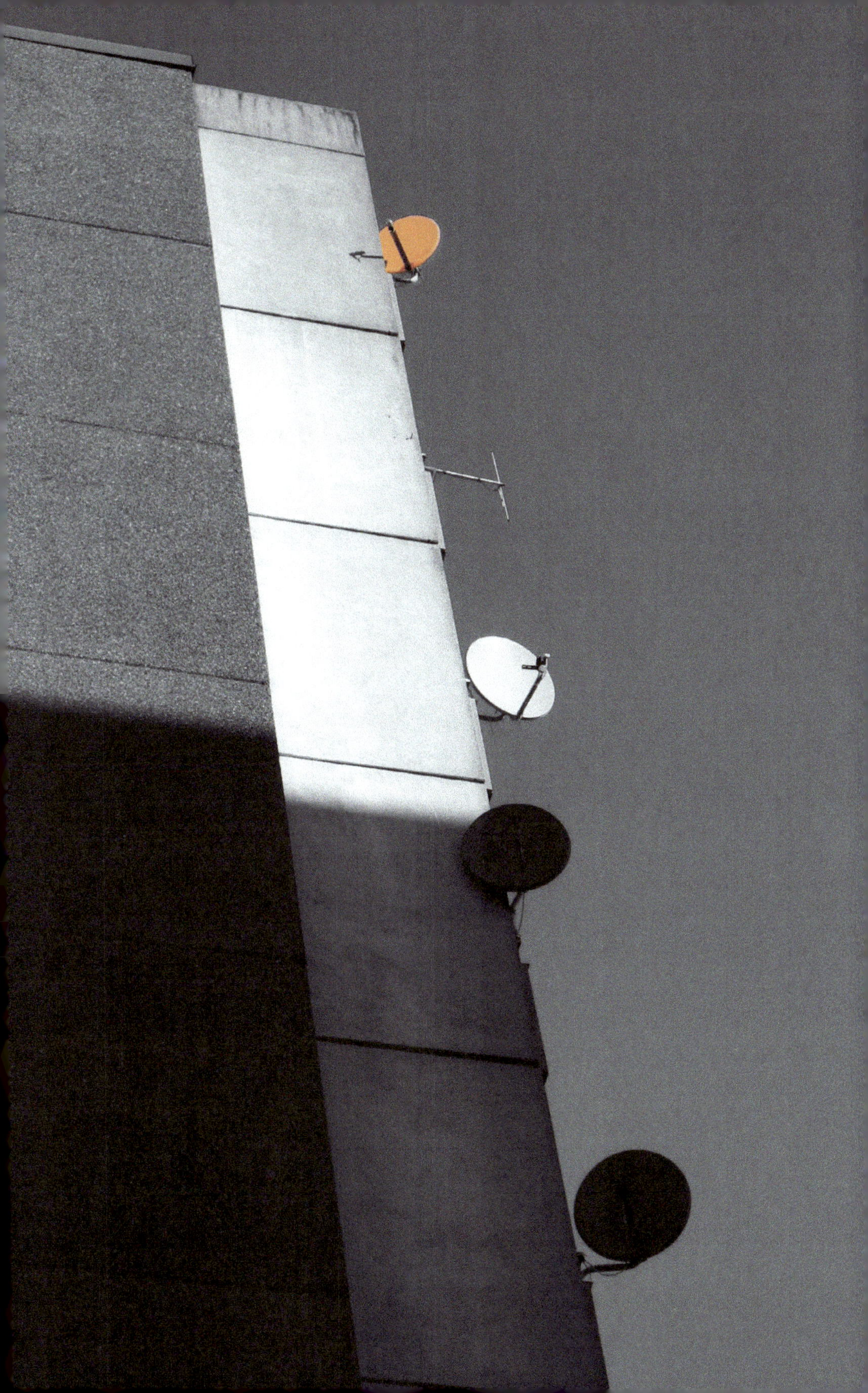

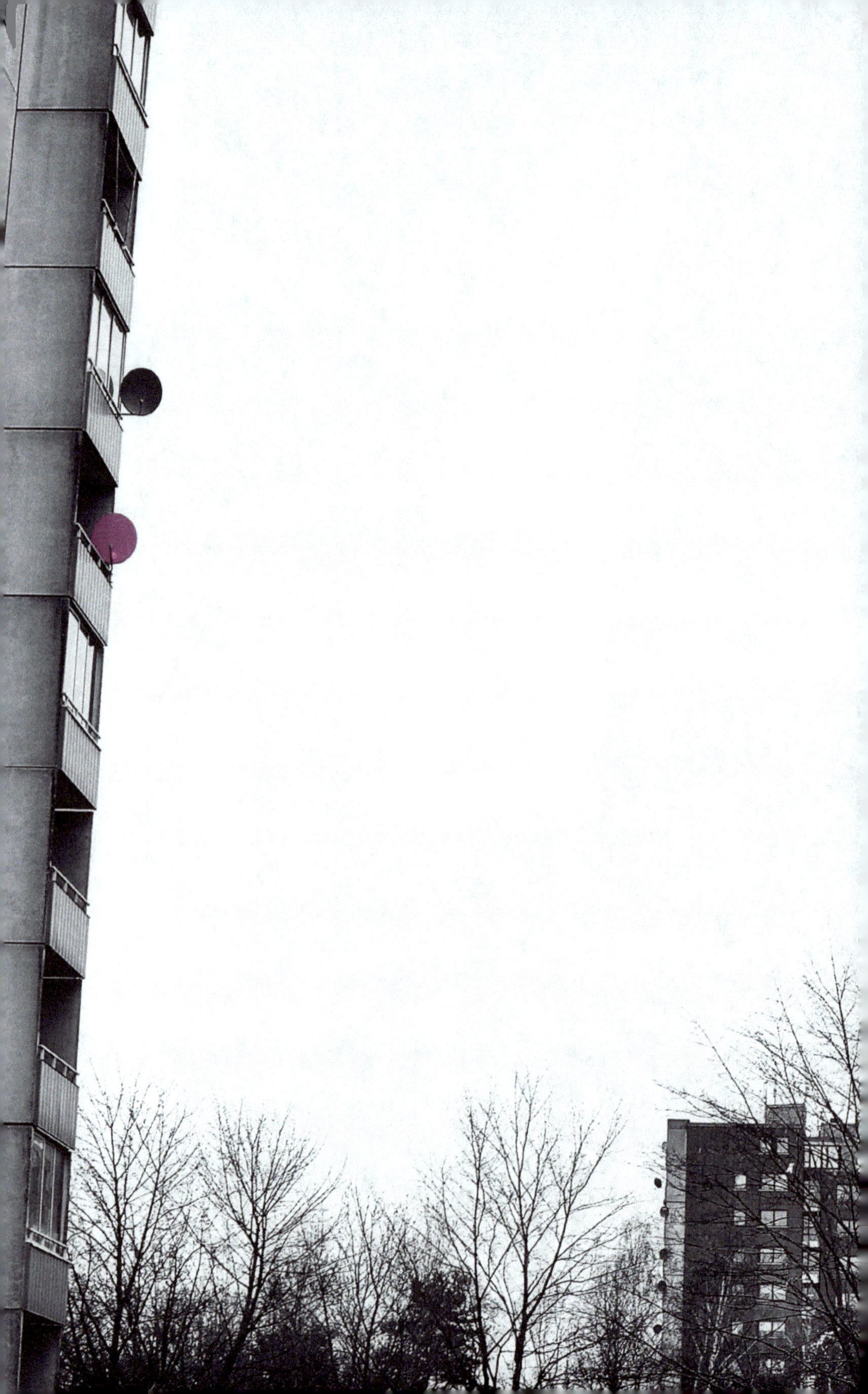

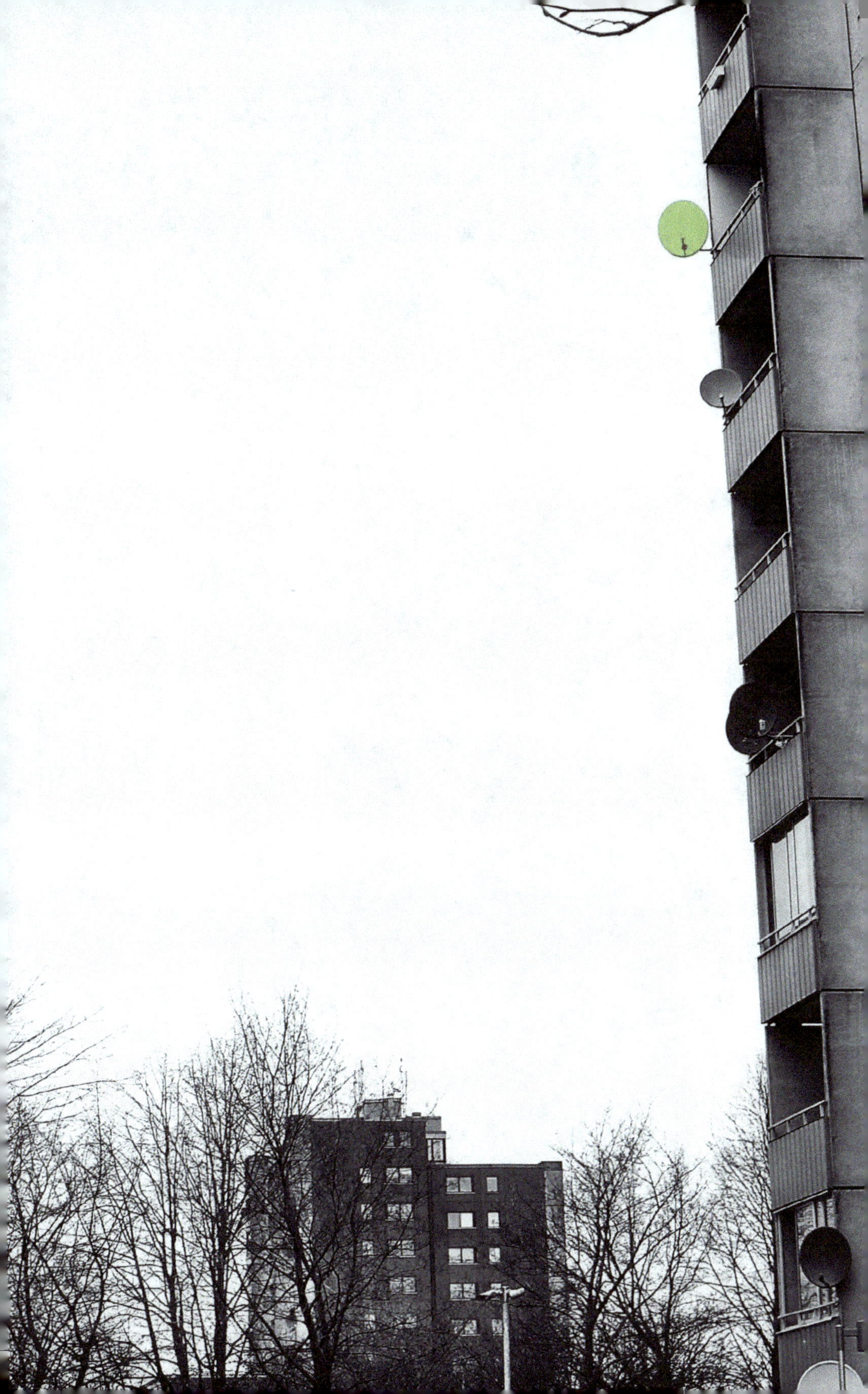

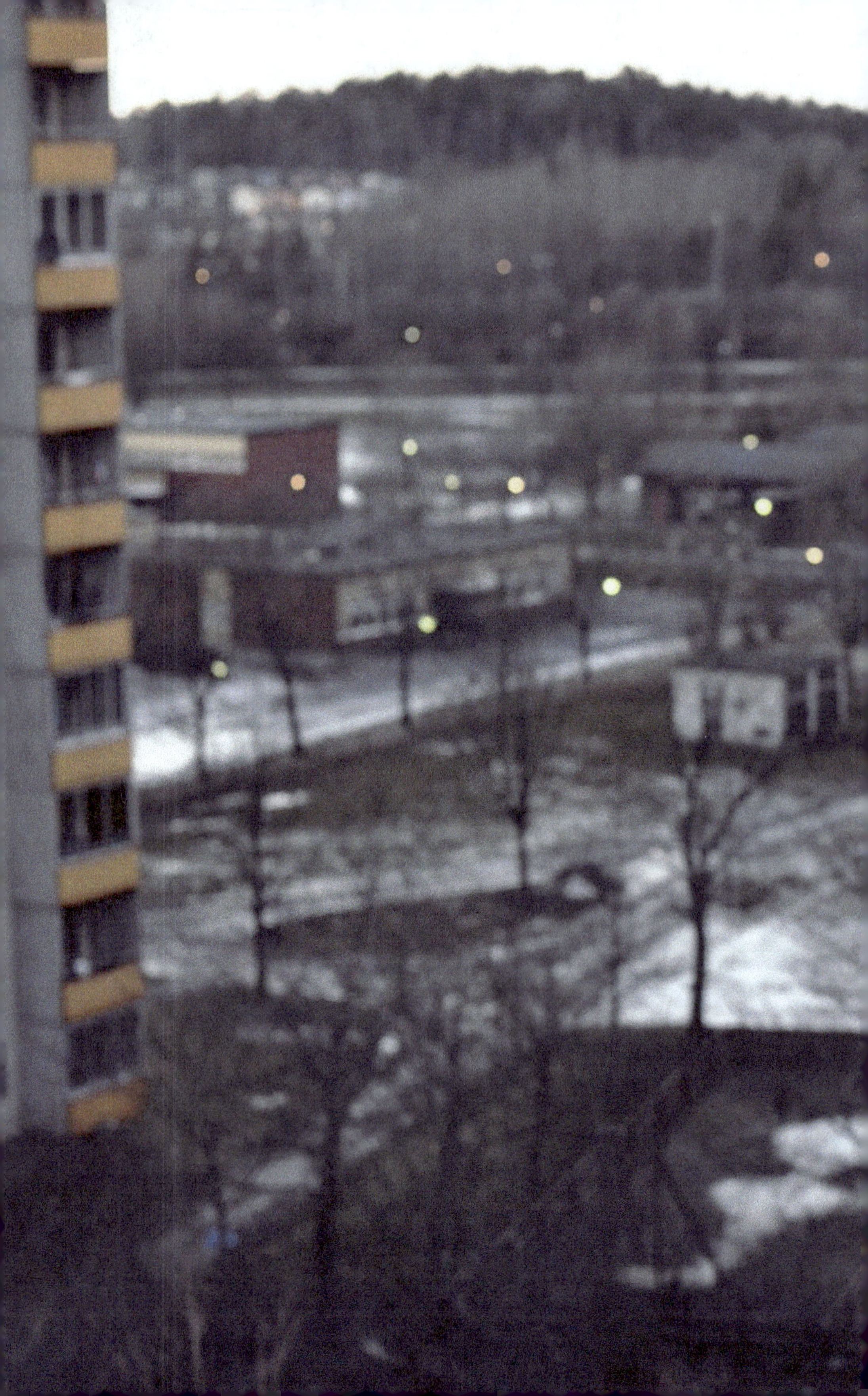

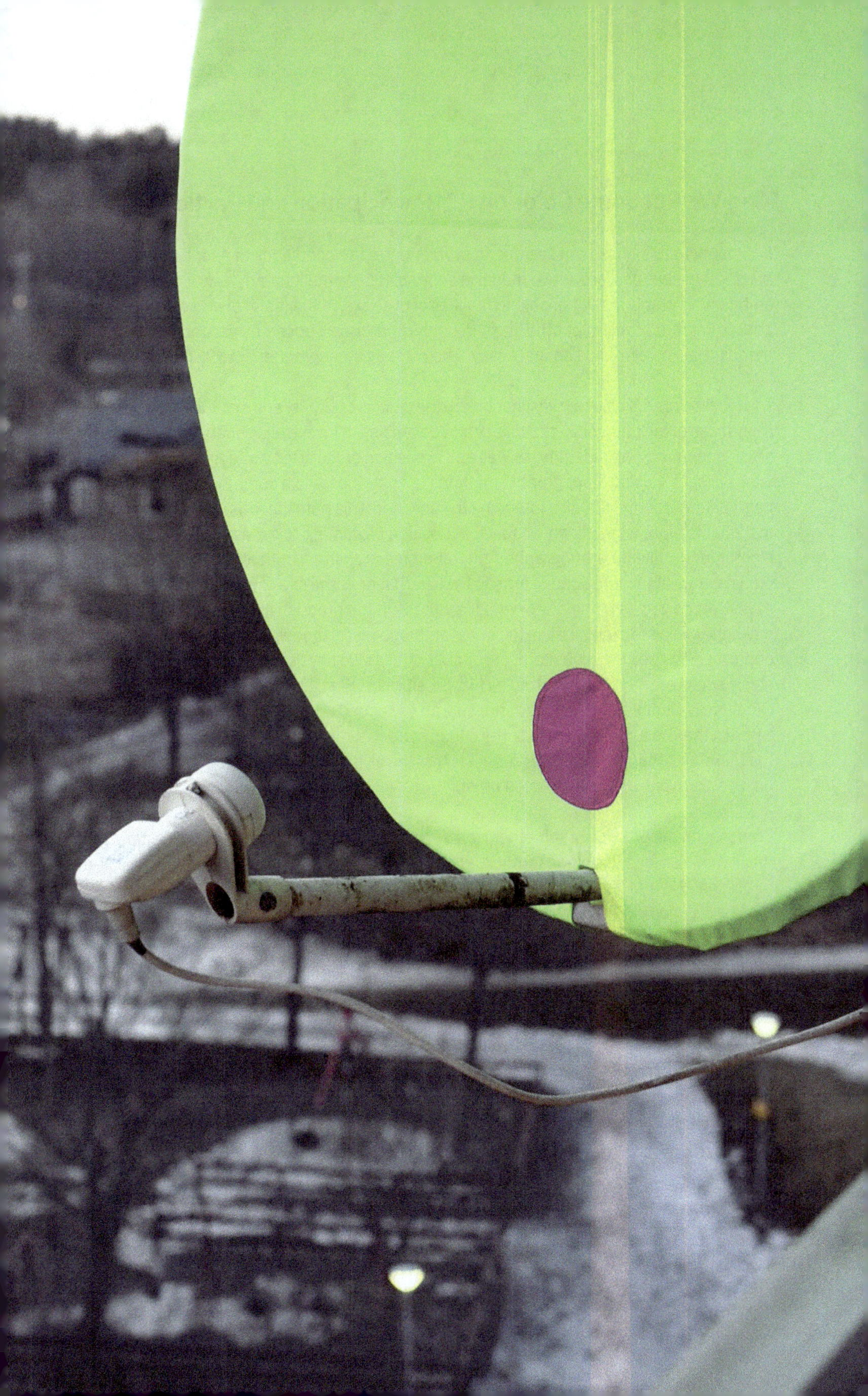

Satellitstaden, *installation view. Images by the author.*

## "Can We Put Some Color on It?" Participation and Participants

If throughout this book I am seeking to problematize the conditions of alterity in the city by placing the 'plan' as a projective model in contradiction to the 'human', as well as placing the ambitions of utopia in relationship to realities of dystopia, in the realm of art I cannot escape addressing the problem of otherness in contemporary art posed by art and architectural theorist Hal Foster in the seminal essay 'The artist as ethnographer?' (1996).

The focal points of Foster's investigation are the politics of alterity and institutions of art, especially those of the bourgeois-capitalist tradition tending to favor exclusionary definitions of art, artist, community, and identity, as well as the position of the artist working with site-specific works allegedly using ethnographic methods to come closer to a community both as an ethnographic 'authority' but also intending to subvert it. This puts the artist and art institutions in a double bind, a seemingly unsolvable position of wanting to get as close as possible to a community, like an ethnographer, but albeit maintaining a criticality towards this method. Foster posits that the site of artistic transformation is the site of political transformation, always perceived as being *elsewhere*. He writes, 'in the productivist model, with the social other, the exploited proletariat; in the quasi-anthropological model, with the cultural other, the oppressed postcolonial, subaltern, or subcultural',[72] as we have already seen. The perception of this *elsewhere* could be distorted by two possibilities. First, by a *realist assumption*, that the Other has an authenticity lacking in the Self; and a second possibility, a *primitivist assumption*, wherein there is a mapping over of the Other, such that the here-and-now Self is superior to the there-and-then Other. Foster suggests that the artist must resist the tendency to project political truth onto this constructed other.

Even though the practice of self-othering is important to a critical practice of art, Foster warns that it may also lead to 'self-absorption, ethnographic self-fashioning, and narcissistic self-refurbishing'.[73] In addition, Foster concentrates especially on site-specific art (which is the case for *Satellitstaden*), and examines a variety of problems that arise when art institutions and artists try to follow the ethnographic principles of participant-observer research methods – which rely on the cultivation of personal relationships with local informants as a way of learning about a culture – in such a way that it involves both observing and participating in the social life of a group as if one were a part of it. The main thrust of his argument is that reflexivity (as we have seen in Ulrich Beck and Zygmunt Bauman in Chapter 1) is essential for the artist, unless she over-identifies with the Other in a way that alienates and compromises it. Foster shows that even in modern art, the notion of the Other is fundamental, but maybe not named as anthropology per se, or even identified as another discipline. Foster expands on this:

> But why the prestige of anthropology in contemporary art? Again, there are precedents of this engagement: in Surrealism, where the Other was figured in the subconscious; in

72 Foster, *The Return of the Real*, p. 302.
73 Foster, *The Return of the Real*, p. 306.

> Art Brut, where the Other represented the anti-civilizational; in Abstract Expressionism, where the Other stood for the primal artist; and variously in the art of the 1960s and 1970s such as in Land Art with its earthworks, the art world as anthropological site, and so on.

Anthropology and its methods are nonetheless appealing for art. He describes,

> First, anthropology is prized as the science of alterity; in this regard it is second only to psychoanalysis as a lingua franca in artistic practice and critical discourse alike. Second, it is the discipline that takes culture as its object, and it is this expanded field of reference that postmodernist art and criticism have long sought to make their own. Third, ethnography is considered contextual, the rote demand for which contemporary artists share with many other practitioners today, some of whom aspire to do fieldwork in the everyday. Fourth, anthropology is thought to arbitrate the interdisciplinary, another rote value in contemporary art and theory. Finally, fifth, it is the self-critique of anthropology that renders it so attractive, for this critical ethnography invites a reflexivity at the center even as it preserves a romanticism of the margins.[74]

Foster was writing in the mid-1990s when contemporary art was beginning to acquire a vocabulary of 'relationality' and relational aesthetics[75] within the context of institutional critique. At this time, the 'institution of art,' he continues,

> (...) could no longer be described simply in terms of physical space (studio, gallery, museum, and so on): it was also a discursive network of practices and institutions, of subjectivities and communities. Nor could the observer of art be delimited only phenomenologically: he or she was also a social subject. (...) The other is admired as one who plays with representation, subverts gender, and so on. In all these ways the artist, critic, or historian projects his or her practice onto the field of the other, where it is read as not only authentically indigenous, but as innovatively political! Of course, this is an exaggeration.

And there is therefore ample space for a scathing understanding of alterity in all levels.

We can say that decades later, this view has been expanded with additional elements of Foster's 'anthropological turn' in Claire Bishop's 'social turn' wherein the globalization of contemporary art, where we see a proliferation of artists, curators and initiatives across the world grappling with issues of alterity in many different ways. This is expressed in the

74 Foster, *The Return of the Real*, p. 305.

75 The term relational aesthetics was created by French curator Nicholas Bourriaud in the 1990s to describe the tendency he noticed in fine art practice to make art based on, or inspired by, human relations and their social context. The text attempts to reveal the principles that structure the thoughts of artists seeking an aesthetic of the inter-human, of the encounter, of proximity, of resisting 'social formatting'. This institutional critique, however, was circumscribed within the art institutional world and practices of relationality with archives, audiences, and critique of institutional models. See also Nicolas Bourriaud, *Relational Aesthetics*, Dijon: Les Presses du Réel, 1998.

proliferation of art residencies, international exchange programs and the number of doctoral programs in the arts, for example, which have provided an opening of these dialectic structures of otherness in artistic research, or in research-based art. Along with the unfolding of postcolonial and decolonial studies, the location of alterity in such 'ethnographic' works has begun to focus on the extent to which contextualization is indeed relevant when dealing with the display of alterity and outsiderness.

Some critics of Foster's ideas point to a large number of contributions from 'southern based' art practices and/or representations of self and other, in relation to the 'north-south nexus'[76] that are better understood through modes of knowledge and artistic production outside a Western paradigm. One of my criticisms, or laments, towards the academic dialectics in Foster and in Bourriaud (who even signals towards a 'creolization' of art) is that their Eurocentric reductionism puts all artistic experiences, European and North American in the 1960s and 1970s in the same 'bag' while completely disregarding any 'relational' practices held in the Southern hemisphere in those same time periods in their writing. Many of the practices of participation, social aesthetics, ethnography and the like, were already introduced as early as the 1960s by artists who undertook a critique of European modern art and expanded them into an embedding into everyday life, thus bridging the gap between aesthetics and local social realities. For instance, the works of Brazilian artists Hélio Oiticica, Lygia Pape and Lygia Clark serve, in their own specificity, to relationality in terms of shaping environments and sensory experiences and creating new modes of sociability between and within art and life, with works embedded in local cultural contexts seeking a synthesis of art and lived experience, of Self *and* Other.[77]

## Social Aesthetics in Nordic Suburbs

Perhaps there is another such 'turn' worth considering as 'social aesthetics', coined by Danish art historian Lars Bang Larsen, about such an involvement of 'other' methods that enter the repertoire of the contemporary artist when she chooses to include art as a part of larger social processes, and in contexts not necessarily managed by the art system specifically in the Nordic context. Bang Larsen has been involved in art historical and artistic research that has been conducted in the specific typology of the Scandinavian suburb, and proposes another definition for this kind of socially oriented art project, or even projects that involve the social, but without the academic competition with other disciplines such as anthropology, which Foster rightfully problematizes. In an article written not too long after Foster's seminal essay, Bang Larsen defines the social aesthetic artwork that 'involves a utilitarian or practical aspect that gives a sense of purpose and direct involvement'.

76 Please note the eurocentrism in using words such as 'southern' or 'north-south nexus,' which are used to indicate practices outside of the established art worlds of Europe and North America.

77 See also Kris Rutten, An van Dienderen, and Ronald Soetaert, 'Revisiting the Ethnographic Turn in Contemporary Art', *Critical Arts: South-North Cultural and Media Studies*, Vol. 27 (2013): 459–473, for references in recent contemporary art projects and exibitions that expose the conditions of alterity and a critique of Foster's 'ethnographic turn'.

He continues,

> In the construction of the subject's interaction with culture it could be said that social aesthetics discusses a notion of the lasting phenomenon that substantiates a critical cultural analysis, a reason for one's existence. It is a way of involving the metaphorical value of artistic concepts and projects on other professional spheres, such as architecture, design, financial structures, etc., either as an understanding integrated in an artistic project, or as a process of decoding and actualizing art-related activity within its cultural location. In this way, artistic work assumes a general focus on performance in a social perspective, either by means of its own nature as an ongoing project without closure or by the real activity it occasions. This often involves collective organization and an employment of art's capacities for going against professional specialization.[78]

While I acknowledge Foster's critical approach to alterity and difference in the artist and the need to address the 'ethnographic' in art projects (especially in projects that straddle the boundaries of the art institution and the academy), I believe it leads to a self-awareness that may be paralyzing. I tend to side more with Bang Larsen's ideas because he speaks of an artist involvement which is 'direct', inspired by the activist dynamics of direct action, and even attending to an existential and collective dimension which is appealing for artists conducting field research within the philosophical-theoretical approach I use here. He writes,

> What I choose to call "social aesthetics" is an artistic attitude focusing on the world of acts. It also experiments with the transgressions of various economies (...) [in which] common to the understanding [of social aesthetic projects] is that the dynamic between artistic activity and the realms that are traditionally relegated to the fabric of the social, fails to properly describe a dialectic. Social and aesthetic understanding are integrated into each other. Here, some forms of social aesthetic activity have deliberately been launched within the art circuit as art projects; others qualify as art, or qualify for artistic discussion, after their actualization in other contexts.[79]

To Foster's question of the place of otherness in art, Bang Larsen's essay may offer an interesting response: 'The distinction between art and other realms of knowledge is made operative in the osmotic exchange between different capacities to do things, which opens up the creation of new subject positions and articulations of democratic equivalence'.[80] The notion of practicing social equality, and not just creating a social aesthetic, is important to emphasize.

An artist often cited by Bang Larsen in the context of art, activism and the activation of democratic processes is Danish artist Palle Nielsen, working with similar issues of the poverty

---

78 Lars Bang Larsen,'Social Aesthetics: 11 Examples to Begin with, in the Light of Parallel History', *Afterall Journal*, (Autumn/Winter 2000), https://vam.afterall.org/journal/issue.1/social.aesthetics.11.examples.begin.light.parallel.

79 Bang Larsen, 'Social Aesthetics'.

80 Bang Larsen, 'Social Aesthetics'.

of the new urban spaces created in newly built concrete block housing estates in the late 1960s in Denmark. At the time, Nielsen created a specific type of research that was coupled to spatial activism, inspired by Kurt Lewin's action-research from 1946. Nielsen understood that the need for social practice within research can best be characterized as research for social management or social engineering. According to Lewin, it is a type of action-research, 'a comparative research on the conditions and effects of various forms of social actions, and research leading to social action. Research that produces nothing but books will not suffice'.[81]

The context of Bang Larsen's research on Nielsen's action artworks bears similarity to the context I was working with in the Stockholm suburb and satellite city of Fittja. A similar construction overhaul occurred in Denmark concurrent to the *miljonprogram* in Sweden in the 1960s and 70s, stirring much criticism about the new modern lifestyle for being homogenizing, mechanistic, and inhumane in both contexts. The poverty of spirit in the public spaces of the new housing complexes had inspired social actions aiming to include citizens in this rapid urbanization process, and both artists and artists' collectives felt compelled to participate in this movement by way of aesthetic actions. Palle Nielsen made a series of works and developed action-research methods into projects he identified as 'playground activism'.[82] By using activist methods for reclaiming ground for the purposes of children and play in these new suburbs built on barren land in the outskirts of Copenhagen, he drew attention to the lack of citizen participation in the decision-making process of constructing these new satellite cities, with special attention to building spaces more hospitable to children, and to everyone.[83] As Bang Larsen writes,

> Palle Nielsen's projects introduced a reflexivity between play and production which must have seemed somewhat frivolous in the light of the era's will to revolutionary upheaval. On the one hand, play qualified large-scale communication as a way of stating that political artistic engagement doesn't exist in terms of practical politics, but as reform works with the prospect of change. On the other hand, play had to be organised and set free, seeing that society no longer offered integrated possibilities for living in

81 The history of action research has in some ways become the history about the relationship between research and democracy, where it proposes democratic arenas as a method to create responsibility and avoid authoritarianism. See also Kurt Lewin, 'Action Research and Minority Problems', *Journal of Social Issues*, 2.4 (November 1946), p. 35.

82 Bang Larsen, 'Social Aesthetics'.

83 'During one Sunday in the spring of 1968, the artist Palle Nielsen built a playground in the slum of Copenhagen's Northern Borough. Together with a group of left-wing architecture students, he planned to clear the court of a neglected housing scheme and erect new facilities for children. At seven o'clock in the morning the group went around to all the residents with a bag containing two cinnamon rolls and a paper attached to it with an image of two children playing on the kerb. The text read: '(...) Do you know that the authorities are empowered to give grants and are willing to invest in children's well-being if you demand it? It is your attitude towards the needs of adolescent children that decides the size of investment that funds increased clearing of backyards, better play facilities in future developments and new designs of municipal playgrounds.' Sensible facilities for play mean that the children stop making noise in the entries and stairwells. They won't have time. They'll be playing.' Bang Larsen, 'Social Aesthetics'. See also: Palle Nielsen and Lars Bang Larsen, *The Model: A Model for a Qualitative Society* (1968). Barcelona: MACBA, 2010, p. 35.

> its regulated, specialised spheres. To introduce social processes in the art institution is, according to Nielsen, socially irrational. Social processes should happen where people are, in direct relation to what they do. But since social reproduction is in dire straits, there is a strong need for the production of participation, and for accessible metaphors of freedom.[84]

Even in Nielsen's case, whose projects can be considered to be social aesthetic framing devices to attain a particular action that leads to a social change, there is always the danger that the artist may be using certain participatory processes only to aestheticize participation. The difference from Nielsen's project and mine is that Nielsen was attending to an urgent need of that community – the children did not effectively have spaces to play; they needed a space to play, so let's make a space for them to play. In my case, even though the presence of satellite dishes was contentious, it was not necessarily an urgency expressed by the community itself. I rather chose to reveal an aspect of the community by way of their use of satellite dishes in order to expand the discourse on the ethics of hospitality, from the micro level of the community to the macro level of the way in which a country relates to the presence of the Other as a part of society at a national level. On the other hand, by highlighting a specific contentious zone in the history of the community, what I was trying to do was to change, albeit temporarily, the way in which Fittja could be perceived from the outside by taking an element that was viewed negatively and, with the artistic means of putting color on the satellite dishes, creating a new image of the site which, later on, would help to represent the community differently and dispel some of the common stereotypes associated with the perception of suburbs as 'othered spaces'. During the course of that reversal from a negative to a positive *image*, the residents themselves would be the agents of that symbolic shift through a participatory strategy within the project.

To bring this discussion into a 'north-south nexus', I associate this aspect of participation and agency to artistic experiments with participation in certain processes within Brazilian art, concurrent to Nielsen's 'actions'. Hélio Oiticica, one of the major figures in Brazilian contemporary art and an early practitioner of participatory strategies, installations and immersive environments beginning in the early 1960s, reflects on a certain uneasiness caused by the very definition of what it means to participate, as in the root definition of participantion as 'taking part of an experience'. In a letter to artist Lygia Clark, sent from his exile in New York to her exile in Paris:[85]

> What I find is that the formal side of the issue (of participation) was overcome long ago by the 'relationship in itself', by the dynamic of incorporating all lived experiences that are precarious or not entirely formulated. Participation is a detail of the work of art,

84 Bang Larsen, 'Social Aesthetics'.

85 Both artists, like many others, had been in exile in Europe or the United States during most of the 1970s, when a hard-line military dictatorship in Brazil persecuted artists, writers and intellectuals. This period of exile also marks the historical moment when the experiments in Brazilian art become visible overseas, at the same time as exile influences Brazilian art tremendously. By the mid and late 1970s, most artists returned home and initiated a very fecund moment in the 1980s and the return to democracy in 1985. This also brings in the discourse of artists in exile closer to the discussion of hospitality.

> because in fact the artist cannot measure this participation, as each person experiences the artwork in a different way. The relationship in itself, the event, the imponderable and immaterial of the work is that it can extend the world and change it, even if in small parts. Experience is not just factual: "this and that"; the words and the choice of terms and the construction (as in a poem) are important in giving dimension to the story of the thing. I am bothered by the emergence of a culture of participation, or rather, of a participatory mannerism that leaves the discovery/invention of the artist to be reduced to an idiosyncratic pettiness of the viewer that eventually disappears. Those who experience what you give, Lygia, either live it or they don't, but never stay in the position of 'watching' as outsiders, as art voyeurs.[86]

In the last lines, Oiticica was referring to Clark's abandonment of the art object and her strict focus on the relational aspect that an artistic experience could engender between individuals taking part in equal terms of the experience. Clark transformed her practice from the object-based and sculptural to a purely psychological relationship, to the extent where she redefined her practice as therapy. People would undergo an aesthetic experience as part of an existential healing process and not as part of the art system. This occurred in 1961 and is one of the earliest and most radical positioning of a conceptual artist I know of – to withdraw from the art system altogether and to turn to participation in a more elemental way, where an aesthetic object simply becomes a mediator between the viewer and experience, but has no intrinsic value in and of itself.[87]

In developing the participatory strategy for *Satellitstaden*, I was naturally concerned with the gap between the artist and the project participants, and in understanding the ethical boundaries of participation in projects that cannot be fully realized without the participation of a community, for example. The terms of involvement, indeed the terms of hospitality first in approaching and then in relating to the Other within a participatoty project are crucial to consider. Claire Bishop's declaration about this gap between artist and participant was reassuring.

She writes,

> In the research I have done, I would say that this gap is largely a fantasy projection on the part of the viewer who is uncomfortable with being confronted by people of another class or race. The reality is that no socially-engaged project would even happen without clear and exhaustive communication between the artist and participants. Artists (...) are, in my experience, incredibly engaged in the process of interviewing, explaining and contextualizing the project to the people they work with. (...) I have interviewed people who have performed in such works and the last thing they feel is exploited; more usually they feel thrilled to be centre of attention. Simplistic

86 Author's translation. Luciano Figueiredo (ed.) *Cartas 1964–74*, Rio de Janeiro: Editora UFRJ, 1998, p. 45.

87 See also Lygia Clark's work 'Caminhando' (1961) and 'Relational masks' (1964–1968), *Lygia Clark: The Abandonment of Art, 1948–1988*, Museum of Modern Art, 2014, https://www.moma.org/calendar/exhibitions/1422.

> critical accusations of exploitation don't take into account the complex psychological motivations of both artist and performer.[88]

If residents were indeed participants in my idea, I would also need to somehow anticipate the nature of their participation. Were they participants or collaborators? British art critic Dave Beech proposes a distinction, which fits within the parameters of an ethics of hospitality as it depends on an invitation:

> (...) the participant typically is not cast as an agent of critique or subversion but rather as one who is invited to accept the parameters of the art project [..] participation always involves a specific invitation and a specific formation of the participant's subjectivity, even when the artist ask them simply to be themselves. [..] Collaborators, however, are distinct from participants insofar as they share authorial rights over the artwork that permit them, among other things, to make fundamental decisions about the key structural features of the work.[89]

The importance of the invitation is – as in Chapter 2 with Derrida's elaboration on the implications of the invitation and of welcoming – a defining factor for a project like *Satellitstaden*. In *Satellitstaden*, participants were invited to take part as well as to contribute with new ideas for the project. I am unsure if they could be called collaborators in Beech's terms in such a way that they would be able to claim authorship in the work itself. Rather, it would be more appropriate to claim the resident's role as *co-generators* of the installation: more than participants that follow a pre-established program but not exactly collaborators in terms of the authorship of the entire endeavor as Beech claims, but more importantly as part of a more complex and layered system where residents took on multiple roles as hosts, participants, agents, consultants, critics, assistants, co-workers, to name only a few of the capacities. The blurry distinctions between these roles reveal the insufficiency and generality of the catch-all term 'participation' used in contemporary art vocabulary and we are left with words that merely approximate the terms of engagement of each member in any complex project. Finally, somehow this distinction became more useful in defining my own role in the project as an author, and, to use a vocabulary of hospitality, a *host* of a proposition who *invites* people to help make it come to life and allowing participants to suggest improvements to the project by opening it to several iterations along its path, here more akin to the philosophy and methods proposed in action-research, not necessarily altering the general premise of the project but allowing enough openness that allowed it to improve and change over time. Although not entirely open-ended as an artwork as the aesthetic of the project was well-defined from the outset, the way in which the process would unfold as well as the final expression of the project was something entirely dependent on the logic of participation within the project.

88 Barok Dusan, 'On Participatory Art: Interview with Claire Bishop', 2009, https://www.academia.edu/771895/On_participatory_art_Interview_with_Claire_Bishop.

89 Dave Beech, 'Don't look now! Art after the viewer and beyond participation', in Jeni Walwin (ed.) *Searching for Art's New Publics*. Bristol: Intellect, 2010: 15–31.

## Co-generating the Satellite City

The most difficult task in *Satellitstaden* was finding and inviting residents to participate. Without the agreement of each resident, it would be impossible to reach the satellite dishes, and thus there would be no artwork. In this sense, one could argue that the residents were more than participants: they were the co-generators of the artwork. Co-generating has the connotation of 'creating form together' and established a mutual dependence and responsibility between the instigator of a proposal and the participant, where both are equally important in creating something. The idea of co-generation opens up a much more creative capacity and distributed authorship of an artistic proposition. Throughout the process of *Satellitstaden*, the participants gave me many ideas that enriched my first general proposition, and the project grew from the ability to leave the initial proposition open to people's inputs without challenging or changing its core. In this sense, co-generation seems more appropriate than 'participation' pure and simple.

The on-site installation then becomes a collective endeavor where each participant plays a vital role, and where artist and participant share the same goal in the project – to make Fittja as colorful as possible and lift it from years of façade deterioration, to change the perception of this locality both from inside and outside, and stimulate community participation from the bottom up. The process of recruiting participants is complex and requires presence, persistence, and also a personal touch. For the first six months, I pushed the project forward by all means possible: contacting members of the konsthall's Citizen's Council I had helped to form, presenting the project to local authorities, presenting at local association meetings, giving artist talks at the local library and at the research institute, meeting women informally in the collective laundry rooms, spending time at *Verdandi* and engaging local service providers, conducting workshops at the local youth center, collaborating with the area's administrators and local businesses, living in the local artist's residency, socializing on the streets, making friends, and even recruiting teenagers as translators.

I quickly understood which means were more effective than others. For example, posters (which are depersonalized) pinned on common areas and flyers in restaurants and cafés were ineffective insofar as they did not convert any participants. Making cold calls by knocking on doors was intrusive and altogether unpleasant. On the other hand, face-to-face connections, recalling Lévinas' importance of the face, were by far more effective, espcially when facilitated by members of the community. A presentation at the 'Neighbor Hour' monthly meeting with approximately fifty attendees yielded about 6 participants in one go, a 5–10% turnout. However, this meant that recruiting was a slow process. I reached 16 participants in the first three months, working full-time and going to Fittja everyday. Once a participant was found, the process was intensive, requiring many phone calls that sometimes remained unanswered, booking appointments that ended up cancelled for one reason or another, or turning down willing participants for technical reasons if their satellite dishes were physically out of reach.

Seeing my frustration, Shakhlo gave me very useful advice: to recruit people more effectively each participant would also recommend a friend, neighbor or relative to participate. In this way, the participants would become more involved in the project and have more agency in the installation. The dynamics of participation became similar to the behavior in social media: I *make visible* the project to people, participants then *like* the idea and adopt it, they *comment* on it and generate a discussion among their family and neighbors and *share* it with someone else in their social network. In this way, the project would cease to be a centralized network with me at the center and would become a distributed network where each participant in the project became a node that generated a link to a new node.

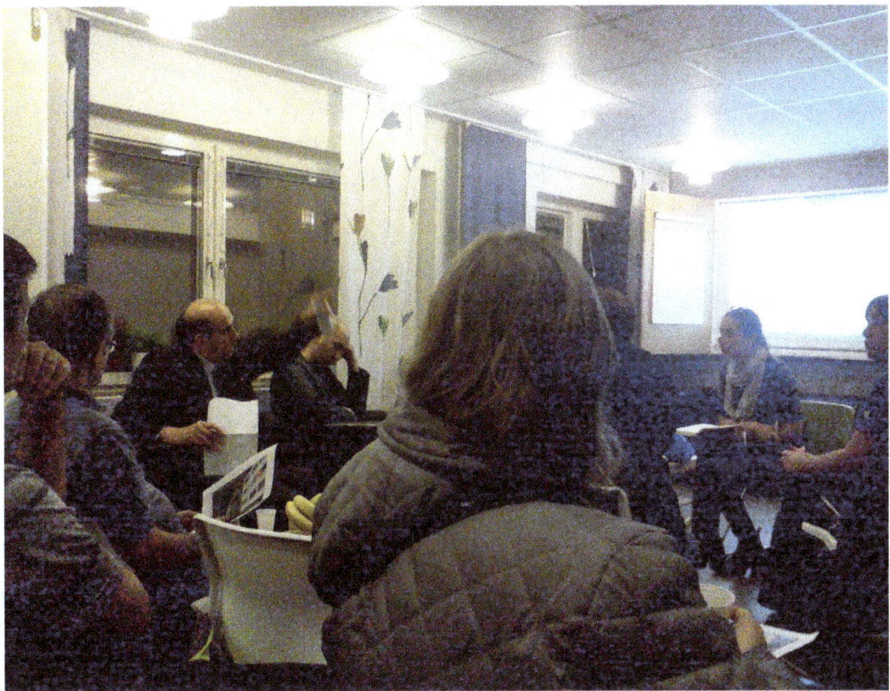

*Figure 38 – Presenting at 'Neighbor Hour' meetings on two different occasions, in September and November 2011.*

Already six months into the project, the recruitment was still slow, largely due to the coming winter. It was too cold to meet residents on the street, and too dark to work outside in the balconies hanging the 'parabol dresses'. So I paused the project until the spring the following year. In addition, sometime in the middle of the winter, a strong windstorm[90] had blown away most of the 16 covers I had installed in the fall, which made me go back to square one. I took the opportunity to redesign the textile cover more effectively and make it more wind-resilient, manufacturing them anew and reinstalling them one by one in the spring. It was also a useful moment to reconsider all the strategies, and I even considered stopping the project altogether, until *Satellitstaden* was reviewed in a local

90 Fittja was built on a flat empty pasture at the edge of Lake Mälaren, and there is always a draft, even in good weather. In the winter of 2012, a windstorm blowing at over 80 km/h had caused some damage to the buildings, and all the satellite covers were blown away. I re-designed the 'parabol dress' with more reinforcements to better withstand the wind and re-installed every single one of them again.

newspaper in February 2012.[91] In response to the article, Dhikra Merza had sent me an email, and three weeks after our first meeting she managed to invite twenty of her friends and neighbors to participate. *Satellitstaden* gains real momentum and colored dots begin to appear in the façades at a fast pace. Within two months, now into the spring, I managed to reach fifty participants, with as many dots along Fittja's façades, and as many interviews conducted with each participant and as many stories to tell. Dhikra is more than a participant, she becomes a co-generator of the project, my main informant, and a friend.

Another participatory strategy was doing workshops with local organizations, as with the youth organization *Ungdomens Hus*,[92] a youth center where many Fittja young people ages 16 to 24 go to in the late afternoon after school and evenings to meet each other, have sports lessons, hang out at the café, record music, and an array of recreational and social activities. In the workshop, I was interested young people's perception about their own satellite city, their perceptions of the urban environment and of the life there. The exercise we did together was to collectively draw a map of the neighborhood, and in so doing, the perception of the place, the choices of elements to be put into the map and the conversations that happen during its making were relevant to the project and to the research. The group began drawing the map with the most visible physical markers: the subway line, the central mall, then the individual blocks and the parks. Then they located and named familiar places and inserting themselves and their family on the map according to where they lived. I asked them to place their friends and family with different colors and draw lines of connection between them. Soon a graphic expression of the network of relations appeared.

According to the conversation and the negotiations in drawing the map, this network of relations seemed to be the most important feature of this neighborhood. Despite the rigidity of the architectural design, the human network was fluid and affective. The verticality of their movement through space, from building to building, up and down elevators and across the very few streets and courtyards did not impede diagonal movements by connecting the dots through and across buildings as relationships are played out. 'We are all quite visible here, everybody knows everybody, we feel safe here', they said. This is where I had the insight to draw a network map of the people I met in Fittja. This is also where I understood that what the project could reveal was the network of people, and in order to draw this map of relations, I had to tap into relationships from the inside. From this day forward, every participant would be required to recommend at least one more person to the project. This way, the art project would have produced its own network through existing ties that mirror the strength of the bonds within the community.

91 Anders Björklund, 'Paraboler ska sätta färg på Fittja', *Mitt i Botkyrka*, 7 February 2012.
92 Ungdomens Hus was closed in 2018 following a decision by local politicians.

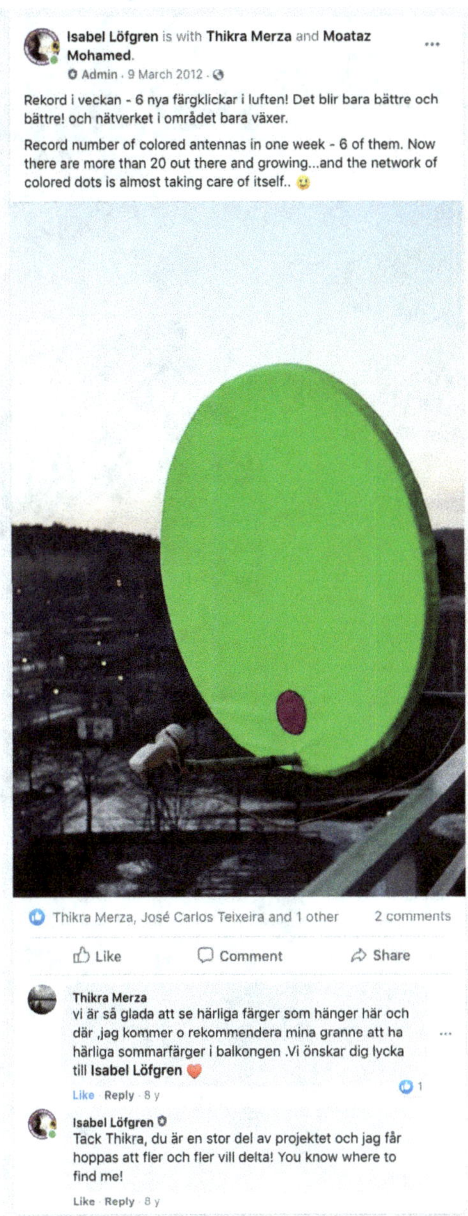


*Figure 39 – Screenshot of Satellitstaden's Facebook page. During the entire length of the project, I posted regularly on social media, as another means of gathering participation. While social media channels did not yield a single new participant, it helped make the project visible to other audiences on a continuous basis. Dhikra Merza's comment reads: 'We are so happy to such great colors here and there. I will recommend my neighbors to have these summer colors on their balconies. We wish you good luck!'*[93]

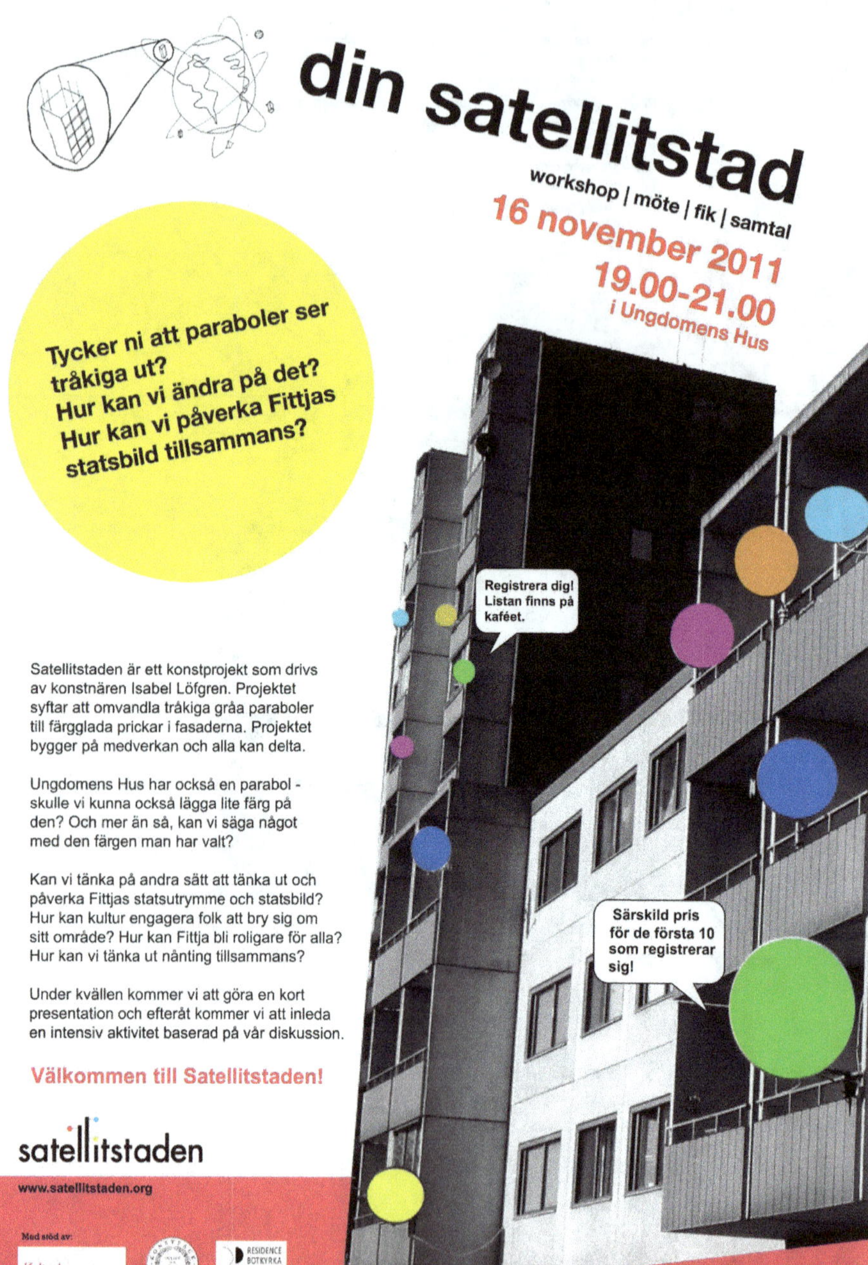


*Figure 40 – Poster for the workshop at the Youth Center (Ungdomens Hus). It reads: 'Your satellite city. Satellitstaden is an art project led by Isabel Löfgren. The project aims to transform the gray satellite dishes into colorful dots on the façades. The project is collaborative, and anyone can participate. Ungdomens Hus also has a satellite dish. Can we put some color on it? Can we say something with that color too? Can we think about new ways to change and improve Fittja's urban space and urban image? How can culture engage people to begin*

*to care about their neighborhood? How can Fittja be more enjoyable for everyone? Can we think of something together? We will make a short presentation and then produce a collective artwork based on our discussion'. Graphic design by the author, November 2011.*

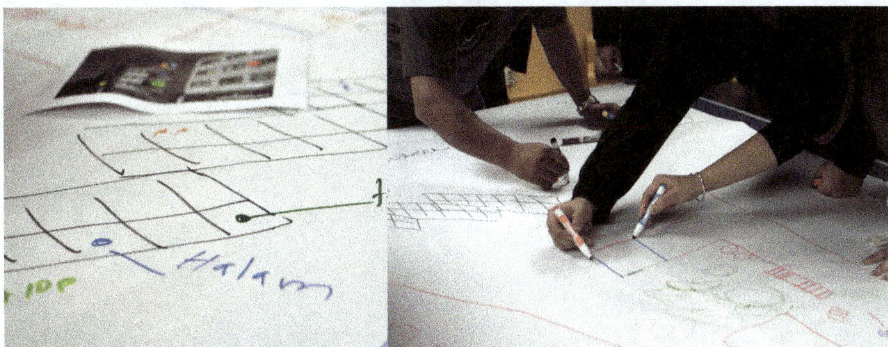

*Figure 41 – Photographs from the workshop, November 2011. The first activity entailed a presentation, then a joint brainstorming process for the design of Undomens Hus satellite dish design. In the collective map, participants began by drawing the subway line as what defines Fittja. They saw their own neighborhood as a station on the subway line. From there, they began drawing the towers, identical, one after another. I asked them to locate the buildings where they lived. After that, they spontaneously added dots and names to signify where their family and friends lived. One of the activities was drawing a collective map of Fittja, and see what emerged during the drawing session, and trying to decipher how the young people saw their neighborhood from the inside out. At the end, the physical markers of the areas such as buildings, the station, shops, etc. were superimposed with the social networks, friends, family and memories that defined their lives. Photo: Lara Szabo Greisman.*

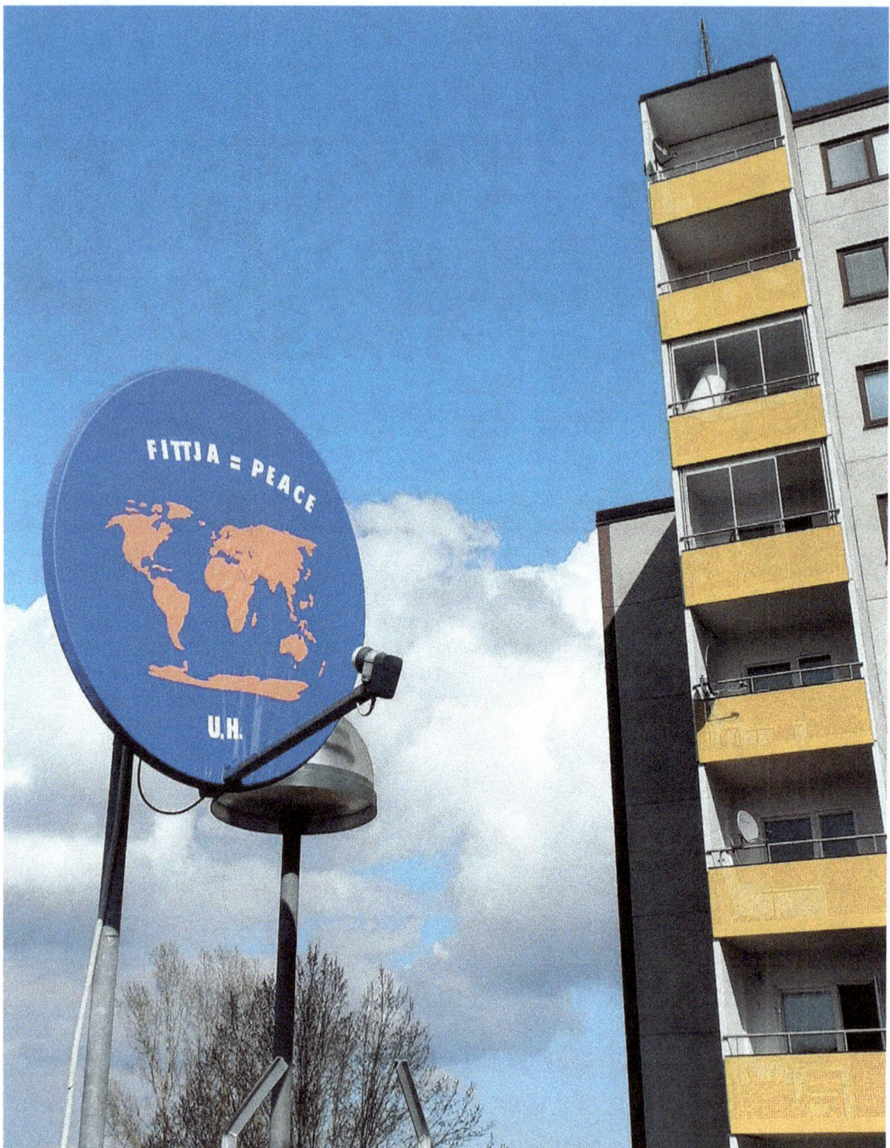


*Figure 42 – If the satellite dish could emit a message instead of just receiving a signal, what would it say? Participants brainstorm possible message that would represent the Youth Centre. For their satellite dish cover, the group decided to draw a world map to represent that the entire world is represented in Fittja and decided to use a slogan well-known to all the young people: 'Fittja is Peace'. Image by the author*

## Satellitstaden and the Logic of Situated Social Networks

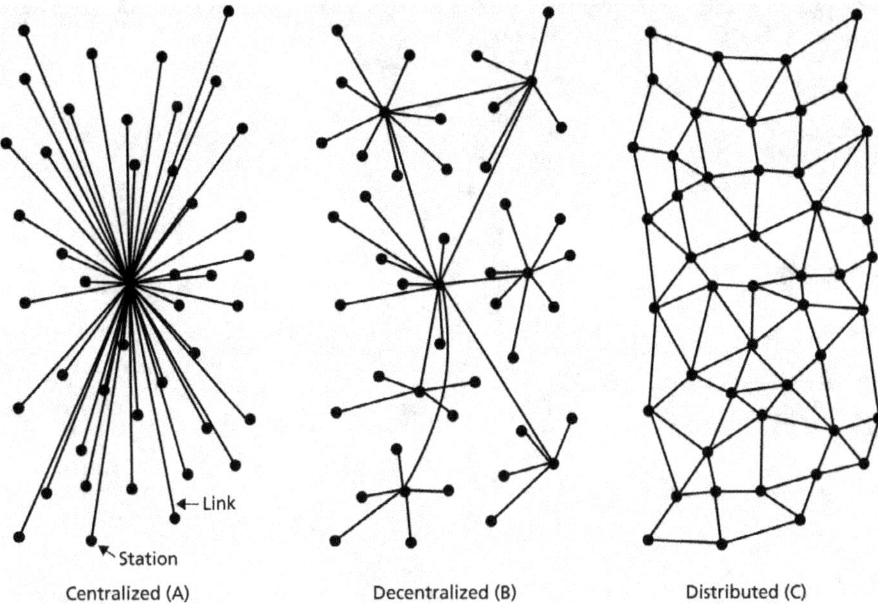


*Figure 43 – Network diagrams created in 1964 by Paul Baran, a Polish-American engineer who invented several technologies related to network architecture. His work on centralized versus decentralized architecture during the Cold War, was inspired by the need to design an information and defense network that could withstand a nuclear attack. The distributed network would be the optimal arrangement. Even if one of the nodes of the network is destroyed, the network would still remain intact.*[94]

As participants began to recommend each other to the project, it became possible to map the network between people and the quality of their bond. According to Baran's model, the 'traditional' network architecture is the centralized network, 'where all nodes send their data to one central node (a server), which then sends the data to the intended recipient. Then there is the distributed network where there is no central server and each node is connected to various other nodes; data simply 'hops' through whichever nodes allow for the shortest route to the recipient. Finally there is the decentralized network which could be characterized as a distributed network of centralized networks'.[95] The network diagram of *Satellitstaden* provides a portrait of the connections made during the project and contains elements of centralized and decentralized networks but never reaching the state of an evenly distributed network.

94 See also Paul Baran, 'On Distributed Communications Networks', *Communications Systems*, IEEE Transactions on 12.1 (1964): 1–9.

95 Geert Lovink and Miriam Rasch (eds) *Unlike Us Reader: Social Media Monopolies and Their Alternatives*, Amsterdam: Institute of Network Cultures, 2013.

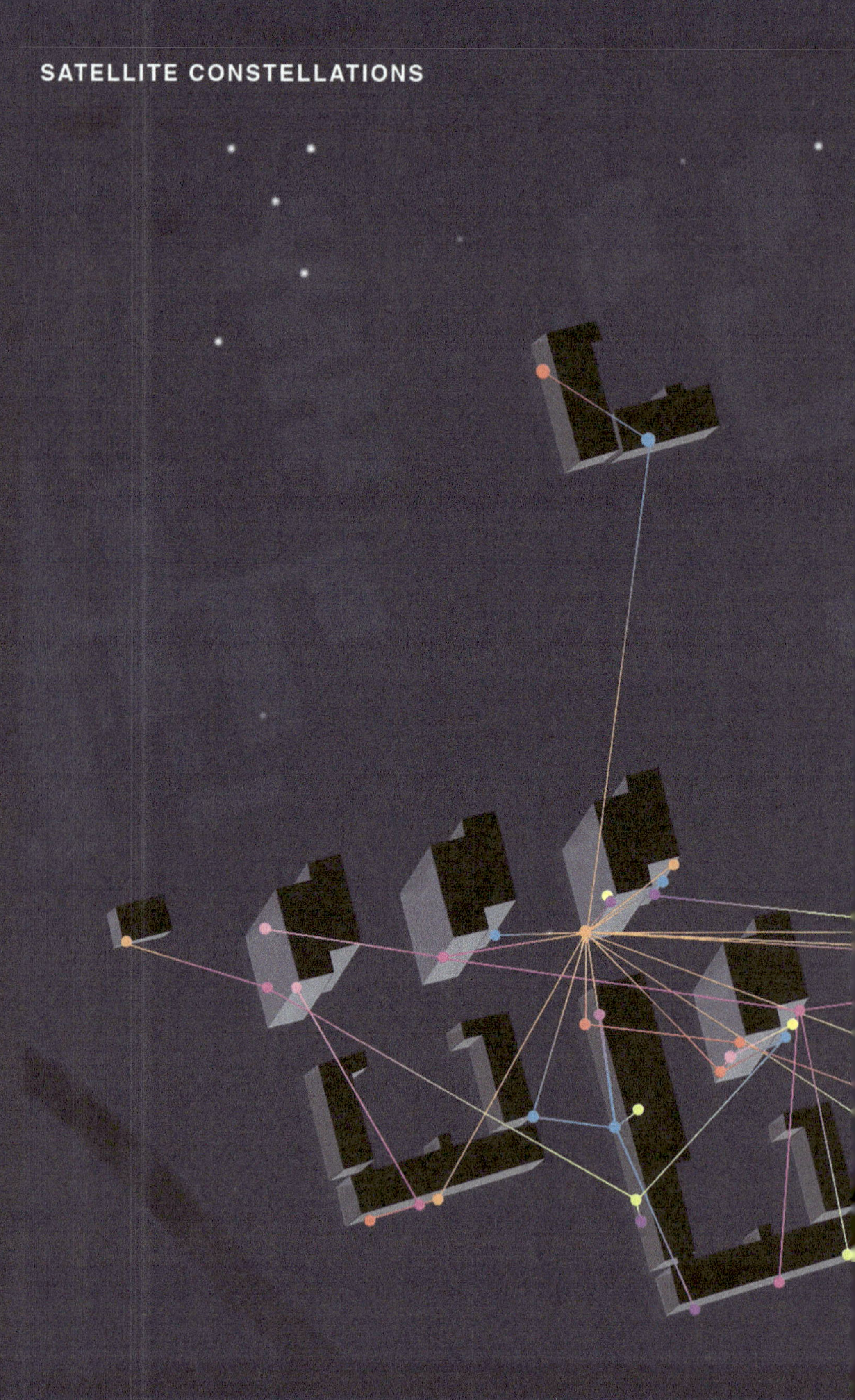

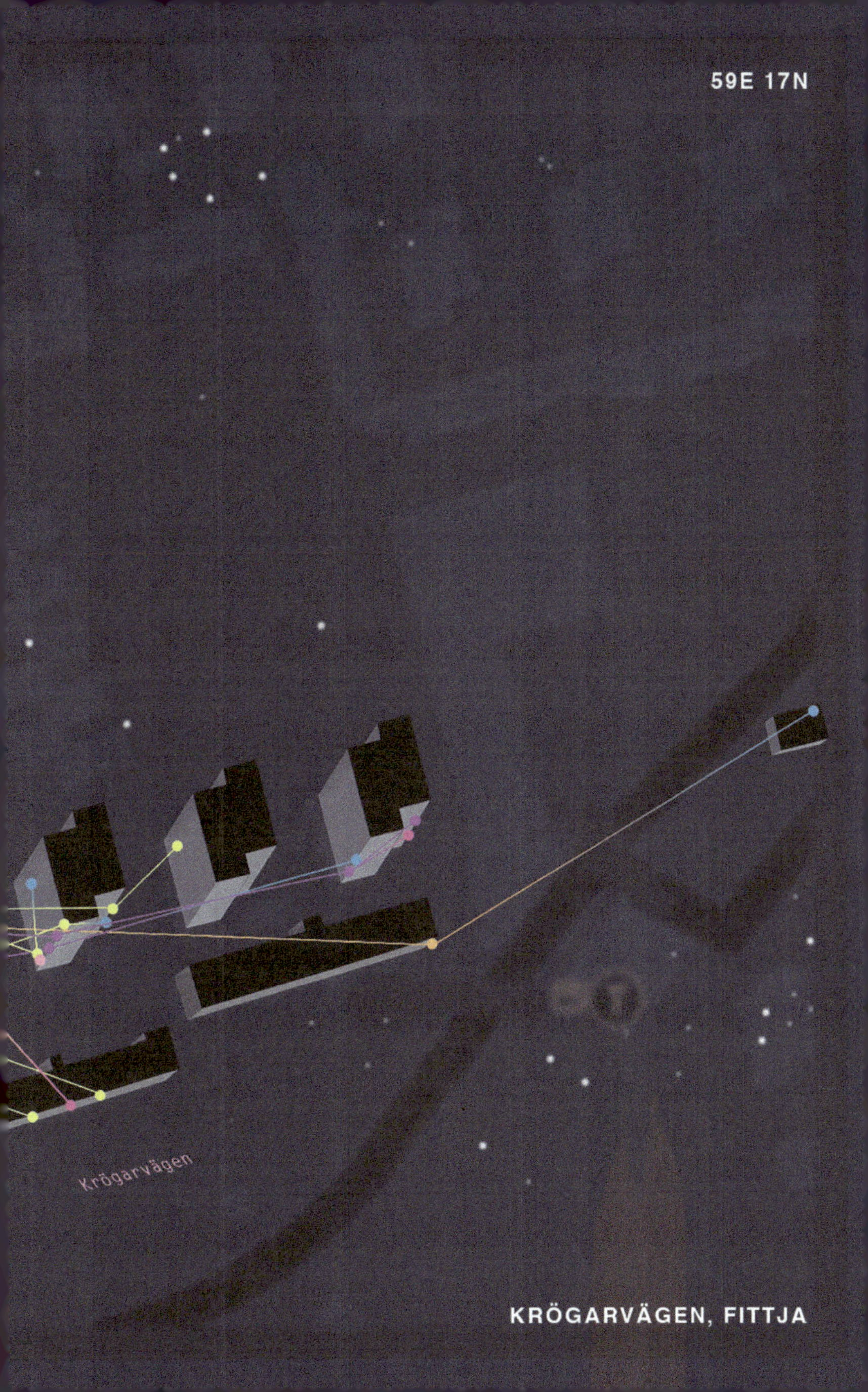

59E 17N

Krögarvägen

KRÖGARVÄGEN, FITTJA

*Figure 44 – Constellation diagram in Satellitstaden over an isometric plane. The colored dots represent satellite dishes, and the different colors represent the actual colors chosen for them by their owners. This diagram is composed of eight overlapping constellations that include different groups with different types of affinities, relatives, or neighbors. In this diagram there are eight overlapping constellations. Image by the author.*

The central node in the diagram begins at Residence Botkyrka, the orange dot in a centralized network. It has the most connections in the diagram since I am the agent that creates the connections between Residence Botkyrka and new nodes, and also the agent between new nodes expanding from them. This diagram represents the first phase of the project, up until the point where I decided that each participant should recommend a friend to the project as a condition of participating. These connections have nothing in common with each other, except for the colored satellite dish. Therefore, this network can be considered rather formal, and reveals little of how the participants relate to each other, if at all. As the diagram tells, there is only one degree of connection from the orange dot to another, except for two instances where participants recommended other people into the project (red and blue dot on top, and the last two green dots on the far right). Also, the only node in this network that was a spontaneous call were the blue and red dots on the building at the top of the diagram. The means of connection are made through the tactics of recruitment described in the previous section.

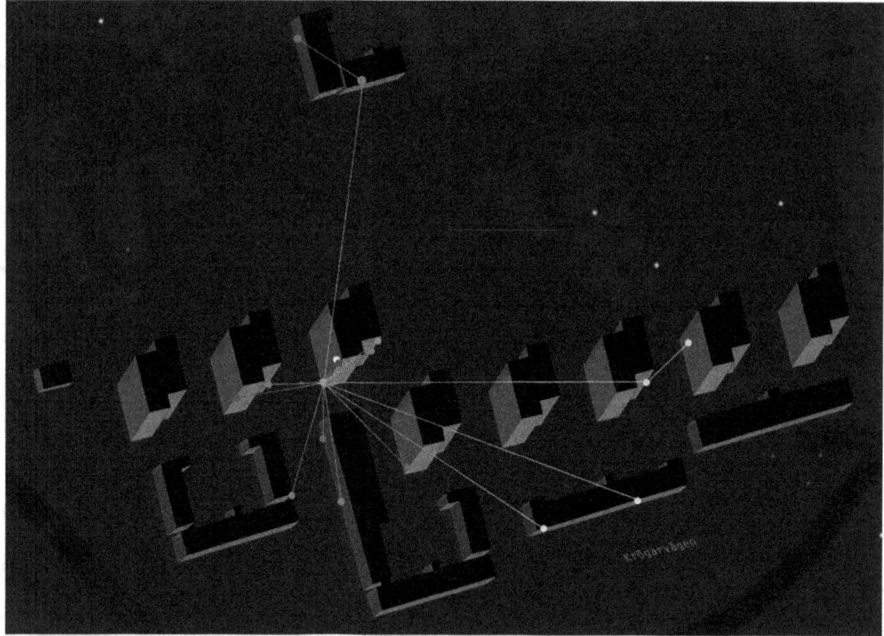

*Figure 45 – Centralized network with its central orange node in Residence Botkyrka. This constellation represents the first three months of the project, before participants recommended each other. Image by the author.*

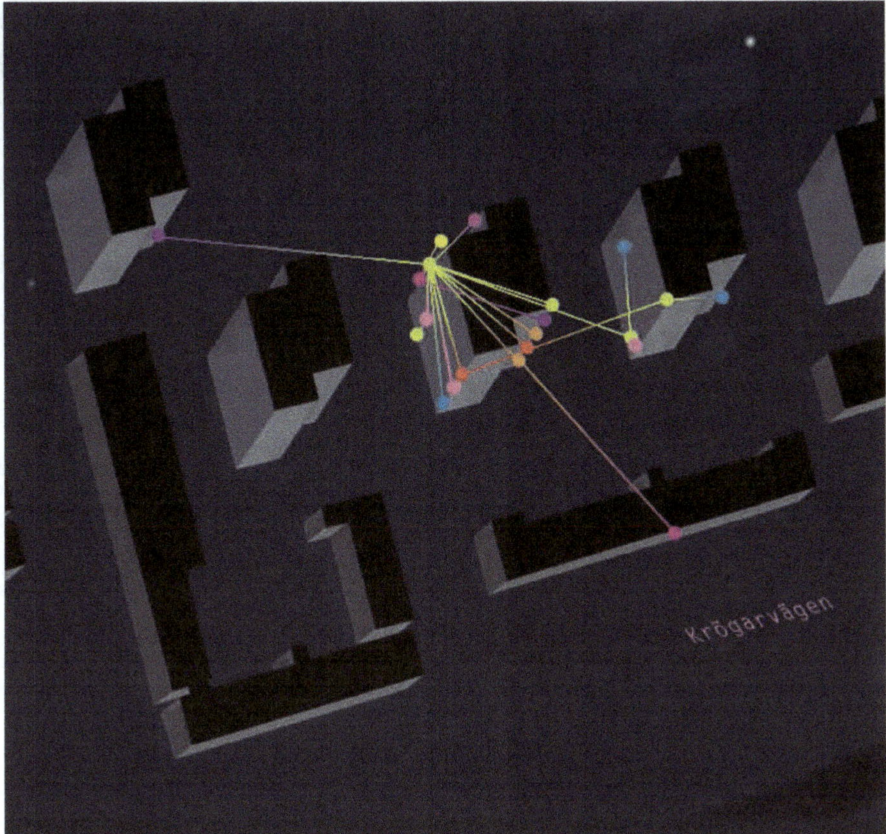


*Figure 48 – Centralized network with Dhikra's green dot in the center. Differently than the constellation above that I initiated, the connections in this network all share previous affective with the central node as friends, neighbors, relatives or countrymen. Image by the author.*

When Dhikra enters the project after responding to the article on the local newspaper, her green dot becomes a central node in the network. She recommends twenty people directly and indirectly. We can notice that whereas the nodes connecting to the orange dot in Residence Botkyrka are widespread in the area, Dhikra's green dot has strong connections in her own building and in the immediate vicinity. It was her building that looked the most colorful in the installation, and it instilled a form of pride amongst its residents. It also assured Dhikra's position as a leadership figure in her building, thus revealing to me how cohesive the people living in a single building can be.

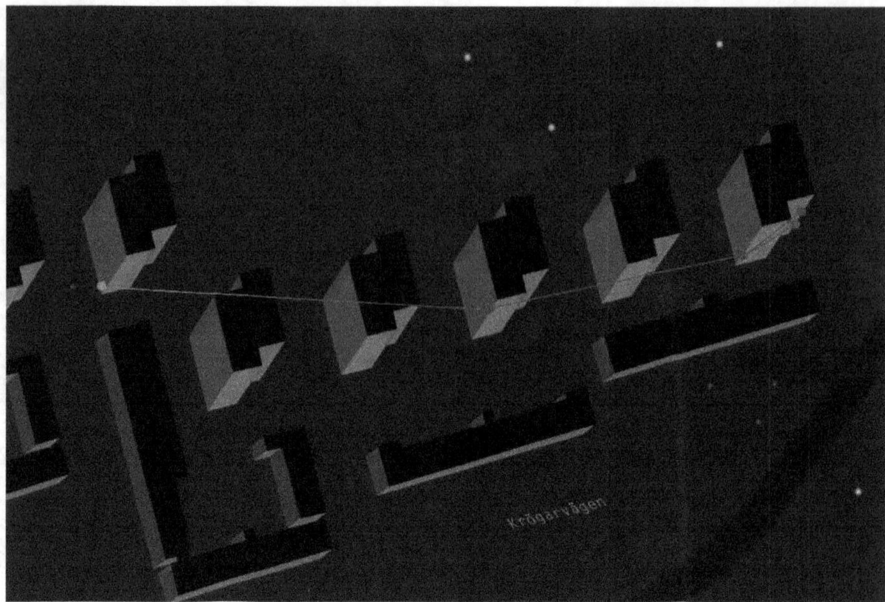


*Figure 49 – Zaliha Agrali's family. Whereas there is no central node in this constellation, it initiates on the orange dot at the Residency which represents me. The other four dots are connected via family ties, first Zaliha, then her daughter-in-law, followed by the daughter-in-law's cousin and the daughter-in-law's cousin's sister. Image by the author.*

Even though I spent considerable time at the café at *Verdandi*, speaking frequently with several women who spent their afternoons there while waiting for Pero to sew the week's orders, it took several months until some of them decided to participate. They were very shy at first, and by getting to knowing me better, they began to open up. I never understood if this delay happened because they needed permission from their husbands to let me into their homes (most of them were Kurdish older women who still live in the old order of their homeland culture and have limited sovereignty over their homes – or their lives – as I would understand later), or if they mistakenly thought they needed to pay to participate. In any case, after about six months, Zaliha, one of the women I grew closest with, sent me to her daughter-in-law's home, who in turn sent me to her cousin, who then recommended me to her sister, and so on. Through this family constellation, one quickly realizes that the villages of Kulu and Tavsanqali near Kolya in Central Turkey, have relocated to Fittja.

Beneath the stark linear appearance of the *miljonprogram* with its monolithic towers is a busy network of family connections, making Fittja a 'city of cousins', as one of the ladies called it. These strong ties are of course a result of a policy of family reunification for immigrants, but also makes Fittja a satellite city not only of Stockholm, but of Kolya as well. The satellite dish and satellite television extend this metaphor to the realm of the televisual, which, as suspected, played a central role in the everyday life of these families, which I investigated further through a series of interviews with each participating family.

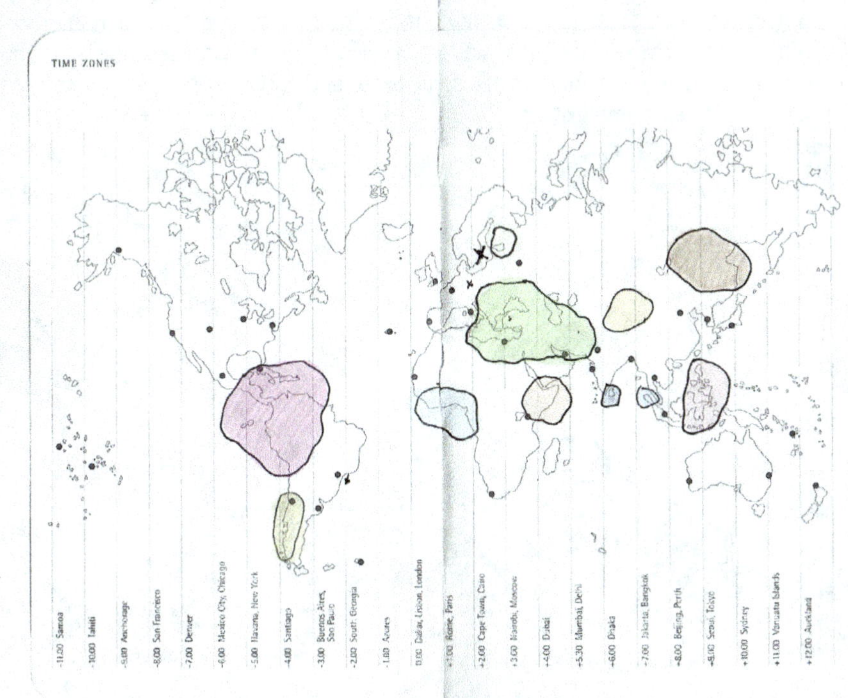


*Figure 50 – World regions where Satellitstaden participants come from. Sweden, Finland, Serbia, Kosovo, Greece, Turkey, Syria, Egypt, Lebanon, Iraq, Pakistan, Bangladesh, Kazakhstan, Uzbekistan, Somalia, Ghana, Chile, Cuba, Venezuela, and Brazil (me). Image by the author.*

## The Suburb as Avant-Garde: Where Others Meet

In the two years following Satellitstaden, I reflected and wrote extensively about the project, and also had the opportunity to present the project in a few conferences and events, usually in the context of participatory strategies in art projects done in peripheral urban contexts like suburbs, or in the dialogue between art and architecture, the 'social turn', etc. Many interesting issues emerged from these discussions which prompted a critical reflection about artistic, political and ethical aspects involved in working in such sites, especially regarding the agency of the artist, the agency of the community, the role of art institutions, and the dynamics between all these actors. In this period, I also became a regular visitor to Residency Botkyrka/Botkyrka konsthall's program and events, where some of these discussions were held and further developed upon. These discussions also prompted me to go back and reflect over many of the experiences in *Satellitstaden* and the ethics of working in Fittja as an artist, and therefore as a representative of the creative or culture class.

To illustrate the complexities of the ethics, and of hospitality in working in contexts like Fittja, I will turn to another example of an event also curated by Botkyrka konsthall, the *New Biennial for Art and Architecture*, held in September 2014, as a means to frame *Satellitstaden* in a wider framework of similar projects, from local and international perspectives. My intention is not to analyze artworks presented nor the curatorial proposal of the event per se. Rather, I will work with the criticism expressed in an opinion article written in response to this event, and then relate to art theory and criticism and some experiences of *Satellitstaden* as a means to unpack some of these complexities.

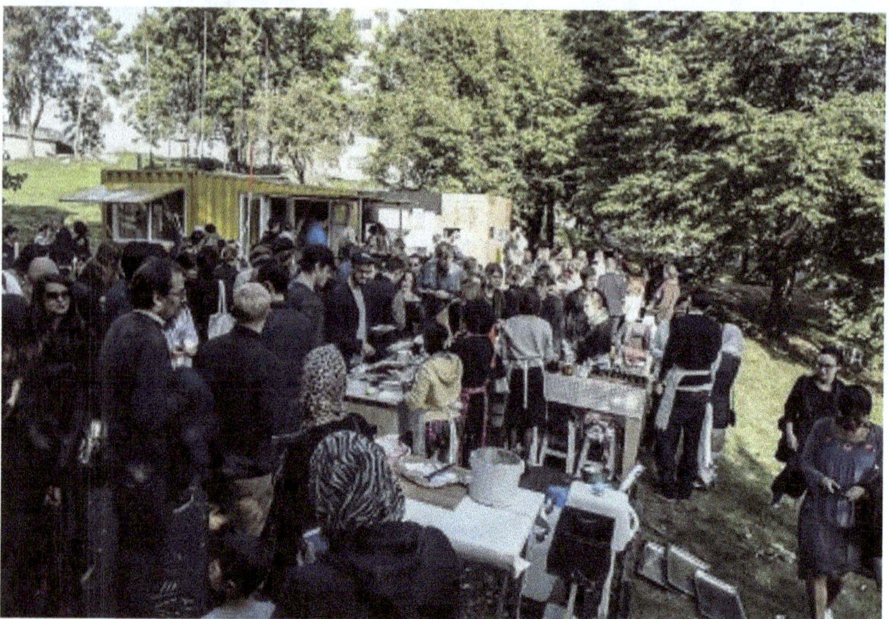

*Figure 51 – The New Biennial for Art and Architecture, Residency Botkyrka/Botkyrka konsthall, September 2014. At the far left, a pop-up exhibition in a container designed as a community kitchen, in Fittja's public space. Image source: ETC,* **https://www.etc.se/**.

The container in the image above is a temporary structure for housing temporary exhibitions and performances curated for the *The New Biennial for Art and Architecture*, an event where contemporary art meets architecture, with activities, performances and artworks meant to activate the neighborhood with an array of locally sited artworks involving international and local artists and architects. The curatorial statement of the event, which resulted from a series of propositions presented at a *Fittja Pavillion* at the Venice Biennale earlier in the same year, reads: 'What role can an art institution play in our times? What can it become? (...) Can the *Million Programme* [the plan to build one million housing units during the years 1965–75 in Sweden] with its modernist grand-scale planning, and its weakly defined public spaces, be reevaluated? Can it even bring about another kind of contemporary art?'[96]

The *New Biennial* focused on an open kitchen located inside a container placed next to the Fittja subway station, and designed by South African architect Michael Orchard, featuring the open work OPENrestaurant with artist Ayhan Aydin. This container became an architectural intervention and a platform for conversations about the social aspects of

96 'Fittja Pavilion during the 14th Venice Architecture Biennale', *E-flux*, 30 May 2014, https://www.e-flux.com/announcements/31046/fittja-pavilion-during-the-14th-venice-architecture-biennale/.

food-making, architectural and artitic exchanges in Fittja, with a program that included an array of sound artworks, performances and activities with local artists and art collectives, as well as with international artists. These events usually receive public funding from the municipality, as it is a public arts institution, in addition to a network of different exchanges and funding sources from a variety of local, national and international organizations.

In a short Op-Ed article in *ETC.*, an independent Swedish newspaper,[97] Nabila Abdul Fattah, an articulate activist from Alby, a suburb not too far from Fittja expresses her skepticism towards art in Fittja:[98]

> No, I'm not finished. I'm not finished with trying to explain what the temporary integration, cultural and recreational projects and other initiatives do to people in socio-economically disadvantaged areas. I'm not finished with describing the overall frustration that people who live and work in these areas feel as they do not have access to the same pot of money for their own ideas (...) Today, it seems to be easier to obtain money for new, experimental and 'innovative' ideas than for long-term activities and methods we already know have been proved to work. (...)
>
> To end discrimination and to diminish class problems, we must bring awareness about people's rights in society, and investing in schools, for example, does not seems glamorous enough. (...) Instead we get (...) an art container from South Africa in the middle of Fittja in a place that is associated with something completely different than art, namely drug dealing.
>
> Fittja is also the neighborhood in Botkyrka where unemployment has increased the most, now between 14 and 15 percent. I'm tired of authorities who send people to experiment in our suburbs instead of supporting solid businesses that are created by and for the people. I'm tired of experiments by people who take advantage of this system for their own personal gain, to show they have been in a *concrete safari*[99] and done "good." (...) We don't want to be your lab rats. We want the same terms as everyone else, and this fact alone is not "innovative," not glamorous, not "new thinking" – but equally important.[100]

Abdul Fattah's reaction expresses a real demand for more agency of residents in cultural initiatives that are held within their own constituencies. It is especially true in peripheral areas of the city where, coincidentally, the effects of failed multiculturalist policies are more salient. During the course of *Satellitstaden,* I had heard similar comments from some residents in a presentation I made at a monthly resident's association meeting in September 2011. 'Thank

97 ETC., Http://www.etc.se.

98 Nabila Abdul Fattah, 'Stop turning us in the suburbs into lab rats!' *ETC.*, 16 december 2014. Author's translation. Nabila Abdul Fattah is a project leader for young people in Skärholmen, southern Stockholm, 3 subway stops from Fittja.

99 *Concrete safari* is slang for 'tourist trip to the suburbs/peripheries'. Variations include 'favela safari' in Brazil, for example.

100 Abdul Fattah, 'Stop turning us in the suburbs into lab rats!'.

you for your wonderful idea, but we don't need this kind of thing in Fittja,' said Juan, from Chile, who had been living in Fittja for more than thirty years, 'We have more important problems to solve here! And I am by no means against culture. My son is an artist. I used to make film. But we need to do things on our own terms according to our needs'.[101]

In a follow-up discussion with Juan after the presentation, we agreed that along with lowering crime rates, art and culture can work in parallel, each with their own specificity, to destigmatize a depressed part of the city. This symbolic dimension however needs to come from an internal urge for signification, from something real, and not from the outside, he said. The question posed by Abdul Fattah is correct: who is legitimated to do this, and why? On what terms? For whom does it serve? Whose voices are being heard, and which voices remain silent? It is not surprising that cultural initiatives by outsiders, such as visiting artists, are met with skepticism and distrust.

Indeed, it does not help if the art (and the public funding that accompanies it) comes from people from the outside; only the community itself sees and understands its own needs. However, this is also not enough reason to dismiss cultural and artistic activity in places like Fittja altogether for it is not a matter of culture or art per se, but of the dynamics of the art world. What Abdul Fattah and Juan grieve about is that they do not feel involved, their knowledge of the area is not considered as a resource, they become objects for artworks they do not need rather than agents of the transformation they actually need or in terms of reciprocity as Abdul Fattah writes. What causes the distrust and sense of exclusion from top-down cultural initiatives is the way in which the community is approached, the underlying ethics behind this approach, and the positionalities and power dynamics involved, notwithstanding the dynamics of the art world.

Of course, no matter how careful I was about the ethics of participation in the project, this type of observation/criticism towards *Satellitstaden* was unavoidable, as I was effectively representing the established art world, or representing a member of what Rosler called the 'culture class'[102]. I found Juan's criticism very constructive, even essential to understand the dynamics at play. In the eyes of a community tired of being scrutinized for its 'exceptional status' as an immigrant community, I was exactly that – a white person from the outside doing a temporary publicly funded art project[103] that had no bearing in the long-term problems in the community, with local participation as stepping stones to achieve something that would ultimately end up in an illustrated art catalogue in an archive somewhere, such as this book. Or, that it would look good as an image *a posteriori* (but hopefully more). They were right: the project looked great in print and Fittja's colorful façades drew enough media attention for a

101 Author's notes.

102 Rosler, *Culture Class*, p. 39.

103 Satellitstaden's funding was mainly public: a public arts fund, Kulturbryggan, seed funding from CuratorLab at Konstfack (a publicly funded arts institution), the Residency Botkyrka stipend for two months (a publicly funded arts institution), and additional support from Botkyrka municipality's arts council (government). The only private funding came from a crowdfunding site, with a small amount that required three times as much effort to acquire than all of the time spent in the application process for the above-mentioned public funds.

full-page article in the culture section of Sweden's largest newspaper on April 19, 2012.[104] All the work I did in Fittja for two years, the intensity of the conversations I had, all the people I met in a variety of ways, all the stories I heard were summed up on a single photograph.

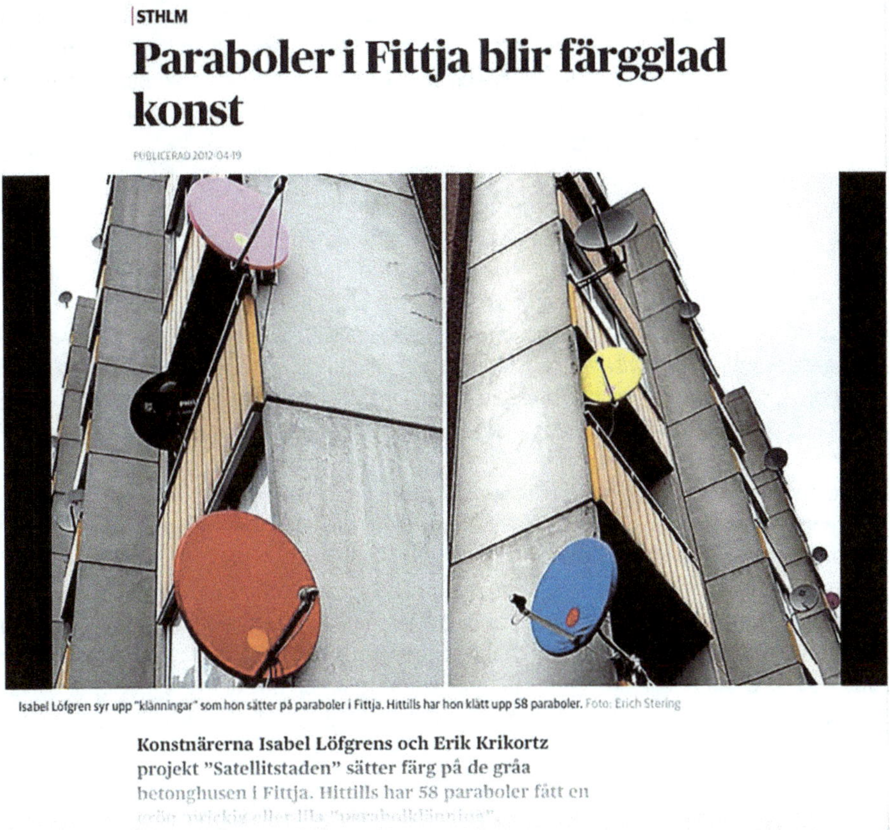

| STHLM

**Paraboler i Fittja blir färgglad konst**

PUBLICERAD 2012-04-19

Isabel Löfgren syr upp "klänningar" som hon sätter på paraboler i Fittja. Hittills har hon klätt upp 58 paraboler. Foto: Erich Stering

**Konstnärerna Isabel Löfgrens och Erik Krikortz projekt "Satellitstaden" sätter färg på de gråa betonghusen i Fittja. Hittills har 58 paraboler fått en**

*Figure 50 – 'Satellite dishes become colorful art', full-page newspaper magazine in the cultural section of Dagens Nyheter, April 19 April 2012.*

Expectedly, Juan did not agree to participate in *Satellitstaden*. However, in the same evening, five other people did agree to participate. When I asked why they agreed to participate, they said that they had liked the idea, and that they appreciated the fact that I addressed them as a community in their own forum. When I asked them about the project not really helping the community more deeply, they agreed that it was true, but the fact that I was there made a difference, and Fittja could indeed use a bit more color on the streets, and it did not cost anything.

104 'Paraboler blir färgglad konst', *Dagens Nyheter*, 19 April 2012, https://www.dn.se/sthlm/paraboler-i-fittja-blir-fargglad-konst/.

Residents of satellite cities like Fittja, or Skärholmen nearby, where Abdul Fattah comes from, are tired of seeing poor areas being treated as areas of exception, and the manipulation of local residents as interesting outsiders in well-intended projects that ultimately benefit the creators and sponsors of the projects is ultimately harmful. She criticizes State directives that support this view by giving away funding to projects that 'fit the bill' but are of marginal relevance to local populations. In other words, there is a market within the academic and cultural sectors for projects that deal specifically with concepts like 'otherness', 'marginalization,' and 'social inclusion' of which only one side benefits. These are entirely legitimate concerns which may end up instrumentalized by other agendas.

These projects and practitioners of socially engaged art often use an activist rhetoric of emancipation and decolonization that may be subtly appropriated by the government 'in order to justify public spending on the arts'.[105] It is not surprising to realize that those who occupy the positions in the public arts funds and decide on the distribution of resources are the same ones who have attended art schools with some 'socially engaged' practitioners, or attend the same events in the *konsthalls* (art centers) in the suburbs where the discourses on social aesthetics, participation, etc. are presented in extensive conferences, workshops and exhibitions. Has participation and the 'social turn' in contemporary art become another mannerism?

In the mind of Mexican curator Cuauhtémoc Medina, yes. He claims there has been a 'periphery fever' in recent years.[106] It is yet another form of colonization, with the same mask of goodwill that the Jesuits presented to the 'heathen' natives upon landing in the New World. Contemporary art, he claims, has become the scapegoat of the right wing. Abdul Fattah understood the game: art is glamorous and relatively cheap way to produce, a good value for the money. Education and structural changes, though cumbersome and slow, are necessary but are less profitable in the short run. The extent to which any of these 'periphery fever' projects, *Satellitstaden* included, provides any form of structural change in the community remains to be seen.

In addition to the specificities of the art sector itself, this may sometimes be inscribed in a larger discourse of creative economies. Claire Bishop writes:

> The rhetoric of 'everyone is creative' is a euphemism for introducing yet more independence from the welfare state. All this is important for contemporary art, because it means that certain terms that it holds dear now need to be urgently recontextualized: creativity, but also community and participation.[107]

---

105 Claire Bishop, *Artificial Hells: Participatory Art and the Politics of Spectatorship*, London: Verso Books: 2012, p. 13.

106 Lecture notes from Cuauhtémoc Medina, 'Biennial Interventions: Margolles in Venice, Cannibal Dominoes and Manifesta 9', *IASPIS*, Stockholm, Sweden, 18 August 2011.

107 Miranda Johnson, 'Hell is Other People: Ethics, Aesthetics and Participatory Art', Undergraduate Honours Methodology paper, University of Western Australia, 2013. Available at: https://www.academia.edu/4019730/Hell_is_Other_People_Ethics_Aesthetics_and_Participatory_Art.

Here she invokes Richard Florida's ideas about the creative economy,[108] where 'everyone is creative' if they try hard enough. This is based on the assumption that today there are more people able to get compensation for their creative output than before and that this also benefits cities as a whole. Even though Botkyrka municipality, as we have seen, is largely inspired by the concept of creative cities as a possibility for intercultural societies to become more visible and engaged in their own visibility, Bishop here is ironic: she reveals yet another means of instrumentalization of culture away from the sphere of citizen's rights and support systems. Furthermore, using community-based participatory art programs in lieu of economic redistribution to strengthen social bonds in deprived areas is an argument often used to justify the financial support of participatory art projects, as if they acquire a function inside a community beyond the aesthetic experience in itself. Bishop considers this attitude disingenuous. It is an appropriation of participatory art projects acting as a cover-up for ingrained inequality, rather than discussing why this inequality exists at all.

This is by no means an exclusive phenomenon in Fittja or Sweden. Claire Bishop's positioning stated above is an adequate response to changes in cultural policy in the UK and in the Netherlands since the early 2010s, with similar contexts. In these countries, sustained support for arts projects and initiatives had recently entered a recessionary régime.[109] Instead of long-term support for arts institutions or long-term bursaries for independent artists, both institutions and artists now apply for the same funding lines for isolated projects. Long-term support for projects thus requires several application rounds, and there are no guarantees for continuity. In so doing, the budgets for culture get renewed every year and get slowly depreciated with every change. The same is true for Sweden where the State is the main funder for cultural activities. It follows that artistic projects, such as *Satellitstaden,* having participated in several funding rounds, tend to be shorter and temporary so as to guarantee any funding at all. Temporariness means that the terms of engagement of projects with the communities may be more fragmented and short-lived than long-term initiatives that have the time to accumulate knowledge and experience to make more substantial contributions. Furthermore, while private funding for the arts in Sweden is growing, it is still very small in comparison to the State support, that has historically been the main sponsor of experimental and non-profit cultural activity. This makes an independence from the State cultural policies very difficult. On the other hand, state support for cultural projects lends a character of responsibility for the use of public money, and there is a democratic component to the responsibility with which these funds are used and accounted for. But the scenario is nonetheless complicated. Slavoj Žižek may succeed in elucidating these contradictions, and in using Lacan's distinction between knaves and fools as a metaphor to identify the ideological battle between different positionalities, he writes:

> Today's right-wing intellectual is a knave, a conformist who refers to the mere existence of the given order as an argument for it and mocks the left for harboring utopian

---

108 See also Florida, *Cities and the Creative Class.*

109 See my article about the cutbacks in public funding for the arts in the Netherlands and in Europe. Isabel Löfgren, 'Collateral Damage', *Paletten,* no. 114 (Autumn 2011): 141–156.

> plans that will necessarily lead to totalitarian or anarchic catastrophe; while the left-wing intellectual is a fool, a court jester who publicly displays the lie of the existing order but in a way that undercuts the sociopolitical efficiency of his speech. After the fall of socialism, the knave is a neoconservative advocate of the free market who cruelly rejects all forms of social solidarity as counterproductive sentimentalism, while the fool is a multiculturalist, 'radical' social critic who, by means of ludic procedures designed to subvert the existing order, actually serves as its supplement.[110]

Are we the fools or knaves in this equation?

Moreover, both Bishop and Abdul Fattah seem to put forth that we should not accept art's instrumentalization for populistic purposes nor the privatization of the creative class to justify budget cutbacks in any socio-immunological system, such as culture. Furthermore, in her critique, Abdul Fattah also implies that people in *miljonprogram* communities do not have access to cultural funding for their own ideas, which points to a segregation in the art field that mirrors segregation patterns in society-at-large. Even though funding opportunities for culture and art is in principle available to all citizens, in practice the knowledge about this opportunity does not reach people in marginalized and peripheral territories as they should, thus highlighting the need for a wider access to these resources for those outside the establishment and across issues of race and class, if culture is to be truly democratic. On the other hand, there is a visible mobilization in terms of alternative cultural scenes in marginalized areas outside of the establishment that shows the dynamism and energy of the creative potential of non-hegemonic cultural practicioners, where new forms of cultural expression find a fertile ground.

In any case, belonging to a more formal 'creative class' may certainly be the aspiration of many young people living in suburbs, and there certainly are many initiatives that try to fill the gap of unemployment and lack of opportunity with cultural initiatives that benefit both the young and the city as a whole in the form of outreach programs within established art institutions. But these initiatives are still located in the context of a co-dependency between communities and institutions, and the knowledge needed to make the funding opportunities visible for these young artists and cultural workers in the peripheries so that they can create autonomous practices still remains opaque and inaccessible. This signals an opportunity for art institutions to distribute this knowledge more widely in order to amplify the possibilities for autonomous voices to speak on their own terms, so that the subaltern may effectively speak even more loudly. And more than that, to be listened to.

Just like we understand the migrant as the Other to the host, we can also ask, what is the Other to the museum? We can argue that, while art in the peripheries may be somewhat different in character from the museums downtown, and often more experimental, it is altogether not so different in nature – it still falls under a canonical definition of art. We may wonder, is it the same art system just situated elsewhere? Art in the peripheries could be seen as extensions of the discourses that happen in the realm of biennales, symposia, residencies and

110 Žižek, 'A Leftist Plea for 'Eurocentrism'', p. 1005.

conferences, and as such add to the art system as a remote facet of the museum, but not always as its antithesis, or, its Other. Marginality, one of the preconditions for experimentalism, is thus lost. In fact, the relation is rather one of co-dependency: just like the satellite city is to the city, the art residency in the suburb is to the museum. Both are equally segregated from but all the while dependent on the 'center' to legitimize themselves, yet never fully reaching its own autonomy. Residencies and the 'experimental' are then relegated to the status of alternative locations for meeting the same art crowds and their attendant rituals during the *vernissage*, despite the inclusion, invitation and participation of communities in such events. As such they are not as radical as they intend themselves to be – radical in the sense of proposing a new ontology of art making and art spectatorship altogether, but rather act as extensions of it. Maria Lind, a Swedish curator and former director of Tensta konsthall, an arts center located in the northern Stockholm suburb of Tensta, also part of the *miljonprogrammet*, states:

> Social practice still mainly operates within the "minor" strands of the art world – as opposed to the spectacularized and consumption-oriented mainstream institutions in the "major" strand. These minors are self-organized initiatives, artistic and otherwise, as well as small-scale public institutions with precarious economies and they are the source of most of the new ideas in art. Sharing certain features with Gilles Deleuze and Félix Guattari's "minor literature," written by members of a minority but using and corrupting the language of the majority (like Franz Kafka) in order to maintain maximum self-determination, the minors of the art world keep a calculated distance from the "majors".[111]

Mexican curator Cuauhtémoc Medina mentions in a lecture I attended while I was enacting *Satellitstaden* that, at least in the world of contemporary art biennials, the sense of adventure and experimentality of the site-specific gesture has been lost. Like oil painting, site-specificity has become an artistic genre, he claims. Within this genre, a certain type of expressionism has evolved: the community-based occupation disguised as Situationist politics that, according to him, has become 'bad politics'. 'Don't get too Situationist', he warns. This led to me ask myself, within the community-based 'occupation', has migration become just another aesthetic texture?

And yet, we need to be attentive to the nuances, for it is in these interstitial spaces between center and periphery that an opening towards new paradigms, even with its inherent contradictions, may happen. Nonetheless, the presence of culture and art institutions in these areas are fundamental in terms of expanding artistic activity and discourse, and as such gradually broadening the range of practices of cultural production and spectatorship in order to stimulate ever more critical voices. The type of art of the 'social turn', or what is today called 'social practice' in art seems to be more appropriate in the alternative circuit as the art 'that makes situations happen' in the words of the British artist Jeremy Deller. Art is not only a commodity that can hang in museums or galleries to be consumed readily by an art market

111 Nato Thompson, *Living as Form: Socially Engaged Art from 1991–2011*. Cambridge, Mass.: MIT Press, 2012, p. 56.

and its systems of valuation. Rather, here we may see another order of activity operating in art spaces and initiatives in border situations that helps to expand the notion of a *border aesthetics* (an aesthetics that brings border situations into the régime of the sensible and of the visible), which is not inscribed with the logic of styles nor artistic movements, but rather acts as a conceptual trigger to make visible the diversity of subjectivities and experiences wherever they are located. Cultural institutions in the peripheries of Stockholm show a growing awareness of this potential, and in recent years there has been a dedicated effort to continuously improve inclusion, promote local participation, and expand contemporary art discourses into socially engaged propositions and act as *aggregative networks* within communities, as per Franco Berardi's suggestion, which needs to expand even further. Perhaps what is needed is, in fact, a diasporic turn[112] in the contemporary art field that accurately represents and supports artists with diasporic backgrounds in art institutions, collections and programs, and the creation of specific cultural policies that break new ground in this domain, more attuned to the demands of racialized, minorotized or marginalized cultural practitioners.

## The Hospitable Turn

Cuauhtemóc Medina's reminder of one of the most fundamental functions of art – its capacity of subjective transformation – can be linked to Greek-Australian art theorist Nikos Papastergiadis' definition of hospitality within the cultural realm as a cultural practice of 'reception' and a fundamental gesture that facilitates the encounter and understanding between strangers. In an interview, he states that,

> These interactions are now heavily framed by suspicion and threat, and the willingness of an individual to express empathy, or extend solidarity is less and less likely. However, the same media can be and has been used to achieve the opposite ends, and I am interested to note that in recent years there has been a conscious effort by numerous artistic and political agencies to address the *empathy deficit*, and close what they call the empathy gap in relation to migration and asylum issues. This might enable new forms of hospitality.[113]

For Papastergiadis, migration is not just another aesthetic texture and neither is the refugee, or better, the expelled as a subject to be feared, in his effort to disentangle the connection between terrorism and the refugee, which is what feeds the 'ambient fear' in the public

112 From 2016 to 2020, I was a co-founder of an independent art collective, Institute for the Decolonization of Art (IDA) together with art historian and critic Macarena Dusant and artist and educator Estella Burga, where we developed a series of investigations and performative artworks looking into the possibility of creating a diaspora art archive, having interviewed artists with diasporic backgrounds across generations, analyzed the representation of such artists in public art collections; analyzing policies of the inclusion of diversity in art academies; and even working with migrant youth in publicly funded film projects that narrate experiences of flight and diaspora, some of which highlight very clearly the complex host and guest relationship of newcomers struggling with their asylum claims. For more information, see *Institute for the Decolonization of Art*, http://www.idakonst.wordpress.com.

113 Nikos Papastergiadis, *Cosmopolitanism and Culture,* Cambridge: Polity Press, 2012.

imaginary, recalling Stuart Hall's notion of 'moral panic'.[114] Instead, in *Cosmopolitanism and Culture* (2012), Papastergiadis proposes to understand the politics of fear as part of the ideas of mobility and difference in artistic practices. In doing so, migration could also be disentangled from moral imperatives and legal recourses, and be considered, in consonance with Flusser, as a creative force.

The entanglement of art and politics, especially in areas that have been stigmatized by exclusion from the media and cultural systems, which as Abdul Fattah points out cannot be overlooked, is essentially dialectical. For Papastergiadis, the danger of putting political intervention in the realm of experience (art) is that it turns the artist into a political agent, without necessarily addressing the fundamental aspect of mediation that an artwork requires, nor of the pragmatism that politics requires. Using aesthetic experience *tout court* as a political tool means to put it at the service of a political aim. In this sense, he claims, the danger is that the polarizing effects that this entanglement creates become all too foreseeable. What is interesting in contemporary art, or art in general, is that it is involved in the process of changing subjectivities and in transforming perceptions of the world, creating, among other things, archives that have not been planned, as well as effects that cannot be predicted, and thus able to imagine new forms of mediation. In sum, if art has a function, its function could be to glitch existing systems, approximate subjects in experiences and situations beyond the habitual, confront familiarity and foreignness, and ignite new modes of relating to one and the Other.

Within this new paradigm of the unforeseeable, there are many possibilities. If the fixed *konsthall* in the suburb can be said to be a satellite of the museum world only sited elsewhere, then perhaps the 'South African container' – which I will now call a pop-up assemblage in a public space – shows that the orbital quality of both the *konsthall* and its residency program has spawned its Other. The same *vague terrain* that is hospitable to drug dealers, as Abdul Fattah tells us, with its own set of guests and hosts can be equally hospitable to an art event with another set of guests and hosts, albeit in another temporality. These are not necessarily mutually exclusive. It is in this public space's doubleness of character where hospitality becomes a form of networking, as a practice of affinities, such as potlatch and gift-giving – as in the theory of reciprocity first identified by Marcel Mauss int the 1920s[115] – which have long been recognized as binding the kinship and friendship arrangements that lie at the heart of social reproduction, or in what I call the making of presence.

In his book, Papastergiadis redirects attention away from the much-debated dyad 'art-and-politics' and introduces the triad 'cosmopolitanism, politics, and aesthetics'. He introduces the concepts of a 'cosmopolitan imaginary' and an 'aesthetic cosmopolitanism' by exploring the roles of artists in reclaiming the conditions of hospitality, sometimes within the genre of 'social practice' which Lind presents as a viable alternative, but which Medina warns about. Even though Abdul Fattah, in her reaction against the objectification of the

114 See Hall, '*Policing the Crisis: Mugging, the State, and Law and Order*'.

115 See Marcel Mauss, *The Gift: Forms and Functions of Exchange in Archaic Societies*, trans. Ian Cunnison, London: Cohen & West, 1966 (1925).

immigrant suburb within the 'experiments' of art, and Bishop, in her critique of the instrumentalization, or 'artificial hell' of participation in cultural projects are entirely justified in their claims, I would argue that the encounter of the artist with the Other in the space of the Other becomes a productive 'border situation' to reveal and make clearer structures of Otherness and exclusion. Hospitality, in this case, helps us to rethink not only the ethics of participation, but to break apart the very logic of participation which remains in a binary order of us/them, one/other. Hospitality helps us to prompt the essence of the invitation itself and begin by inverting and blurring the roles of hosts and guests. It is in these zones of mediation between guests and hosts, in the establishment of a relationship of mutuality inherent to hospitality where the perception, and even the condition of exclusion can be questioned, problematized, and transformed. We could even say that in this case the term 'social turn' is not sufficient as it directs attention to the social but doesn't necessarily turn it around. Rather, we should think of a 'hospitable turn' in contemporary art where these confrontations, mediations and transformations can be more adequately addressed by cosmopolitanism, politics and aesthetics together, and not separate from each other.

One of the public art projects commissioned by the Agency of Public Art in Sweden in 2016–17 in *miljonprogram* areas across the country[116] addresses the entanglement of hospitality philosophically, artistically and politically, and exemplifies the hospitable turn proposed above. Sandi Hilal, a Palestinian architect and scholar of hospitality resident in Sweden created the installation *Al Madhafha/The Living Room* in Boden, an industrial city in northern Sweden. Boden is a small but growing city that has a past as city of refuge in the northern edges of the Baltic Sea. First, it functioned as a military outpost for foreigners awaiting entry to the nearby border city in neighboring Finland, and it has recently become a destination for refugees and asylum seekers thus reawakening the city's vocation as a site of hospitality. With this history in mind, Hilal has researched the role of the refugee and the dynamics of host and guests within this particular context. She highlights the fact that refugees may be stuck in an eternal condition of asylum seekers and as such become eternal guests. She wonders, on whose terms is integration meant to happen? How can refugees claim the right to become hosts and act as hosts, the right to invite and set their own agenda?

Hilal's artistic proposition for a public artwork included collaborating with residents who have recently arrived in Sweden with asylum status and physically transforming a residential apartment into a semi-public living room where refugees can exercise the right to become hosts in the space. Can we change society from a living room? – she asks. I interpret 'living room' metaphorically as a 'room for generating new life and new lifeforms' and a 'room where

116 'The government gives a mandate to the National Public Art Agency and the National Arts Council to conduct the culture initiative in the public areas of the Million Program (...) The initiative now includes a total of SEK170 million and will run from 2016 to 2018. The Public Art Agency, in collaboration with local stakeholders, will develop practical examples of how the Million Program's public spaces can be enriched artistically, while the Swedish Arts Council will allocate funds to operators of local civil society. The government has earmarked two million dollars for preparation during 2015. This project has already been concluded with several interventions ranging from installations to performances to collaborative projects in several *miljonprogram* areas across all of Sweden. *Public Art Agency Sweden*, http://www.statenskonstrad.se.

life is invited', to use some of the terms discussed in previous chapters, and the living room as part of a socio-immunological framework and support system. For newcomers, a living room may not always be a part of the first modest accomodations offered upon arrival, and its absence denies the new resident the right to host for lack of a space to be a host within. In the project, Yasmeen Mahmoud and Ibrahim Muhammad Haj Abdullah played a central role by being the hosts in this new living room space inviting guests on their own terms, which opens up a physical as well as a subjective space for exchanging experiences, knowledge, and social mobilization between persons who otherwise may become entrapped in an eternal guesthood. The right to host, and the right to a space of being a host, embodied in the space of a living room, is the first condition for this invitation to take place.[117] In this sense, the directness of the face-to-face encounter, unmediated by institutional conditions, and in the semi-public sphere of the living room inside the residential apartment, is where the responsibility embedded in this encounter with the Other, in the first philosophy proposed by Lévinas, may materialize.

117 Sandi Hilal, 'The Living Room: The Right to Host', *Obieg*, Vol. 11 (2019), https://obieg.u-jazdowski.pl/en/numery/goscinnosc/the-living-room-the-right-to-host

# CHAPTER 5: TRANSNATIONAL MEDIA AND HOSPITALITY

# CHAPTER 5: TRANSNATIONAL MEDIA AND HOSPITALITY

> When I leave home to conquer the world, I lose myself. When I come home to find myself again, I lose the world. This pendulum is political consciousness, and political consciousness is always unhappy. There is no political paradise. There is no cultural paradise, there is no identity paradise, there is no housing paradise. There is only a silent agreement to appease this conflict, and the mechanism that appeases contradiction is habit. Habit blunts the edges of perception, distances us from curiosity, at the same time habit it also forms a grounding, a reference point we somehow return to.
>
> – Vilém Flusser[1]

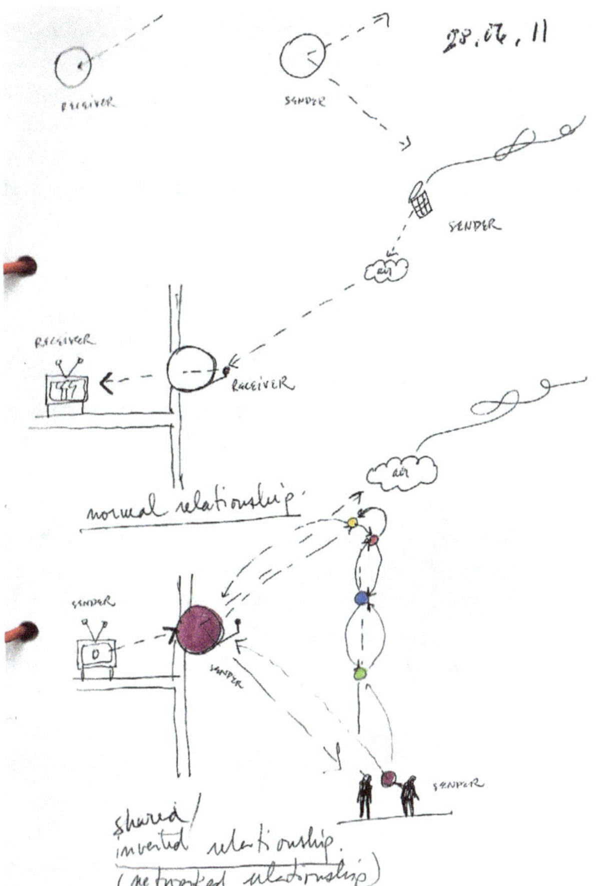


*Figure 51 – A diagram describing the emitter-receiver relationships within Satellitstaden. Image by the author.*

1 Vilém Flusser Archive, *We Shall Survive in the Memory of Others.*

In this chapter we will step out of the street and go inside the homes of Fittja residents where the ethnographic research took place, with conversations and interviews held over kitchen tables and living rooms, often where a television set displayed satellite transmissions from each resident's distinctive homeland or region. But first, let me provide some theoretical perspectives to contextualize the media practices observed and discussed with each resident with some theoretical perspectives on television, viewerships and diasporic media life practices.

In Flusser's analysis of television and politics, he illustrates the case where the sender and receiver of television is private as it begins at a private source, inside the television studio, then crosses the air waves through a technical-political apparatus, satellite and cable infrastructure in the public realm, and ends again in the private sphere of the television device, in the living room, that is, in the space of the home. As such, Flusser contends that the notion of public space – by 'public' he means the agora, the political space of discourse – is made insignificant.[2] With satellite technology, the public-political space is embodied in the intensity of air waves, or in the extension of visible or invisible cables, or even in the antennae – all the elements in the apparatus matter. These politics are reified into an image, which is what we evidence on the television screen, as presentation (*Vorstellung*), as Samuel Weber conclaims. The flickering stream of images that appear on screen are merely symptomatic of this entire transmission system, and in its content, we find multiple instances and representations of always distant realities.[3]

As such, in a state of 'connected exile', the connection to one's homeland from afar has a double function. While it helps to maintain a relationship to one's homeland and mitigate the severance from it, it also makes it easier for people to live a life apart. It is equally telling of a specific relationship that immigrant communities have to broadcast media and how this access affects everyday life and the formation of a specific subject that develops under these conditions. The access and distribution of television channels from the homelands, now available through a series of media developments in the past two decades,[4] creates an open channel for one's referential culture, where migration as a 'process' unfolds accompanied by media objects, such as satellite dishes, and content, such as homeland channel programming, that acquire a real and symbolic status in the everyday life of diasporic communities. By focusing on the satellite dish as a site for situating a notion of belonging, it is implicit that the network culture we are discussing is connected to the televisual medium; television as a social apparatus that bears significance within a discussion of the ethics of contemporary hospitality.

While the television set is merely an object that carries and presents the stream, on the screen, Flusser suggests that [historical] events begin to accelerate towards the image, where every

2 Flusser, 'The City as a Wave-Trough in the Image-flood', trans. Phil Gochenour, *Critical Inquiry* 31, Winter 2005. https://www.academia.edu/260662/The_City_as_Wave_Trough_in_the_Image_Flood.

3 Samuel Weber, *Mass Mediauras: Form, Technics, Media.* Palo Alto: Stanford University Press, 1996, p. 23.

4 I refer to the expansion of several broadcast media from the Middle Eastern and Caucasus regions in the past two decades: Al-Jazeera, Turkish television soap operas, NBC in Arabic, Kurdish channels; in addition to dozens of channels from around the world that are broadcast through satellite technology.

event (even the event of the possibility of the broadcast itself) is an image, with its accompanying apparatus. Back to the context of this study, the real experience of the homeland, for those who consider television broadcasts from their homelands as a lifeline, is triggered by this *image*.

What happens behind the image does not really matter – it is, as Flusser says, 'the result of technical voodoo'. Yet the real experience is elsewhere as it occurs in the space of the room between the screen and the body that watches it. This image is received in the form of 'familiar vibrations',[5] but also in the space between the receiving device and the emitter, the thousands of kilometers that connect Earth and sky through an orbital signal that invisibly pierces the airspace and materializes in the intimate sphere of the living room. What I want to stress is that the space produced between these distant images and *Being* forms a heteroptopic notion of home where host and homeland get confounded into one – I am sitting *here* but watching images and events from *over there* – in a temporal and spatial contingency. The experience and mediation have thus become increasingly deterritorialized but has also been embodied in different practices.[6]

While the technical apparatus can be explained rationally, the affective qualities that conjoin the apparatus, the image and the motivation for viewing something into creating a sense of home, can only be inferred from field study and observation. According to David Morley's seminal analysis, television constitutes the key home-making technology mediating family relations including those of power and gender.[7] 'The privileged role of the home', he writes, 'does not consist in being the end of human activity but in being its condition, and in this sense its commencement'.[8] I contend that counter to claims that media are considered alienating and deem spectatorship as a passive practice, media is not only a substitute for the notion of home and homeland but may constitute a home in and of itself where active spectatorship occurs. The television broadcast made possible by the infrastructure of satellites, signals, receivers and screens produce a space of inhabitation, and from this point of view we can begin to discuss the notion of media beyond the emitter-receiver paradigm and consider the mediation of the signal as an intensive capacity that constitutes space in and of itself, certainly belonging to one of the kinds of space Henri Levebvre theorized as resulting from different production modes.[9] This space of home-making is mediated by host and guest relationships within a practice and an ethics of hospitality in a media context, which opens up for further investigation into the realm of *hospitable media*.

The satellite dish, as an object that receives of signals that precipitates the flow of inhabitable images as a television flow, in its full implications may constitute such a site of mediation within an ethics of hospitality. According to Bruno Latour's actor-network theory (ANT), 'human and non-human (e.g. artifacts, organization structures) should be integrated into the same conceptual framework and assigned equal amounts of agency'.[10] In a classical example,

5 Vilém Flusser Archive, *We Shall Survive in the Memory of Others*.
6 Jan Aart Sholte, *Globalization: A Critical Introduction*. New York: Palgrave, 2005, p. 61.
7 Morley, *Family Television: Cultural Power and Domestic Leisure*, p. 54.
8 Lévinas, *Totality and Infinity*, p. 152.
9 Lefebvre, *La production de l'espace*. Paris: Anthropos, 1974.
10 Latour, *Reassembling the Social: An Introduction to Actor-Network-Theory*, p. 13.

a human and a car are both complex systems that acquire a different potential, meaning and agency when they are assembled into one network (i.e., driver+car). Likewise, the car itself is a network consisting of a set of actors (parts). Of course, it does not mean that they have an independent agency in the sense of will; the agency of the car (or one of its parts) comes to the fore when it breaks down (and the network collapses, losing function and meaning). Similarly, different *assemblages* arise as the people use media, and in this sense all media technological objects (from phones and tablets to satellite dishes) can be treated as a site and an actor at the same time. Thus, the satellite dish as space, and as a site of heterotopia, can be said to be part of an extensive sign-system, a 'site of cultural atmospherics'[11] within the socio-material reality of a spatial theory of communications. Here, notions of media temporality and spatiality are not merely a technical result of a given apparatus but play a constitutive role in communication and how it shapes built and social environments.

## A Timeless Present

In an interview about television in 1989, Vilém Flusser claimed that when historical events are played out in the 'timeless present' as live media events, we enter into the 'post-historical circularity of technical images'.[12] In this sense, he says, the television and satellite transmission of the lone man confronting a row of tanks in the Tiananmen Square protests, for instance, or of the last hours of Romanian president Ceauşescu and his wife before and after their execution, and the fall of the Berlin wall in that same year, were played out in a virtual geography that collapsed the present and the past into the *now*, a *now* manifest on the television screen. 'Post-history' for Flusser is where temporality occurs outside of the realm of cause and effect and becomes dictated only by events. Flusser passed away in late 1991, long enough to witness yet another manifestation of the timeless present: the spectacular live-sent beginning of the Persian Gulf War on television. Differently than the 'Living Room War' which invaded US families' living rooms with footage from the war in Vietnam in the 1970s, this time there would be no delay in transmitting the war. 'The real-time quality of television war reporting elevated the live remote broadcast to a stylistic necessity while eliminating the temporal distance required for the work of journalism. The ultimate temporal distortion was the tacit but immediate denial of history with regard to the development of this conflict, as real time obliterated both past and future,' say Jeffords and Rabinovitz in *Seeing Through the Media: The Persian Gulf War,* written soon after the conflicts and in full accordance with Flusser's temporal concept.

The Gulf War inaugurated the live declaration of war with the innovative 'night-vision' footage of real-time US bombing of Baghdad transmitted from a portable satellite antenna by CNN's reporter Peter Arnett. Rovert Wiener, a CNN executive producer infamously exclaimed, 'we are a 24-hour news network looking for a 24 hour news story, and one just fell from the sky', about the spectacular SCUD missiles appearing on the TV screen as green flickers behind the reporter in the distance. The type of rhetoric used in Arnett's reporting style seemed no different than sports journalism, narrating events occurring on the field as they unfold before

11 Franke, *B-Zone: Becoming Europe and Beyond*, p. 309.

12 Vilém Flusser Archive, *We Shall Survive in the Memory of Others*.

the eyes of the audience, neither presenter nor spectator knowing the final outcome, but all addicted to the game. I personally remember the uneasiness of watching these scenes of conflict on television, not knowing what was a *mise-en-scène* or what was real. One thing was certain: watching real bombings on television had the same wonderment as watching fireworks in the sky, and the unclear image in low light and low resolution most definitely contributed to the uncertainty of what was happening. And such is the doubleness of the spectacle of war: it is as seductive as it is horrifying – and we cannot stop watching.

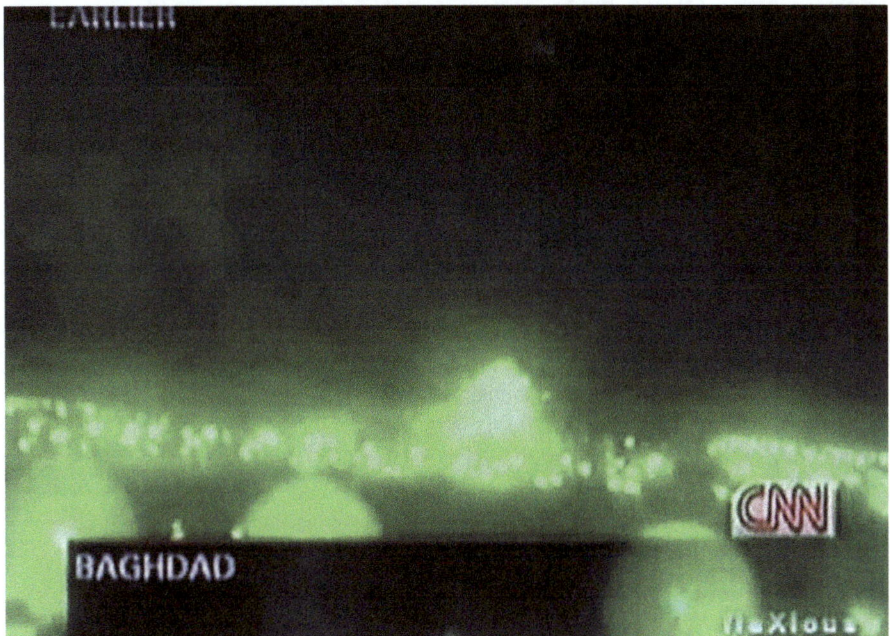


*Figure 52 – Still frame of CNN live broadcast of the Baghdad bombings, January 16, 1991, as I remember watching them at the time. See also the documentary film Live From Baghdad (2002), based on a true story of CNN's coverage of the Gulf War.*

In *Echographies of Television: Filmed Interviews,* one of the questions addressed by Jacques Derrida in conversation with Bernard Stiegler is: what does it mean to speak of the present in a situation of 'live' recording? Derrida is here referring to both being filmed as he is being interviewed (like a sort of performance), but also more philosophically about what tools we can use to deconstruct the speech, as in the enunciation and the grammar of a live event on the television medium. Derrida points to the inherent doubleness of the televisual medium and its mystifications, 'while continuing to remind people and to demonstrate that the "live" and "real time" are never pure, that they do not give us intuition or transparency, a perception stripped of interpretation or technical intervention'. I go back to my own puzzlement in watching CNN that day in 1991: did the bombings actually happen, how could we be sure? Derrida: 'Everything (...) even violence, suffering, war, and death, everything is constructed, fictionalized, constituted by and for the media apparatus. Nothing really happens. There is nothing but simulacrum and delusion.' As a guard against this neoidealism and a denial of the event, Derrida urges us that 'a consistent deconstruction is a thinking of singularity, and therefore of the event, of what ultimately preserves of the irreducible, but also that 'information' is a contradictory and heterogeneous process'.[13] In this case, the broadcast would last several days, interrupting regular television programming. In the war that followed between Iraq and the Coalition forces, what did not appear on screen was the 'event' of thousands of Iraqi refugees who were forced to relocate elsewhere. Among this displaced population was Dhikra Merza, 40, and her family. After a long voyage from a war-ridden Baghdad in the early 1990s through the Caucasus and into Europe, they managed to find refuge in the calm and austere suburbs of Stockholm, Sweden, where she and many fellow countrymen now live.

## Television and Difference

For the past two decades, especially with the expansion of satellite communications and information technology, transnational media have become central to the media practices of immigrant populations in Europe. According to Aksoy and Robins in *Banal Transnationalism: The Difference that Television Makes* from 2008, 'migrant groups (...) are now able to make use of transnational communications to gain access to media services from the country of origin. This has been an entirely new phenomenon (...) which has very significant implications for how migrants experience their lives, and for how they think and feel about their experiences'.[14] Moreover, the implications are also commercial and political. This has been made possible by several factors including available technologies, national media policies and the availability of a variety of new television channels from the regions where the immigrants of certain areas come from, most notably in the Middle East, the ex-Soviet republics, but also Africa, Asia and the Americas. The conjoining of these factors is embodied in a growing transnational media infrastructure where satellite signals can be captured from simple satellite dishes in most homes of those who live far away from their countries.

In Morley's nuanced analysis of television watching preferences, he draws attention to the power dynamic present in the programming choice, but also to variation and fragmentation inside the audience, moving away from seeing it as a monolithic, generalized subject. The meaning and the use of television can only be understood in the context of domestic life, family relations and other (leisurely) activities, and the results will be really diverse for different segments of the audience: 'Watching television' cannot be assumed to be a one-dimensional activity which has equivalent meaning or significance at all times for all who perform it'.[15] Yet, arguably, the context must be extended to include all aspects of personal/communal 'space of experience'. After all, Paddy Scannell's problematization of how television appears generally understandable and interpretable to everyone, in spite of the broad variation in the audience and the content, appeals to the same experiential plane and common frame of reference.[16]

---

13 Jacques Derrida and Bernard Stiegler, *Echographies of Television: Filmed Interviews*. Cambridge: Polity Press, 1996, p. 17.

14 Kevin Robins and Asu Aksoy, 'Banal Transnationalism: The Difference that Television Makes' in *Diversity and Diaspora: Arab Communities and Satellite Communication in Europe. Global Media and Communication*, No. 4, (December 2008), p. 278.

15 Morley, *Family Television: Cultural Power and Domestic Leisure*, p. 3.

16 Paddy Scannell, 'For a Phenomenology of Radio and Television', *Journal of Communication*, 45(3), 1995: 4–19.

In *Spotting the Satellite Dish: Populist Approaches to Infrastructure*, Parks describes how the satellite dish functions 'not only as a sign of cultural taste and class, but also of ethnic identity, (trans)national belonging, and global media integration'.[17] The spatial dimension of communication networks also provides a means of sociability by the production of communication, exchange of information capital, and the subjectivity of those who use, affect and are affected by these global networks. In her analysis of the satellite landscape in the new states formed at the end of the Balkan war in the 1990s, [18] Parks describes the effects of the establishments of transnational satellite networks:

> First, it allows new national broadcasters to circulate their signals alongside those of other nations, positioning them as participants in a global economy. Second, it stages the "liberalization" of a formerly socialist media system by showcasing the "free" exchange of new "states" signals to other parts of the world. Third, television provides a mean with which to construct and transnationally project or beam new national identities around the world. (...) Finally, it enables new national identities to target and maintain contact with 'diasporic' communities no longer called "Yugoslavs" but now recast in nationally ethnic terms (as Croats, Bosnians, Slovenes, Serbs, Kosovars, etc.).[19]

While Parks focused on former Yugoslavia for her study, my study in Fittja involves this former Yugoslav footprint and many other footprints of diasporas, both satellital and cultural, overlapping with each other. Even though there is a Kurdish majority in the area and Assyrians are well represented, the remaining groups are so diverse that it would be difficult to attribute a single nationality or ethnicity to Fittja. Most of these people in diaspora depend to some extent on access to broadcasts from the homeland to connect to political networks in their home countries, especially those who come from war zones such as Syria, or from countries that impose tight information controls on their population such as Iran or Cuba. Fittja is unique in this aspect: it does not concentrate any one diaspora, but many.

The idea of the 'ethnoburb', a term geographer Wei Li uses to describe the emerging phenomenon of suburban areas where many ethnic groups live together, may be more appropriate to describe the urban and social formation under one term, but would require adapting it to the European context and its connection to the architecture of public housing.[20] Since the focus of the research was not to study satellite television usage within a specific group, but rather study the phenomenon as it covers one city block, looking at how media, space and community interact, we must therefore take into account the heterogeneity of the interviewed population. In fact, these populations and their dispersed histories crisscross each other in every space of the area, converging into the common life of the neighborhood.

---

17 Lisa Parks, 'Technostruggles and the Satellite Dish: A Populist Approach to Infrastructure', in Göran Bolin (ed.) *Cultural Technologies*, Routledge, 2012.

18 Many residents in Fittja hail from the former Eastern bloc, particularly former Yugoslavia and the new states that were created after the Balkan wars (Serbia, Bosnia, Croatia, Slovenia, Kosovo, Macedonia and Montenegro). Their access to satellite television from the region today is a result of the new satellite distribution geography described by Parks, 'Postwar Footprints', p. 306–348.

19 Parks, 'Postwar Footprints', p. 343.

20 Wei, *Ethnoburb: The New Ethnic Community in Urban America*, p. 55.

Therefore, it becomes difficult to trace specific patterns in a single population and use it as comparison to others.[21]

Screen-based media, television especially, are still a central feature in modern homes. David Morley states that television use is primarily a home-based activity (among the principal home-making tools) and can only be made sense of in the context of other leisurely activities.[22] Stina Bengtsson suggested that media use functions as a modern ritual, maintaining social norms as well as boundaries between different spaces and activities (such as work and leisure) in everyday life. According to Bengtsson, 'the modern separation of public and private spheres does not mean, even on a microanalytical level within the household, that the private sphere – which is perhaps most private when we are also alone – can be characterized by any kind of lack of social norms [...]. The symbolic significance of the media in everyday life, thus, maintains as well as loosens up the strict boundaries between private and public spheres in modern everyday life'.[23]

Unlike the cinematic experience, which is much more distanced from everyday reality as it does not happen *live*, television is not exclusively a space of exception or alienation in the everyday. It is also neither alienation nor inclusion – yet it is exceptional, alienating and including at the same time. In *Television-Video-Architecture*, American conceptual artist Dan Graham claims that 'TV gains much of its effect from the fact that it appears to depict a world which is immediately and fully present. The viewer assumes that the television image is both immediate and contiguous as to time with the shared social time and the parallel 'real world' of its perceivers – even when this may not be the case. This physical immediacy produces in the viewer(s) a sense of psychological intimacy where people on TV and events appear to directly address him or her'.[24]

An idea of home consequently leads to an idea of the construction of oneself, and by extension, of the society that self may inhabit. In this sense, television, when seen within the framework of the ethics of hospitality, presents a possibility where technology and media allow the subjectivities of both host and guest to blur and overlap. In *Critique of Everyday Life*, Henri Lefebvre drew together concepts that have been inseparable ever since, namely space and everyday life. He conceived this dialectic relationship such that space and the everyday are never in step but always somehow disjointed from historicity as the kind of distance that enables the self to perceive itself in the third person.[25]

This very estrangement references the subjectivity of the exile underpinned throughout everyday life and space through varying degrees of cultural, if not existential, disorientation. We cannot seem to get our bearings in a brave new world without borders even if the illusion of

21 See Chapter 4 for a profile of the Fittja community.

22 Morley, *Family Television: Cultural Power and Domestic Leisure*, p. 76.

23 Bengtsson, 'Symbolic Spaces of Everyday Life', p. 130.

24 Dan Graham, *Video-Architecture-Television: Writings on Video and Video Works 1970–1978*, New York University Press, 1979, p. 63. Available at: https://monoskop.org/File:Graham_Dan_Video_Architecture_Television_1979.pdf.

25 Lefevbre, *Critique of Everyday Life Vol. 3*, London: Verso, 2005 (1981), p. 27.

grounding oneself through information deludes one into a suspended space of momentary belonging. In a television broadcast, a familiar voice using familiar words in a language we recognize as belonging to something intrinsic in us – our identification of origin – becomes flickering points of light on the formless grid of this estrangement. A cultural disembedding of any sort in the space of the everyday beckons in its turn a compensating process of reembedding to accommodate us in seemingly faceless surroundings, when stronger, more communal bonds are absent. Watching television from the homeland may just as well soothe the pain of homesickness, and deny, albeit temporarily, that there is a world outside that is strange and incomprehensible. How, then, is the life of the migrant changed by the availability of transnational television? How does it aid or deter the process of cultural and political integration and what are its implications in assessing the level of hospitality granted and felt by the migrant in the host country?

## The Interviews

> To approach the Other in conversation is to welcome his expression, in which at each instant he overflows the idea a thought would carry away from it. It is therefore to receive from the Other beyond the capacity of the I, which means exactly: to have the idea of infinity. But this also means: to be taught. The relation with the Other, or Conversation, is a non-allergic relation, an ethical relation; but inasmuch as it is welcomed this conversation is a teaching.
>
> – Emmanuel Lévinas[26]

Beyond the artistic intervention, the second most important component of the project was a series of interviews with project participants. In fact, the artwork was a device to initiate a conversation about Fittja resident's use of transnational media and how this media usage impacts their notion of home and belonging in their host country. My general interest in the presence of satellite dishes in Fittja and my specific interest in learning about Dhikra's and all fifty participants' television habits was to understand the effect of transnational television on the lives of those who are living in exile, or who are part of a diaspora.

I began with very simple questions, such as why the respondents have a satellite dish, their favorite programs, who watches what and at what times. Then I get into more sensitive questions about their opinion on forbidding the satellite dishes, what they think of Sweden and Fittja, the best and worst aspects of living in Sweden and what they miss the most about home – and what they consider 'home' to be. At the end, I asked if they would like to make a statement to be published through the project as a way of making parts of this conversation public. The interview process happened both ways. As I interview the participant, they also interview me, in a reciprocal relationship which I considered to be fair. Often, their curiosity is what drove the conversations.

26 Lévinas, *Totality and Infinity*, p. 51.

**WHY DID YOU CHOOSE THIS COLOR FOR YOUR SATELLITE DISH?**

My sister picked yellow for me but I prefer orange.

Everything feels better with a little extra color.

Purple is MY color.

**Blue matches my curtains.**

The satellite dishes look nice with more color. Why aren't our balconies colorful too?

**Green because I wish there was more green in my country. Now it's only desert and war.**

Blue like the sea in Greece.

Neon orange is the coolest color.

Green like nature, and the color of Islam.

Pink like my note book, my rug, and my coat.

**Purple like the Assyrian Democratic Party flag.**

Blue is not because of the Serbian flag. We just really like it.

Green looks bright even in the evening.

Red like the Turkish flag (of course).

Yellow like the sun.

The whole world should live in pink, in peace and love for everyone.

I chose green because I only wear green.

Orange makes me happy, it reminds me of oranges.

Blue is like the sky, closer to the clouds.

**Pink is like spring flowers.**

**WHY DO YOU HAVE A SATELLITE DISH, WHAT DO YOU WATCH ON TV AND WHY?**

When I just arrived, I felt isolated. I got a satellite
as soon as I could so I could listen to Spanish. It wa
just about the language but a way of thinking an
expressing oneself which was closer to my o

Turkish soap operas are cool because one of them is filmed in Belgrade where my parents come from.

Half my family
lives back hom
so I have to keep
eye on the news
and football to

Now there are many Turkish series dubb
in Arabic. I prefer Turkish and Indi
series, and never watch American sho

I want to see news from all ov
the world, in our language, to
able to tell the lies from the tru

**The satellite dish is part
my culture, it's my nee**

If I spoke better Swedish, I would watch Swedish news. I am newly arrived so it's tough with the language, but a half hour everyday would help me learn. The children, though, all watch Bollibompa.

**I watch the news fr
home everyday. W
things get better, it
be time to go home –
plan to move back
soon as possible.**

When I bought the satellite dish,
Swedish got worse. But we have to wat
TV from back home...what to d

One day I want to turn on the TV and see only good news from home. We miss the happiness of our people.

Swedish news are too sh
need the real news from h
It's important especially fo
who come from the Middle

Maybe people could pay a little ext
to avoid the ugliness of all the
things hanging from the balconi
(I only have one because of my wi

Without the satellite dish, I feel like in a pris

**When I hear familiar soun
coming from the TV, it feels li
I am back home – like a mira**

I want all possible windows to the world,
bought the largest satellite dish in all of Fit

I just want to come home and chill out watching TV. I think better if I watch stuff in my own language.

Turkish soap operas
fun and dramatic,
the actors are rea
handsome, hehehe :)

This is a democracy. We have t
right to watch whatever we wa

WHAT WOULD YOU DO IF THEY TOOK AWAY THE SATELLITE DISHES?

ew technology is still o expensive. We will ep the satellite dish long as possible.

The TV makes me feel like home and not so outside society. I feel safer, it makes my life easier. I just moved here.

they take away the satellite shes, I will protest in Sergels Torg!

ey take away the satellite hes, everyone here will l watch their own TV on computer. But the old ople need it most, and y don't use the computer.

Take away the satellite dishes! People are chained to their living rooms, locked to their own cultures and don't learn anything new.

atellite dishes are considered a mbol of immigrants. To allow us keep our satellite dishes shows spect for people from other cultures.

y husband would move back to Iraq the satellite dishes are forbidden.

el free in this country, were blinded back me. It feels like whole new world ens before my eyes.

Let me keep my antenna!

It's nice to have a connection back home.

we let go of satellite dishes, then a transformation ld begin to happen. Watch Swedish channels and cott all others! Out with the ugly satellite dishes!

feel naked without ny satellite dish.

ould be unfair to take them ay. The older folks miss ir homeland very much and TV is a way for them to like they still belong there.

There is nothing special about satellite dishes, and I am used to seeng them everywhere, just like in Turkey. Why do they make such a fuss about it here?

TV is my friend.

IF YOU COULD SEND A MESSAGE BACK TO THE SKY, WHAT WOULD IT BE?

Parents, bring up your children safely, don't let them hang out with the wrong friends.

It's difficult to be happy here if we are treated differently than everybody else

We are foreigners here but we should also have a say in the society where we live now

There are no jobs for women. We deserve to be fully employed. For us Muslim women it's more difficult – they don't say it, but we know.

People should know that Fittja is a good place where people respect each other like brother and sister. I don't want to move anywhere else

I can bake the best bread. Hire me, I need a job

With the Latins, I am Latin. With the Swedes, I am a Swede. But regardless where we come from and where we end up living, we should never forget our roots

Missing home doesn't help much We have to look forward and not just sit at home in front of the TV

I believe in working together so that we can change the place where we live. We can only count on ourselves.

Everyone is only concerned about work here in Sweden Back home it people worry less and have more time to socialize

I don't have a job because my Swedish is not perfect

Sometimes people get into fights here, but it's not my problem

I only like the people out here. The buildings are ugly

The whole world meets here. We can communicate and get to know each other if you are up for it.

We can't just classify immigrants like in the media There are good ones and bad ones, just like the rest of society. There should be no difference between us

If I have fewer possibilities than other citizens, I also feel like less of a person.

Don't believe what you see in the media this is not a slum Come and see for yourself, welcome!

Yes, Fittja's image is negative But life here is not negative

Don't come here! I liked it here before, but now it got worse

I just want to say that life is good here

*Figure 53 – Printed matter containing citations from the interviews conducted in Fittja as responses to the following questions: 2011–2012. Graphic Design by 2Typer (Sepidar Hosseini and Moa Schulman).*

During the interviews I also ask if I may take a photograph of their living room where the television is, which became the photographic essay, *Television is my homeland,* see Chapter 4. These images uncover another aspect of domestic life and television through the life of objects inside people's homes. This is inspired by Flusser where he makes an analysis of material possessions in exile as a substitution for owning land. Material possessions take another symbolic order in the life of the exile as the home becomes a microcosm where fragments of the homeland coinhabit the living space in the host country. Television here is seen as an object in the house, with the power also to provide a virtual and temporal dimension of the homeland inside the house – a type of heterotopia where different temporal dimensions and multiple spaces coexist in the same place.

This also resonates with Dan Graham's thoughts connecting the living environment to television and social, lived realities:

> An architectural code both reflects and directs the social order. In the not too distant future one can envisage that this code will be supplemented, modified and in part supplanted by a new code, that of television. As cabled television images displayed on wall-sized monitors connect and mediate between rooms, families, social classes, "public"/"private" domains, connecting architecturally (and socially) bounded regions, they take on an architectural (and social) function. Video in architecture will function semiotically speaking as window and as mirror simultaneously, but subvert the effects and functions of both. (...) Architecture defines certain cultural and psychological boundaries, video may intercede to replace or re-arrange some of these boundaries. Cable television, being reciprocally two-way, can interpenetrate social orders not previously linked; its initial use may tend to de-construct or re-define existing social hierarchies.[27]

What is more important, I was interested in how the image of Dhikra's own home country, as represented by the television networks affects her emotional perception of her homeland, whether it makes a difference for her life or not. Inversely, I am also curious to understand how she sees herself reflected in Sweden, what her views are on integrating into a culture different from her own and how this virtual proximity to the homeland, by way of satellite television, may or may not mitigate a sense of loss that seems to permeate all those in exile. We may even consider if 'loss' is even an appropriate term, or if living in exile in times of intense connectivity provides a freedom from isolation – not a living apart, but a *living-with*. Of course, these perspectives change through time. While many of those in exile live in the hopes of returning to their homelands when order is restored, many like Dhikra have made the firm decision to never return. Return to what? – many have replied.

From Dhikra's balcony, where her green satellite dish hangs pointing to the sky, we can spot details of how these areas have become problematic in contemporary Sweden. I see a rusty and bleached balcony front threatening to detach from the façade. A window is taped together

27 Dan Graham, *Video-Architecture-Television: Writings on Video and Video Works 1970–1978*, p. 64.

to avert the glass from breaking and falling in the children's play area below. The concrete is cracking at some stress points of the façade, as any façade made of precast concrete is prone to do. Tens of satellite dishes hang from every balcony window in what looks like an improvised notation of dots over the façade pointing in all directions. Fittja's buildings, like many similar suburbs in its vicinity and built in the same time period, have not seen renovations since the time of its construction in 1973 and the original concepts of living have become outdated. In contrast, from her balcony I can also see a vast and beautiful meadow bordering a lake, and small gardening allotments tended by the community, as well as well-equipped green areas with walking paths and park areas. Yet, Dhikra is proud to live there, is a well-regarded member of the community and neighbors, and it is visible that she has made a happy home there, where I was welcomed many times – her role as a host within her community represents the embodiment of hospitality.

## 'The Satellite Dish that Unites Us!!' Transnational Media and Life in Exile

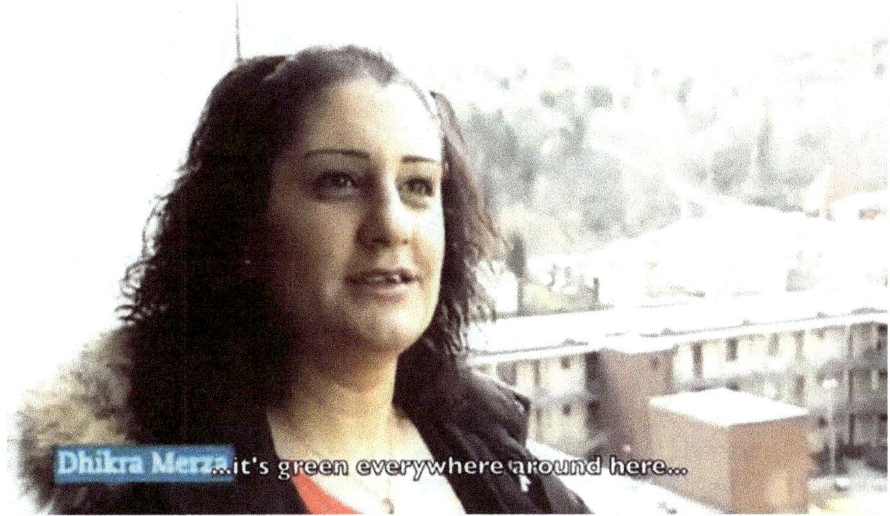


*Figure 54 – Dhikra kindly agrees to appear on a television reportage about Satellitstaden. Her motivation for choosing green is that she wishes her country, Iraq, to be as green as Sweden someday. Her comment is nostalgic. Dhikra has never returned to Iraq since she arrived in Sweden almost thirty years ago. 'Satellitstaden', Sveriges Television, 4 May 2012, 4'32'.*

During our first interview in early March 2012, Dhikra tells me over coffee and cake in her kitchen about her and her family's journey. It is still winter, and the days are still very short. I arrived early at her house to get the last glimpse of daylight so that I could install her green cover properly. She, like many other Iraqi Assyrians of Christian descent live in Botkyrka municipality. She lives with her husband, William, and three teenage children on the seventh floor of one of Fittja's highrise towers. As the working-class profile of these new estates gradually gave way to the increasing and changing character of immigration to Sweden in the past 40 years, they have been stigmatized as segregated areas. They offer cheaper rents, are reasonably well connected to the rest of the city, besides the security of living closer to their kin and to their homeland communities.

As we sit in the kitchen, we can hear the television set in her living room, which is turned on to CNBC Arabia, in Arabic.[28] And yet, when she arrived in Sweden, even though satellite television was already well established, television channels from the Middle East, especially from Iraq, were unavailable. Nevertheless, she and her husband William bought a satellite dish and watched whatever they could in Arabic. The Internet did not exist, and communication with the homeland and other family members was done by telephone (which was very expensive) or by letter (which sometimes never reached their addressees in the homeland) causing frustration, worry and isolation. The history of transnational television in Arabic along with technological advancements in satellite technology and the popularization of satellite culture would somehow change all of that. It would be stimulated by the period after 1990 and the reshuffling of power relations in the region occasioned by the Gulf War:

> A phenomenon born in the aftermath of Iraq's 1990 invasion of Kuwait, Arab satellite television was dominated during the first half of the 1990s by broadcasters so closely allied to governments that they had far more interest in shaping public opinion than in reflecting it. Initially, therefore, the new transnational medium's power to liberate viewers from tight government censorship was not realized. So when Al-JAzeera emerged on the scene during the second half of the decade, its appetite for airing controversy and reporting dissent shocked most Arab governments. (...) As millions of viewers equipped themselves to receive Al-Jazeera's programs, a new generation of other broadcasting hopefuls elbowed their way into an increasingly popular satellite television arena, eager to benefit in one way or another from the chance to transmit to Arabic-speaking audiences inside and outside the Arab world.[29]

The Syriac/Assyrian population in Sweden is the largest in the world living in diaspora, and has made Södertälje, Sweden, its international capital, only 15 kilometers away from Dhikra's apartment in Fittja.[30] At a population of around 150,000 in Sweden currently, many of them have settled in areas dominated by *miljonprogram* architecture such as Fittja. Assyrians are the descendants of an ancient people from the central valleys of Iraq, northern Iran, spanning into Central Turkey and parts of northern Syria. Until the second invasion of Iraq in 2003, roughy 5 percent of the Iraqi population, or 1.5 million people, had Christian affiliation. After the invasion, violence against Christians rose with abduction, torture, bombings, evictions and killings, and many have been pressured to convert to Islam under threat of death or expulsion. Christians have since then successively migrated to nearby Syria and Jordan, and from there on to the world to join the existing diasporas of displaced Chaldean Catholics and Coptic Christians around the world. The Assyrians and the Kurds are considered ethnic groups

28 *CNBC Arabia*, https://www.cnbcarabia.com/.

29 Naomi Sakr, 'Maverick or Model? Al-Jazeera's Impact on Arabic Satellite Television', in Jean K. Chalabi (ed.) *Transnational Television Worldwide*. London: I.B. Tauris, 2005, P. 66.

30 Assyrians first arrived in Sweden in 1967, with 2,000 individuals that were expelled from Turkey, and settled in Södertälje, 15 kilometers west of Fittja. In 2007 the arrival of Syriacs, a Christian population i Syria and Assyrians from Turkey and Iraq has trebled in comparison to previous years.

that do not have their own homeland and can be said to be the 'expelled of the expelled'. The Assyrian homeland today can be described as a virtual homeland whereby the multiple communities in different countries connect via family ties and by sharing common media, such as satellite television. In the early 2010s, the strengthening of bonds across this 'virtual geography' of the Assyrian homeland has led to the successful crowd-funding in support of an Assyrian army against the advances of the Islamic State.[31]

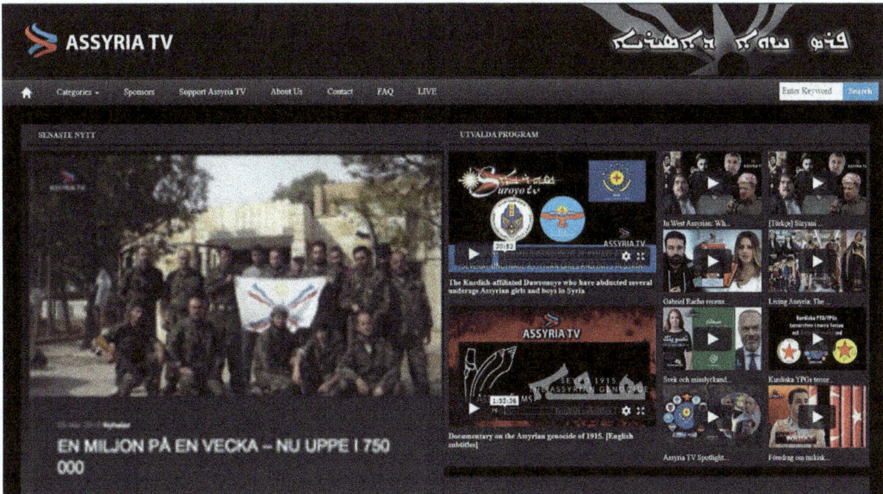


*Figure 55 – Screenshot of Assyria TV, the Assyrian television channel in Sweden. This video is part of the crowd-funding campaign 'One million in one week' to raise 1 million SEK to support the 'Nineveh Protection Unit' in Iraq. Source: Assyria TV,* **https://www.assyriatv.org/**.

Since Dhikra's arrival in the early 1990s, the reputation of areas like Fittja has deteriorated while the media have denounced them as eyesores, ugly places of social failure, where everything that progressive Sweden sought to overcome exists: poverty, inequality, unemployment, criminality and urban decay. However, some populations like the Assyrians are one of the few immigrant groups in Sweden to have begun transforming the built landscape by self-organizing and buying property to build their own church, banquet halls, and other community facilities that the original *miljonprogram* planning did not initially accommodate. This kind of self-organization made in dialogue and negotiation with formal urban planning authorities is one of the possibilities of emancipation from urban blight that could be seen as a model for accommodating and incorporating multi-cultures in the city, and an instance of hospitality that can be put into practice in the future. The Assyrian community dominates, for example, the small town of Geneta, not too far from Fittja, which was completely transformed into a 'new city' by the *miljonprogram* and is now seeing a new phase where a new aesthetic

31 Many Assyrians in Sweden have enlisted to participate in an opposition army to Isis, the 'Nineveh Protection Unit.' The numbers are yet unknown. Organized by political leaders for the 400,000-member Assyrian community in Iraq, and 'working alongside an Assyrian-American political action group, the American Mesopotamian Organization (AMO) vetted and enlisted the first tranche of displaced volunteers from among 2,500 applicants to compose the NPU's inaugural battalion.' See also 'Assyrian Christians crowdfund an army to reclaim homeland from ISIL', *Al-Jazeera*, 26 February 2015.

paradigm, one that is not normalized by traditional Swedish taste now symbolized by Ikea, is showing how newcomers can make Sweden a place of their own.[32]

In 1997, the Assyrian community founded Suroyo TV[33] with a grant by the Swedish government. Their slogan says 'The Satellite Dish That Unites Us!' and is a voice for the Assyrian/Chaldean/Syriac people and their cultural heritage, history and language. Suroyo TV is transmitted in five languages: Syriac, Arabic, Swedish, English, and Turkish, and currently has a wide range of content ranging from programs designed for children to political and cultural debates to sports programs, from historical documentaries to religious and national events, and from film reviews to musical video clips and educational programs. Furthermore, with its daily news programs that are broadcast in Syriac (eastern and western dialects) as well as in Arabic, it is an alternative news channel serving the members of the Assyrian/Chaldean/Syriac community scattered all around the world.

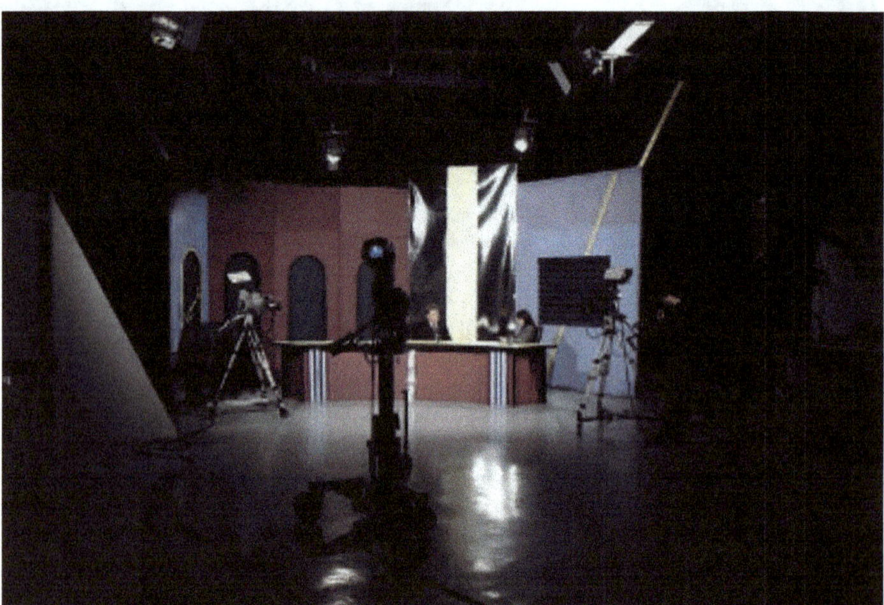

*Figure 56 – Sabri Isho, a radio and television journalist from Iraq who has been in Sweden since 1979, and Sargonta Oshana (right) host 'Tahrazto Ditonoyto' (Special Topic), a live call-in television talk show, at the Suroyo TV studios in Södertälje, 15 km from Fittja, and the largest Syriac community in diaspora in the world. The live show is broadcast internationally once a week. Source: Assyria TV.*

## Media as Life Support

Dhikra, and many others I interviewed for the project say that even though she has adopted Sweden as her home country, she sees her ability to connect to the culture of her homeland via television as something beyond entertainment or a banal consumer choice. For her, it is

32 Lecture notes from Jennifer Mack, 'Urban design from below', Arkitekturmuseet, 1–2 June 2015.
33 Suroyo TV, http://old.suroyotv.com/index.php/live.html.

a life necessity – media as life support, or a media life support, in line with Mark Deuze's theories of 'media life'. This media practice has become 'an indispensable thing'[34] completing the mediatization of her lifeworld as a 'mediatized world'.[35] Even though she speaks Swedish fluently as an acquired language, she feels the need to be in contact with her referential language in everyday life.

During one of our afternoons together, her brother Hassan joined us. He presented the opposite view, blaming the satellite dishes for making people passive and unable to integrate into Swedish society, and blaming it for the rampant unemployment that give Fittja its 'deserved bad reputation', he claims. Hassan says that the passivity and the group mentality that affects many immigrant groups deters them from a better life in Sweden, and homeland television should be discouraged – except for the older generation that still believes, like Mahmoud, that they will return to the homeland one day. The brother says vehemently that most immigrants live in a sort of collective denial that they are still living in their villages and that nothing has changed. In addition, he believes that easy access to welfare makes life too comfortable and further plunges many people into an existential apathy, unable to evolve and to create a new life. He says that under these circumstances, people cease to learn. When I asked his opinion about getting rid of the satellite dishes, he agreed that it would be for the best: 'This way, people would finally get out of their sofas and begin to interact with real people and hopefully learn how to speak Swedish and begin to function like normal people in society'.

For others such as Dalia, also an Iraqi Assyrian and Dhikra's neighbor two floors down, the access to all television is regarded as a fulfillment of a longing for freedom. During our interview she told me that 'in the time of Saddam we were kept in the dark – here I have the freedom to choose what I see, my mind can expand and learn new things.' She expresses a sense of openness that the West is able to provide and revealed to me the importance of a newly found concept of democracy in her life. She moved to Sweden only two years before due to remarriage to an Iraqi who had already been living in Sweden for several years. Even though she is still not conversant in Swedish and misses her homeland, the advantage of freedom as a Christian and all the benefits of a democracy justify her life and discomfort in exile, that is, the distance to her extended family, her culture and her language.

Differently from Dhikra who has made Sweden her home, other Iraqis in Fittja like Mahmoud, a Muslim who lives two doors away from her, still entertain the idea of returning to their homeland 'as soon as the situation there gets better', he tells me when I visit him in his apartment. The situation, however, is not getting any better, and Mahmoud, like thousands of others live in a sort of never-ending waiting game. Like many other immigrants and refugees who see Sweden as a temporary home, Mahmoud benefits from having a satellite dish on his balcony that allows his children to watch Iraqi TV children's programs in Arabic. Hoping that they manage to move back, Mahmoud would like his children to be somewhat integrated into Iraqi culture, and television is, in his opinion, the fast-track to a quicker integration back to the homeland. Language is Mahmoud's homeland in exile.

---

34 Jansson, 'Indispensable Things'.

35 Hepp and Krotz, *Mediatized Worlds*.

In this sense, Mahmoud implicates his family into the logic circularity of technical images and embeds this mediatic flow into the existential and cultural lifestyle of his family. Mahmoud's living room, and by extension most living rooms in Fittja, are dominated by a 60-inch flatscreen television encircled by oversized and very comfortable leather sofas. The modern-classical style of the sofas and their large-scale clashes with the stark lines of the building's brutalist design and the intimate scale of the living room with its low ceilings and measurements made to fit standard Swedish wood furniture.

There are interesting historical parallels between the history of Fittja and satellite networks arising from the research. Parallel to Fittja's construction as part of the *miljonprogram* in 1973, we have seen the growth and consolidation of transnational satellite networks since the 1970s when satellite broadcasts were first made widely available to a worldwide audience and enabled by a robust investment by developed nations in the creation of satellite technology infrastructure. Until that moment, television consisted of national networks covering the footprint of national territories. Usually land-based, television infrastructure could not reach internationally, to such an extent that international programming on any particular national network needed to be purchased and then aired locally. Programming could thus not be shared synchronically, and barriers of language and translation also caused an additional lag in the broadcasts. In a paper commissioned by Unesco to evaluate the social and cultural impact of satellite television in 1974, before the full roll-out of this technology, Tomo Martelanc states that:

> At the outset, television was basically a national mass medium. Owing to certain of their technical features, television signals are limited in range: they can reach only points and areas within line of sight of the point of transmission. Thus, in its infancy television was, for technical reasons, essentially confined to a limited geographical territory. The next stage began with the introduction and subsequent increase of international exchange of television programs. This marked the international stage in the development of television as a means and carrier of cross-cultural communication. International exchange has, indeed, become a regular feature of television programming (...). Very powerful satellites will be able to broadcast television programs directly to home receivers without the intermediate aid of a ground station. Eventually this may open the possibility of region-wide, even word-wide television, that is, of global television.[36]

The concept of real-time broadcasts was only made possible when the first satellite technology was made commercially available. Consequently, the shift from national television closed networks to both cable and satellite open networks allowed for the exchange of television programming from different countries and time zones simultaneously. If we assume that technological changes affect the way in which the world is perceived and experienced, so satellite television brought the world closer together by means of live and real-time images across national territories and time zones.

36 Tomo Martelanc, *Social and Cultural Impact of Satellite-based Television*, UNESCO, 1974. Available at: https://unesdoc.unesco.org/ark:/48223/pf0000011244?posInSet=2&queryId=dfeffdab-1609-48e2-9af9-7aa61a27c182.

In Sweden, national television only offered two public advertising-free channels until the mid-1980s when commercial television licenses were allowed to compete in the television market.[37] Satellite television networks entered rather late in the country. Nelson, a Chilean lawyer and political dissident arriving in the early 1970s, and living in Fittja since its construction, told me that his first decade in exile in Sweden was tough without cable or television media in his native Spanish. 'As soon as the first satellite dish was available, I bought it. I missed hearing my language at home and also missed the Latin cultural touch. Since the Chilean satellite was too far away, the Spanish channels were enough', he said to me in an interview at Fittja's local Bürek café on a November evening in 2011. For Nelson, it was important to be connected to a certain style of thinking as well as to his native language. By the time he acquired his satellite dish in the 1980s, most European countries were able to transmit their channels internationally. Also, by then, the decade without Spanish television brought him closer to Swedish culture, and marriage to a Swede. Today, the Chilean satellite is still too far away, but the Internet now supplements Nelson's needs for connection to his home culture. Does the absence of direct everyday media contact with the homeland country elicit deeper ties to the host country and culture? Does the availability of satellite television cause a distancing from the host country? Here is the paradox of satellite cultures: the closer one is to one's homeland culture, the more indirect becomes the access to the host culture. The farther one is from one's homeland culture, the closer it brings the exile to the host country. This perhaps to a subjectivity of the exile that changes by contamination, in a spectrum of contact with the guest or host wherein a satellite subjectivity occurs – one that orbit around several homelands through different intensities of signals from homeland and land of arrival in a dialogical relationship. It creates a quasi-proximity or quasi-distance depending on the distance from the signal one is orbiting around, never static, ever revolving, in, as mentioned earlier, suspended states of belonging.

Martelanc's language from the 1970s may seem outdated but it brings us closer to a state of the world in which Nelson found himself in his first years in Sweden. Martelanc's paper prognosticates some of the fundamental structures affecting the future of television which would change the realities of exiles like Nelson, exposing some technical, economic and cultural barriers, towards the utopia of a worldwide global audience. Martelanc mentions the interesting term 'spill-over' which is the capacity of a satellite footprint to 'spill over' onto another satellite footprint and by so doing opens up the possibility of two satellite providers to eavesdropping, or stealing the airtime, on one another. Interestingly enough, national satellites are made to beam over a given national territory, and, since a satellite footprint does not necessarily conform exactly to national borders as they are drawn on a map, its shadows may overlap each other creating these spill-over zones. These can be taken advantage of

37 In Sweden, public television is seen as a high-quality and highly valued public service that provided a mixture of in-house children's programs and documentary production as well as international film selections and news services. In Europe, most television models follow a national public service profile such as the BBC, SVT1 and SVT2, and others. The North American commercial model arrived late in Europe, but eventuallly found its place. Commercial television directly financed the expansion of satellite networks that required large investments. Today, the commercial model dominates the television market, even though most countries still maintain state-owned and subsidized pubic television channels.

commercially as well as politically, where a 'deliberate spill-over may also have a political character as a very effective means of propaganda from one neighboring State to another having a different ideology and a different political social order'.[38] But this spill-over may also take more metaphorical connotations as interstitial zones where different televisual cultures overlap. Zones where there is no 'homeland' media, but a media that enables other forms of constitutencies at the border of national apparatuses.

## Freedom for Speech: Media Non Grata

If David Harvey claims that the right to the city is a fundamental human right, we could perhaps create a hypothesis that access to media is also a human right (tapping into the welfare state democratic ideal of public service media model). Who has the right to media? By observing the type of television setup each family had in their living room, I found a parallel between the many types of migration that create the social aggregates in Fittja (asylum seekers and asylees, refugees, relatives of immigrants, naturalized immigrants, etc.) and the different types of access and provenance of equipment: piracy (unauthorized appropriation of existing technology), smuggling (unauthorized transportation and trade of foreign goods), and commercial packages available in the market. These modes of circulation of people (migration) and of technology (decoders, cable TV subscriptions, pirated signals, etc.) reveal a parallel economy that enables the questions of freedom. It creates a 'network architecture of hospitality', which I define as the media apparatus overlaying the concrete architecture of social housing and the social architecture of the satellite city while connecting both.

In Flusser's conception of the city, the city is as much a system of buildings as the system of threads, wires and signals where a mediatic nerve pulsates with information. It is a weaving of nerves; a nervous system. The system between city, media and people works in all directions: people connect the wires and signals though the city, thus creating the city's social spaces. The city enables people and media to connect, media enable people in cities to connect, etc. They can be local networks as well as national, regional or global. However, the media architecture is larger than the city alone because it is able to connect cities across the world.

The ability, or shall we say, the audacity, to hang a satellite dish on the balcony of her rental apartment could be seen as Dalia's fundamental right to information and expression, despite building regulations that officially forbid her to do so. The building regulations currently disallow residents of hanging objects from the balconies because, in theory, the façade belongs to the realtor while the internal space of the apartment belongs to the resident. On these grounds, Fittja's administration tried to evict one family a few years ago without much success. The community complained so much that the administration decided to tolerate the satellite dishes, and created guidelines for hanging them while very slowly planning 'alternative technological solutions that should cater to the television needs of most people', according to Charley Malm, one of the local area coordinators who became one of my main collaborators during the field research. These alternative solutions are still not in place, and no single television service exists that can provide the hundreds of options needed by this heterogeneous

38 Martelanc, *Social and Cultural Impact of Satellite-based Television*.

community, one of the most diverse in Scandinavia, with dozens of nationalities represented with as many different media wish lists.[39]

And yet, this kind of prohibition in a country like Sweden, notorious for its liberal ideas and freedom of speech, could be reason enough to question what freedom of speech really means. For most residents in Fittja, the freedom of speech is not a given – it is something that was conquered through exile whereas freedom of speech in the homeland was an issue that in some cases may have even prompted the expulsion.[40]

Television enters daily life in Fittja in several ways. When I visited each apartment for the installation of the colored satellite dish cover and the interview, I also paid attention to the equipment used by each household and how they access media in general. In most cases, the apartments have a satellite dish connected to a pirate decoder bought in the store at Fittja Centrum – the local satellite TV shop, the only provider of such services in the area – or another local service provider of this equipment from a different area. While there is no monthly subscription fee, the owner of the satellite shop charges inflated prices for the equipment and installation. Their monopoly of the satellite TV local market causes delays in delivery dates and the use of faulty equipment.[41]

The world of Fittja can be seen as a DIY-world, showcasing DIY-technologies (satellite dishes with hacked access), which we have used the term 'gambiarra' from Brazil – but, as contemporary communities and identifications are characterized by DIY-citizenship, a bottom-up community-building and belonging based on the web and social media, oftentimes running contrary to what is expected of the individual in terms of their spatial location.[42] The world of Fittja reflects a kind of DIY-belonging to both home and host communities, and possibly even a DIY-subjectivity that is actively constructed from re-assembled fragments of identification available from their spaces of experience.

39 The commercial offerings by national media companies are targetted at an average 'Swedish' subject, with very little nuance of Sweden's more 'international' population.

40 Flusser, 'Exile and Creativity*. I here allude to Flusser's use of the words 'expelled' to designate the person in exile and 'expeller' introduced in this essay. Flusser refers to *exile* as a noun and as a condition, and designates the exiled subject as the 'expelled'. This facilitates a dialectic relationship between the expelled and the expeller, which he refers to at the end of the essay. See Chapter 1.

41 When I mounted the colored covers on each antenna for the art installation, I noticed that most antennas were precariously mounted on the balconies. It was therefore very hazardous for me as I needed to perch over ledges to do my work, but also hazardous because they could easily fall onto the pavement below from several stories high. This technical difficulty presented one of the main obstacles in selecting and retaining participants in the project. If their antennas were too dangerously or precariously installed, I had to give up on the participant and on the interview. Nevertheless, 55 participants managed to comply with the technical requirements for participation.

42 Hartley, 'Silly citizenship', p. 240.

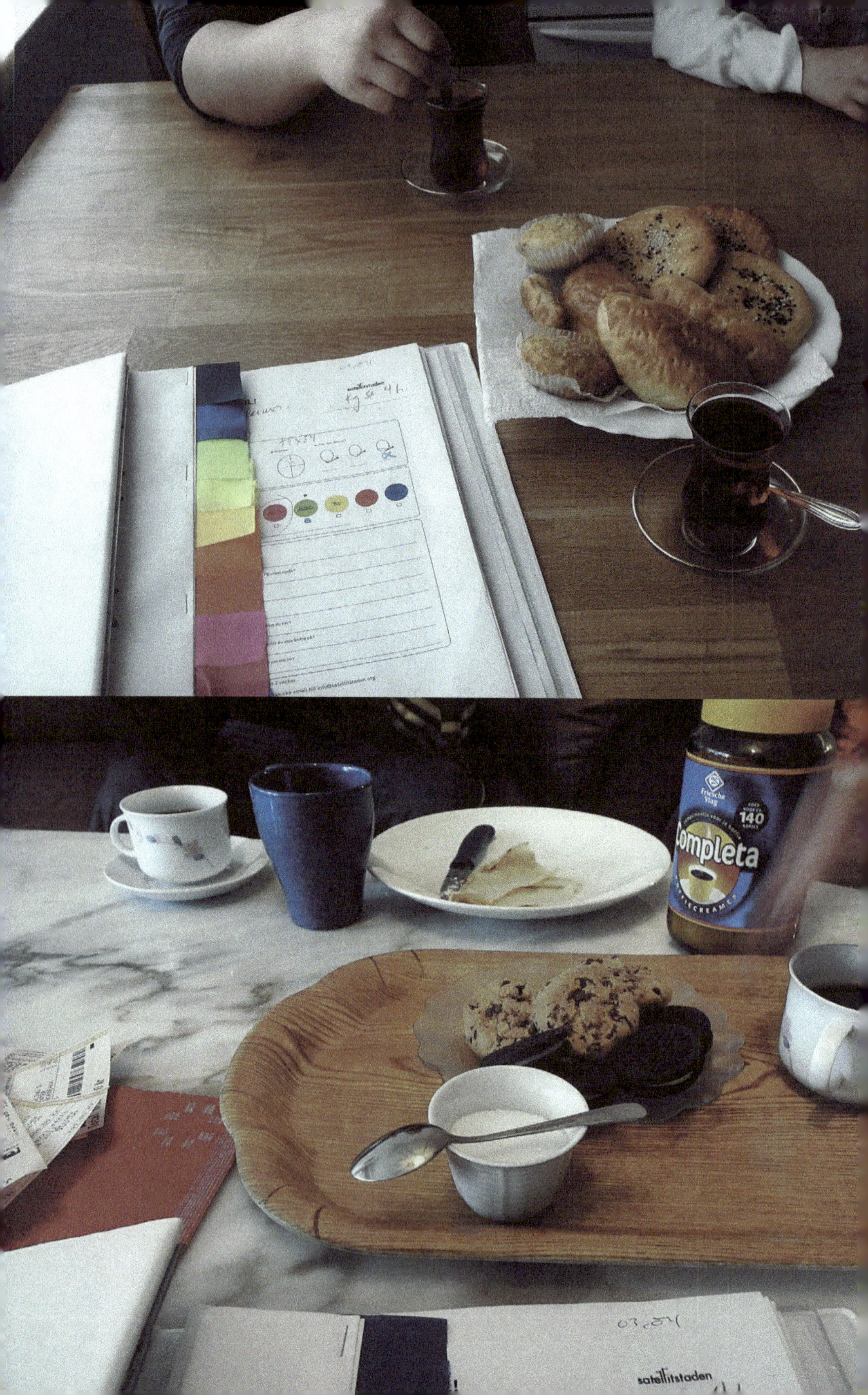

Friesche Vlag
140
Completa

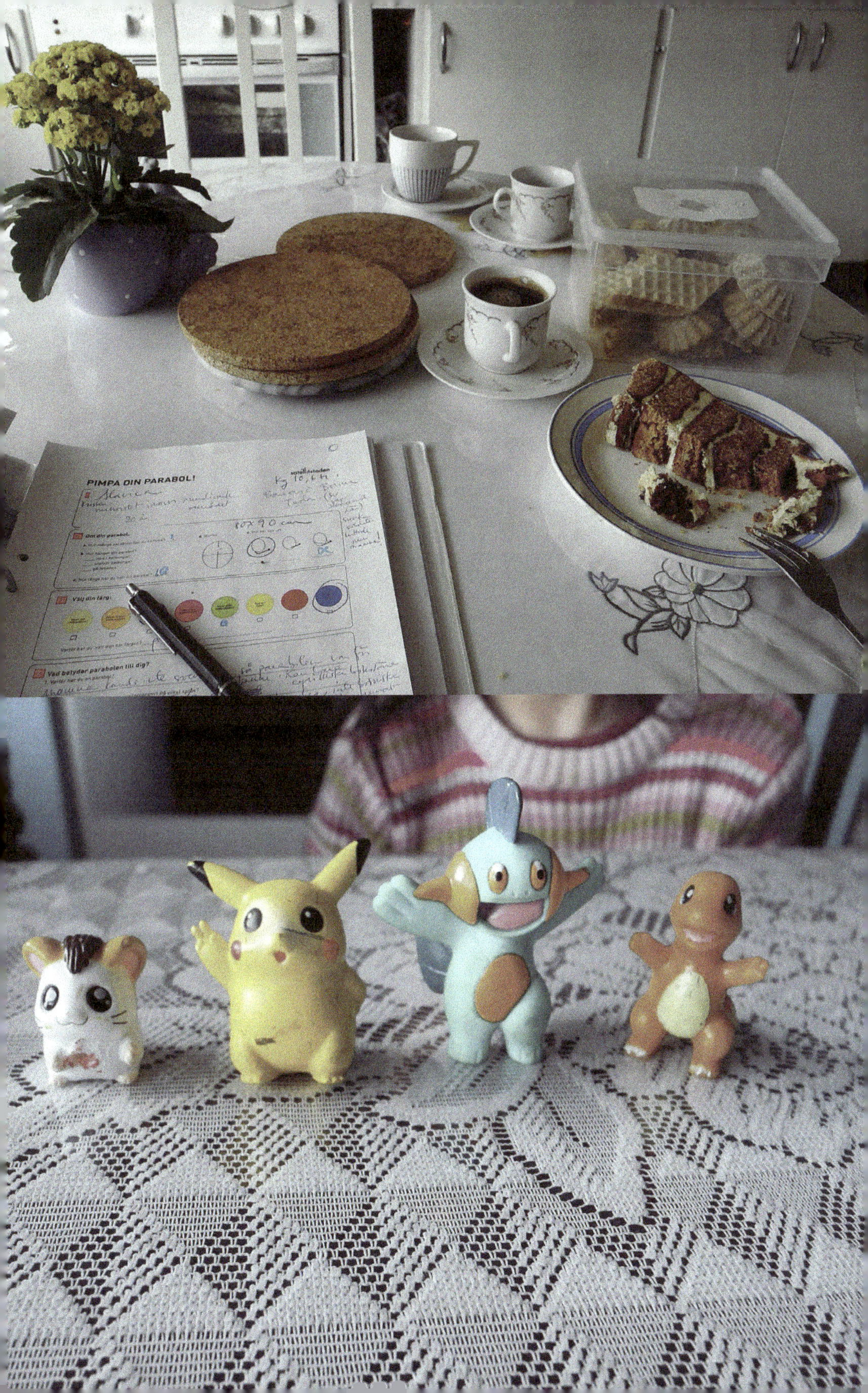
PIMPA DIN PARABOL!
satellitstaden
Om din parabol
80 X 90 cm
Välj din färg:
Vad betyder parabolen till dig?

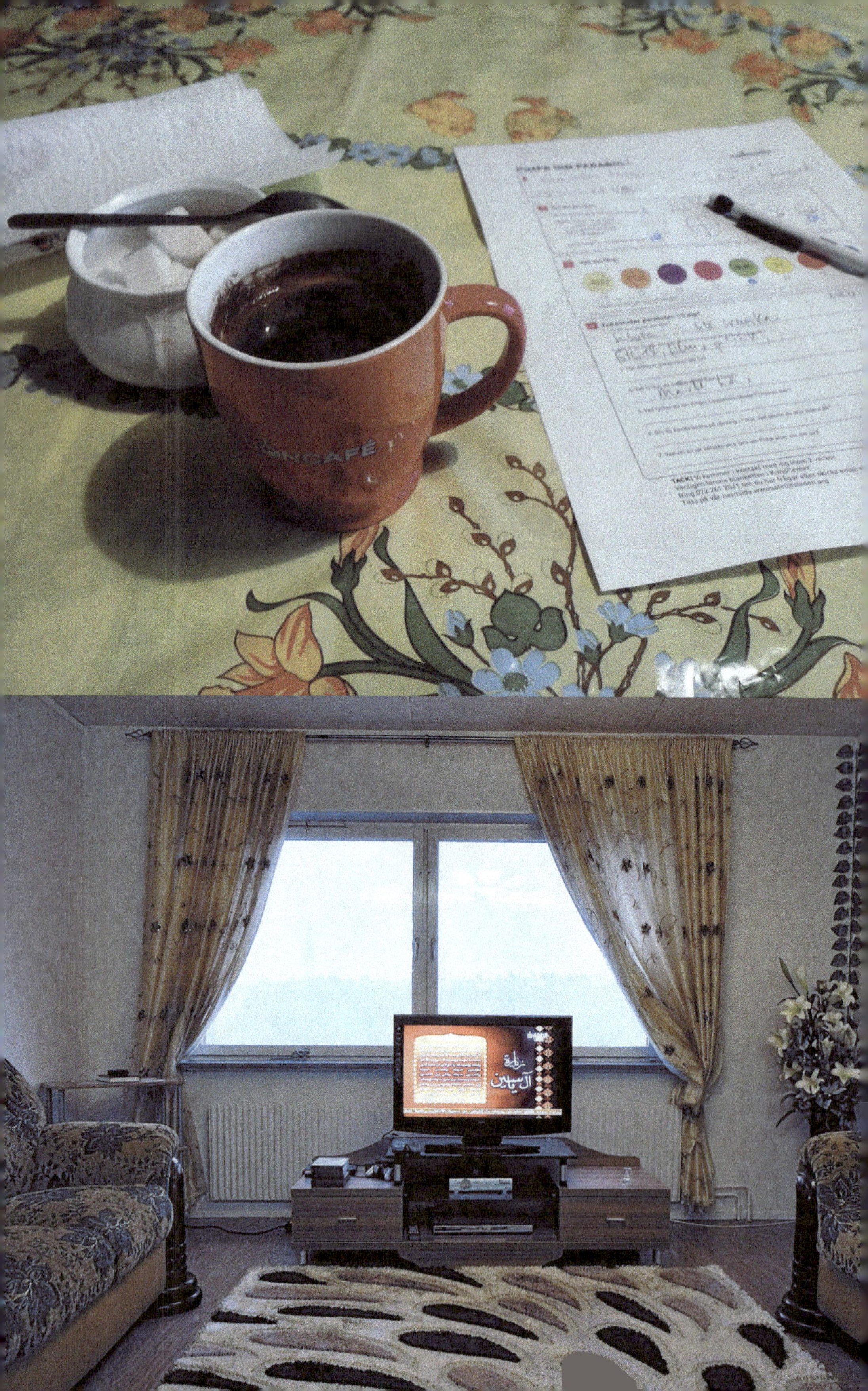

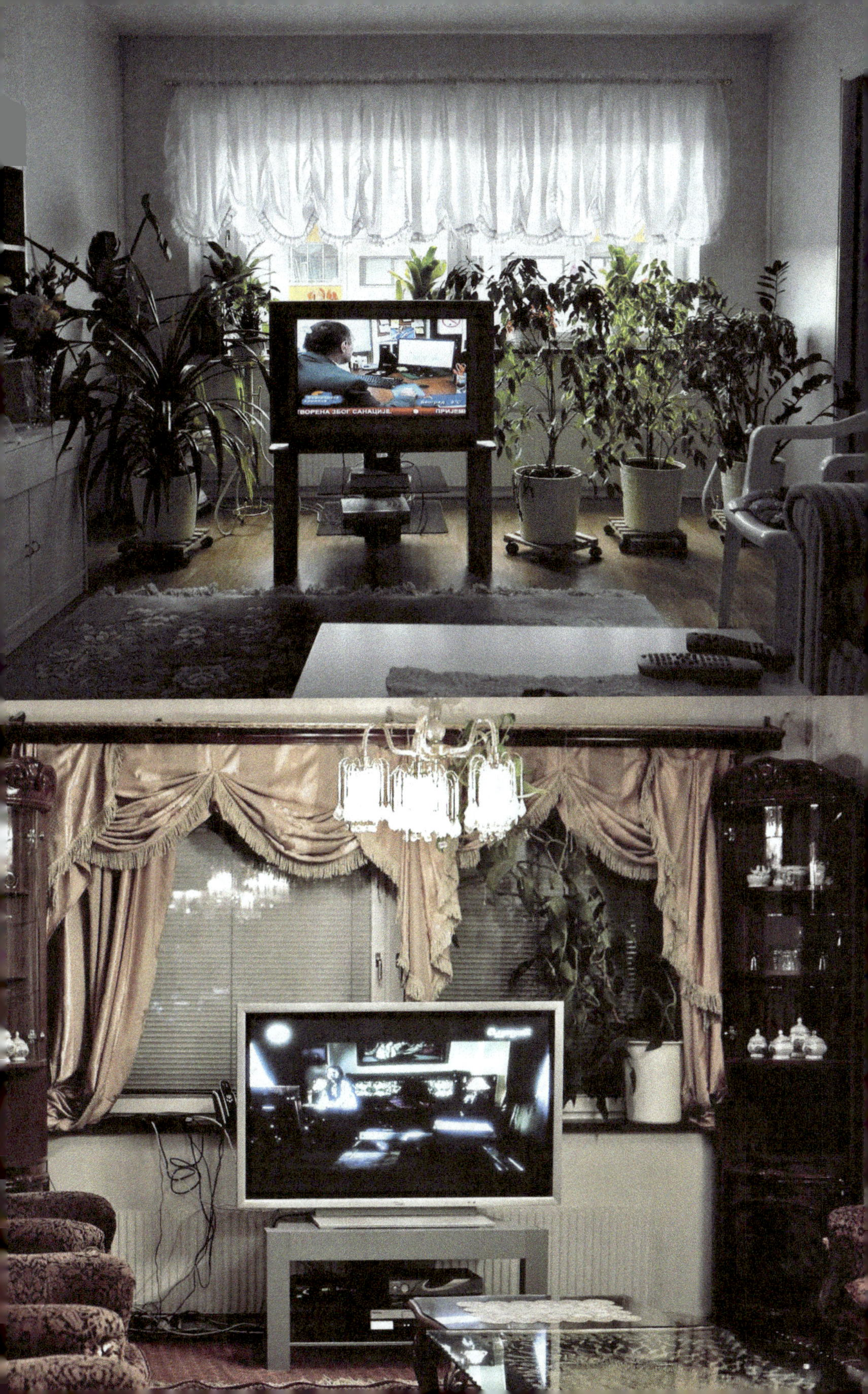
ЗБОГ САНАЦИЈЕ.

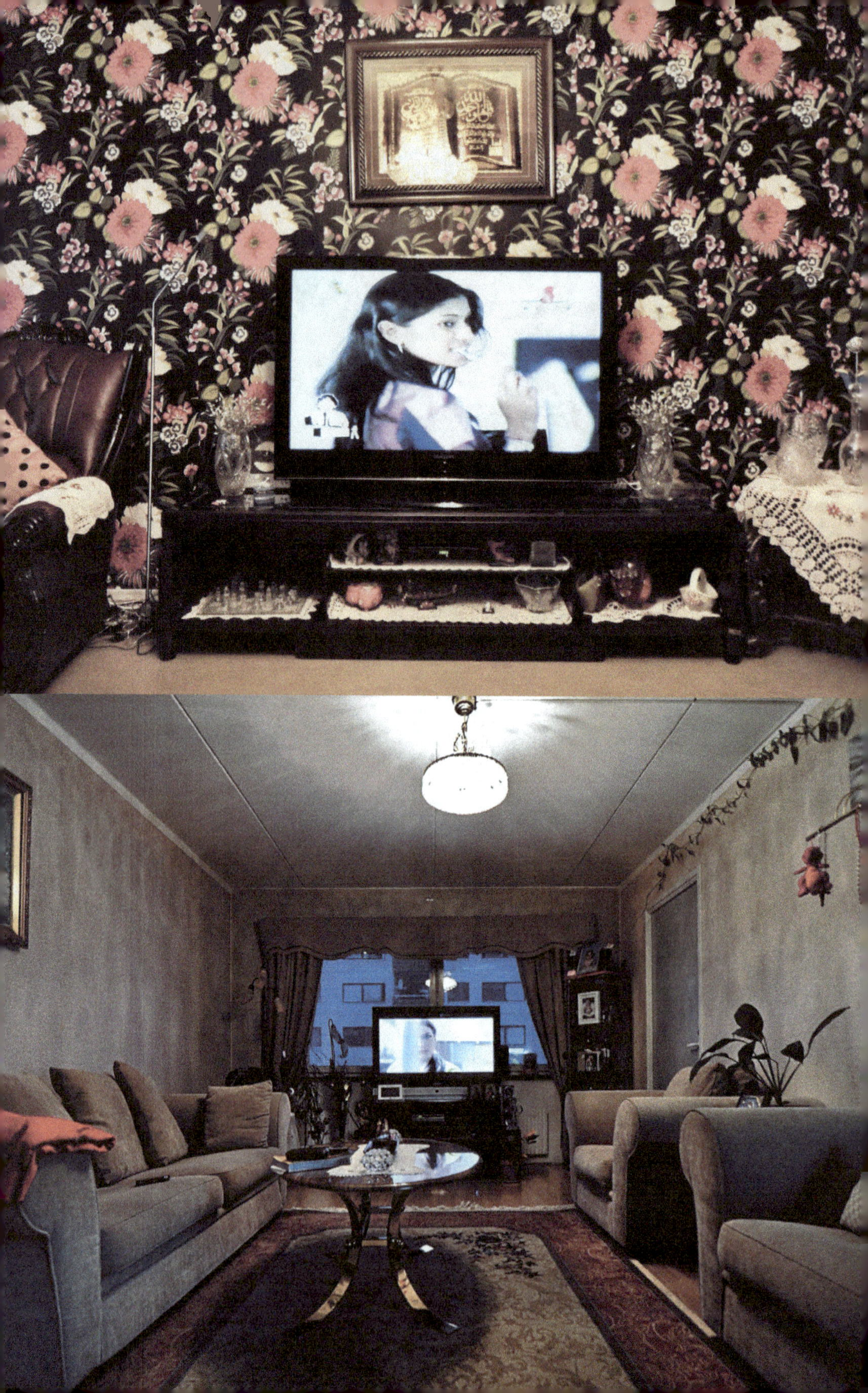

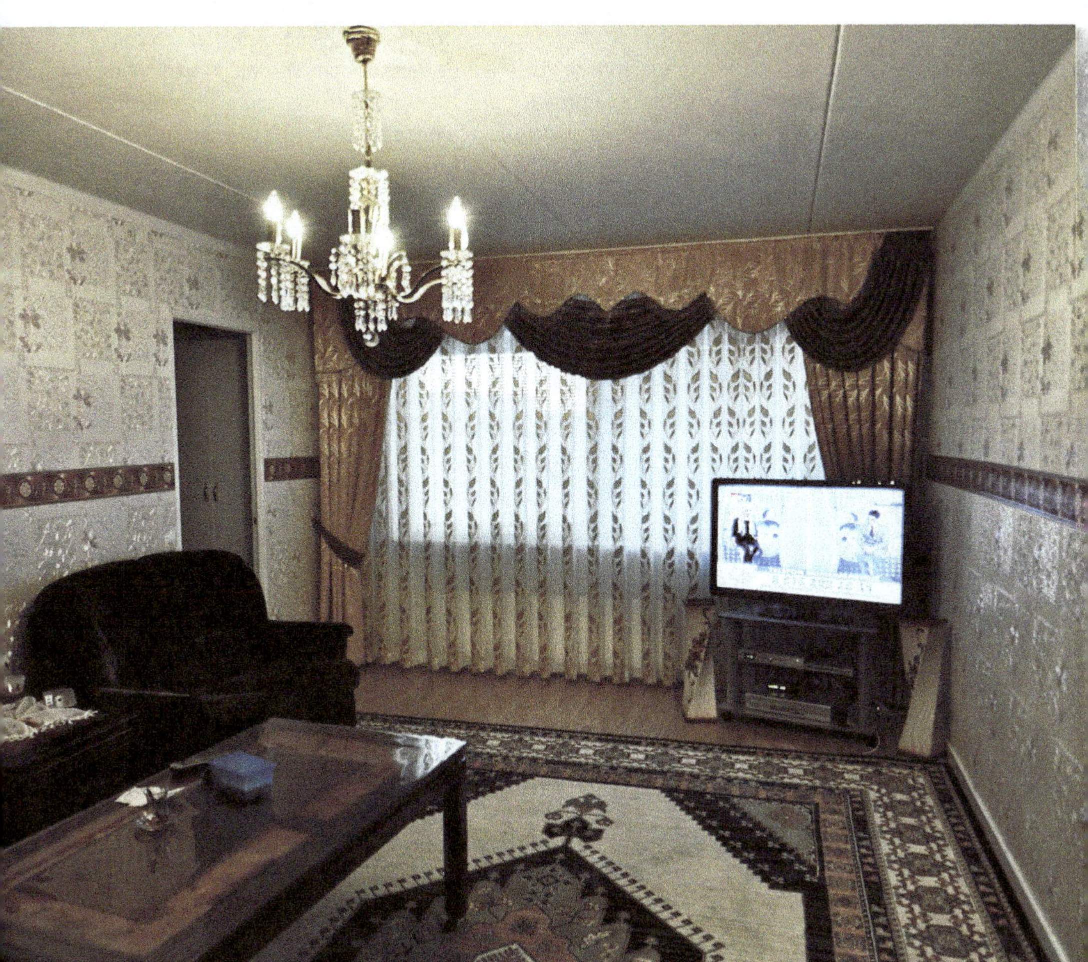

Television is My Homeland series, Satellitstaden, *Photography, 2012. Images by the author.*

Kitchen *and* Living Room *series,* Satellitstaden, *Photography, 2012. Images by the author.*

## The Exile of Things

When describing the 'migrant condition', Flusser describes that one form of identification with one's existence in exile is through things.[43] Things function as a mirror that are not a mimesis of one's own image, but an abstract representation – it is the image of the self *before* the world, her reflection within society. For those in exile, possessions show a human need of owning things, whether materially or territorially, and they become extensions of land ownership. Likewise, the idea of 'homeland' is also a possession, a property and is assimilated and defended as such. When I entered several apartments, they 'felt' Turkish, or Kurdish, or Iraqi, or Assyrian, or Swedish, at first glance because of the presence of these things as extensions of these 'national' identities. But there was something common to them all – a local 'Fittja' style where the interior decoration is 'framed' by the concrete architecture which is common to all. In a sense, the things when framed by the Swedish design lost a certain dimension of genuineness and became something other, something that vaguely alludes to the homeland, but does, in reality, create a new identification that is neither from the homeland nor from the host country. It is not even something that is intermediary to both – it is something unique to itself altogether, a true case of hybridity conceptualized by Homi Bhabha.[44]

Almost all homes I visited had the satellite TV decoder and a cable TV decoder for watching local television programming. Mobile phones and iPads are connected to the Internet, and as in any contemporary home, several devices connected to the Internet are used simultaneously (i.e., watching TV and using social media on the smartphone simultaneously; gaming on iPad while the TV is on; watching/listening to youtube clips on the TV and using the laptop for social media simultaneously, etc.), or complementary to each other (i.e. watching a TV commercial about a specific product on TV may prompt a viewer to access the product's website on the iPhone or iPad).

The Turkish decoders are more than an object from the homeland, however. What makes the clandestine decoder so attractive for those living in diaspora is the appeal and global success of Turkish soap operas: dramas involving complicated love triangles and other complex life situations that offer a distraction from real-world problems and everyday life. Previously state-owned, Turkish television now sports many private channels in an Islamic society that is considered secularized in comparison to regional neighbors. These soap operas, a main Turkish export and translated into several languages, command such a high emotional value for its spectators that all the logistical efforts for bringing in decoders into Sweden, and elsewhere, are well worth it. During the interviews I conducted, approximately one-third of the television sets that were turned on during the conversations were showing these soap operas, including the home of Bosnians and Serbians who were watching dubbed versions of the series in their respective homeland channels as I spoke with them. These soap

43 Flusser, 'Exile and Creativity', p. 108.
44 Bhabha, *DissemiNation: Time, Narrative and the Margins of The Modern Nation.*

operas generally appeal to women, and it is worth mentioning here that most of the interviews I conducted were with women, as the men were usually unavailable during interviews or did not accept to be interviewed.

As a genre, both in terms of production and of consumption, soap opera represents a rich and contradictory ideological and moral space within media culture. The popularity of Turkish serials among women in the European Arab diaspora intensified the ideological tensions and gender trouble around the television set. According to Myria Georgiou, 'soap opera viewing provides female audiences in the diaspora with opportunities to reflect on their own gender identities as distant from hegemonic discourses of gender in their region of origin but as proximate to a moral set of values they associate with this same region'.[45] Indeed, the notions of belonging are not just to the homeland as a territory and a collection of objects, but also to the homeland as a set of values, identifications, and roles. This 'critical proximity' to one's culture via television is an opportunity to reflect and to perform on the new identities that overlap the cultural norms and roles of the host country and the homeland.

In a few homes, placed besides the pirated decoder with free access to an array of satellite TV channels was the so-called *clandestine* decoder. In some Kurdish and Turkish homes, I discovered that the families had bought the decoders in Turkey, paid for subscriptions addressed to a relative in Turkey, and brought them back to Sweden in their suitcases when returning from vacation. In the same suitcases came Turkish curtains, objects, clothing and an array of other products from the homeland nowhere to be found in Swedish markets. Due to high demand of these products, a niche 'homeland' market is developing and creating business opportunities in what could be termed 'the economy of exile,' or even 'the economy of hospitality.' With the television broadcasts, families simulated a homeland environment inside their 'homes away from home', filling it with sounds and images from the homeland all the while being located in Sweden.

The interesting fact about Turkish television is that, unlike other satellite television channels created specifically for diasporas, such as Iranian channels created by those expelled from the Iranian revolution in 1979 at first and only aired outside of Iran,[46] the Turkish population in Turkey and the Turkish diaspora watch the same programming all over the world, at the same time. This distinguishes the potential of Turkish TV to create an experience of a common Turkish medial space from the notion of diaspora TV which exists only outside the homeland. In this way, television is a form of 'uniting' all Turkish nationals in real-time and creating a common television experience for all its spectators at home and abroad.

45 Giorgiou, 'Identity, Space and the Media: Thinking through Diaspora', *Revue Européenne des migrations internationales*, 26.1, (2010).

46 On March 15, 1981, Ali Limonadi launched the first television broadcast representing the Iranian diaspora from a small Los Angeles studio. He named the station IRTV, short for Iranian Television. He believed that the exiled from the 1979 revolution would eventually return after a short while, but this never happened. The relevant fact for this discussion is that diaspora TV for the Iranian community was not only a way for Iranians to retain their language abroad, but also represented a form of political forum for ideas which would have been censored at home. See also 'The Iranian Diaspora in America: 30 Years in the Making', *PBS*, 12 September 2010.

They present a new way of creating connections to the Turkish diaspora in Europe and building a transnational Turkish public.

As the distinction between home and homeland becomes increasingly blurred, the new transnational environment created by this common experience is a mediated space, not home nor homeland. In fact, Turkish television series have emerged as significant instruments of foreign policy and cultural diplomacy, as a sign of Turkey's rising role in foreign affairs, especially as its political influence in the region increases. Turkish soap operas far outreach the TurkSAT's footprint and are dubbed into several languages. The East European population in Fittja, Serbs and Bosnians, also watched the same soap operas as their Turkish and Kurdish neighbors, thus creating one more layer of cultural coexistence between the different groups that live there.

Also, perhaps it is due to the large Turkish-speaking population in Sweden that the Swedish public broadcaster SVT (Swedish Television) acquired the series *Son* (*The End*), becoming the first major broadcaster in Western Europe to buy a Turkish drama in late 2013, thus expanding the viewership of Turkish soaps far beyond regional borders, and away from satellite television. To some critics, this was a way for SVT to attempt a more multicultural policy and broaden its audience. But when all immigrants have satellite dishes, why do they need Swedish public television to show Turkish programs?

According to my research, SVT is not top-of-mind when it comes to television watched by adults in Fittja, but opinion is rather divided. Whereas watching television in Swedish is considered by some to be a useful tool in acquiring the Swedish language, for others SVT does not offer enough in-depth content about the region of origin where most of Fittja residents come from. SVT does not always broadcast international football either and therefore loses much of its audience to other channels and satellite media. On the other hand, all children in Fittja watch SVT's programming. Children, through the common experience of watching children's television, may indeed become the 'artisans of incorporation' that Sassen envisioned as a possibility for a common belonging – based on a shared media memory that becomes the basis for a new definition of 'home'.

This may seem hopeful, as a sign there is a space for hybridity in the future. Even now, the space that Fittja residents are producing – partly out of physical (hyper)local space, partly of the lived, imaginary space contracted and de-territorialized by satellite television's mediation – becomes the site for mediatized hospitality practices, amalgamating the disjointed, discrete points of origin, home and host countries, into a lifeworld where daily experiences and media complement each other and create outlets for breaking beyond the guest-host binary. But this is not simply about imagination; satellite receivers form a part of the hyperlocal media materiality in the neighborhood. Television redefines the home in 2010s Fittja, just as it was observed by Morley in the 1980s. Anachronism? A durable network, rather. Using pirated, sometimes improvized DIY-devices to construct a DIY-belonging, identity and citizenship, the residents of Fittja establish and/or claim their own boundaries, their own spaces, their own rituals, by virtue of this core function of the media. As this is achieved in a network binding together human and technical actors, each action taken by the technology – even in its malfunctioning – is mirrored by social agency, if not outright rebellion, on the part of human agents, inspiring new, dynamic life inside the brutalist shell of the modernist utopia.

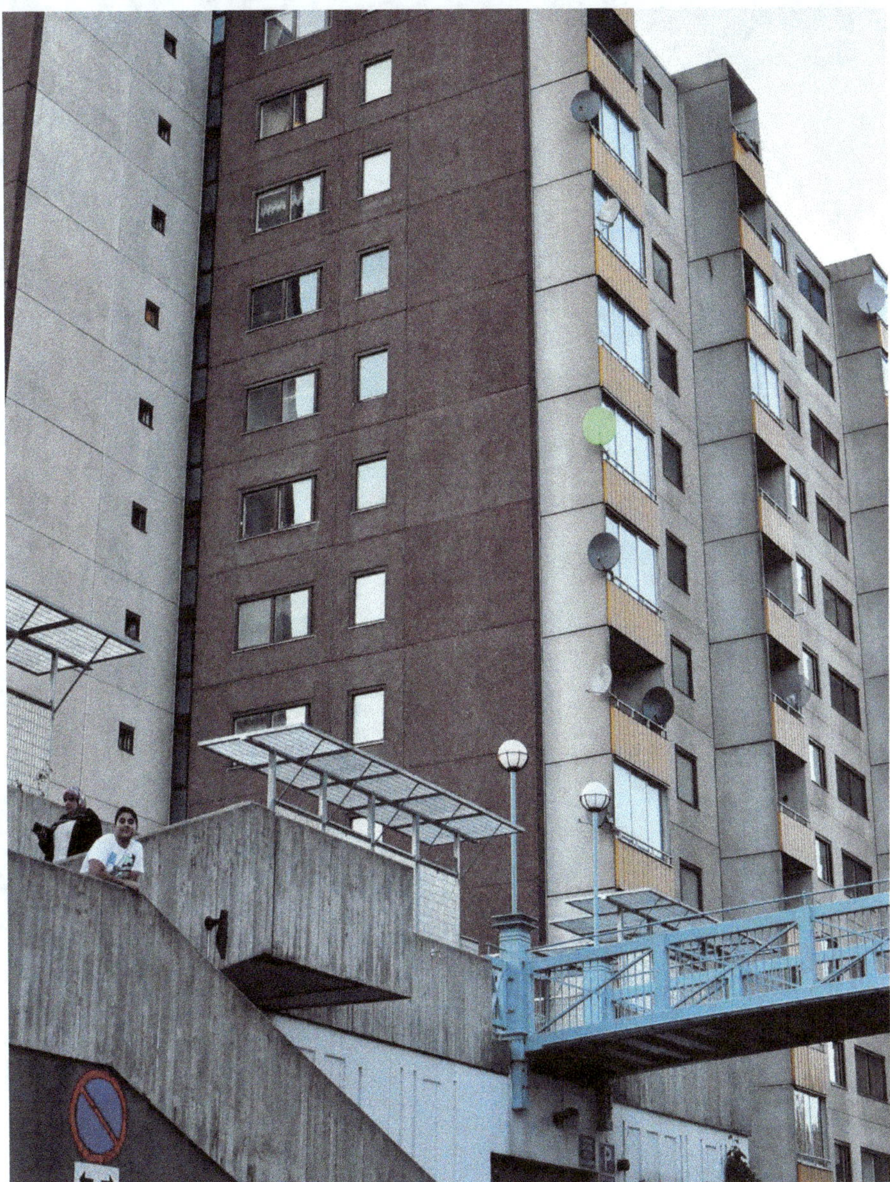

*Figure 57 – View of Fittja, with Shakhlo Altieva's green satellite dish in the background, 2012. Image by the author.*

# EPILOGUE: THE SATELLITE SUBJECT UNBOUND

# EPILOGUE: THE SATELLITE SUBJECT UNBOUND

> If I function within a predictable programmed reality, can I rebel? And how can I do it? The answer comes swiftly. Only malfunctioning programs and apparatus allow for freedom. Only a malfunctioning functionary can hope for freedom. The essence of freedom is unpredictability.
>
> – Vilém Flusser[1]

I am in the Flusser archive in Berlin. In that small room, meant to emulate Flusser's own personal library with rows and rows of unpublished and undated typewritten essays scribbled with a pencil or pen in the margins, in a private dialogue with the philosopher. I meandered in and out of folder after folder, passing my eyes through lines of writing, newspaper cutouts, private letters, photographs, commentaries, as if I was interviewing him, in his own home, just like I had interviewed so many people in Fittja.

Many essays were written in tandem with others by way of letter, in a dialogic dynamic of responses on top of responses that build up to an essay, or to an exhibition idea, or a lecture, in a crescendo over a duration of time. It is not difficult to become close to Flusser this way, for his essays as much as his letters follow a way of speaking. Later I discover that Flusser's essays are meant to be read aloud, to be animated by way of a voice, with exaggerated inflections or purposeful silences – all made to elicit a thought or a response, vocal or not. Everything was there except the physicality of the person, now dead, but as he himself says of media: 'we shall survive in the memory of others'.

As I became more familiar with the philosopher by way of the traces left behind, I understood that Vilém Flusser had great skill for de-familiarizing everyday aspects of human life. This estrangement so typical of the exile may have been an unconscious tool for his survival – to keep the senses sharpened in a state of continuous estrangement towards the world in order to avoid the 'soft blanket' of habit from blunting the sharpness of his perception.

Flusser often created fabulous animals and used them as a mirror in which human behavior should be considered from a non-human perspective. His philosophical creatures somehow embodied the capacity of systems and were in and of themselves little ironies of humankind. In *Vampirotheutys Infernalis*, he fictionalizes biological details of a rare squid considered the most evolved of all species, to both describe and try to trace forward a model for human communication – and the future of art. Flusser also uses the Other, in this case a giant electric squid living deep underwater, to elucidate forms and notions about oneself, or one's civilization.[2] But who is the exile for Flusser, is it another creature, an exception to humankind that is able to hold up a mirror to humankind?

---

1 Flusser, *Post-History*, p. XII.

2 Flusser, *Vampyrotheutis Infernalis*, trans. Rodrigo Maltez Novaes, Minneapolis: Univocal, 2013.

Invoking Flusser here for one last time opens up the possibility of a new subjectivity of alterity to emerge in relation to technology and media. Otherness as a kind of medium, part of a system that, in turn, belongs to a larger, more encompassing apparatus. Flusser's concept of the subject as a knot of relations, as the intersection of various channels of information, out of which the network of a city is formed, is similar to concepts formulated by Maturana and Varela in the 1980s and 1990s, the architects of systems theory and autopoietic systems.[3] This is not the Frankfurt School and Habermasian subject as Flusser no longer refers to an *a priori* autonomous subject that emerges into the public sphere in order to engage in a process of consensus. Rather, Flusser sees interwoven systems of relations functioning to allow participants to discover the manifold subjects within themselves. He considers the city is as a 'dance of masks' rather than a space of parliamentary proceedings. And here, in the metaphor of city of masks, it would be appropriate to bring back Lévinas 'face', the face of the other as the instance of ultimate recognition of the Other...and the mask as a sort of face, no less truthful but perhaps belonging to a performative realm of everyday theatrics. Flusser points to the necessity of dialogic relations between subjects, in constant relation to each other in their own singularity, as an autopoietic process of distinction and subject formation.

In Flusser's view of the subject, dialogic relations provide the subject with an opportunity to explore and develop itself in an environment rather than as a process in which two systems attempt to get in synch with one another in order to increase 'overall system rationality'. Likewise, current state-mandated integration politics is not about a dialogue between identities but the subjugation of one identity into another in a hierarchical manner. For this reason, Flusser's contribution is the ability to deal with technology more reflexively, away from the view where mass media is seen as a source of indoctrination and mediation that eventually leads to alienation. Flusser's interest lies in understanding the way in which media can contribute to a dialogic practice in the formation of active nets of relationships and making the passage from *being* to *becoming*.

While exploring the Flusser archive I could not help noticing that many of the terms Flusser used are considered outdated today. *Cybernetic, informational, systemic*...what do these mean today in the age of dark webs and pervasive social media? Is this vocabulary as obsolete and replaceable as technology itself, to the point where we may not be able to understand what Flusser meant? The same occurs with the doubtful terminology for the immigrant and our twisted tongues as we utter this word. Or shall we say the exile, the refugee, the pioneer, the floater, the paperless, candango, the expelled, the unprotected...the Other. What shall we call this subject which has no beginning, no end, no home and no homeland – which orbits around itself and around the world? Flusser's autobiography, also a philosophy book on its own, has a name: 'Groundless' – the subject without ground, the subject without territory. A subject *unbound*.

3 Flusser, 'The City as a Wave-Trough in the Image-flood', p. 325.

## The Future that Escapes Us

What are the media implications of this, then? The focus of the project was placed on the media as media practices – what people do with the media – and materially located in the liminal zone, between the private sphere of home and the public space of the street, as satellite dishes typically are, blurring the boundary between the private and the public in the spirit of late modernity. Urban architecture and city planning have been considered as a medium, too, and clearly stem from a particular ideological setup that has very similar, if unpredictable, consequences to the communication media, enabling some types of interactions and disabling the other. Practically, satellite television caters to ritualized media practices organizing space and time in homes and fostering belonging in the form close to do-it-yourself citizenship, by way of deterritorialized supranational media 'thickenings'. These media practices reinforce mediatization of the expelled's lifeworlds by virtue of becoming indispensable for their users.

The experience of *Satellitstaden* points out the importance of media materiality as, instead of concealing, it exposed and emphasized technological objects of the mediascape that some seek to remove or hide. Likewise, the accentuation of the satellite dishes as objects in mediascape, and a layer in Fittja's media texture and supranational media thickening, intervened in that very texture/thickening with a purpose to overcome many levels of segregation (media, urban, artistic) by foregrounding rather than de-emphasizing diaspora media with the community ties and identifications it amalgamates for the 'mediatized migrant'.[4] Moreover, embracing diaspora media is also a form of unconditional hospitality. Such approach prioritizes Koselleck's 'space of experience' shared by Fittja's mediatized exile and actively engages with their 'horizon of expectations' in Sweden, both collaborating with it and shifting it. What results from this is the overcoming of the postcolonial 'splitting' of the subject embracing its inherent hybridity as a form of incipient critique.

How is it possible to predict who will inhabit our home in the future? We cannot. Therefore, we must account for this not-knowing, and to find a resting ground in Derrida's suggestion of hospitality as *aporia*. The plan for the ideal city, if any plan is to be part of a future, is thus already an illusion. For the architects of Brasília and of *Our Home*, they were possibly imbued with utopian optimism and reality is only too slow to embody it. As Flusser states in the essay *Our Dwelling*, 'We should (...) learn to love the future that is no longer ours. And we should do it in full knowledge that this envisages the programming that will devour us'.[5]

To claim the city as a part of 'our programming', to use Flusser's terminology, is to see the city as an apparatus. Whether this apparatus is made of metal, sticks and stones or complex networks of host-guest relationships, we can imagine it as part of a 'first philosophy', following Lévinas' definition of hospitality, where the city is where an ethical stance towards the Other can take place. The city is a product of not only human desire, as urban sociologist Robert Park defined it: 'The city is man's most successful attempt to remake the world he lives in

4 Hepp, Bozdag and Suna, 'Mediatized Migrants: Media Cultures and Communicative Networking in the Diaspora'.

5 Flusser, *Post-History*, p. 45.

more after his heart's desire. If the city is the world which humans created, it is the world in which they are henceforth condemned to live in. Thus, indirectly, and without any clear sense of the nature of his task, in making the city man has remade itself.'[6] Also, as Arjun Appadurai suggests, it involves human imagination and performativity,[7] and, as I wish to add, a process of becoming that involves, alongside planning, desire and imagination, an ethics of the Other and otherness – an ethics of *habitability*. Not only a habitability of erected walls and its enclosures, but of habitability in the expanded definition of the term, of an architecture that involves a *telos*, where the architecture is equal to a politics, and in that politics, we see an *ethos*, that is, an ethos of hospitality – an ethics of welcoming the Self and the Other, entangled, and orbiting around each other. Hospitality, no other.

6 Harvey, *The Right to the City*, p. 9.
7 Arjun Appadurai, 'Here and Now', in Nicholas Mirzoeff (ed.) *The Visual Culture Reader*, Routledge, 2002.

# BIBLIOGRAPHY

## Books

Altieva, Shakhlo. *Fittjakvinnors röster!,* Botkyrka kommun, 2014.

Altheide, David L and Robert P. Snow. *Media Logic*, Beverly Hills: Sage, 1979.

Asplund, Gunnar, Wolter Gahn, Sven Markelius, Gregor Paulsson, Eskil Sundahl, and Uno Åhrén. *Acceptera*. Stockholm: Tidens förlag, 1931.

Avermaete, Tom and Serhat Karakayali Marion von Osten (eds) *Colonial Modern: Aesthetics of the Past, Rebellions for the Future*, London: Black Dog Publishing, 2010.

Bhabha, Homi K. *The Location of Culture.* London: Routledge, 1994.

Bachelard, Gaston. *The Poetics of Space*, trans. Maria Jolas, Boston: Beacon Press, 1969.

Baudrillard, Jean. *Simulacra and Simulation*, Ann Arbor: University of Michigan Press, 1994.

Bauman, Zygmunt. *Community: Seeking Safety in an Insecure World*, Cambridge: Polity Press, 2001.

______. *Collateral Damage: Social Inequalities in a Global Age*, Cambridge: Polity Press, 2011.

Beck, Ulrich. *Risk Society: Towards a New Modernity,* Polity Press, 2008.

Benjamin, Walter. *The Arcades Project*, New York: Belknap Press, 2002.

Bentham, Jeremy. The Panopticon Writings, *Radical Writing Series*, Verso Books, 2005 (1791).

Bishop, Claire. *Artificial Hells: Participatory Art and the Politics of Spectatorship*, London: Verso Books: 2012.

Bourriaud, Nicolas. *Relational Aesthetics*, Dijon: Les Presses du Réel, 1998.

Brochmann ,Grete and Anniken Hagelund. *Immigration policy and the Scandinavian welfare state 1945–2010*, London: Palgrave Macmillan, 2012.

Calvino, Italo. *Invisible Cities*, New York: Harcourt Brace Jovanovich, 1974.

Castro, Alex. *Outrofobia*, Rio de Janeiro: Editora Publisher Brasil, 2015.

Castro Senra, Nelson de(ed.) *Veredas de Brasília: as expedições geográficas em busca de um sonho,* Rio de Janeiro: IBGE – Centro de Documentação e Disseminação de Informações, 2010.

Costa, Lúcio. *Registro de uma vivência*, São Paulo: Empresa das Artes, 1995.

Couldry, Nick. *Media Rituals: A Critical Approach*, Routledge, 2004.

Chakrabarty. Dipesh. *Provincializing Europe: Postcolonial Thought and Historical Difference.* Princeton University Press, 2008.

Darwīsh, Ma�mūd and Mona Anis. *Edward Said: A Contrapuntual Reading, Cultural Critique*, Minneapolis: University of Minnesota Press, 2016.

Davis, Mike. *Planet of Slums*, London: Verso, 2006.

Debord, Guy. *The Society of Spectacle*, trans. Ken Knabb, Berkeley:Bureau of Public Secrets, 2014 (1957).

Derrida, Jacques. *Adieu to Emmanuel Lévinas,* Palo Alto: Stanford University Press, 1999.

______. *Of Hospitality (Cultural Memory in the Present),* Palo Alto: Stanford University Press, 2000.

______. *On Cosmopolitanism and Forgiveness (Thinking in Action),* London: Routledge, 2001.

______ and Bernard Stiegler, *Echographies of Television: Filmed Interviews.* Cambridge: Polity Press, 1996.

Fanon, Frantz. *The Wretched of the Earth*, trans. Constance Farrington, New York: Grove Weidenfeld, 1991 (1961).

Fickers, Andreas and Catherine Johnson (eds) *Transnational Television History: a Comparative Approach.* London: Routledge, 2012.

Figueiredo, Luciano (ed.) *Cartas 1964–74*, Rio de Janeiro: Editora UFRJ, 1998.

Flew, Terry. *The Creative Industries*, Sage, 2011.

Florida, Richard. *Cities and the Creative Class*. Routledge, 2004.

Flusser, Vilém. *Post-history,* Siegfried Zielinski , trans. Rodrigo Maltez Novaes, Minneapolis: Univocal, 2014.

______. *'The Shape of Things'*, in *A Philosophy of Design*, London: Reaktion Books, 1999.

______. *Vampyrotheutis Infernalis*, trans. Rodrigo Maltez Novaes, Minneapolis: Univocal, 2013.

Foster, Hal. *The Art-Architecture Complex*, London: Verso, 2011.

______. *The Return of the Real: The Avant-garde at the End of the Century.* Cambridge, Mass.: MIT Press, 1996.

Franke, Anselm (ed.) *B-Zone: Becoming Europe and Beyond*, Barcelona: Actar, 2005.

Georgiou, Myria. *Diaspora, Identity and the Media: Diasporic Transnationalism and Mediated Spatialities*, NY: Hampton Press, 2006.

______. *Media and the City: Cosmopolitanism and Difference*, Cambridge: Polity, 2013.

Gilroy, Paul. *After Empire: Melancholia or Convivial Culture? Multiculture or Postcolonial Melancholia*. London: Routledge, 2004.

Glissant, Édouard. *Poetics of Relation*, trans. Betsy Wing, Ann Arbor: The University of Michigan Press, 1997.

Graham, Dan. Video-Architecture-Television: Writings on Video and VideoWorks 1970–1978, New York University Press, 1979, p. 63. Available at: https://monoskop.org/File:Graham_Dan_Video_Architecture_Television_1979.pdf.

Guattari, Félix. *The Three Ecologies*. London: Athlone Press, 2000.

______. and Suely Rolnik, *Molecular Revolution in Brazil,* New York: Semi(o)texte, 2007.

Hafez, Kai. *The Myth of Media Globalization*, Cambridge: Polity, 2007.

Hall, Stuart. *Questions of Cultural Identity,* London: Sage, 1996.

______ (ed.) *Policing the Crisis: Mugging, the State, and Law and Order*, New York: Macmillan, 1978.

Harvey, David. *Rebel Cities: From the Right to the City to the Urban Revolution*, New York: Verso, 2012.
______. *The Condition of Postmodernity: An Enquiry into the Origins of Cultural Change.* Oxford: Blackwell, 1990.

Hayden, Dolores. *The Grand Domestic Revolution: A History of Feminist Designs for American Homes, Neighborhoods, and Cities*, Cambridge, Mass.: MIT Press, 1981.

Hecht, Gabrielle. *Entangled Geographies: Empire and Technopolitics in the Global Cold War,* Cambridge: MIT Press, 2011.

Hepp, Andreas and Friedrich Krotz (eds). *Mediatized Worlds: Culture and Society in a Media Age*, Basingstoke: Palgrave Macmillan, 2014.

Hesmondhalgh, David. *The Cultural Industries,* 4th ed, Sage, 2018.

Ebenezer Howard, *Garden Cities of To-Morrow,* London: Faber and Faber, 1946 (1902).

http://urbanplanning.library.cornell.edu/DOCS/howard.htm.

Howkins, John. *The creative economy: How people make money from ideas*. Penguin Books, 2001.

______. *Invisible Work: The Hidden Ingredient of True Creativity, Purpose and Power.* September Publishing, 2020.

Huizinga, Johan. *Homo Ludens: A Study of the Play-element in Culture*, Boston: Beacon Press, 1955.

Jacobs, Jane. *The Death and Life of Great American Cities,* New York: Vintage Books, 1992 (1961).

Jenkins, Henry. *Convergence Culture: Where Old and New Media Collide*, New York: NYU Press, 2006.

Kant, Immanuel. *Perpetual Peace: A Philosophical Essay,* trans. M.Campbell Smith, New York: The Macmillan Company, 2017 (1795). Available at: https://www.gutenberg.org/files/50922/50922-h/50922-h.htm#tnote.

Kittler, Friedrich A. *Gramophone, Film, Typewriter*, Palo Alto: Stanford University Press, 1999.

Koselleck, Reinhart. *Futures Past: On the Semantics of Historical Time*, NY: Columbia University Press, 2004.

Latour, Bruno. *Reassembling the Social: An Introduction of the Actor-Network Theory*, Oxford University Press, 2005.

Lévinas, Emmanuel. *Totality and Infinity: An Essay on Exteriority,* trans. Alphonso Lingis, Pittsburgh: Duquesne University Press, 1969.

Lévi-Strauss, Claude. *The Savage Mind*. Chicago: University of Chicago Press, 1968.

Le Corbusier (Charles-Edouard Jeanneret), *Towards an Architecture,* transl. John Goodman, Los Angeles: Getty Research Institute, 2007 (1923).

Lefebvre, Henri. *The Urban Revolution*, trans. Robert Bononno. Minneapolis: University of Minnesota Press, 2003.

______. *La production de l'espace*, Paris: Anthropos, 1974.

______. *Critique of Everyday Life*, Vol. 3, London: Verso, 2005 (1981).

Letta, Enrico. *Andare insieme, andare lontano*. Rome: Mondadori, 2014.

Li, Wei. *Ethnoburb: The New Ethnic Community in Urban America*, Honolulu: University of Hawaii Press, 2009.

Lovink, Geert. *Networks Without a Cause: A Critique of Social Media*, Cambridge: Polity Press, 2013.

______ and Miriam Rasch (eds) *Unlike Us Reader: Social Media Monopolies and Their Alternatives*, Amsterdam: Institute of Network Cultures, 2013.

Löwgren, Jonas and Bo Reimer, *Collaborative Media: Production, Consumption, and Design Interventions*, Cambridge, Mass.: MIT Press, 2013.

Mattson, Helena and Sven-Olov Wallenstein. *Swedish Modernism: Architecture, Consumption and the Welfare State.* London: Black Dog Architecture, 2010.

Mbembe, Achille. *Necropolitics*, Duke University Press, 2019.

More, Thomas. *Utopia*, transl. Paul Turner (ed.) Penguin Classics, 2003 (1516).

Morley, David. *Family Television: Cultural Power and Domestic Leisure*, London: Comedia Publishing Group, 1986.

Moser, Benjamin. *Cemitério da Esperança*, Editora Cesárea, 2014.

Mumford, Per Eric Paul. *The CIAM Discourse on Urbanism – 1928–1960*, Cambridge: MIT Press, 2002. http://designtheory.fiu.edu/readings/mumford_CIAM_discourse.pdf.

Myrdal, Gunnar. *Rich Lands and Poor*, New York: Harper and Row, 1957.

______ and Alva Myrdal. *Kris i befolkningsfrågan.* Bokförlaget Nya Dox, 1997 (1934).

Newman, Oscar. *Creating Defensible Space*, Collingdale: DIANE Publishing, 1972.

Nielsen, Palle and Lars Bang Larsen, *The Model: A Model for a Qualitative Society* (1968). Barcelona: MACBA, 2010.

Lisa Parks, *Cultures in Orbit: Satellites and the Televisual*, Durham: Duke University Press, 2005.

Perec, Georges. *Life: A User's Manual*, New York: David R Godine Pub, First Edition, 1987 (1978).

_____ and John Sturrock. *Species of Spaces and Other Pieces.* London: Penguin Books, 1997.

Papastergiadis, Nikos. *Cosmopolitanism and Culture,* Cambridge: Polity Press, 2012.

Ptak, Anna (ed.) *Re-tooling Residences: A Closer Look at the Mobility of Art Professionals*, Warsaw, Poland: Centre for Contemporary Art Ujazdowski Castle, 2011.

Ramberg, Klas. *Allmännyttan: Välfärdsbygge 1850–2000,* Stockholm: Byggförlaget, 2000.

Rosello, Mireille. *Postcolonial Hospitality: The Immigrant as Guest,* Palo Alto: Stanford University Press, 2002.

Rosler, Martha. *Culture Class*, Berlin: Sternberg Press, 2013.

Rudberg, Eva. *Sven Markelius Architect*, Stockholm: Arkitektur Förlag, 1989.

Sassen, Saskia. *Cities in a World Economy*, 3rd edition, London: Sage, 2006.

Schérer, René. *Zeus hospitalier: l'éloge de l'hospitalité*. Paris: La Table Ronde, 2005.

Schimanski, Johan and Stephen F. Wolfe (eds) *Border Aesthetics: Concepts and Intersections.* Berghan, 2018.

Schirmacher, Wolfgang. *Homo Generator: Media and Postmodern Technology*, New York, 1994.

Scholte, Jan Aart. *Globalization: A Critical Introduction*, New York: Palgrave, 2005.

Scott, James C. *Seeing Like a State: How Certain Schemes to Improve the Human Condition Have Failed*, New Haven: Yale University Press, 1998.

Serres, Michel. *The Parasite*, University of Minnesota Press, 2007 (1980).

Sennett, Richard. *The Foreigner*, Notting Hill Editions, 2011.

Sholte, Jan Aart. Globalization: A Critical Introduction. New York: Palgrave, 2005.

Sloterdijk, Peter. *Sphères: Écumes, sphérologie plurielle, Volume 3*, Paris: Pluriel, 1982.

_____. *You Must Change Your Life: On Anthropotechnics*, Polity Press, 2013.

Spivak, Gayatri Chakravorty. *A Critique of Postcolonial Reason: Toward a History of the Vanishing Past*, Cambridge, Massachusetts: Harvard University Press, 1999.

Staal, Jonas. *Nosso Lar/Brasília*. Capacete/JAP SAM Books, Rio de Janeiro, 2014.

Tafuri, Manfredo and Francesco Co. *Modern Architecture*, New York: H. N. Abrams, 1979.

Tafuri, Manfredo. *Architecture and Utopia: Design and Capitalist Development*. Cambridge, Mass.: MIT Press, 1976.

Thompson, Nato. *Living as Form: Socially Engaged Art from 1991–2011*. Cambridge, Mass.: MIT Press, 2012.

Virilio, Paul. *Speed and Politics*, NY: Semi(o)texte, 2006.

Wallace Brown, Garrett and David Held (eds). *The Cosmopolitanism Reader*, Cambridge: Polity Press, 2010.

Weber, Samuel. *Mass Mediauras: Form, Technics, Media*, Palo Alto: Stanford University Press, 1996.

Xavier, Francisco Cândido. *Poetry from Beyond the Grave*, trans. Vitor Pequeno, Uitgeverij, 2013.

______. *Nosso Lar.* Brasília: International Spiritist Council, 2006 (1944).

______. and André Luiz (Spirit), *Nosso Lar/The Astral City: The Story of a Doctor's Odyssey in the Spirit World*, Christian Spirit Center, 1986.

Žižek, Slavoj. *The Metastases of Enjoyment: Six essays on Woman and Causality*, New York, 1994.

**Book Chapters**

Appadurai, Arjun. 'Here and Now', in Nicholas Mirzoeff (ed.) *The Visual Culture Reader*, Routledge, 2002.

Beck, Ulrich. 'The Cosmopolitan Manifesto', in Wallace Brown, Garrett and David Held (eds). *The Cosmopolitanism Reader*, Cambridge: Polity Press, 2010.

Beech, Dave. 'Don't look now! Art after the viewer and beyond participation', in Jeni Walwin (ed.) *Searching for Art's New Publics*. Bristol: Intellect, 2010: 15–31.

Benjamin, Walter. 'The Task of the Translator', in*The Translation Studies Reader*(ed.) Lawrence Venuti, London: Routledge, 2000.

Bhabha, Homi K. 'Foreword', in Pnina Werbner and Tariq Modood (eds) *Debating Cultural Hybridity: Multicultural Identities and the Politics of Anti-Racism*, Zed Books Ltd, 2015, p. II–VII.

Couldry, Nick, 'Transvaluing Media Studies: Or, Beyond the Myth of the Mediated Centre', in James Curran and David Morley (eds) *Media and Cultural Theory*. Abingdon: Routledge, 2009, pp. 177–191.

Derrida, Jacques. 'On Cosmopolitanism', in Garret W. Brown, Garrett and David Held, eds., *The Cosmopolitanism Reader*. Cambridge: Polity Press, 2013, pp. 413–422.

Flusser, Vilém. 'Taking up Residence in Homelessness', trans. Erik Heisel, in Andreas Ströhl (ed.) *Writings*, Electronic Mediations, vol. 6. Minneapolis: University of Minnesota Press, 2002, pp. 91–103.

______. 'Exile and Creativity', trans. Erik Heisel, in Andreas Ströhl (ed.) *Writings*, Electronic Mediations, vol. 6. Minneapolis: University of Minnesota Press, 2002, pp. 104–109.

Ferreira da Silva, Denise. 'The 'Refugee Crisis' and the Current Predicament of the Liberal State', in L'Internationale Online (ed.) *Subjects and Objects in Exile*, 2017, pp. 154–163. Available at: https://d2tv32fgpo1xal.cloudfront.net/files/05-subjectsandobjectsinexile.pdf.

Foucault, Michel. 'Of Other Spaces', in Nicholas Mirzoeff (ed.) *The Visual Culture Reader*, London: Routledge, 2002.

Hall, Stuart. 'The Spectacle of the Other', in Stuart Hall (ed.) *Representation: Cultural Representations and Signifying Practices*, London: Sage, 1997.

Hepp, Andreas, Cigdem Bozdag, and Laura Suna. 'Mediatized Migrants: Media Cultures and Communicative Networking in the Diaspora', in Leopoldina Fortunati, Raul Pertierra and Jane Vincent (eds) *Migrations, Diaspora, and Information Technology in Global Societies*, London: Palgrave, 2012: 172–188.

Hepp, Andreas and Nick Couldry, 'What Should Comparative Media Research Be Comparing? Towards a Transcultural Approach to 'Media Cultures', in Daya Kishan Thussu (ed.) *Internationalizing Media Studies*. Abingdon: Routledge, 2009: 32–48.

Hirsch, Nikolaus. 'A Model World', in Andrea Phillips and Fulya Erdemci (eds) *Social Housing-Housing the Social: Art, Property and Spatial Justice*, Amsterdam/Berlin: SKOR/Sternberg Press, June 2012.

Jansson, André. 'Indispensable Things: On Mediatization, Materiality, and Space', in Knut Lundby (ed.) *Mediatization of Communication*. Berlin: De Gruyter, 2014: 273–296.

Lacan, Jacques. 'The Mirror Stage as Formative of the Function of the I as Revealed in Psychoanalytic Experience' (1966), *Écrits: A Selection*, trans. Bruce Flink, New York: W. W. Norton & Company, 2004.

Mauss, Marcel. *The Gift: Forms and Functions of Exchange in Archaic Societies*, trans. Ian Cunnison, London: Cohen & West, 1966 (1925).

Parks, Lisa. 'Postwar Footprints: Satellite and Wireless Stories in Slovenia and Croatia', in Anselm Franke (ed.) *B-Zone: Becoming Europe and Beyond*, Barcelona: Actar, 2005, p. 306–347.

______. 'Technostruggles and the Satellite Dish: A Populist Approach to Infrastructure', in Göran Bolin (ed.) *Cultural Technologies*, Routledge, 2012.

Racek, Jacob. 'Strategies of Weakness', in Ptak, Anna (ed.) *Re-tooling Residences: A Closer Look at the Mobility of Art Professionals*, Warsaw, Poland: Centre for Contemporary Art Ujazdowski Castle, 2011.

Rosas, Ricardo. 'The Gambiarra: Considerations on a Recombinatory Technology', in Boler, Megan (ed.) *Digital Media and Democracy: Tactics in Hard Times*, Cambridge, Mass.: MIT Press, 2010, pp. 343–354.

Sakr, Naomi. 'Maverick or Model? Al-Jazeera's Impact on Arabic Satellite Television', in Jean K. Chalabi (ed.) Transnational Television Worldwide. London: I.B. Tauris, 2005.

Spivak, Gayatri Chakravorthy. 'Can the Subaltern Speak?', in Cary Nelson and Lawrence Grossberg (eds) *Marxism and the Interpretation of Culture,* Basingstoke: Macmillan, 1988, p. 271–313.

**Journal Articles**

Agamben, Giorgio. 'We refugees', *Symposium: A Quarterly Journal in Modern Literatures*, 2.49 (1995): 114–119.

Arjun Appadurai, 'Disjuncture and Difference in the Global Cultural Economy', *Public Culture,* 2.2 (1990): 1–24.

Baran, Paul. 'On Distributed Communications Networks', *Communications Systems*, IEEE Transactions on 12.1 (1964): 1–9.

Bauman, Zygmunt. 'Utopia with no topos', *History of the Human Sciences*, 16.1 (2003): 11–25.

Bengtsson, Stina. 'Symbolic spaces of everyday life', *Nordicom Review,* 27.2 (2006): 119-132.

Berry: John W. 'Immigration, Acculturation, and Adaptation', *Applied Psychology*, 46.1 (1997): 5–34.

Boyd, Dana M. and N. B. Ellison. 'Social Network Sites: Definition, History, and Scholarship', *Journal of computer-mediated Communication*, 13.1 (2007): 210–230.

Brubaker, Rogers and Frederick Cooper. 'Beyond "Identity"', *Theory & Society*, 29.1 (2009): 1–47.

Brunsdon, Charlotte. 'Satellite Dishes and the Landscapes of Taste', *New Formations*, 15 (Winter 1991): 23–42.

Buck-Morss, Susan. 'Hegel and Haiti', *Critical Inquiry*, 26.4 (Summer 2000): 821–865.

Couldry, Nick. "Theorising Media as Practice', *Social Semiotics*, 14.2 (2004): 115–132.

Deuze, Mark. 'Media Life', *Media, Culture and Society*, 33.1 (2011): 137–148.

Flusser, Vilém. 'The City as a Wave-Trough in the Image-flood', trans. Phil Gochenour, *Critical Inquiry,* 31 (Winter 2005): 320–328. Available at: https://www.academia.edu/260662/The_City_as_Wave_Trough_in_the_Image_Flood.

Fraser, Nancy. 'From Redistribution to Recognition? Dilemmas of Justice in a 'Post-Socialist' Age', *New Left Review,* I.I.212, (July–August 1995).

Georgiou, Myria. 'Identity, Space and the Media: Thinking through Diaspora', Revue Européenne des migrations internationales, 26.1 (2010).

Goffman, Erwing. 'On Face-work: An Analysis of Ritual Elements in Social Interaction', *Psychiatry*, 18.3 (1955): 213–231.

Hartley, John. 'Silly Citizenship', *Critical Discourse Studies,* 7.4 (2010): 233-248.

Haque, M. Shamsul. 'New Public Management: Origins, Dimensions, and Critical Implications', *Public Administration and Public Policy*, Vol. I (2013): 13–27.

Kelly, Sean. 'Derrida's cities of refuge: toward a non-utopian utopia', *Contemporary Justice Review* 7.4 (2004): 421-439.

Larsen, Håkon. 'The Legitimacy of Public Service Broadcasting in the 21st Century: The Case of Scandinavia', *Nordicom Review*, 35.2 (2015): 65–76.

Lewin, Kurt. 'Action Research and Minority Problems', *Journal of Social Issues,* 2.4 (November 1946): 34–48.

Löfgren, Isabel. 'Collateral Damage', *Paletten*, 114 (Autumn 2011):141–156.

Nilsson, David. 'Sweden-Norway at the Berlin Conference 1884–85: History, national identity-making and Sweden's relations with Africa', *Current African Issues*, 53 (2013).

Owens, P.A. 'Xenophilia, Gender, and Sentimental Humanitarianism', *Alternatives*, 29.3 (2004): 285-304.

Pratt, Mary Louise. 'Arts of the Contact Zone', *Profession* (1991): 33–40. Available at: https://www.jstor.org/stable/25595469.

Racek, Jacob. 'Strategies of Weakness', in Anna Ptak (ed.) *Re-tooling Residences: A Closer Look at the Mobility of Art Professionals*, Warsaw, Poland: Centre for Contemporary Art Ujazdowski Castle, 2011.

Robins, Kevin and Asu Aksoy. 'Banal Transnationalism: The Difference that Television Makes' in *Diversity and Diaspora: Arab Communities and Satellite Communication in Europe. Global Media and Communication*, No. 4 (December 2008): 277–300.

Ross, Kristin. 'Henri Lefebvre on the Situationist International', *October,* 79 (Winter 1997). Available at: http://www.notbored.org/lefebvre-interview.html.

Ruist, Joakim. 'Free Immigration and Welfare Access: The Swedish Experience', *Fiscal Studies*, 35.1 (March 2014): 19–39.

Rutten, Kris, An van Dienderen, and Ronald Soetaert, 'Revisiting the Ethnographic Turn in Contemporary Art', *Critical Arts: South-North Cultural and Media Studies*, Vol. 27 (2013): 459–473.

Sassen, Saskia. 'Expelled: Humans in Capitalism's Deepening Crisis', *Journal of World Systems Research*, 19.2 (2013): 198–201. Available at: https://doi.org/10.5195/jwsr.2013.495.

______. 'At the Systemic Edge: Expulsions', *European Review,* 24.1 (2016): 89–104.

______. 'Local actors in global politics', *Current Sociology,* 52.4 (2004):649–670.

Scannell, Paddy. 'For a Phenomenology of Radio and Television', *Journal of Communication*, 45.3 (1995): 4–19.

Van Dijck, José and Thomas Poell. 'Making Public Television Social? Public Service Broadcasting and the Challenges of Social Media', *Television & New Media*, 16.2 (2015): 148–164.

Vernadsky, Volodymyr I. 'The Biosphere and the Noosphere', *American Scientist*, 33.1 (1945): 1–12.

Westmoreland, Mark W. 'Interruptions: Derrida and Hospitality', *Kritike*, 2.1 (June 2008): 1–10.

Yegenoglu, Meyda. 'Liberal Multiculturalism and the Ethics of Hospitality in the Age of Globalization' *Postmodern Culture*, 13.2 (2003), https://search-proquest-com.till.biblextern.sh.se/docview/1428990315?accountid=13936.

Žižek, Slavoj. 'A Leftist Plea for 'Eurocentrism', *Critical Inquiry*, 24.4 (Summer 1998): 988–1009.

**Online magazines**

Lars Bang Larsen,'Social Aesthetics: 11 Examples to Begin with, in the Light of Parallel History', *Afterall Journal*, (Autumn/Winter 2000), https://vam.afterall.org/journal/issue.1/social.aesthetics.11.examples.begin.light.parallel.

Bishop, Claire. 'The Social Turn: Collaboration and its Discontents', *Artforum* (February 2006), https://www.artforum.com/print/200602/the-social-turn-collaboration-and-its-discontents-10274.

Barak, Dusan. 'On Participatory Art: Interview with Claire Bishop', 2009. Originally published on *Multiplace* theory mailing list. Available at: https://www.academia.edu/771895/On_participatory_art_Interview_with_Claire_Bishop.

Goodhardt, David. 'Too Diverse?', *Prospect*, 20 February 2004, https://www.prospectmagazine.co.uk/magazine/too-diverse-david-goodhart-multiculturalism-britain-immigration-globalisation.

Hilal, Sandi. 'The Living Room: The Right to Host', *Obieg*, Vol. 11 (2019), https://obieg.u-jazdowski.pl/en/numery/goscinnosc/the-living-room-the-right-to-host.

Holdstock, Nick. '"Artisans for incorporation" – An interview with Saskia Sassen', *Citizenship in Southeast Europe*, 17 December 2012, http://citsee.eu/interview/%E2%80%98artisans-incorporation%E2%80%99-interview-saskia-sassen.

Höller, Christian and Achille Mbembe. 'Africa in Motion: An Interview with the Post-colonialism Theoretician Achille Mbembe', *Metamute*, 17 March 2007, https://www.metamute.org/editorial/articles/africa-motion-interview-post-colonialism-theoretician-achille-mbembe.

Hübinette, Tobias and Catrin Lundström. 'White Melancholia: Mourning the Loss of "Good Old Sweden"', *Eurozine*, 18 October 2011, https://www.eurozine.com/white-melancholia/.

Lagnado, Lisette. 'O malabarista e a gambiarra', *Trópico*, (October 2003). Available at: http://www.caoguimaraes.com/wordpress/wp-content/uploads/2012/12/o-malabarista-e-a-gambiarra.pdf.

Malik, Kenan. 'The Failure of Multiculturalism: Community Versus Society in Europe', *Foreign Affairs*, (March/April 2015), https://www.foreignaffairs.com/articles/western-europe/2015-02-18/failure-multiculturalism.

Preciado, Paul B. 'Nós dizemos revolução', Universidade Nômade do Brasil, 24 March 2013, http://uninomade.net/tenda/nos-dizemos-revolucao/.

Ranstorp, Magnus, Linus Gustafsson, and Peder Hyllgren, 'From the Welfare State to the Caliphate: How a Swedish suburb became a breeding ground for foreign fighters streaming into Syria and Iraq', *Foreign Policy*, 23 February 2015, https://foreignpolicy.com/2015/02/23/from_the_welfare_state_to_the_caliphate_sweden_islamic_state_syria_iraq_foreign_fighters/.

Rosler, Martha. 'Culture Class: Art, Creativity, Urbanism, Part I', *e-flux*, 21 (December 2010), https://www.e-flux.com/journal/21/67676/culture-class-art-creativity-urbanism-part-i/.

Sanandaji, Nima. 'Influence of 'creative class' ideas in Sweden', *New Geography*, 11 November 2008, https://www.newgeography.com/content/00389-influence-creative-class-ideas-sweden.
Sassen, Saskia. 'The Language of Expulsion', *Truthout*, 30 April 2014, https://truthout.org/articles/the-language-of-expulsion/.

**Online encyclopaedias**

Song, Sarah. 'Multiculturalism', in Edward N. Zalta (ed.) *The Stanford Encyclopedia of Philosophy,* Summer 2015 Edition, https://plato.stanford.edu/archives/sum2015/entries/multiculturalism/.

Beyer, Christian. 'Edmund Husserl', in Edward N. Zalta (ed.) *The Stanford Encyclopedia of Philosophy,* Summer 2015 Edition, http://plato.stanford.edu/archives/sum2015/entries/husserl/.

**Blogs**

'Interview with Per Hasselberg', no date, http://perhasselberg.wordpress.com/konsthall-c/.

'Nosso Lar, Brasília', *31a. Bienal – How to Become Things that Don't Exist*, 14 September 2014, http://www.31bienal.org.br/en/post/1520.

**News articles**

Abdul Fattah, Nabila. 'Sluta göra oss i förorten till labbråttor!' *ETC.*, 16 December 2014, https://www.etc.se/ledare/sluta-gora-oss-i-fororten-till-labbrattor.

af Kleen, Björn. 'Det ockuperade landskapet: Idyllen som gisslan', DN Fokus, *Dagens Nyheter*, 10 May 2015, https://fokus.dn.se/det-ockuperade-landskapet/.

'Agne, ett av alla offer för svensk rasbiologi', *Dagens Nyheter*, 30 March 2010.

'Assyrian Christians crowdfund an army to reclaim homeland from ISIL', Al-Jazeera, 26 February 2015.

'Benefits Tourism Not OK', *The Economist*, 15 November 2014.

Beckman, Petter. 'Konsthögskolan kommer till Fittja', 12 April 2012, https://www.stockholmdirekt.se/sodra-sidan/konsthogskolan-kommer-till-fittja/cbbldl!9w9kgZuf2vrNPq3NXudgbA/.

Björklund, Anders. 'Paraboler ska sätta färg på Fittja', *Mitt i Botkyrka*, 7 February 2012.

Broström, Anna. 'Paraboler i Fittja blir färgglad konst', *Dagens Nyheter*, 19 April 2012, https://www.dn.se/sthlm/paraboler-i-fittja-blir-fargglad-konst/.

'Como nasce uma cidade: com quantos goianos se faz uma utopia', *Correio Braziliense*, 18 June 2011, https://www.correiobraziliense.com.br/app/noticia/cidades/2011/06/18/interna_cidadesdf,257450/como-nasce-uma-cidade-com-quantos-goianos-se-faz-uma-utopia.shtml.

'Como nasce uma cidade', Correio Braziliense, 13 April 2012.

Costa, Gilberto. 'Censo populacional de 1959 revela quem eram os candangos que construiram Brasilia', Agência Brasil, 21 April 2010, http://memoria.ebc.com.br/agenciabrasil/noticia/2010-04-21/censo-populacional-de-1959-revela-quem-eram-os-candangos-que-construiram-brasilia.

'Efter rapport om utsatta områden: Polisen: Fittja har faktiskt blivit tryggare', *Stockholm Direkt*, 30 June 2017, https://www.stockholmdirekt.se/nyheter/efter-rapport-om-utsatta-omraden-polisen-fittja-har-faktiskt-blivit-tryggare/repqfv!NE8msk9Ps@PfmmqSbpYkkQ/.

'Enklaste vägen ut är att flytta', Jessica Ritzén, *Dagens Nyheter*, 22 May 2013.

'Fittja skakat av våld och upplopp', *Dagens Nyheter*, 19 January 2010. 'Fittja Pavilion during the 14th Venice Architecture Biennale', *E-flux*, 30 May 2014, https://www.e-flux.com/announcements/31046/fittja-pavilion-during-the-14th-venice-architecture-biennale/.

'Greek Premier Condemns Europe's Response to Migrant Crisis', *New York Times*, 30 October 2015. https://www.nytimes.com/2015/10/31/world/europe/tsipras-migrants-aegean-eu.html.

'Germany Opens Borders, Expects 7,000 Refugees and Migrants from Hungary Over Weekend', *NBC News*, 5 September 2015, https://www.nbcnews.com/storyline/europes-border-crisis/germany-opens-borders-expects-7-000-refugees-migrants-hungary-over-n42233.

Gudmunsson, Per. '55 'no go'-zoner i Sverige', *Svenska Dagbladet*, 28 October 2014, https://www.svd.se/55-no-go-zoner-i-sverige.

'The Iranian Diaspora in America: 30 Years in the Making', PBS, 12 September 2010.

'Managing the refugee crisis: Immediate operational, budgetary and legal measures under the European Agenda on Migration', *European Commission*, 23 September 2015, https://europa.eu/rapid/press-release_IP-15-5700_en.htm.

'Merkel says German multicultural society has failed', *BBC News Europe*, 17 October 2010, https://www.bbc.com/news/world-europe-11559451.

Mirzoeff, Nicholas. '"Social Death" in Denmark – The European country is isolating and excluding asylum seekers until they disappear from society completely', *The Nation*, 20 January 2019, https://www.thenation.com/article/denmark-refugees-asylum-europe/.

Nougayrède, Natalie. 'Europe's tide of migrant tragedy can be stemmed only in Africa', *The Guardian*, 15 May 2015, https://www.theguardian.com/commentisfree/2015/may/15/europe-migrant-tide-tragedy-africa.

'Nicolas Sarkozy joins David Cameron-Angela Merkel view that multiculturalism failed', *Daily Mail*, 11 February 2011, https://www.dailymail.co.uk/news/article-1355961/Nicolas-Sarkozy-joins-David-Cameron-Angela-Merkel-view-multiculturalism-failed.html.

'Paraboler blir färgglad konst', *Dagens Nyheter*, 19 April 2012, https://www.dn.se/sthlm/paraboler-i-fittja-blir-fargglad-konst/.

'Polisen: Positiva tecken i utsatta områden', *Aftonbladet*, 3 June 2019. https://www.aftonbladet.se/nyheter/a/zG9E49/polisen-positiva-tecken-i-utsatta-omraden.

Truc, Olivier. 'Sweden Pays the High Price of Segregation', *Le Monde*, 3 June 2013, https://worldcrunch.com/culture-society/sweden-pays-the-price-of-segregation.

'The Iranian Diaspora in America: 30 Years in the Making', *PBS*, 12 September 2010.

**Reports and Legal documents**

*Botkyrka and Växjö – A Situation Analysis*. Responsibilities of cities in counteracting racism sustainably, *ECAR (European Cities Against Racism)*, 2012. Available at: https://bgz-berlin.de/files/ecar_se-_summary__situation_analysis_botkyrka_-_vaexjoe.pdf.

Martelanc, Tomo. *Social and Cultural Impact of Satellite-based Television*, UNESCO, 1974. Available at: https://unesdoc.unesco.org/ark:/48223/pf0000011244?posInSet=2&queryId=dfeffdab-1609-48e2-9af9-7aa61a27c182.

*Potential Nordic population in 2030*, Nordregio (Nordic Centre for Spatial Development), 2014, https://archive.nordregio.se/en/Metameny/About-Nordregio/Journal-of-Nordregio/2008/Journal-of-Nordregio-no-1-2008/Potential-Nordic-population-2030/index.html.

*En nationell översikt av kriminella nätverk med stor påverkan i lokalsamhälle,* Rikskriminalpolisen, Underrättelsesektionen, October 2014, p. 8. Available at: https://polisen.se/siteassets/dokument/ovriga_rapporter/en-nationell-oversikt-av-kriminella-natverk.pdf.

*Riksdagens protokoll 2005/06:60*, Swedish Parliament, 24 January 2005, https://www.riksdagen.se/sv/dokument-lagar/dokument/protokoll/riksdagens-protokoll-20050660-tisdagen-den-24_GT0960/html.

*Sweden in the Creative Age*. Irene Tinagli, Richard Florida, Patrik Ström, Evelina Wahlqvist (eds) School of Business, Economics and Law, Göteborg University & Creativitygroupeurope, June 2007. Available at: http://www.creativeclass.com/rfcgdb/articles/Sweden%20in%20 the%20Creative%20Age.pdf.

**Websites**

Abdullah Yüçel, https://abdullahyucelisvectebirturkoncusununhayati.wordpress.com/.

Assyria TV, https://www.assyriatv.org/.

Botkyrka konsthall, http://www.botkyrkakonsthall.se.

Botkyrka municipality, http://www.botkyrka.se. CNBC Arabia, https://www.cnbcarabia.com/.

Data Cities, https://data-cities.net/from-garden-cities-to-data-cities.

Historieberättarna, http://historieberattarna.se/kontakt.

Ekonomifakta http://ekonomifakta.se.

Fittja Open 2011, https://botkyrkakonsthall.se/evenemang/fittja-open-2011.

Fondation Le Corbusier, http://fondationlecorbusier.fr/.

Fundação Athos Bulcão, https://www.fundathos.org.br/.

Google Earth, http://earth.google.com.

Instituto Brasileiro de Geografia e Estatística – IBGE, https://cidades.ibge.gov.br/brasil/df/brasilia/panorama.

ICORN – International Cities of Refuge Network, https://www.icorn.org/.

Ingen människa är illegal, https://www.ingenillegal.org/.

Institute for the Decolonization of Art, http://www.idakonst.wordpress.com.

International Lexicon of Aesthetics, https://lexicon.mimesisjournals.com/international_lexicon_of_aesthetics_item_detail.php?item_id=70.

Konsthall C, http://www.konsthallc.se.

Megafonen, Alby är inte till Salu!,http://megafonen.com/alby-ar-inte-till-salu/.

Megafonen, https://www.facebook.com/Megafonenorten/.

Memorial da Democracia, http://www.memorialdademocracia.com.br/card/construcao-de-brasilia/5.

Mensagens Espíritas, https://mensagensespiritasapp.wordpress.com/2012/12/14/mapas-de-nosso-lar/.

Moderna museet, https://www.modernamuseet.se/stockholm/sv/aktiviteter/adrian-paci-och-tomas-rafa/.

New Biennial for Art and Architecture, https://botkyrkakonsthall.se/evenemang/nya-biennalen-for-konst-arkitektur-i-botkyrka/.

Papal Encyclicals, https://www.papalencyclicals.net/alex06/alex06inter.htm.

Public Art Agency Sweden, http://www.statenskonstrad.se.

Refugees Welcome, https://refugees-welcome.se/, https://www.refugees-welcome.net/

Slave Voyages Database, https://www.slavevoyages.org/assessment/estimates.

Stadsmuseet, https://stadsmuseet.stockholm.se/.Suroyo TV, http://old.suroyotv.com/index.php/live.html. Swedish Migration Authority, http://www.migrationsverket.se.

Swedish government, http://regeringen.se.

Tensta konsthall, http://www.tenstakonsthall.se.

Tomas Rafa, http://your-art.sk/.

UNHCR 1951 Refugee Convention, https://www.unhcr.org/1951-refugee-convention.html.

UNHCR, https://www.unhcr.org/globaltrends2019/.

*United Nations Human Rights Office of the High Commissioner (OHCHR)*, https://www.ohchr.org/EN/Issues/Migration/Pages/HumanRightsFramework.aspx. *Ungdomens Hus Fittja*, https://www.facebook.com/ungdomens.

*Valmyndigheten*, http://www.valmyndigheten.se

**Films**

*A Cidade é Uma Só?* (dir. Adirley Queiroz, 2011). Available at: https://youtu.be/vVlqCVKdlxA.

*A Perfect New World/Europe's Brasília* (dir. Carl Pontus Hjorthén, 2017). Available at: Available at: https://youtu.be/UDhuA4efq0A.

*Bye Bye Brasil* (dir. Carlos Diegues, 1980).

*Conterrâneos Velhos de Guerra* (dir. Vladimir Carvalho, 1991). Available at: https://youtu.be/wWRmY-2rxD4.

*I'm a Fucking Panther*, (dir. Anders Rundberg, Leo Palmestål and Jennifer Perez, 2014). Available at: https://youtu.be/PMulaOoNX3Y.

*Förvaret: Migrationsverkets låsta rum*, (dir. Anna Persson and Sharon Chakraborty, 2014).

*Globo: Beyond Citizen Kane* (dir. Simon Hartog, 1993). Available at: https://youtu.be/-bR8AkMaG1g.

*Koyaanisqatsi* (dir. Godfrey Reggio, 1982). Once There was Brasilia (dir. Adirley Queiroz, 2017). Available at: https://mubi.com/films/era-uma-vez-brasilia.

*Powers of 10*, (dir. Charles Eames, 1970). Available at: https://youtu.be/0fKBhvDjuy0.

*Push*, (dir. Fredrik Gertten, 2019). Available at: https://vimeo.com/ondemand/pushthefilm.

*The Matrix* (dir. Wachowsky Brothers, 1999–2003).

*We Shall Survive in the Memory of Others, featuring Vllém Flusser*. (dir. Center for Culture and Communication Foundation, Budapest in cooperation with the Vilém Flusser Archive Universität der Künste Berlin, 2011).

*White Out, Black In* (dir. Adirley Queiroz, 2014).

**Television Programs**

'Satellitstaden', *Sveriges Television*, 4 May 2012, 4'32".

### Lectures/Conferences

Berardi, Franco. 'Life at Work', *Transmediale 2011*, Berlin, 30 January–2 February 2011.

Mack, Jennifer. 'Urban design from below', Arkitekturmuseet, 1–2 June 2015.

Medina, Cuauhtémoc, 'Biennial Interventions: Margolles in Venice, Cannibal Dominoes and Manifesta 9', *IASPIS*, The Swedish Arts Grants Committee, 18 August 2011.

Sassen, Saskia. Keynote speech at the *2014 Creative Time Summit,* Stockholm, 13–16 November 2014, https://www.youtube.com/watch?v=EwqNuFugYRg.

Stenberg, Erik. *Miljonprogrammet – framtidens stad*, Stockholm, 12 September 2012, https://youtu.be/pxplKifguLA

### Monographs

Johnson, Miranda. 'Hell is Other People: Ethics, Aesthetics and Participatory Art', Undergraduate Honours Methodology paper, University of Western Australia, 2013. Available at: https://www.academia.edu/4019730/Hell_is_Other_People_Ethics_Aesthetics_and_Participatory_Art.

Sönmez, Emrah. *Abdullah Yücel: En marginell man – en diskursanalytisk studie om poesi och identitetsskapande i en svensk-turkisk migrationskontext*, Sociology Department, Stockholm University, Stockholm, Sweden, 2014, http://su.diva-portal.org/smash/record.jsf?pid=diva2%3A732009&dswid=85740896.

### Exhibition Catalogues

*1930/80 ARKITEKTUR-FORM-KONST*, Kulturhuset, Stockholm, Sweden, 6 May -24 October 1980.

*New Babylon – Constant Nieuwenhuys,* Haags Gemeetenmuseum, The Hague, 1974. https://stichtingconstant.nl/system/files/1974_new_babylon.pdf.

*Satellite, Border, Footprint,* Hartware Medienkunstverein (ed.) Dortmund 2011.

### Exhibitions

*Lygia Clark: The Abandonment of Art, 1948–1988*, Museum of Modern Art, 2014, https://www.moma.org/calendar/exhibitions/1422.

*Washed Out* (Curated by Isabel Löfgren, Corina Oprea, Judith Souriau, Valerio del Baglivo, Milena Placentile), *Konsthall C*, Stockholm, Sweden, 2011, http://apexart.org/exhibitions/washedout.htm.

### Radio programs

'Bland satelliter och pimpade paraboler i Fittja', *Kulturradio P1*, Sveriges Radio, 11 June 2012, https://sverigesradio.se/sida/artikel.aspx?programid=3050&artikel=5143268.

'Lättare att ha parabolantenn', *Sveriges Radio*, 25 July 2006.

### Facebook posts

Satellitstaden, 'Record number of colored antennas this week', Facebook group update, 9 March 2012, https://www.facebook.com/groups/satellitstaden.

# ACKNOWLEDGEMENTS

First and foremost, my gratitude to the careful guidance, inspiration and friendship of my supervisor, Geert Lovink, who never gave up hope that one day I would publish this book. I thank my partner, Mats Hjelm, who endured my moments of doubt and still wonders why my PhD thesis became a book only now. Thanks to our families for their love, trust, and tremendous support throughout this long journey.

There are many people and institutions that made this research possible. In Fittja, I thank the women at *Verdandi/Garaget* for their company and affection; Pero Dag and Leila Sözen for their professionalism, collaboration and friendship; Shakhlo Altieva for intelligent dialogue; Dhikra Merza for her enthusiasm; and the fifty families in Fittja for their participation and involvement in *Satellitstaden*, including Gülüzar Aykut, William Merza, Firat Güzel, Gülüzer Eker, Mayra Eker, Gülsum Bardaci, Habib Samandar, Halla Chamoun, Hacer Kücükyasa, Halime Demirel, Hoda Daoud, Josef Charro, Ulf Hansson, Dalia Kamala, Kristina Nedeljkovic, Lamia Abboudi, Marian Ansultani, Minhaaj Rehman, Mamasa Sacko, Moataz Tawfik, Rabia Surme, Radmila Storsic, Sargan Oshana, Shakhlo Altieva, Shaista Sahi, Serap Karadaz, Sukram Kaja, Sallam Muse, Slavica, Suna, Tisha Molla, Turkan Sözen, Teodora Touma, Yasar Kosikaslan, Zoran, Yildis Agrali, Zaliha Agrali, Ezmer Agrali, Zenahaida, Özlem Umal, Hadeel Fatimah, and Nelson. Thank you for welcoming me so warmly in your homes.

Thanks to Renée Padt and the CuratorLab program at Konstfack University College of Arts, Crafts and Design in Stockholm for giving me a reason to come to Sweden and opening up the pathway for a collaborative and research-oriented approach in my artistic and academic practice. Thanks to curator Miriam Andersson Blecher at Botkyrka konsthall/Residence Botkyrka for the first introduction to Fittja, and Anneli Bäckman for continued support throughout these years. My friends Laercio Redondo and Birger Lipinski for introducing me to curator Joanna Sandell at Botkyrka konsthall/Residence Botkyrka – without her encouragement and crucial support to work on site for nearly two years, Satellitstaden would have been impossible. The Vilém Flusser Archive in Berlin for accessing Flusser's original and unpublished manuscripts. Mother Tongue (Tiffany Boyle and Jessica Carden) for commissioning the essay from which I began to build the thesis. Per Hüttner and Vision Forum, for refining my vision on collaboration and hospitality in contemporary art research. Erik Krikortz, who collaborated with the project in its initial stages. The research team at Mångkulturellt Centrum (MKC), Leif Magnusson, Mikael Morberg and Tobias Hübinette for directing me to precious sources and for patiently listening to the developments of *Satellitstaden* as the project unfolded. Parvaneh Sharaffi at the Citizen's Office in Fittja for local connections and data. Pernilla Hellman, secretary for culture in Botkyrka Municipality, and Björn Schenholm-Ristborg at Botkyrkabyggen, for supporting my vision. Charley Malm and his dedicated team at Botkyrkabyggen for sharing their knowledge and helping me find ladders when I needed. Lara Szabo Greisman for climbing balconies with me and helping with documentation, and many other collaborators who are part of this journey.

Most of this research was made possible with funding from Konstfack CuratorLab, Kulturbryggan, Crowdculture.se, Botkyrka Municipality and Botkyrka Konsthall/Residence Botkyrka for *Satellitstaden*. In 2012, the Council of Europe awarded *Satellitstaden* the *Council of Europe's Culture, Heritage and Diversity Label for Intercultural Cities* award.

Thanks to Alex Castro, Jeremy Fernando, Yvonne Bezerra de Mello, Paola Madrid Sartoretto, and Mats Hjelm who contributed greatly in reading and revising parts of the manuscript, and the careful academic edit by Roman Horbyk, who revised this document especially for this book edition. Lastly, special thanks for the wonderful staff at the Institute of Network Cultures (INC) for publishing this book.

Most of this work was done between the passing of my stepfather, Alvaro, and the birth of my son, Theo. I dedicate this work to both of you, as you are my definition of absolute, unconditional love and hospitality.

Stockholm, June 2015/October 2020

# ABOUT THE AUTHOR

Isabel Löfgren is a Swedish-Brazilian artist, researcher and educator based in Stockholm, Sweden and Rio de Janeiro, Brazil.

She completed her doctoral degree from the European Graduate School's division of Media & Communications (now the division of Philosophy, Art and Critical Thought), Saas-Fee, Switzerland, in 2015. She is currently a Senior Lecturer in Media and Communication Studies at Södertörn University, Sweden in parallel to her artistic practice.

The cultural politics, the media philosophy of diaspora and cosmopolitanism in the fields of art, media and media activism are the key focus areas of her research. She has participated in artistic research collectives in Brazil and Sweden and in research collaborations internationally.

www.isabellofgren.com www.satellitstaden.tv

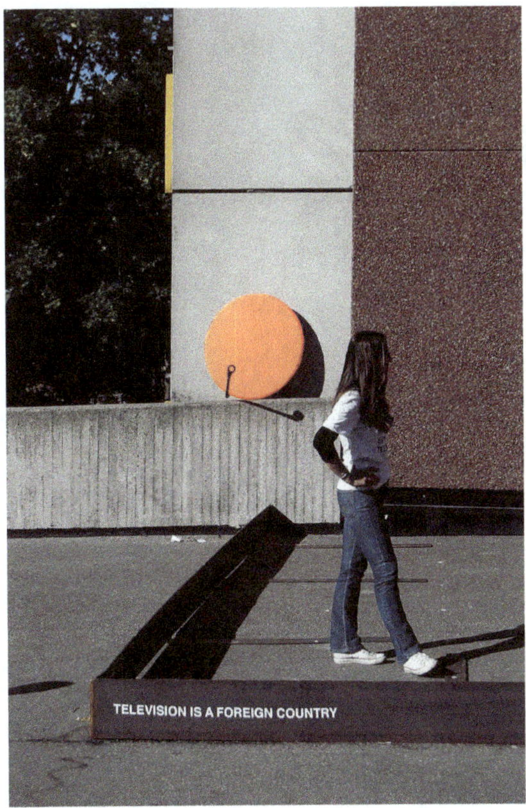

www.ingramcontent.com/pod-product-compliance
Lightning Source LLC
LaVergne TN
LVHW020506100826
845148LV00003B/708

*9789492302694*